Spiritual Healing

© Copyright S. Gregg, 2016

www.susangregg.com

First Edition

All rights reserved. No part of this book may be reproduced or transmitted in any form or by any means whatsoever, including graphic, electronic, or mechanical, including photocopying, recording, taping, or by any information storage or retrieval system, without written permission from the author.

Published in English
by Dr. Susan Gregg, LLC
PO Box 1006
Kurtistown, HI 96760 USA
http://susangregg.com

If you wish to learn more about what I do
or be notified about future books
please go to
http://www.susangregg.com/nextbook/

Spiritual Healing Quick Reference Card

Creating a Daily Routine

Decide what you are going to do on a daily basis to assist you in your spiritual healing. Then put the list on your bathroom mirror so you won't forget to do them.

Here is a list of suggestions. Pick a few and make sure you do them for yourself every day.

- Meditate
- Journal
- Go for a walk
- Affirmations
- Pray
- Do breathing exercises
- Exercise
- Eat well
- Get enough rest
- Yoga
- Tai Chi
- Jog
- Spend time with yourself
- Read
- Relax
- Listen to mellow music
- Do at least one nurturing thing

Making a List of Nurturing Things

When we're feeling judgmental toward ourselves it is hard to remember to be kind, loving, and supportive to ourselves. I find it helpful to have a list of things I can do for myself that I can refer to. I can remember to pick an item off the list even when I can't think of a single thing that will make me feel better.

This is a list of things I enjoy – you can use it as a starting point to create a list of your own. Make sure you allow yourself to feel the benefit as you are engaging in the activity.

- Take a hot bath
- Make a cup of hot tea
- Watch a sunrise or sunset
- Go for a walk in nature
- Call a friend
- Read an uplifting book
- Engage in your favorite hobby
- Get a massage
- Buy yourself some flowers
- Make a nice meal for yourself, set the table, light candles
- Sprinkle your favorite scent around the house
- Burn a candle
- Play your favorite music
- Dance
- Exercise

Talking to Yourself in the Mirror

Look into the mirror and look directly into your own eyes. Repeat the following to yourself in a loving and gentle manner until you begin to really believe them.

- I love and accept myself just the way I am.
- I am perfect just the way I am.
- I am learning how to be my own best friend
- I deserve to be happy and to feel free.
- I am never alone. I am always surrounded by the love of the universe. *(Then let yourself feel that love)*
- I am love. I am lovable. I am loved.
- Add several positive statements of your own.

Contents

Part 1   **Your Journey Toward Wholeness**   **1**

Chapter 1: What is Spiritual Healing Anyway?   3

Chapter 2: The Fall From Grace   17

Chapter 3: The Paradox or Why Bother?   29

Chapter 4: Beware, the Snake Oil Salesman   41

Part 2   **So, What's Available**   **53**

Chapter 5: Alternative Medicine   55

Chapter 6: Altered States   67

Chapter 7: Body Therapies   79

Chapter 8: Energy Work   93

Chapter 9: Spirit Stuff   103

Part 3   **Making Your Mind Your Own**   **117**

Chapter 10: There is No "Out There"   119

Chapter 11: What Did I Just Say?   131

Chapter 12: My Emotions Made Me Do It   143

Chapter 13: Dynamics of Change   155

Chapter 14: Journaling   167

Part 4   **When Your Body Yells, Listen**   **179**

Chapter 15: Mind/Body/Spirit Connection   181

Chapter 16: But It Hurts So Good   193

Chapter 17: Shake Your Booty   205

Chapter 18: Eating Mindfully   217

Part 5 **The Spirit That Moves You** **227**

    Chapter 19: Prayer, Connection, and Inner Guidance   229

    Chapter 20: I Give Up, I Surrender   241

    Chapter 21: Nature as Healer   253

    Chapter 22: Love, Compassion, Judgment, and God   263

Part 6 **Putting It All Together** **275**

    Chapter 23: Coming Up with a Formula   277

    Chapter 24: Relationships   289

    Chapter 25: Who Am I and What Do I Want To Do?   301

    Chapter 26: Finding a Happiness That Lasts   313

Part 7 **A Vision For The Future** **325**

    Chapter 27: Planetary Healing   327

Appendixes:

    A: Suggested Reading   337

    B: Organizations   341

Dear Reader,

Several years ago I was asked to speak at a high school on the Big Island of Hawaii. On the flight over I was very nervous, I had no idea what I was going to say to several hundred teenagers. When I walked up on stage I expressed my nervousness and told them how I'd decided what I was going to talk about. I told them I'd imagined myself in their place and wondered what someone could have said to me that would've made a difference in my life. I spoke about that for well over an hour and the student's attention never wavered.

When I sat down to write this letter I asked myself the same question. What could someone have said to me at the beginning of my journey that would've made my life easier? If I'd really listened this is what would've helped me.

You're about to give yourself the most incredible gift there is.
This process will be a long and at times arduous journey but it will be worth every moment. You may cry, get angry, and want to quit. Whatever you do don't give up on yourself. When your mind says stop go a few steps further. When you want to run away, stay. Be gentle with yourself and trust your process.

This book is a wonderful beginning. Read it from cover to cover or skip around, enjoy it but remember to do all the exercise especially the ones you really don't want to do. Follow the directions; doing it your way won't work.

At some point in your journey you'll know why you're doing it and you'll smile. Before the end of your journey you'll have reclaimed yourself; you will love yourself and your world with an open heart; you'll accept yourself as a human being with shortcomings and love even them; you'll have the ability to be happy no matter what is happening around you. You'll be free. Your life will be a magnificent reflection of your divinity.

You've begun a wonderful journey; don't give up on yourself five minutes before the miracle. Thanks for allowing me to be a part of your journey.

In love and light,

Susan

Introduction

When I began my journey of emotional and spiritual healing I spent years reading books, going to lectures, and studying. When I first began in the early seventies there wasn't much information out there. This book is the result of those years of research.

Our journey toward spiritual wholeness is very personal and the gifts we receive as the result are immeasurable. I hope you allow yourself to enjoy your journey. Avoid the trap of wanting to be further along than you are. This is the only time you will be able to be able to experience this particular moment, to be right where are, and to know exactly what you know now. You're already a different person form the one who started reading this sentence. It is no mistake you are thinking of reading this book.

Be gentle with yourself and enjoy your process. This book was designed to help you explore and move toward a deeper sense of happiness and wholeness as rapidly as possible. The first sections are informational, while the later sections are full of exercises to help you break free from your limitations.

You are a limitless being inside a physical body experiencing a world that seems to be full of limitations. The world as you now see it is an illusion. Read on and learn how to set yourself free.

Part 1, "Your Journey Toward Wholeness," gives you an overview of spiritual healing, it outlines some of its benefits, and helps you decide if it's something you really want to do.

In **Part 2, "So, What's Available?"** we explore many of the alternative healing methods available. There are methods for healing your body, your mind, and your spirit.

We are composed of three parts: our minds, our body, and our spirits. In the next three sections we explore each part of this miraculous trinity.

Part 3, "Making Your Mind Your Own," shows you how to retrain your mind so it is your servant instead of your master.

Part 4, "When Your Body Yells, Listen," explores the needs of your body, including how to free yourself from addictions.

In **Part 5, "The Spirit That Moves You,"** we explore ways to connect with your spirit.

Part 6, "Putting it All Together," will help you create a formula that works for you, that will allow you to heal your life. You will be shown how improve the quality of your relationships and how to be happy no matter what's happening in your life.

Part 7, "A Vision for the Future," talks about the world as a whole and the role we can play in helping the world be a better place.

In addition to the wealth of information on the pages you will find little nuggets in the these boxes:

Smoke & Mirrors

These boxes include warnings, they will help you avoid the pit falls we can encounter on our spiritual quest.

Clarity Corner

These boxes will give you definitions and more in depth explanation of key concepts

Sage Advice

You'll find quotes and short vignettes that will help lift your spirits and keep you on track. They're wonderful thoughts to put on index cards placed strategically on your bathroom mirror or on your refrigerator door.

Spiritual Shortcuts

In these boxes you'll find exercises, meditations, and other bits of information that will help you move more rapidly along your path.

Acknowledgements

I would like to first thank all the people that helped me along my path. I extend my deepest love to Jennie Lang my first teacher who loved my long before I could love myself. I'd like to thank my students who push me to continue to grow and don Miguel Ruiz and Sister Sarita who showed me the path of personal freedom.

I'd like to thank my agent Sheree Bykofsky and Randy Ladenheim Gil for giving the opportunity to write this wonderful book.

Special Thanks to the Techincal Reviewer

Spiritual Healing was reviewed by an expert who doubles-checked the accuracy of what you'll learn here, to help ensure that this book gives you everything you need to know about spiritual healing. Special thanks are extended to Richard A. Lavin.

Richard A. Lavin has been a hypnotherapist, trance channel,, counselor, lecturer, aurthor, and computer consultant for 20 years. He works globally, providing individuals and groups with practical spiritual assistance in person, by telephone, and through the mail. You can learn more about Richard's work at *http://www.richardlavin.com*

Part 1
Your Journey Toward Wholeness

Spiritual healing is a journey in which you will find yourself. It is a journey in which you will remember who and what you really are. You will learn how to love yourself unconditionally and accept yourself completely. It is a journey into wholeness as well as into your holiness.

Every journey has a beginning, middle, and end. This journey is often filled with confusion, exhilaration, and at times sadness and fear. It is the greatest gift you will ever give yourself.

In this section we will talk about the journey as a whole. I will give you some historical insight and reasons for taking this journey. Along the way we will get to know one another.

I hope you enjoy the journey.

Chapter 1

What is Spiritual Healing Anyway?

In This Chapter

- ➤ Definitions of spiritual healing.
- ➤ Why you should bother.
- ➤ How grand can your life really be.
- ➤ How can you get there.
- ➤ Staying on course.

Five years from now it will be five years later and you'll be five years older. Time will pass regardless of what you do but the quality of your life depends on how you use that time. Would you rather be homeless or living in the lap of luxury? The quality of your life isn't a matter of luck, it is a matter of the choices you make on a daily basis. Spiritual healing isn't an abstract concept, it is a tool that will show you how to make choices that will create a life filled with joy and happiness.

In this chapter we will explore some of the definitions of spiritual healing. I will explain how spiritual healing can affect your life and why you might want to pursue it. When I first heard the term spiritual healing I had a mental image of a ghost with a bandage on it. Nothing could be further from the truth. Your spirit is fine, always has been, always will be but chances are your connection to it is a little bit fuzzy. In this chapter we will begin to explore how to improve that connection.

Definitions

I have always loved words. As a child I spent hours reading the dictionary. Sometimes merely changing our definition of a word can change our entire experience of the people and events in our lives. (We'll be talking a lot more about this in later chapters.) So what are we talking about anyway?

Clarity Corner

SPIRIT

The word spirit originally came from a Latin word that meant breath. Around 400 AD it gradually replaced the word soul. In many ancient traditions it is believed that the spirit and breath are one because the spirit connects with the body through the breath.

Spirituality

Spirituality is our ability to focus on and nurture our spirit. Long ago I heard it said that we are spiritual beings having a physical experience rather than physical beings searching for our spirit. I think of spirituality as a road map guiding us toward a direct connection to our own divinity.

Spirituality can take on many shapes and forms. Spirituality can become a practice that is something you do on a regular basis such as meditation or yoga but it doesn't have to. Spirituality is very personal and intimate. Your spiritual connection is your connection, let no one else tell you it is right or wrong. It is yours and yours alone. Spirituality is your personal roadmap to your divinity. Religion is a roadmap designed by someone else.

Healing

Healing means to make whole or to purify. The dictionary also defines it as overcoming an undesirable condition. Healing can happen in an instant but generally it takes time and requires us to take actions.

Healing can refer to your physical body or it can refer to your emotions. We can apply healing to anything including inanimate objects like our car. When I think of healing I usually think holistically, I think about healing all areas of my life.

What areas of your life would you like to heal? Relationships? Finances? Your body? Emotions? Take a minute and list all the things you'd like to change in your life.

_____
_____
_____
_____
_____

Spiritual Healing

Okay, so we have definitions of spirituality and healing. What is spiritual healing? Spiritual healing affects your body, mind, and spirit. As you proceed on this journey your life will change completely. You will learn to see life differently, the flowers will smell sweeter and the sky looks more vibrant. You will be more alive than you thought possible and you will love yourself and others more deeply.

Spiritual healing will:

- Create abundance in your life.
- Assist you in being happy no matter what.
- Fill your life with a sense of inner peace and ease.
- Make miracles become an every day occurrence.
- Improve the quality of your relationships.
- Help you to feel safe and loved.
- Allow you to see the bigger picture.
- Release you from your limitations.
- Free your mind and spirit.
- Relax your body and improve the quality of your life.

The list can go on and on but what is spiritual healing? Ultimately spiritual healing is a journey in which you will find yourself. It takes many shapes and forms. In the first two sections of this book we will explore various methods of healing your mind, body, and spirit. In the last five sections I will show you how to apply spiritual healing to your life.

Spiritual healing is a process, it is a journey, and it is a destination. Enjoy the ride! Throughout this book I will remind you to at least allow for the possibility. Allowing for the possibility is a very powerful elixir for change. If you allow for the possibility that miracles can happen they will. If you allow for the possibility for anything to happen you open the door and let it enter your life. So allow for the possibility that your life can be better than your wildest imaginings and that this journey of healing can be fun.

Sage Advice
"The most important decision we can make is whether this is a friendly or hostile universe. From that decision all other's spring."

Albert Einstein

Spiritual Shortcut

You are at the beginning of a wonderful journey. I suggest you take the time to begin a journal. Write about your process, in the days to come it will be gratifying to look back at it and see where you started. You could begin by doing what I call a daily weather report. Before you start your day take a few minutes to record you thoughts and feelings. Is your mood sunny and warm or wild and windy. You only need a few words. Learning to keep a journal is a process that is well worth the effort.

Perhaps this weekend spend a few hours writing about what you'd like to let go of and what you'd like to create in your life. Imagine waking up, it's five years from now - what would your day look like, who would be there, and how would you feel about what you're doing? Let your imagination fly high and then allow for the possibility that your life will be far grander then you could ever imagine.

Beginnings, Middles, and Ends

Clarity Corner

pro·cess
According to the dictionary a process is a systematic series of actions directed toward a specific end. It is also the act of being committed to continuing to take action or actions. Spiritual healing is a process, it does take a commitment on your part to follow through and to take actions.

Life is a series of beginnings and middles and ends. Each ending is the start of a new beginning and each beginning is the start of a new ending. Often we have a hard time letting go and trusting the process. We fearfully hold onto something when it is time to let go and miss the joy life has to offer.

Learning to honor your process will make your life much easier and you'll be happier. Each of us has a unique process, no two of us experience life exactly the same way. Even though our beliefs and definitions may seem similar they are not the same. No one has the exact same perspective on life as you do. Celebrate your uniqueness, celebrate and honor exactly where you are in your process.

The truth is that at any given moment you are where you are. Kind of obvious but at times it is hard to accept. No matter what you do, what you say, or how you feel about it you are going to be exactly where you are in life and in your process. If you accept where you are it is easier to move forward. With acceptance you can change where you are. But if you fight being where you are you'll make it much harder on yourself. Our resistance to accepting where we are often makes change impossible.

Where you are is your starting point. If a pilot is sitting on a runway at an airport and knows where she is she can fly anywhere. But if a pilot is sitting on a runway and refuses to admit where she is she can't get anywhere. So it is with life, admit where you are and make choices to move on. "But I hate where I am. I am not happy. I'm in pain. I don't have what I want. I . . .." On and on go the demands of your mind. In section three you will learn how to retrain your mind, for now just practice accepting where you are. Allow for the possibility that you are right where you need to be because you need to be there. Take a deep breath and at least try to enjoy it. A sense of humor often helps. As a species we certainly have the ability to create wild and wonderful dramas in our lives; lost loves; jobs ending; friendships falling apart; huge fights with employers or lovers. You name it, we create it and we usually excel at doing it. So as strange as it seems, enjoy your creation.

The Purpose of Life

Why are we here? As a T-shirt I once saw asked, "Why are we way out here at the edge of the universe spinning around this sun on this tiny speck of dust called a planet?" When I was a young girl my grandfather told me the day we stop learning is the day we die. I believe we are here to learn about our relationship to the world and to ourselves. We are here to learn how to love. I also think we are here to have fun, experience joy, and hopefully leave the world a little better place because of our existence. Ultimately we are here to remember our true nature.

Sage Advice

"A man walking across a field encountered a tiger. He fled, the tiger chasing after him. Coming to a cliff, he caught hold of a wild vine and swung himself over the edge. The tiger sniffed at him from above. Terrified, the man looked down to where, far below, another tiger had come, waiting to eat him. Two mice, one white, one black, little by little began to gnaw away at the vine. The man saw a luscious strawberry near him. Grasping the vine with one hand, he plucked the strawberry with the other. How sweet it tasted!"

ZEN Parable

Take a few moments and think about your life's purpose. Why do you believe you are here? What would you like to accomplish with your life?

_____
_____
_____
_____

One of my mentors suggested I go to the library and read passages from some of the great philosophers, then decide for myself what the purpose of my life was. It assisted me in understanding where I was and where I wanted to go. As Plato said, "A life unexamined is not worth living."

Sage Advice

Thousands of starfish had washed up on the shore. A small girl began to pick them up and throw them back in so they wouldn't die.

"Don't bother, sweetie" her mother said, "it won't make a difference."

The girl stopped for a moment and looked at the starfish in her hand.

"It will make a difference to this one."

7

Be All That You Can Be

Sage Advice

"What lies behind us and what lies before us are tiny matters compared to what lies within us."
Ralph Waldo Emerson

All of our lives we've been told things about ourselves that just aren't true. We've been told we aren't smart enough, or thin enough, or tall enough, or good enough, or a hundred other things. As long as we believe these things we are limited by them, we can't be all that we were meant to be. The worse part is that eventually we begin to repeat these things to ourselves. We worry about things, we worry about not having enough money, or about not being happy, or . . . the list goes on and on. Have you ever noticed how many of the things you worry about never happen?

Being all that we can be is a decision. It is a decision to learn how to love ourselves unconditionally and to do whatever it takes to free ourselves from our limiting thinking. In chapter 12, I will go into great detail about how you can change your thought patterns. Part of the process of spiritual healing is beginning to see yourself as you truly are rather than how you've been trained to think you are. As you stop seeing yourself through the filters of the past you will begin to see yourself as the magnificent person you really are.

So How Do I Get There?

Sage Advice

"Life does not consist mainly or even largely, of facts and happenings. It consists mainly of the storm of thoughts that is forever flowing through one's head."
Mark Twain

Getting from where you are to where you want to be is a process that will take time and effort. Only you can decide whether it's worth it. I know it was for me. Once you make the decision to make the journey this book will act as a detailed, easy to follow road map.

Your journey of healing is like a flower with many petals. Each petal represents a different part of your process. As the flower unfolds its beauty and true essence is revealed. If you try to hurry the process by pulling the petals apart the flower will be ruined. Hurrying your process won't work either, allow your process unfold naturally.

Spiritual healing is a process much like climbing a spiral staircase. As you reach the landing the view may look the same but it isn't, you're at a different level. Issues will continue to reveal themselves at deeper and deeper levels. And each time you explore your issues and release them your happiness will deepen as well.

After all, you are a spirit that happens to reside within a body. Your spirit is limitless, it is without bounds, it is immortal, and it is infinite. Anything that stops you from experiencing yourself as that spirit limits your joyous experience of life. Step by step you can begin to experience yourself as your spirit, as that energy that keeps your body going.

The only way to get anywhere is one step at a time. If someone showed up at your door right now and delivered all the food you were going to eat for the rest of your life you'd be overwhelmed by the sight of it. Your first reaction would probably be "I can't possibly eat all that." You can't change everything all at once either.

It will help if you remind yourself:

- Always be gentle with yourself.
- Healing is a process that takes time and effort.
- You can do it.
- Maintain a sense of humor.
- Set yourself up for success by taking small, manageable steps.
- It's okay to say I don't know and to ask for help.
- There is nothing inherently wrong with you.
- You can change or accept anything.
- And above all else be gentle with yourself.

Clarity Corner

UNCONDITIONAL LOVE

Unconditional love is something we rarely experience. It is the ability to accept someone exactly as they are (including ourselves), to respect them for who they are, to support them, to honor them, and to enjoy being in their presence without the need or desire to change them in anyway. It is love without any conditions placed upon it. There are no expectations of rewards, we love period. The love is truly without limits.

You might want to write some of these things on index cards and hang them up in places you can see them. When I began my spiritual healing I carried a stack of index cards and would read them whenever I was feeling unsettled. I wrote down quotes from famous people, from books I was reading, and things I knew I needed to remember.

We often get impatient or irritated with our progress. Once we decide we want our lives to be different, we want everything to change right now. But this journey takes time and our impatience only stops us from enjoying the process. This is the only time you will be experiencing exactly what you are experiencing right now, in this moment. "Tell me something new," your mind says. If you knew tonight was the last opportunity you'd ever have to see a sunset would you take the time to savor that sunset? If today was the last time you'd ever see your closest friend would that time together take on a special meaning?

Sage Advice

"Life is a quarry, out of which we are to mold and chisel and complete a character."
Goethe

Today is the only time you will ever get to experience today. Savor ever moment of every day, even if you don't like what's happening. Learn to celebrate your limitations. As I look back at my path my only regret is that I didn't savor even my most irritating limitations. When I smoked, I didn't savor smoking. When I quit smoking I hated quitting, I judged myself and how long it was taking to get over the desire. I missed both the experience of smoking and the of joy of stopping.

As you proceed with your path of spiritual healing each issue, every belief, and all of your limitations are gifts. The gifts they bring are a deeper understanding of yourself, your beliefs, and your assumptions about life. Our limitations allow us to see ourselves as we believe we are, releasing them allows us to see the truth. You are a limitless being able to experience joy in every moment.

If you want to change something in your life judging it, wishing it would go away, or just trying to get rid of it won't work. The key to releasing anything is embracing it. If you push an issue away you can't understand it. By embracing an issue you can get close enough to examine it and really understand what it is about for you. Every limiting thought or belief you have was originally created as a survival tool. That tool no longer serves you but you must remember how it served you in the past if you want to successfully let go of it.

Sage Advice

"A bad habit cannot be simply thrown out the window. It must be coaxed down the stairs one at a time."

Mark Twain

Spiritual Shortcuts

EMBRACING AN ISSUE

How do you embrace something you want to let go of? The dictionary defines embrace as: to avail oneself of or to influence or to change. If you embrace an issue you can understand it, you make it part of yourself, and then you can change it. Embracing an issue allows you to become large enough to include the issue within yourself. You can avail yourself of all the information a particular issue brings to you.

Embracing anything begins with the knowledge that it isn't your enemy or opponent, it was once your friend and protector. Embrace it, love it, understand it, and then you can let it go. To embrace something you must first accept it.

For example let's say your issue is being fat. You must first accept the fact that you are overweight, you may still want to change your weight but judging yourself and your body is not embracing the issue. Embracing the issue is learning to love your body just as it without any emotional charge. Embracing an issue is a process in itself and it is a necessary step. If we don't embrace the issue we won't be able to fully understand it and then we won't be able to change it.

Embracing an issue is just like embracing a person. We hold the issue near to our heart so we can understand what it is really about.

Step by Step

Change is a process that has very definite steps. It is like a recipe, if you carefully follow the recipe the dish will come out fine every time. If you don't follow the directions your results will vary, the dish may very well be inedible.

Recipe for Change

- Realize there's something you want to change.
- Decide you're willing to change it.
- Define the issue thoroughly.
- Understand the issue's benefits and limitations.
- Recognize what 'makes' you do it.
- Explore your options.
- Make new decisions.
- Experiment with alternate behaviors.
- Replace your old beliefs, assumptions, and agreements.
- Practice your new choices.
- Evaluate the results you are getting.
- Modify if necessary.
- Move on to the next issue.

If you fully complete each step you can successfully change anything. Chapter 14 will be dedicated to exploring these steps in great detail. In this chapter I will only give you a brief overview.

Realize there's something you want to change

This may seem like an obvious step but it isn't. People often spend years in a job they hate or a relationship that doesn't support them before they decide there's something they want to change. We usually know exactly what our friends need to change long before they do *(that's conditional love or as it's better known judgment)*.

If you look back at your life there's probably something you've changed that seemed quite acceptable earlier in your life. I know I've changed things and then in hindsight wondered why I ever put up with them for so long. So step one is to realize there is something you want to change about yourself or your life but not about someone else.

Decide you're willing to change it

Getting to the point you are willing to change something is often a process in itself. You may decide you want to change something but you may still be unwilling to change it. As an example take smoking, many people want to quit but are unwilling to give it up yet.

Making a decision is an ongoing process until we finally make the decision. A decision is the act of making up your mind once and for all; it is a choice to move beyond the need for debate; it is a firm resolve to act and think in a certain way. Making a decision can take a lot of work. At times you may make a decision to change, go on to the next step of defining the issue only to notice you're vacillating and then you have to make the decision again.

Define the issue thoroughly

As the saying goes, we are seldom upset for the reason we think we are. It is difficult to see the true nature of an issue because what we really see is our filter system. Defining an issue requires you to look deep within yourself, beyond your inner filters. Issues are like dandelions. If you merely cut off the top of the dandelion it will grow right back. Dandelions have deep roots that must be thoroughly removed. Issues also have deep and tangled roots. Issues are often interrelated and overlap and unless you remove the roots it will keep returning.

Writing is an excellent tool for defining issues and I will devote an entire chapter to this later on in the book. Sit down and just write about the issue until you have nothing else to say. Give yourself permission to rant and rave and say whatever you need to say. Have a sense of curiosity and let the issue talk to you.

Understand the issue's benefits and limitations

Embracing the issue is a necessary part of your explorations. In order to understand the issue you must view it from all sides. You must understand how it serves as well as how it limits you.

Remember every one of your issues served you at some point. Often as young children we make decisions about life that haunt us as adults. We had to make sense out of the chaos around us and we did the best we could at the time.

Sage Advice

The world is a looking glass. It gives back to every man a true reflection of his own thoughts.
Thackery

Clarity Corner

FILTER SYSTEM

You can think of your filter system as a huge computer that changes the meaning of everything that goes through it. We are unable to see reality as it is because of our filter system. We actually remember the past and see the present through it. We literally filter what we see and what we hear. No two people live in the same world, we live in a world created by our filter system.

We developed our filter system as a child and our parents, our siblings, our friends, and society as a whole assisted us in that task. Our filter system acts like a fun house mirror distorting everything we see. As we begin to understand our filter system we can change it.

Recognize what 'makes' you do it

Most of our behaviors have what I call triggers. My mother used to have this look – when she looked at me that way I automatically went into defense mode. I would lie, run away emotionally, or just disappear rather than face her wrath. As an adult if someone looked at me that way I would unconsciously revert to the same behaviors. The look would trigger my behaviors.

Each of us has a host of triggers. It could be a look, a smell, a tone of voice, or the way the light is coming into the room. Emotions and situations can also be triggers. Once we understand our triggers we can make new choices.

Explore your options

What other choices do you have? How else could you act? How else could you interrupt an event? How would you like to act? What results would you like to get in your life? Ask other people what they would do in a similar situation. Read, observe, and watch others. New behaviors are usually foreign concepts because they aren't a natural part of thought patterns. Pretend you're your favorite fictional character and imagine what she or he would do.

Clarity Corner

ASSUMPTIONS

Once we assume something we think we know the answer. Our assumptions are always based on our filter system and are usually wrong. One definition in the dictionary of assumption is arrogance. Assume nothing, always ask the other person what they mean or believe before you assume you know. Always go deep within yourself to find your assumptions and then ask yourself if that is really the truth.

When we assume (ass-u-me) something we make an ass out of you and me. A good adage to keep in mind as you move through your life.

Your options are limitless, take the time to explore them. Use your imagination and see how far it can take you.

Make new decisions

Decide to act differently. Decide to think differently. Life is a series of choices and outcomes. If you want a different outcome make a new choice.

Pretend, play act, do anything it takes to allow you to act differently. Dress differently. They once did a study and found people tend to wear clothing that corresponds to their mood. So dress for the new part.

Experiment with alternate behaviors

Play, experiment. Try a new behavior and observe the results. If you like the results do it again. If you don't like the results try another new behavior.

Use your curiosity. Observe other people. Read a biography of someone you really admire and emulate their behavior. Pretend you are successful and you will be.

Replace your old beliefs, assumptions, and agreements

By this point in the process you will have realized what your old beliefs, assumptions, and agreements about this particular issue are. Experiment with ones that are less limiting. Affirmations are a wonderful tool for doing this if they are used properly.

Spiritual Shortcuts

AFFIRMATIONS

Affirmations are positive statements designed to assist you in releasing old, limiting beliefs. It is important to first use them as a tool of discovery so you don't just cover up the old belief. Begin by writing your new affirmation and listening for the yeah buts. For example you write "I am lovable" and your mind says yeah but your too fat. You remind yourself your not too fat. Then you again say "I am lovable" and your mind says yeah but your mom never thought so. You remind your self that mom's opinion doesn't matter. You keep writing your affirmation until your mind agrees. At times it feels like you're sweeping the ocean out with a broom but just keep doing it.

Another thing you can do is write your new affirmations on different colored index cards. Read them at least once a day, more often if possible. Take small squares of the same colored paper and hang them everywhere. Put one on your car's rear view mirror, on your computer, on the refrigerator, any pace your eye is apt to notice them. Your mind will subconsciously remember the affirmation because it associates it with the color.

Repetition is the key to using affirmations.

Ultimately our goal is to move beyond beliefs and assumptions and agreements but the first step in that process is to move toward less and less limiting ones.

Practice your new choices

You learned your old behaviors by doing them over and over again. Do the same thing with your new choices.

Evaluate the results you are getting

Decide if you like the changes you've made. Do you like the results you are getting? Is there anything else you need to change or modify?

Do you need to go back to step one again? Do you need to repeat any part of the process to get exactly what you want in your life?

Modify if necessary

Change what ever needs to be changed. Then . . .

Move on to the next issue

Once you get to the top of the mountain you will find another mountain waiting for you on the other side. Take time to enjoy the view and when you're ready start hiking up the next hill.

Spiritual Butterflies

Time and time again I have observed people quit just before their lives were about to change profoundly. Unconsciously they will get close to a core issue and run away from it. They will decide it is time to try something different or that whatever they are doing isn't working or they decide they're just too busy. They will stop doing the very things that were about to create the miracle in their lives. These aren't conscious decisions and often when I talk to them about their decision they really believe whatever they are telling themselves. Fear can cause us to react in very strange ways.

One of my students used the term spiritual butterflies. They never stay long enough anywhere to finish their work, they flit from thing to thing much as a butterfly does with flowers. If you look at your past history you will know if you are a butterfly. Does your attention often wander? Do you lose interest in things? Do you like to change jobs or relationships or friends? Drool over the latest new car? Do you read several books at once? Do you have a hard time finishing things? Does the grass look greenery over there? If you are a butterfly I suggest you decide right here and right now to stick with your process. Follow all the directions and stick around for the miracle.

> ### *The Least You Need to Know*
>
> ▸ Spiritual healing is a process, a journey, and a destination
>
> ▸ You are a spiritual being living inside a physical body
>
> ▸ Change can be easy if you follow the recipe
>
> ▸ The miracle will happen if you don't quit first

Chapter 2

The Fall From Grace

> **In This Chapter**
>
> ➤ The history of healing
>
> ➤ From goddess to god
>
> ➤ Which way do we go?
>
> ➤ Paradise lost

Early in the development of civilization we had a very limited understanding of how our world operated. As a race we were very superstitious, we weren't even sure if the sun would rise the next day unless we appeased the gods. We spent a great deal of time trying to keep the gods happy and really had no idea how to do that.

We got sick emotionally, spiritually, and physically. Life didn't go as we planned, crops failed, lovers left, and people died. We tried to make sense of the chaos around us, for that matter we still do. We came up with theories to explain the universe and religions to explain the needs of the gods. We learned to think about life instead of living it. We are still trying to explain the universe but now we have a world-view that is based on technology and has very little to do with spirituality.

In the Beginning

It's hard to tell what was going on before written history; no one left us any notes. By studying cave drawings, burial practices, tools, and the garbage we left behind we can make certain assumptions. One of them is that early humans were very superstitious. The world was filled with things beyond their control; they felt unsafe and small in comparison to the world around them. They developed stories or myths in their attempt to make sense of the chaos. They banded together and formed alliances. Slowly society developed and the power of the individual gave way to the power of the group. We began to let others tell us what to think and how to feel about things. Seers would interpret the signs and spiritual leaders would decide what people needed to do in order to appease the gods.

Throughout early history humans struggled to understand the causes of physical and emotional sickness. Early humans didn't view death and sickness as a natural part of life. They believed illness and death were due to an imbalance of some sort. They believed the person's spirit was out of harmony with nature, themselves, and with the gods and goddesses. They believed an evil spirit or some sort of spell had caused the great earth mother to withdraw her love and support.

The people of earth decided that if they kept the goddess happy food would be plentiful and the members of the tribe would remain healthy. They didn't understand the correlation between their actions and the outcomes they were achieving. They had to blame their distress on something. The idea that the climate was changing or that they had overgrazed an area was beyond their comprehension. The only thing that made sense to them was that the cause of their happiness or discomfort was due to an external source, beyond their control. They had in some way displeased the forces of nature.

From the beginning of time we've searched for answers, we've looked for someone to tell us how to fix our bodies, our minds and our spirits. We've tried to find explanations for life that allowed us to feel safe. We developed gods and rules for their behavior. The ancient Greeks and Romans built temples to the *Asclepius*, the god of healing. They believed that if you slept in the temple the god would come to the person and cure them or at least tell them what they needed to do if they wanted to heal.

Clarity Corner

Asclepius was considered the god of medicine or healing by the ancient Greeks (Asklepios) and Romans (Aesculapius). He was the son of Apollo (god of healing, truth, and prophecy) and the nymph Coronis. Zeus was afraid he would give immortality to humans so he killed him with a thunderbolt.

On Cos, an island situated off the coast of Turkey there was a temple dedicated to Asclepius. It later became a health resort and the first school of medicine in ancient Greece. Hippocrates, long thought to be the father of modern medicine was one of its more famous residents.

We wanted to believe that we could control our world. If we did something in a certain way we wanted to believe we would get the results we wanted. If we did a fertility ritual in the spring food would be plentiful. We wanted to understand our place in the cosmos and we wanted to know how to wrestle happiness out of life on a consistent basis. Life was harsh and we wanted an explanation that would make it feel gentle and safe. From the beginning of time we have looked for external guarantees and there aren't any *(there are internal ways to guarantee happiness but we'll talk a lot about that later)*.

Creation Myth

All societies have a creation myth. A myth is a narrative or imaginative story that a group of people believes explains the true nature of reality. A creation myth is a symbolic explanation of the beginning of the world as viewed by a particular tribe or group of people. Each society has its own creation myth. It gives order and structure to that societies' universe; it helps the world make sense for them. This myth forms the basis of society; all other practices derive from this myth.

These myths not only explain how the world came into being but they also explain the role human beings play in that universe. They also define the way men and women treat each other. Earlier in history mankind believed they were part of the universe and that they were meant to work in harmony with the earth mother and all of her creatures. As society progressed the myths changed and mankind became a ruler and the sense of separation deepened. Most myths place the earth at the center of the universe and elevate mankind to a place of either supreme ruler or loving caretaker of the earth.

There are five major themes for all of the world's creation myths.
- **Supreme Deity.** This theme is usually found in societies with a highly developed social structure. A single supreme being creates an idyllic world and humans are eventually thrown out of that paradise for offending the being.
- **Emergence.** Human beings are born out of the chaos or the underworld by a great earth mother.
- **World Parents.** The world is the product of the union between the primordial mother and father often represented by the symbols of earth(mother) and sky(father).
- **Cosmic Egg.** Is symbolized in many ways by many cultures. The egg symbolizes the totality from which creation springs forth. The breaking off the egg leads to the rise of individual consciousness.
- **Earth Divers.** The water represents the chaos before creation and then an animal plunges into the water at which point humans are born. The animal often represents a pre-human species. In some myths the diver is the devil and the myth sets up the battle between good and evil as well as the creation of the universe

Creation myths always attempt to explain our place in our world. How we feel about the world and ourselves depends to a very large degree on that myth. If that myth describes a loving, nurturing, and supportive relationship we will tend to feel safe and loved. If the myth describes a judgmental and controlling god we will feel fearful and unsure of ourselves.

A Short History of Healing

Early spirituality and religions were based on the concept of goddess worship. 40,000 years ago the focal point of Stone Age society was the bond between a mother and her child. The people of the earth focused on their sacred relationship with the land and the cycles of nature. Nature was honored with rituals and celebrations. The people considered themselves part of nature, they worked with it rather than trying to control it. They were nomads, following their source of food.

In early society men and women were considered equal and there was no hierarchy. Women were revered, honored, and respected. Since women were able to give birth and create life, they were considered to be part of the goddess. Women's bodies were fully adorned with their worldly possessions when they were buried but men were also buried with a great deal of respect. It was obvious that men and women were considered equal. Women were the healers and counselors. They remained profoundly connected to the earth and their spirituality. The goddess reigned supreme. Harmony with each other and the earth was highly valued. They were peaceful people that coexisted with each other and with the land.

Sage Advice

"Miracles happen, not in opposition to nature, but in opposition to what we know of nature."

St. Augustine

Sickness was considered to be the result of an imbalance between a person and their spirit. Magic and religion played a pivotal role in their healing practices. In many areas of Europe and in Peru they cut small holes in the skulls of sick people to allow the illness or evil spirit to escape. People were often buried with amulets and talisman that obviously didn't work in curing the disease.

Then around 6,000 years ago people began to cultivate crops and society changed drastically. Once we became an agricultural society people no longer surrendered to nature. There was no longer any need to follow the crops. Nature was viewed as a resource, something to be overcome and controlled. Men began to conquer one another and women slowly lost their place of honor. Spirituality and healing were no longer linked together. Domination became a way of life. Warlords ruled society and they were buried with incredible treasures. Women were no longer revered and the commoners were buried without adornment. Society slowly shifted to a patriarchic society.

Laws and rules took the place of a person's inner guidance. Love of self, the sacredness of nature, and respect of others no longer governed life. Priests and lords became intermediaries between a person and god. Women were forced further and further away from the center of society. The goddess took a back seat to a rather controlling male god. As the separation between an individual and their spirit deepened the greater the need for spiritual healing became.

Sage Advice

"Your vision will become clear only when you can look in to your own heart."

Carl Jung

By the Middle Ages women healers were called witches and burned at the stakes. Between 1200 AD and 1800 AD between 4 to 8 million women were killed for being witches. Their property was seized and turned over to the rulers. In the late 1300's, around the time of the Black Plague the Catholic Church proclaimed that healers had to be physicians and must have a degree. Only upper class men were able to go to the universities so women and the lower classes were excluded from the healing arts. Midwives were condemned by the church for easing the pain of childbirth and teaching women about birth control. They continued to practice their art in secrecy with the threat of death looming over them.

As a society we moved further away from a sense of connection to the earth and to one another. Domination became more prevalent in society and the happiness of the individual was hardly a consideration anymore. Healing was taken out of the hands of the people. Healing became something external and done by others to us.

Earlier healing therapies stressed a holistic approach. By the 1700's this was no longer the case. The balance between the mind, body, and spirit was seldom considered.

Witch Doctor?

A witch doctor is defined as a healer or benevolent worker of magic in a non-literate society. Healing really is a form of magic. It requires us to let go of what we have been doing and allow change to occur in our lives. Healing is seldom possible without our participation.

Of course you could try going to one of the temples dedicated to Asclepius but it might be easier to find help locally, in your own neighborhood. In the second section of this book we will explore in detail many of the various healing modalities that are available to assist you.

After my mother died I went to see a medium. She told me I had a curse and to free myself I had to bury all my mother's jewelry on her grave. Then she asked me where she was buried. I told the medium her ashes had been scattered at sea and she looked most distressed. So much for her stealing the family jewels.

A friend later sent me to a woman who called herself a spiritualist. She helped me tremendously with my grief and sense of loss. There are people out there that will help you as well as unscrupulous people who want your money or your adoration. Make a decision to find people that will really help you heal. Spiritual healing is like any other service, make sure you shop around and find the best.

Smoke & Mirrors

Spiritual Healing is a fertile ground for rip off artists. When we are in emotional, physical, or spiritual pain we very vulnerable. There are people out there who will gladly take advantage of you. There are also people out there that honestly want to help. Knowing the difference can be difficult. Ultimately you must learn to trust your inner voice but until then ask other people you trust for recommendations.

If someone guarantees they have all of your answers run away, as fast as you can! If someone wants you to do something that really goes against any of your principles, refuse. If a person tells you to stop having contact with your friends or family, leave immediately.

Some people feel ripped off if a healer charges for their services. I remind people that in earlier times the village always supported their healer. At harvest time they were given the best of everything, they didn't need to charge. In our society we exchange energy by exchanging money.

When you think about your healing the first decision is what needs healing the most? Is it your mind, body, or spirit? Ideally any approach you decide upon will address all three aspects. Without that balance happiness will remain elusive.

Magic and spirituality played a huge role in the medical practices of primitive human beings. Early healers knew the importance of treating the whole person. They knew the mind, body, and spirit needed to be in harmony if the person was to achieve happiness in their life.

The Paths Diverge

In society today everything, including healing, tends to be very fragmented. One day I was sitting at a light waiting for it to turn green. I watched as car after car went by. After a few minutes I started to laugh. I was struck by the fact that we had really taken our sense of separation to the extreme. We had even created small tin boxes that deepened our sense of isolation from each other and from the earth.

When the Catholic Church banned women from being healers the paths of healing diverged sharply. Healers trained in the university no longer treated the whole person, they treated their body. The mind and spirit belonged to the priests.

The rift between body, mind, and spirit continues to deepen. In mainstream society you go to a medical doctor for your body, a therapist for your mind, and a priest or minister for your spirit. They tell you what to do and how to do it. Luckily these divisions are slowly starting to dissolve.

It is very important for you to balance all aspects of your life. I once read about a study done by a group of graduate students. They found that people who maintained a good balance healed much more rapidly. People that failed to balance these aspects either grew worse or remained the same.

Take a few minutes and answer these questions for yourself:

When in your life have you felt the happiest and most fulfilled?

_____

_____

_____

What were you doing?

_____

_____

_____

Clarity Corner

A PATH

The ancient Hawaiians believe there are many paths to the top of the mountain. Each path has different and unique twists and turns but all paths lead to the top of the mountain. Regardless of the path, the view from the top is the same for everyone.

Sage Advice

"The soul is created in a place between Time and eternity: with its highest powers it touches Eternity, with its lower Time."

Meister Eckhart

Has there ever been a time you felt totally balanced and in alignment with yourself?

_____

_____

_____

What did that sense of balance feel like? What did you do to achieve that feeling?

_____

_____

_____

If you haven't what do you imagine it would feel like and what would it take to get there?

_____

_____

_____

What is your definition of spirituality? _____

_____

What is your definition of being connected to your spirit? _____

_____

_____

When you think of being on a path, what does that meant to you? _____

_____

_____

It is time we returned a sense of balance to our lives. It is time for the three aspects of healing to converge and work as one again. You are a multidimensional being – you are a spirit, you have a body, and you have a mind. You operate at all three levels simultaneously so you must learn to balance all aspects of yourself. A gymnast couldn't remain balanced if they only concentrated on keeping part of their body in balance. Can you imagine what someone would look like on the parallel bars if their legs and arms were going in two different directions as they dismounted? It wouldn't be a very graceful landing.

Paradise Lost

In the Judeo-Christian myth of creation Adam and Eve were thrown out of paradise for eating of the tree of the knowledge of good and evil. They stopped listening to their inner voice; good and evil became something that was measured externally. In that moment they began to listen to their heads instead of their spirits and paradise was lost.

What does it really mean to have lost paradise? Symbolically we can view it in many ways. We can view it as the loss of our connection between our mind and spirit. Paradise lost means we've been kicked out of the garden where we were intimately connected to god, where all our needs were met, and we were loved and cared for. As soon as we left the garden we stopped listening to our spirit or our heart and began listening to our mind. We started listening to the voice of fear instead of the voice of love.

In the Judeo-Christian myth Eve listened to the serpent that told her she wouldn't die if she ate the apple from the tree of the knowledge of good and evil. And he was right. The snake is a symbol that has always been associated with the goddess. In the past the women had been the seers, the ones sought after for their guidance. They had learned to trust their inner wisdom to guide them. Their inner voice had the ability to assist them in making decisions. After all the goddess caused man's fall from grace. One of the many messages was don't trust your inner knowing the price is too high.

The women or feminine aspect has become synonymous with the path of inner wisdom, intuition, with the path of the heart and spirit. The male or masculine aspect has become associated with the mind and with the ability to take external action. The woman draws in the energy of creation while the male aspect harnesses it. In this myth the woman betrays the man and persuades him to eat the apple. The feminine aspect is not to be trusted. Action not intuition is of value. Another message is don't listen to your heart or your spirit only your mind can be trusted.

As a species once we lost paradise we believed we had to fight for everything we got. It reflects the change of attitude that took place in society toward nature and life as a whole. It explains life's hardships in an understandable manner and it deepens the division between a person's head and their heart. Paradise is lost

Clarity Corner

HEART

When I refer to our heart I am not referring to the physical or emotional heart. I am referring to our connection to our spirit. We can't connect to our spirit through our mind; a spiritual connection is something we feel rather than something we think about.

I use the term heart to mean the center of our essence, the part of us that contains our intuition, spirit and feelings.

as soon as we lose our connection to our spirit or our divinity. Once we value our rational, linear mind more than we value our inner knowing paradise no longer exists.

In the Judeo-Christian myth one of the first things that happens after Adam and Eve have a few children is the kids start killing each other. Violence becomes a way of life. As a species we start hurting one another; we implement laws in an attempt to control the actions of the individual, which is impossible. We no longer feel a profound connection to our world. We feel alone. We are seldom present in the moment experiencing life instead we spend most of our time thinking about what's happening. As we learn to think about life we lose our ability to actually live it.

Losing paradise is a process. We slowly shifted our focus from our spirit to our mind. When we lose paradise we also lose our godself. This loss of connection is at the very core of our need for spiritual healing. Once we view history from this perspective events take on a new meaning. The further away from our spiritual connection we move the more violence there is in society.

What did we really lose? We lost our ability to feel safe, to feel loved, cared for, and protected. As we learn to reconnect with our spirit paradise can once again be found.

Coming Full Circle

Spiritual healing is really a process in which paradise is recaptured by our heads and our hearts. When we remember we are part of the whole much of our fear and discomfort leaves us. We find an inner sense of peace that was previously missing in our life.

A state of grace is defined as receiving unmerited love freely and openly. It is also defined as the influence of spirit operating in a person's life. Once we open our hearts and reconnect to our spiritual essence we step back into a state of grace. We fell from grace when we lost our connection to our spirit and ourselves. We can live in a state of grace every moment of every day once we reestablish that connection. Spiritual healing is a process of remembering of that connection; it returns us to a state of balance with the world about us and with ourselves.

When we come full circle and reconnect with our spirit we learn to live life from our heart while we use our head as the wonderful tool it was meant to be. Our rational, linear thinking no longer enslaves us. We become the master of our fate and life becomes a joyous expression of our divinity.

Practice does make following guided meditations easier. Relax and enjoy the process. Allow it to be whatever it needs to be for you. Make it uniquely your own and don't judge your experience. It is after your experience and no one else's.

Guided meditations are a wonderful way to get in touch with hidden information and feelings. The most important thing to remember is to avoid judging your experience. When I first start working with someone they usually feel they aren't doing it right. The only way you can "do this wrong" is by not doing

Spiritual Shortcuts

MEDITATION

Find a place you won't be disturbed for a few minutes. Unplug the phone and put up the do not disturb sign. Take some time just for yourself. You could read the mediation into a tape recorder, have someone read it to you, or just read it over a few times and do it by memory. Give yourself permission to relax and enjoy the process.

You can't do this wrong, just play along. Make believe you can see what I suggest you see and you will. Everyone "sees" differently but we all have the ability to see, if we didn't we wouldn't be able to think. If I say imagine a red fire truck you might not clearly see a picture of it but you would know it was there, somehow. Well that's the way you visualize or mentally see things. Some people see mental pictures, some people hear sounds, and some people just have a feeling. It doesn't really matter how you do it the most important thing is to let yourself do it.

it and even that isn't wrong. Even if your mind wanders and you feel like you aren't getting anything out of the experience you are. The more frequently you meditate the easier it will be, as the saying goes practice makes perfect.

Start by focusing your attention on your breathing. Really notice your breath. Notice how it feels as it comes in through your nose and how it feels as your lungs expand and contract. Take a few minutes to really notice your breathing, and while you are doing that, mentally give yourself permission to relax. As you continue to observe your breathing, notice how your chest relaxes. With each breath, really allow your chest to relax. Let out a few heavy sighs, take a few really deep breaths, and let yourself relax. *(Long pause)*

Settle back into your spirit: settle back into your body. Just follow your breath and let it flow into a gentle rhythm. Follow that rhythm; become that rhythm. Just let your breath relax you. Take some time to notice how good it feels to relax and let yourself sink into that feeling of relaxation. *(Pause)* If your mind wanders, just allow that to relax you even more. Bring your attention back to your breathing and relax.

Become aware of the muscles in the top of your head, around your scalp and your ears, and just gently invite them to relax. Focus your attention on the front of your face. Relax your face and all the tiny muscles around your eyes. Take a deep breath and give yourself permission to go deeper, to relax, to let go. Remind yourself that you could open your eyes any time you want, but it feels so good to relax that you just let go. Take a deep breath and go even deeper.

Relax your jaw, let your tongue fall to the floor of your mouth, allow your jaw to part slightly and just relax. Feel the relaxation floating down your spine: feel it go down vertebrae by vertebrae, relaxing you totally and completely. Feel your chest filling with a deep sense of relaxation. Feel your chest opening, relaxing, and letting go. Feel that feeling going down into your stomach. *(Pause)*

Now feel it going down your legs and out your feet. Imagine yourself totally surrounded by an energy of peace, of love, and of deep relaxation. Notice how your body feels. Let the energy of relaxation and peace flow through you. And relax, just breathe deeply and relax. *(Long pause)*

Imagine yourself sitting on top of a hill looking out at the countryside. The air is warm and the wind is gently caressing your skin. You feel totally at peace, relaxed, and safe. The sky is incredibly blue and there are beautiful, fluffy, white clouds floating by. You lie back and take a deep breath and just watch the clouds. You feel so relaxed, so at peace.

Now, allow yourself to feel one with the sky. Imagine yourself becoming a cloud, just floating along. You are part of the magnificent sky. Feel your connection to everyone and everything. Feel the wind, feel the sky and let yourself relax into the feeling.*(Long Pause)*

Imagine yourself being loved. Imagine yourself being loved by all of nature. Really allow yourself to feel the love. Feel that sense of self-acceptance flowing through you, embracing you and filling you with a deep sense of peace and love. Imagine yourself connecting fully and completely with your spirit and yourself. Allow yourself to feel totally loved and accepted.*(Pause)*

Just relax into the feeling of being one, of being loved. Clouds contain the sun and the moon and the stars. They are one with everything we eat or drink. They hold the water of this planet and nurture all of life. Let yourself be a cloud and let yourself be loved. Stay with the experience for a time. *(long pause)*

When you are done, gently and lovingly bring yourself back to this room.

Take at least a few minutes to bring yourself back. Get up slowly and give yourself some time to become oriented to the room again. You might want to stretch gently and take a few deep breaths.

You might want to take a few minutes to write about your experience.

The Least You Need to Know

> Society went from worshipping the goddess to worshiping god

> The advent of agriculture drastically changed society

> The loss our sacred connection to nature affected all of life

> We can regain paradise as we regain our spiritual connection

> Spiritual healing helps us to feel safe and loved again

Chapter 3

The Paradox or Why Bother?

> **In This Chapter**
> - Let's make sense of what doesn't make sense.
> - Resistance really is futile.
> - Don't take anything personally.
> - You only have to find the eye of the tiger.
> - Life is a journey–not a destination.

When I decided my life wasn't working and I wanted to do something about it the last thing I wanted to do was begin a spiritual journey. Spirituality was for monks and losers, certainly not for me, or so I thought. Over the years my thinking about almost everything has changed drastically and clearly my opinion on that one changed. I've learned to question my beliefs, embrace confusion, and focus on the process rather than the goal.

Mentors and friends would suggest I go inside, to connect with my spirituality and I thought they were crazy. Why should I bother doing all that work? Today all that 'work' is a pleasure. I enjoy life moment by moment and focus on what I have instead of what I don't have. Today I know life is glorious even in the midst of chaos.

That Just Doesn't Make Any Sense

The idea of spiritual healing itself seems to be a paradox. Why do we need to heal? What do we need to heal? If we only want to improve the quality of our life why do we have to look inside? Why do we need to heal our relationship to our spirit if we are that spirit? If we are that spirit we're already perfect so why do we have to change? How will healing the relationship we have with our spirit improve the quality of our physical life? After all if we just had more money, a better job, a great place to live, a sexier body, or a perfect relationship we'd be happy. Why should we do all this other stuff?

A paradox seldom makes sense but then again neither does listening to your inner voice. Learning to listen to your inner guidance may at times seem downright crazy, foolish, and outrageous but it is a process and a valuable one at that. During my early explorations I found it was important to put aside the cynical part of my being.

Sage Advice
"True wisdom is less presuming than folly. The wise man doubteth often, and changes his mind; the fool is obstinate, and doubteth not; he knoweth all things but his own ignorance."
— Akhenaton

A paradox is a statement or assumption that seems to be a contradiction but may in fact be the truth. As I proceeded with my spiritual explorations I ran in to so many paradoxes I decided the process of spiritual healing was really just a series of paradoxes. At first the paradoxes drove me crazy but eventually I got excited because whenever I ran into one I knew I was getting closer to the truth.

Spiritual Shortcuts

YOUR INNER VOICES

Pay attention to your inner world for a few days. Notice the various ways in which you talk to yourself. Make a game of it. Carry a small notebook with you and every fifteen minutes stop and ask yourself: "Who said that?" Then listen to what you were saying and write it down. After a while you will have a whole list of characters.

If you can't remember to ask yourself "who said that" get a watch with an alarm. Even if you don't write down the comments this is a very powerful exercise. Whenever you are feeling any discomfort or you have to make a decision ask yourself this question. You'll be amazed at the answers you get. Eventually you will be able to listen more to the gentle, loving voices instead of the harsh, judgmental ones. Once you do that the quality of your life will improve drastically.

Within each of us there is a symphony of voices each singing a different tune. There is the voice of the cynic, the voice of the wounded child, the voice of your parents, the voice of reason, and the quiet voice of your inner wisdom just to mention a few. If you're going to learn how to act in life instead of reacting you have to learn to listen to the voice of your inner wisdom. That voice will always guide you toward your greater good. Your inner voice always makes choices based on love instead of fear. At first listening to your inner voice makes very little sense but not listening makes even less sense.

Have you ever had the feeling to do or not do something and not listened to yourself only to regret the decision later? Hindsight of course is twenty-twenty. That feeling is generated by our inner voice and learning to differentiate it from the other voices is an integral part of this journey. For now, just start listening to yourself.

Don't Take it Personally

Believe it or not nothing in life is personal. Life just happens and we happen to be in the way. Once you are able to stop taking things personally it is very freeing. At one level when someone is angry they aren't really angry with you they are angry and you just happen to be there. "Now just wait a minute," you say. Believe me this will be a long conversation we will have in stages.

You only take things personally when you already believe what is being said. Let's say your friend is angry with you because they thought you were inconsiderate and thoughtless. If you believe in yourself and know you weren't thoughtless you'd realize they were just in a bad mood and you wouldn't take their anger personally. If you have an emotional wound in this area of course you would believe they were angry with you and react to their anger.

What your mind says to you isn't personal either. Today you'll repeat 95% of the same thoughts you thought yesterday. Your mind was trained to think in a certain way, it isn't speaking to you personally it is just repeating what it learned. Now, if your mind isn't directing its thoughts at you personally why would someone else? Think about it. Not taking things personally is incredible freeing. We react to the people in a habitual way and it really isn't personal.

Smoke & Mirrors

EMOTIONS

Not taking things personally DOES NOT mean don't feel your emotions. It also doesn't mean that you're doing something wrong if you do react to events in your life. Once you start to have an emotional reaction it is too late not to feel it. When we do have an emotional reaction it is most useful to acknowledge it and instead of blaming it on an external source realize we have an emotional wound. Then we can talk lovingly to ourselves about it. If your best friend came to you all upset hopefully you wouldn't just tell them to get over it. You'd comfort them and let them talk about it. Give yourself a chance to understand why you are reacting. Avoid judging yourself.

Realize that emotions are a call to action. When you are feeling something ask yourself what you need. Reacting to the external event isn't the answer. That just causes more turmoil and takes us further away from the real solution. What we really need to do is go inside and find out what our emotional needs are. Do we need to nurture ourselves? Get more rest? Set boundaries with someone? Call a friend? The most important thing we can do is get quiet, look inside, and ask ourselves what we need to do to take care of ourselves.

Ironically we seldom hear what others say either. We filter all incoming information through our filter system so it is all distorted. Someone can tell you they love you and you'll hear you're a dumb idiot. What we hear and what we see totally depends upon our filter system. Life really isn't personal.

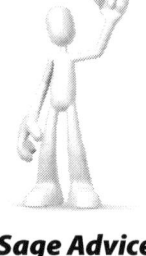

I Just Want to be Happy

Since life isn't personal your happiness doesn't come from external sources either. One of the many gifts of not taking life personally is that we can be happy regardless of what is happening around us. If we want to be happy we just have to change what we are telling ourselves.

We can decide if life is half empty or half full. No event in our life has emotions automatically attached to it. We attach the emotions by what we tell ourselves about the event. Back to the friend who thinks you're thoughtless. You can accept the anger and be miserable, you can react to it and have a fight, or you could be a loving and caring friend and find out what's really going on.

Picture this: Your friend, Bob, comes into the restaurant and starts yelling at you about your thoughtlessness. You don't take it personally and realize this is totally out of character for Bob. You respond very lovingly. You acknowledge that he feels you've been thoughtless and you express you're regret that he feels that way. You gently and lovingly ask him what happened. Eventually he tells you his had a huge fight with his boss early that day and lost his job. When you called and asked him out for dinner he was worried about money and decided it was thoughtless of you to ask him to spend money. The mystery is solved.

Scenarios like that are played out daily in our lives. Unfortunately we usually take the feelings personally and react to them. We aren't able to choose how to act as long as we take things personally. When we are able to act we can choose how we feel about any situation in our life.

So if you really want to be happy stop taking things personally. Start choosing what you tell yourself about life instead of believing your mind.

Sage Advice

"Just as a picture is drawn by an artist, surroundings are created by the activities of the mind."

Buddha

Sage Advice

"A good rule for mental conduct – think whatever it makes you truly happy to think."

Black Elk

But They Said...

A useful question to ask yourself is, "Do you want to be right or do you want to be happy?" When you are upset by or with someone you have to hold onto what you're telling yourself about their actions in order to stay upset. If you want to be happy all you have to do is tell yourself something different about what they did or said.

You're walking down the street and someone yells an insult out of the car window. You get furious at the comment and you walk down the street thinking of all the things you could have said. You rage about how dare they say such a thing. You take what they said personally and allow your mind to run with it. They pushed on one of your emotional wounds; that place where you don't feel good enough. You are really reacting to your wound, not them. If you no longer have a wound you can easily dismiss what they say. You realize that what they said has more to do with how they feel about themselves then is does about you.

I've always loved my blue eyes. If someone insults my eyes I have no emotional reaction, I can laugh about it. Most of my life I was overweight and felt very inadequate about being fat. Until I healed that wound whenever someone made fun of my body I couldn't help but react.

So what 'they say' doesn't really matter unless we believe it. When someone likes me it has nothing to do with me. I just remind them that they love themselves; I push on their self-love button. When someone dislikes me it isn't me they dislike it is a part of themselves they don't like, I merely push on that emotional wound.

The gift in all this is that if we take responsibility for our emotional reaction we can use our reactions as guideposts to our wounds and heal. As long as we point a finger at them we can't heal. The blame game keeps both parties trapped in the swamp created by our emotional wounds.

Can't do This to Get That

One of the hardest things for me to learn was that I couldn't do my spiritual healing in order to get something. When I didn't have enough money to pay the bills and I tried doing my healing so I'd have enough money for everything it didn't work. When I pursued my spirituality just to pursue my spirituality the money came. I never understood why that worked, I just observed that it did work every time.

Control and manipulation are the tools most often used by our wounded-self. Our wounded-self feels small and insignificant, it is fearful most of the time. But if our wounded-self is in control, if the wounded-self knows how to manipulate the world to get what it wants then it feels happy. Our wounded-self only feels safe when it's in control. If you are trying to manipulate someone into loving you by being loving it won't work. People pleasing or codependency won't get us what we want.

> **Sage Advice**
> "Happiness is a butterfly which, when pursued, is always beyond our reach, but if you will sit down quietly, may alight upon you."
> Nathaniel Hawthorne

What's in it for me?

First you have to define it. Frequently in life we have many un-negotiated expectations. We do something for a friend and then we expect them to do something in return. That's fine if we tell them first, but we usually don't and then we get disappointed. Many relationships are seriously damaged by un-negotiated expectations. Our relationship with ourselves can be affected as well. When I began doing my healing work I wasn't aware that I had a lot of expectations. At first I wasn't really on a spiritual journey, I was on a quest to get a better job, find a great place to live, and find my life's partner.

I was placing conditions on things; I'll do this if I get that. When I wouldn't get that I'd get angry and stop doing my emotional explorations. It was a wonderful way for me to focus on things that didn't really matter instead of feeling those pesky emotions I'd so successfully avoided all those years. I'd also judge myself terrible when I wouldn't get what I what I was bartering for, I was sure I'd done something wrong.

Eventually I became aware of my un-negotiated expectations and released them. Now if I have an expectation I make sure it is realistic and that I verbalize it to myself and anyone else it involves. I no longer do my spiritual healing to get things, I do it because I want to and in the process my life improves. Your life will improve dramatically but only if you are doing this just to do it.

Negotiated expectations are an entirely different matter. Each person has an opportunity to say yes or no and to set any necessary limits. Relationships really thrive when we negotiate the nature of our interactions. It is so much easier when everyone knows what is expected of them. If we agree to act in a certain manner it's easy to follow through but when we don't know what's expected of us we can only guess. Since everyone lives in their own private world my guess about what you want is very often wrong. I will act the way I want you to act not necessarily the way you want me to act.

Clarity Corner

CODEPENDENCY

Codependency is a form of addiction. A person is literally addicted to a particular relationship or to relationships in general. When we are a codependent our actions are controlled by our fear of disrupting our relationships. We are controlled and controlling; we are manipulated and manipulating. We lose ourselves in order to maintain the relationship. Codependency affects all areas of a person's life. It is a fear-based way of dealing with the world and it is impossible to be truly loving when we are codependent.

Sage Advice

"Happiness is the absence of striving for happiness."

Chuang-tzu

You can negotiate with yourself about how you want yourself to act as well. Our expectations about ourselves were formed while we were young children and we didn't have the ability to choose back then. Now you can choose how you want to act. One of the most important decisions I made was to act from a place of love rather that fear on a regular basis. Years ago I had a very negative opinion of people who were loving, gentle, and vulnerable I thought they all wanted something and that they were weak. Once I healed that wound I realized how being vulnerable was much more powerful than being angry.

Spiritual Shortcuts

Write down your expectations. What do you expect to get out of this journey? What do you expect from your friends and family? Look deep within yourself. What do you really expect of them? What do you expect of yourself? Perfection perhaps?

For years I unknowingly expected my father to support me. I expected him to give me money whenever I needed it. Until I let go of that expectation I wasn't able to support myself. My relationship with my father was strained and we fought almost constantly.

Take sometime and realize how many unnegotiated expectations you have in your life.

Life as a Sacred Act

Life is sacred. When we live that way life is magical. Even brushing our teeth can become a profound experience. Long ago the people of the earth treated the land and all its inhabitants in a sacred manner. Before an animal was killed its spirit was thanked for giving up its life. The land was honored and cared for, ceremonies were preformed and prayers offered before the crops were planted. We were much more in touch with nature. As a race we were very superstitious and unaware of our own divinity.

Then the pendulum swung to the other extreme. Our mind began to look for scientific explanations for everything. We developed belief systems that supported slavery and human sacrifice. Society moved further and further away from its sacred connection. Happiness became more illusive and the life of the individual was valued less and less.

As we learn to reconnect with that sense of sacredness life becomes richer and more rewarding. Living life as if everything is a sacred act is a beautiful way to live. One of my favorite authors is the Vietnamese Buddhist Monk, Thich Nhat Hanh. He writes about living life mindfully and being consciously aware of the sacred nature of every moment. The way he writes about life is beautiful. In his retreat center in France there is a bell that is rung throughout the day to remind people to be mindful. When he writes about the bell he refers to the bell being invited to sing.

Clarity Corner
A SACRED ACT

When something is sacred it is defined as being entitled to respect and veneration. It is held in high regard and is treated reverently. We take pains to maintain it and nurture it.

When we perform a sacred act we do it with full awareness and with a loving and open heart. We choose our actions carefully and make sure they are respectful and reverent. Within the sacred there is often a sense of wonder and awe. When I treat things as sacred I'm filled with a sense of wonder at the beauty of life.

Making life a sacred act isn't going to change what you do but it will change your experience of doing it. Making life sacred will allow you to be more fully alive than you ever imagined possible. Your enjoyment of life increases immensely. I found the sky was bluer, the air sweeter, and people more beautiful.

Making life a sacred act is merely a choice. It is a matter of how we view things. If we think of something as sacred we will experience it that way. Just think about the difference between a bell ringing and one being invited to sing. The difference is subtle but very powerful. When we perform a scared act we do it lovingly so we have absolutely no ulterior motives. If we are doing anything to get something we aren't being loving we are being controlling.

Me, You, Us, and Them

All of life is a relationship. Life is the relationship you have to me and to you and to all us and to them. We have relationships 'with' people as well as 'to' them. Part of clearing out our filter system is clearing up our relationships.

One of the things we often do is create allies. When we are in the midst of one of our dramas the last thing we want someone to do is point out that it's really our filter system. Instead we find someone who will agree with us. Then we can talk about how terrible they are. We don't want someone to say to us, "Do you think you heard them wrong or made a false assumption?" Every time we run to an ally we get to be right instead of being happy. We will continue to create the same drama until we clear out our filters enough to make different choices.

I decided to change the format of my on-going classes in order to assist people in moving through their emotional wounds more rapidly. The night I announced the changes several people weren't there. A few of the students heard the changes through their filter systems and were afraid of being abandoned. It was too frightening to talk directly to me so they called other classmates who they knew would play the role of allies. Before you knew it we had a huge drama going on. People that weren't there were having feelings about what they heard had been said even though they didn't really know what was said. A few people took the risk of checking things out with me and were able to see their emotional wounds. Once we see the wound we at least have a chance of healing it.

Being aware of the nature of our relationships is so important to our growth. So often we grow up with the mentality of us against them. We spend so much of our life trying to find an 'us' to become our ally against a hostile universe. The only problem is the 'us' keeps turning into 'them' and we are alone with our emotional pain again. When we finally deicide we don't need allies healing will be a much easier process.

As we learn to have an open heart and realize we don't have to defend ourselves life takes on a new dimension. We feel safe enough to face even our most troubling beliefs and let them go.

Sage Advice

Thousands of candles can be lighted from a single one, and the life of the candle will not be shortened. You don't have to blow out my candle in order to make yours burn brighter.

An Ancient Proverb

Resistance is Futile

Whatever you resist persists. If we resist looking at something it doesn't go away. My experience is that if I am avoiding something it becomes more and more prevalent in my life until I can't ignore it. I call that turning up the volume. Eventually the volume gets so loud there is absolutely no way I can ignore. The emotional pain also increases. When we get in enough pain we become willing to deal with the issue. After a while I learned to deal with things before they hurt so much.

When we first begin this journey we generally spend a great deal of our time moving away from emotional pain. At some point I realized I could either move away from pain or move toward pleasure. In order to move toward pleasure I had to stop resisting growth. I had to stop avoiding my issues and embrace them. Moving toward pleasure required that I had to begin looking for my issues before they found me. If I wasn't getting the results I wanted in an area of my life I needed to start looking for the reasons. I had to start uncovering the beliefs that were holding me back and change them.

Resistance is useful but it can also be painful. Without gravity we would have a difficult time moving around on this planet. We need something to push against in order to propel ourselves forward. Gravity also keeps us from spinning off, out into space. If we fall down or bump into something it hurts. Gravity serves a very useful purpose and so does our resistance. Our resistance to seeing our filter system limits us but it also gives us something to push against. We are an unlimited being so when we experience limitations we aren't comfortable. We chafe against the limitations and eventually are propelled into doing something about them.

As with any of the tools you will be introduced to in this book you can either use them to hurt yourself or heal. You can use your resistance to help yourself move forward or to help yourself stay stuck. The choice is yours and yours alone. Use your resistance as a signal telling you which way to go. Your mind will usually tell you to run in the opposite direction but moving directly toward whatever you are revisiting will result in the greatest growth. Remember your mind will always tell you to go in the opposite direction of your growth. Until you retrain it, your mind believes its safety lies in maintaining your filter system. Your mind would rather be right than be happy

Finding the Eye of the Tiger

A tiger, when it is hungry, is intent on its prey and totally focused. It will not fail. If you look into the eye of that tiger you will know what is needed to be success. You would see an unwavering focus and a commitment to do whatever it takes to catch its prey. The tiger knows it must catch an animal or starve to death. Its ability to hunt is a matter of life and death.

Ancient Wisdom: A Korean Folk Tale
The warlord took the woman's husband away to defend his territory. For years the woman prayed for her husbands safety. When he didn't return she started praying for his soul.

After many years her husband came home but he had turned into a bitter, old man. She went to her friend who was a great healer. Her friend told her there was a magic potion that would cure her husband but that she would have to collect all of the ingredients herself.

She traveled to the distant riverbank to collect all the herbs. After many nights he returned and her friend told her she needed one more ingredient. She needed to go into the mountains and collect the whisker from a live tiger. The woman looked shocked and walked away in tears. Her hope was shattered.

She awoke in the middle of the night and knew what she must do. She climbed out of her bed and took a bowl of fresh meat with her. She placed it outside the tiger's den and waited downwind. The tiger came out and smelled the air to make sure he was safe and then he ate the meat before he returned to his den. For many nights the woman watched moving ever closer. One night, when the time was right, she jumped out and grabbed on of his whiskers. She ran all the way home.

The next morning she went triumphantly to her friend's hut. Her friend took the whisker and threw it into the fire. The woman was shocked to see her prize consumed by the flames.

"You have all you need my friend. Take what you learned with the tiger and apply it to your life. With that discipline and dedication you can change anything. When you put your heart and soul into anything you can move mountains."

For us to be successful in life we also have to have that focus. The more we can reach inside of ourselves and find that eye of the tiger the easier change becomes. My cat is well fed; her ability to hunt is relatively unimportant in her life for her it is a matter of sport. There are hundreds of feral or wild cats in Hawaii. When I watch them hunt their focus and the value they place on hunting is very different. For most of them it is a matter of life and death.

I watch my students. Some of them play at doing their healing while some of them do it as if it's a matter of life and death. The results they achieve are very different. If you want your life to transform into a magnificent work of art find the eye of the tiger. If you are half hearted in this journey the results you achieve will reflect your lack of commitment to yourself.

Reaching for the Tool Again: A Meditation

Take a few minutes to relax. Shut off the phone and do whatever you need to do so you won't be disturbed for the next ten or fifteen minutes.

Focus your attention on your breathing. Breath in as you count to ten. Then hold your breath to the count of ten. Exhale to the count of ten and then hold your breath to the count of ten. Do this three times. *(Pause)*

Now take a deep breath and relax. Relax your shoulders and let go of any tension you may be carrying in your body. As you inhale breathe in relaxation and as you exhale let go of anything unlike relaxation. *(Long pause)*

Now imagine that you're a big cat. The sun is warm and you are all stretched out over the limb of a tree. You are safe and warm above the savanna, totally relaxed. Really allow yourself to feel what that would feel like. Feel your muscles. Really let yourself imagine being a big cat and stretch. Imagine what it would feel like to have such a strong and flexible body.

Now think about a cat as it focuses on its prey. Let yourself feel that focus, feel the intensity of that single purpose focus. Now imagine what that would feel like in your life. What would it feel like to have that sort of intensity? Go back and forth between to the two images until you get a clear sense of how that would feel in your life. *(Long Pause)*

When you feel done with this exercise bring yourself gently and lovingly back to this room. Take a deep breath and remind yourself that you did just fine.

Take a few minutes to write about your experience. Write about what it would mean to you and your process if you did have the eye of the tiger. What would you have to do in order to achieve that type of focus and intensity?

Life is a Journey, Not a Destination

You will find your pleasure, your happiness, your joy, and your freedom in the journey not in the destination. If we postpone our happiness until tomorrow it will never get here. Tomorrow never arrives because by the time tomorrow gets here it is already today. If we think we'll be happy when we get something we are almost certain to be disappointed. But if we focus our attention on the present moment and enjoy that, by the time we get to the destination we've already been happy for a while.

Years ago I had a store built for me in a remodeled woolen mill. The building was gorgeous. It sat overlooking a raging river. The windows were twelve feet high and the ceilings were fourteen feet high, made of sandblasted hard wood. I worried so much about the completion date and the money it was costing me I never really enjoyed the process. By the time it was finished I had moved on to worrying about something else. I never really had the time to enjoy my accomplishment. How often have you stopped your enjoyment of the moment by worrying about something that might happen in the future?

We rob ourselves of our happiness by forgetting that it always exists in the moment. If you are driving somewhere and hate every moment of the drive by the time you get there you will be all stressed out. But if you take time to savor the process of getting there you will also be able to enjoy the destination. Life is the same way. As much as possible allow yourself to enjoy the process of healing your life. Don't judge your progress or your process and try not to focus too much on the end result. You will be much happier and your progress will seem to go much faster.

Do you remember how long it took as a child for summer vacation to arrive? As you get older have you noticed how fast do the months go by? When you are worried about paying the bills it seems like you just paid them and here they are again. But if we focus on the moment time no longer matters. So focus on the journey and let the destination take care of itself.

The Least You Need to Know

- If you do your spiritual healing in order to get something it just won't work.

- No sense in taking life personally because it isn't.

- You can be as happy as you make your mind up to be.

- Whatever you resist is like gum on the bottom of your shoe, it doesn't go away.

- Enjoy every moment and the goals will take care of themselves.

- The more sacred you make your life the better it gets.

Chapter 4

Beware, the Snake Oil Salesman

> **In This Chapter**
>
> ➤ Trusting yourself could save your life.
>
> ➤ Discernment is the most important tool there is.
>
> ➤ There are no guarantees.
>
> ➤ Dreams are important.
>
> ➤ There is no such thing as a curse.

A con artist knows that there's a fool born every minute and believe me they're out there looking for them. We tend to begin exploring the concept of spiritual healing when our lives are in flux, when we are unsure which way to turn, and we truly need guidance. When we are in emotional turmoil or at a turning point in our life we tend to be more vulnerable to unscrupulous people that are not really there to help us.

When I began my journey I quickly realized two things. First and foremost I needed to quiet the cynical part of my nature if I was going to truly heal and secondly I needed to be careful where I placed my trust. Ultimately I learned I needed to trust myself but that was hard. My cynical inner voice stopped me from feeling loved so at first it was a juggling act. I would move forward, trust a little, take a risk, and then retreat back into myself. Eventually I learned to tell the difference between a person who truly wanted to help me and a snake oil salesman. By the end of this chapter you'll know how to do that too.

Put a Nickel on the Drum and Be Saved

My grandmother loved to watch TV evangelists. For years she sent money to support their ministries and was horrified when all the sex scandals broke out. She felt betrayed because she had trusted them.

Trust is a funny thing. We seem to spend a great deal of time trying to find people we can trust when the person we really need to trust is ourselves. As a child I was told not to trust anyone. I became afraid of being hurt and that fear isolated me from others. Whenever we make a decision based in fear the best result we can get is to more fear. If we make a decision based in love we produce more love.

So if we trust someone from a place of fear it is almost certain that our trust will be broken. I always tell my students not to trust me. When I say that they look at me in disbelief. Whenever someone trusts me from that desperate place of please don't hurt me the only thing I can do is disappointed them. Their trust comes from a place of fear. They don't trust themselves so they want me to take care of them. Am I there to help them? Absolutely. Will I disappoint them if they trust me? Unfortunately, yes. Do I hurt them intentionally? No, that's just the way fear works.

> **Clarity Corner**
>
> **Snake oil** is any number of liquid elixirs guaranteed to cure everything that won't really cure anything. These potions often had addictive substances in them so the buyers would continue to want more.

But why does fear work that way? We all have emotional wounds and they act like blind spots. Those wounds stop us from clearly asking for what we want. We think we have communicated what we want and need but we haven't. Usually what we actually communicate creates the very events we are trying to avoid. Our emotional wounds prevent us from asking important questions or they prevent us from hearing the answers.

One of my students had a lot of issues around money. Time and time again she had been disappointed when people she trusted hadn't paid her back. She went shopping with me one day when I was in the midst of moving my office. I bought some cleaning supplies and didn't realize I had no cash until I was at the check out. She lent me the money. I more or less forgot about the five dollars until a month later when we were out having lunch. I paid for her lunch and told her to forget it because I'd just remembered I owed her five dollars.

She went on to say that she had been waiting to see if I was going to pay her back. Our relationship had been hanging in the balance and I wasn't even aware of it. Her wound was such that she didn't want to ask me for the money instead her wound told her that five dollars was a test of my trustworthiness. Was it my responsibility to pay her back? Of course, but my forgetfulness had nothing to do with trying to rip her off. It wasn't until years later that she understood the difference and saw where her wound made her choices for her. Did she know I was often forgetful? Yes, but her wound told her to trust me to remember so she could prove that it wasn't safe to trust. Fear would have triumphed once again. If she'd simply asked me for the money trust wouldn't have even been an issue.

What does placing your trust in someone really mean? When we trust a person it usually means we expect them to do something. We expect that person to take care of us, or to do something in a specific manner, or to not do something. Trusting someone generally means we have some un-negotiated expectations. And if we haven't clearly communicated what we want and are assuming that person will do it we are setting ourselves up to be disappointed. We look for someone else to trust because we don't trust ourselves. We try to trust something outside of ourselves to alleviate our fears and all it does is create more fear. That is the way fear works.

If on the other hand we trust from a place of love we create more love. We trust in a way that is nurturing. We clearly ask for what we want and we negotiate our expectations. If I clearly say to you I want you to do something you have the freedom to say yes or no. At least then I can reasonably expect you to do what you said you would do. If you don't I can talk to you about it. People tend to be consistent. If you fail to keep your word on a regular basis I can trust that you will fail to keep your word. I know what to expect.

When we trust ourselves we believe in our basic integrity or wholeness. When we look beyond ourselves for something to trust we usually don't have faith in our own choice making ability. That is why we trust an evangelist who obviously cares more for the money than they do for us and fail to trust the friends that really love us. It is safer that way, fear only feels safe with more fear – love is the real threat to our fear based belief system.

Sage Advice
"A belief is not merely an idea the mind possesses; it is an idea that possesses the mind."
Robert Bolton

I Promise This Time it Will Work

How many times have you promised yourself that tomorrow things would be different? Tomorrow you wouldn't overeat or get angry or in some way change your behavior only to find yourself doing the same thing over and over again. How many times has someone in your life said, "I'm sorry, I won't ever do that again." only to repeat their behavior a few days later?

We place our trust in promises that we know won't be kept and then decide it isn't safe to trust. We try to ignore the fact that we knew the promises were a lie to begin with. The solution lies in learning how to listen to our healthy inner voice. Our belief system will try to tell us it isn't safe to trust. Trust isn't the issue knowing when to trust is. Our wounded inner voice will tell us to trust when we shouldn't and not to trust when we should. That cynical inner voice is the voice of our wounds, it tries to keep us safe but what it really does is keep our wounds in tact. Part of the healing process is learning to know the difference between our wounded self and our true inner self.

We can sell ourselves a lie better than anyone else. We often do 'sales pitches' on ourselves and convince ourselves of all sorts of lies and inconsistencies. We can persuade ourselves to do things we'd never do for someone else. Every morning we wake up, remind ourselves about all our limitations, and then act accordingly.

Part of spiritual healing is learning to know the difference between a sales pitch and the truth. It is important to remember that the best snake oil salesman in your life is yourself. And we get addicted to our lies. It seems so much safer to believe we are limited than to remember our limitless nature.

How do I tell the difference?

If you really pay attention to your body you will always be able to tell when you are trying to fool yourself. When I am about to say something that is not exactly the truth I get a funny feeling in my stomach. One of my students gets a severe pain in her head when she is trying to convince herself of something. Everyone's signals are different. In this exercise you will begin to get in touch with what your signals are.

Finding Your Inner Signals Exercise

Find a place you won't be disturbed for a few minutes. Take a few deep breaths and let yourself relax. Relax your shoulders and focus your attention on your breathing. Gently close your eyes and let your mind drift. Notice your breath and allow it to slow down. Allow it to become easy and relaxed.

Now begin to think about a time in the past when you lied to yourself about something. It could be a time you misplaced your trust or told yourself you were going to do something and didn't. Just let yourself remember. Take yourself back to that time. What were you feeling in your body? Notice any unusual feelings. Back up a few minutes and notice what you were feeling just before the event. *(pause)*

Now move forward and remember what you felt at the time of the event. Now go to another time you sold yourself on something. Review how your body felt. Continue to review events until you get a clear idea what your signals are. If you can't get a clear sense of what they are in the past observe your behavior over the next several days. Chances are you'll begin to notice what it feels like when you are about to step out of integrity with yourself.

Take sometime to write about your feelings both physical and emotional. What does it feel like when you think about lying to yourself? Does if feel uncomfortable to even admit to yourself that you lie? Write until you feel done. *(How do you know when you feel done? You'll know, just begin to trust your inner knowing.)*

Our minds would much rather be right than be happy. Our minds feel more comfortable reliving the past than they do stepping out into the unknown. We tend to go to work the same way, eat in the same places, and do the same things because it's familiar. Our minds equate familiarity with being safe. Some people feel safe by never doing things the same way. They thrive on change. In an odd way they are both the same behavior even though they seem to be in opposition to one another. The person who avoids change and the person who craves change still consistently do the same thing. They repeat the same behavior, even if that behavior is not repeating behaviors. One consistently avoids change while one consistently craves it, either way they both repeat the same behaviors over and over again.

Our minds are like an incredibly efficient bio-computer. They are amazing. They can process information long before we even consciously aware of the data. They filter out hundreds of bits of information and choose where to focus our attention. Without a conscious thought on our part they translate all the events, sights, and sounds of the world so they fit neatly into our belief system. If we believe something, anything our mind will translate all incoming messages to reinforce that belief. So the key to healing of any kind is becoming aware of our belief system and changing it. Then things really will be different tomorrow. It is time to stop selling your old beliefs to yourself. It is time to let them go so you can create whatever you'd like in your life.

Sage Advice
"It is wrong to think that misfortunes come from the east or from the west; they originate within one's own mind. Therefore, it is foolish to guard against misfortunes from the external world and leave the inner mind uncontrolled."
Buddha

A Promise You Can Keep

We are so often disappointed in our lives primarily by those closest to us and by ourselves. We make promises we just can't keep, we want to but we can't. So how do we make promises we can keep? By learning how to make promises we can keep.

The first thing to do is to make the promise small and attainable. At the beginning of my journey I made myself a promise to do at least three things every day. Every morning I'd make the list of my three things. I never set myself up to fail by making them huge. I made them small and manageable. If I needed to clean the house and it was a real mess, I broke it down into smaller steps. When I needed to do my taxes I didn't just write "Do my taxes." I listed getting the forms, gathering the information, and computing my taxes as separate items. I would even spread them out over several days.

Spiritual Shortcuts
One of the ways to begin learning how to keep your promises to yourself is by making a list. Each day list three things you will accomplish and don't go to bed until they're finished. If you make the list and consistently put things off realize you're really trying to disappoint yourself and make a new choice. This exercise is an easy way to learn how to keep commitments and it takes some discipline on your part.

At first make one of the items on the list to make the list. Make all of the items small and easily doable. Allow for the possibility that learning to keep promises can be easy and fun. Then do it!! Why not start your list right now? When you check them off at night make sure you joyously acknowledge your accomplishment. I'm sure you beat yourself up when you fall short of your expectations so begin praising yourself whenever you make progress no matter how small it is.

If I wanted to do something a lot bigger like quitting smoking or losing weight I could promise myself to do something each day that would bring me closer to achieving that goal. Writing a little bit about the habit each day until I fully understand it would be a good first step.

Sage Advice
"Unless you try to so something beyond what you have already mastered, you will never grow."
Ralph Waldo Emerson

Disappointment is avoidable but if you feel it you can use it as a road sign directing you toward part of your wounded self. When we use it that way it isn't really disappointing at all. In part three we'll talk all about how to do that.

The Cursed Curse

One day when I was wandering around New York City feeling sad and lonely I went into a storefront to have my fortune told. The kindly older woman told me I had a curse and I would never find happiness until I had it removed. Of course for a fee she would remove it. Now it's funny but that day, if I'd had the money I would have gladly given it to her.

There is no such thing as a curse or negative karma. We don't ever have to pay for our mistakes. Life is merely a series of choices and outcomes. Karma is really just that, if we make a particular choice we are stuck with that outcome. If we change our choices we get different outcomes. If I kill someone in this lifetime it certainly doesn't mean I'll get killed in another life. If I get caught and live in a state that has the death penalty I may get killed. But that isn't karma it is just choice and outcome. If I choose to live my life based in anger I will get angry results. If I chose to live my life based on love and joy I will have love and joy reflected to me.

Clarity Corner

KARMA

Karma is a concept based in Indian philosophy. It is a Hindu concept that is also embraced by several other philosophies. It is a mechanical process, God plays no role and forgiveness or growth is excluded. If you act in a particular way in life those actions are bound to show up in the next life. It is a concept that is used to explain the seeming inequities in life. It is often used to make a person feel better about some event. We feel less threatened if we know others will get what they deserve eventually. I believe it is part of our wounded-self trying to explain life in a way that makes us feel comfortable.

The only curses that exist are the ones we visit upon ourselves. In a sense every limiting belief we have is a curse. We have cursed ourselves, we have demanded pain and suffering by believing we deserve it.

The most painful curse of all is the belief that there is something wrong with us. That belief causes more emotional pain and suffering than any event in our life ever could. When we believe there is something wrong with us it makes it very difficult to learn or to change. When one of my students isn't aware of that fact they struggle so hard. If I point out one of their limiting beliefs they feel judged and aren't able to look at their belief. They hear me judging them instead realizing I'm really attempting to help them see one of their limitations.

If we believe there is something wrong with us we spend most of our lives trying to defend ourselves. It is rather difficult to change when we are constantly defending our limitations. You are not your beliefs or your mind or your filter system. You are the energy that gives them life but they aren't who you are. Take some time and write about your beliefs – what have you cursed yourself or blessed yourself to experience on a daily basis?

Walking to the Beat of Another Person's Drum

We can't fix a broken computer with a broken computer. We need new ideas to free us from the self-imposed limitations of our filter system. We need help if we are going to truly heal but we always need to remember, healing is a journey back toward wholeness.

In the seventies I lost several friends to cults. At first they seemed happier and the quality of their lives improved. But then slowly, one by one they cut themselves off from their family and friends. As soon as it was evident I wasn't going to join the group I was no longer welcome in their life. It was sad for me, I'd lost a friend but they lost themselves. They no longer thought for themselves. They only listened to the group and followed their guru.

Healing is not about following someone else. It is about releasing our limiting beliefs and clearing out the chatter in our minds enough that we can once again hear our inner wisdom. A good teacher will challenge your old beliefs and at times any group can feel like a cult. When we are wounded emotionally we are often looking for someone to fix us, we want someone to rescue us from ourselves and we are willing to give our power to anyone if they'll just fix us.

Sage Advice
"How to tell the student what to look for without telling the student what to see is the dilemma of teaching."
Lascelles Abercrombie

Beware of anyone who wants you to follow them. Run, do not walk, away from anyone who suggests you cut yourself off from your friends or your family. As you heal emotionally your friends may change but never allow someone to change them for you. Always remember to walk to the beat of your own drum but also realize that drumbeat might be part of your filter system, so be willing to change it.

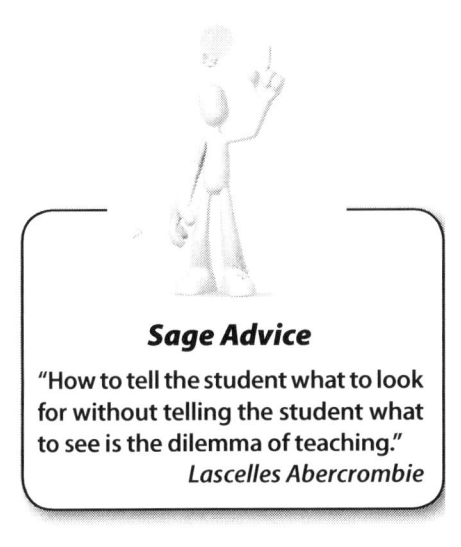

Sit Up and Notice!

When we hear the word cult we tend to think of the more destructive ones, cults in which their members kill themselves or others. In fact most religions are a cult but luckily few of them are truly destructive. There are groups we must be wary of. There are group leaders out there that seem very benign and loving but are extremely destructive.

Beware of the following signs of a destructive cult:

- You are expected to give up your individuality.
- Your relationships with family and friends are threatened.
- You are asked to donate large amounts of money.
- Theirs is the only right way – "Us against them" mentality.
- Your time in no longer your own.
- Guilt is employed as a method of control.
- Sex with the group leader is involved.
- If you don't follow this path you are doomed for eternity.
- You are physically or mentally abused.
- You don't feel safe.
- The leader or the members use intimidation.
- They promise they have all your answers.

> **Sage Advice**
> "It takes a person who is wide-awake to make their dreams come true."
> Roger Babson

When our issues are roaring to the surface of our reality even a loving group may feel threatening but trust yourself to know the difference.

Where Do Lost Dreams Go?

If it seems too good to be true chances are it is. You deserve to live your dreams not be haunted by them. Promises and lost childhood dreams can keep us hopelessly trapped in the past. Knowing the difference between past hopes and present dreams can set us free.

When I was a junior in high school my dad promised me a Ford Mustang when I graduated. My senior year my family lost our house to a fire and had several other financial setbacks. When graduation arrived a new Ford was out of the question and a used VW replace my bright red Mustang. As an adult I still craved that car until I finally decided to let it go. I had stopped myself from enjoying several new cars because of my dream of a red Mustang. Once I let go of that old dream I could chose whatever car I wanted and enjoy it.

> **Sage Advice**
> "Joy descends gently upon us like the evening dew, and does not patter down like a hailstorm."
> Richter

We all have lost dreams. Knowing the difference between what we really want and what we think we want is an important step toward

> **Spiritual Shortcuts**
>
> Journal time again: Take a few minutes to write about your dreams. If you had a magic want and you could create anything, absolutely anything you want, what would you create? What would you change about your life? What did you want to be as a child? What did you dream about? How did you want to look? What did you believe about the world as a child? What old dreams are you still holding on to? How are those old dreams limiting you? How could you update your dreams so they assist you in improving the quality of your life?

freeing ourselves from the past. The advertising industry capitalizes on our desire for old or lost dreams. Youth is an excellent example. Our society is obsessed with youth and with staying young. Look at the billions of dollars spent on hair dyes, skin creams, and plastic surgery. Among other things each wrinkle or gray hair is an opportunity to honor our true self. Instead of holding on to the dream of youth we can let go of that wounded-self. The ego self needs youth but our true self knows it doesn't matter. Only with time can we gain wisdom and with that time comes aging. We can age gracefully once we let go of the need to be young.

What if society was obsessed with age instead of youth? What if the wisdom that can come with age was deeply revered? In Native American traditions the Elders of the tribe are looked to for wisdom and guidance. And you don't get to be an elder by applying for the job you have to earn it over time.

The signature on my E-mail is a quote from my first book. "Only the dreamer can change the dream." We all have the power to live our dreams. What are yours? Part of the healing process is remembering your dreams so you can make choices to create them. If you want to drive your car in a straight line you focus your attention off in the distance. If you focus right in front of you you'll wind up weaving back and forth. Dreams help you focus off in the distance so you don't have to get off track. When you are clear about your dreams finding the most direct route toward achieving them is much easier.

> **Sage Advice**
>
> "Dreams – A microscope through which we look at the hidden occurrences in our soul."
>
> Erich Fromm

We have personal dreams as well as dreams as a society. As a society we collectively dream a lot of ridiculous things and then live life as if they are true. We dream that we can control other people by making laws instead of teaching them how to be loving; we dream that we can stop people from using drugs by fighting a war on drugs instead of teaching people how to stop hurting themselves; we dream money is real instead of just a means exchanging energy; we dream about racial hatred and then try to stop it without looking at our own self-hatred. The biggest dream of all is that this physical universe is real, it is really just an illusion created by our filter system.

Lucid dreaming is the process of waking up in our dreams and then doing whatever we would like in them. In our dreams we can fly, we can jump over buildings, we can do just about anything we want to do. I think of the healing process as lucid living. We wake up in the dream of our life and then do whatever we want to do.

What's Really Real?

Discernment is complex. It is often a paradox. How do we distinguish or define anything? We define reality through our filter system so what we discern or understand today will be different from what we understand a year from now. Discernment is relative and our ability to discern fact from fiction is of paramount importance. We use discernment to make choices and to decide where to place our trust.

Since discernment is relative it is easy to understand why we often make choices that create less than desirable outcomes early in our healing process. A large part of the healing process is clearing out our filter system. As we clear out our filter system our discernment becomes more accurate and our choices become more nurturing.

There's that word process again. Discernment is another skill you need to develop. It is like learning a new language. If you take the vocabulary of a new language and use the wrong grammar no one will be able to understand you. If you take the new information you are gaining and put it into your old filter system it won't make sense. You need to develop the ability to see or discern your filter system.

Clarity Corner

Discernment is defined as the ability or the quality of being able to grasp and comprehend what is mentally obscure. It is the ability to show good judgment and understanding. Discernment allows us to tell the difference between what will really help us and what will hurt us; it helps us tell friend from foe. Discernment keeps us safe in a world that often feels unsafe.

One of the ways I began to see my filter system was to realize that every time I was upset it was because my filter system had been activated. You will always have a filter system and you will always have beliefs. Discernment will allow you to choose what you believe. It will assist you in sorting out what beliefs work for you and which ones don't. After a while it will become second nature to look at your outcomes and if you like them make the same choice. If you don't like the results you're getting you'll use your discernment to find the belief, change it, and then make a different choice.

If you choose to work with a therapist and you don't feel like your getting anywhere you won't give up on therapy, you'll look at the situation and decide if you need to change therapists or work harder. If you join a group and you see warning signs you won't give up on groups – you'll just change groups.

So often we place the blame on something like intimacy instead of looking at our ability to give and receive love. We are never upset for the reason we think we are. Discernment is one of the tools that will help us understand what is really going on.

Remember the old childhood song:
>*Row, row, row your boat*
>*Gently down the stream*
>*Merrily, merrily, merrily*
>*Life is but a dream.*

Life really is a dream and discernment helps us wake up in our dream.

Spiritual Shortcuts

For the next week or two do things in your life differently. If you normally get up on the right side of the bed get up on the left. Brush your teeth differently, go to work a different way, if you're always late be on time, and if you're always on time be late. When you wake up in the morning remind yourself it is time to go to sleep and when you go to sleep at night remind yourself it is time to wake up. Eat differently; dress differently; just shake up all your habits and routines. If you always have to know what you're doing this weekend or tomorrow don't plan; if you never plan anything plan everything. Walk backwards down the sidewalk; try wearing your clothing inside out. You'll be amazed at what happens.

Write about your experiences. Take a few minutes each night and answer the following questions. How do you feel? Can you get yourself to do things differently or is even the thought of it too uncomfortable? What happens when your friends notice the changes? Do you immediately want to do things the old way? This is a very powerful exercise. Play with it for a while and see what happens.

The Least You Need to Know

- Place your trust in yourself.
- Your beliefs keep you trapped in the past.
- Dreams can be guideposts or stumbling blocks.
- There is no such thing as a curse.
- Your ability to discern the truth is one of your most valuable tools.
- Life is merely a dream and you have the power to change it.

Part 2
So, What's Available

Your healing journey is multidimensional. It involves not only your relationship with your mind and your spirit but also with your body. Frequently our complaints manifest in our physical body as well as in other areas of our life. In this section I'll take you on a quick tour of many of the things available out there.

We'll be talking mainly about alternative therapies. Not because mainstream approaches don't work but because there is so much information already available on them. I suggest people be open minded and eclectic in their approach toward healing. Don't get too invested in any one method and be very wary of any method that makes claims that sound too good. There are still a lot of snake oil salesmen out there.

And make sure you explore all of your options. People can die when they ignore common sense approaches. A woman I knew died prematurely of breast cancer because she refused medical treatment and decided to only go with alternative methods. Eastern, western, mind, body, spirit, and shamanic healing are all equally valid and have their own applications. They all work for certain problems but when I want to remove a screw I don't use a hammer. Remain open minded and try to figure out what's the best tool for the job.

Chapter 5

Alternative Medicine

> ### In This Chapter
>
> ➤ Alternative to what?
>
> ➤ Needles, herbs, and tinctures, Oh my!
>
> ➤ Body types–where you fit in.
>
> ➤ What your eyes give away about you.

Alternative medicine or complimentary medicine as it is often called is generally aimed at treating the patient as a whole. Conventional medicine tends to be based on diagnosis; the philosophy is basically find the cause and treat it. In this chapter we'll explore some of the alternative methods. Complementary methods tend to try to activate the body's inherent healing powers to heal itself.

I believe a holistic approach incorporates all available methods into a coherent treatment plan. No need to throw the baby out with the bath water, use all the methods available to you. In this chapter will begin our exploration of alternative therapies.

You Want to Stick That Where?

Acupuncture is an ancient Chinese medical technique that has been practiced since before 2500 BC. It is used for pain relief, curing disease, and improving the health and well-being of the patient.

Acupuncture evolved from the Chinese philosophy of yin and yang. Yin is the female energy that is thought of as passive, cold, damp, still, and contracting. It is represented as the earth. Yang is the male energy that is defined as active, light, heat, dry, and expansive. It is represented as the heavens. Imbalances between the yin and yang cause obstructions in the qi or life energies of the body.

The Chinese have mapped the body's energy system and have defined a number of energy lives called meridians. These meridians act like power lines carrying the qi throughout the body. Along each of the approximately fourteen meridians there are hundreds of specific acupoints where the practitioner inserts the needles. Twelve of the meridians correspond to the main organs of the body. The Chinese concept of organ is much broader than just the organ itself. The heart meridian for instance is related not only to the heart but also to spiritual vitality and the liver is also related to smooth distribution of the qi throughout the body. The other two meridians act as communication lines that link the other meridians.

When I first moved to Hawaii I injured my shoulder and my neck. I could barely move my shoulder or turn my head and I was in a great deal of pain. I went to both the doctor and the chiropractor yet weeks later I was no better. A friend of mine suggested I go to Chinatown and get a treatment. In the back of an herb shop there was an old Chinese man that performed acupuncture. The rooms were small and the walls didn't go all the way to the ceiling. Everything was painted white. First he asked me a number of questions and took my pulses. They check your pulses in several places on your arm in that way they can tell what the energies in your body are doing.

He had me lay down on a small cot in one of the rooms. He inserted several needles in my back, neck, and hand. The smells of the herbs drifted over me, I could hear them chopping herbs, and speaking rapidly in Chinese. I was transported to another time and place. I feel asleep and was awakened as he rolled the cart in to remove the needles. I went back two more times and was completely cured. Since then I have returned to that little shop for colds and a whole variety of ailments. Every time it is a magical experience.

Clarity Corner

Acupuncture is an ancient form of healing first believed to be practiced in Mongolia. Needles are inserted in various points on the body to unblock the energy or qi. It is believed that blocked energy is the cause of disease and disharmony in the body. It has seen a recent resurgence in popularity. **Acupressure** uses the same points in the body, but the pressure is applied by hand rather than needles.

Clarity Corner

The Chinese believe **qi** (pronounced *chee*) is the life force or energy that keeps our body alive. An imbalance in our qi can cause disease or discomfort in our body. Emotional upset, improper diet, stress, and insufficient can all upset our qi. An imbalance between our yin and yang or female and pale aspects of our personality also affects our qi.

> ### Spiritual Shortcuts
>
> **ELIMINATING NAUSEA AND EASING HEADACHES**
>
> If you massage a point approximately two inches above your wrist on the thumb side of your arm you can relieve nausea due to morning sickness, chemotherapy, or motion sickness.
>
> You can also relive headaches by rubbing a point between your thumb and forefinger. You can find acupressure points by their sensitivity to pressure and touch. When you press on them you will feel a dull or sometimes sharp pain. The pressure will definitely cause some sort of discomfort if you are pressing on the correct spot. The pain will abate when it is time to let go.

A treatment usually takes at least a half hour. The practitioner decides where to place the needle by reading your pulses and talking to you about the ailment. The needles they use are very thin, almost hair like. Most of the time you don't even feel them but sometimes you can feel the electrical current rushing down your nerve. The needles are rotated several times. Sometimes a small electrical current is placed on them. When the practitioner feels the treatment is done the needles are removed. The needles used today are disposable and come individually wrapped.

Acupuncture and acupressure have hundreds of uses. The medical world is still unsure why they work. What is certain is that they do work.

Seeking the Pathys

Homeopathy, naturopathy, and osteopathy are three holistic approaches of western origin. Most traditional Western medicine treats the disease rather than the whole person. In a traditional medical practice, the physical symptoms. Seldom is the patient asked about any significant events in his life. The disease is named and the disease is treated. A homeopath, naturopath and osteopath will treat the whole person rather than name and target the disease.

Choosing a Practitioner

Choosing who to work with in any of the healing arts is one of the most important decisions you'll make. It is important to check out a person's

> ### *Clarity Corner*
>
> **Holisim** is a theory that the universe and especially living nature is a series of interacting wholes that are more than the mere sum of elementary particles. **Holistic** medicine attempts to treat both the mind and the body of the patient. The person's body is seen as a whole system rather than a bunch of parts that can be treated separately.

credentials and make sure they are what they say they are. In the appendix there will be a list of professional organizations where you can get referrals as well as check on the practitioner's credentials. But even more important then their credentials is how you feel about them. If you don't trust them or feel comfortable working with them healing isn't very likely.

Ask your friends for referrals. Talk to the person before you decide whether you want to work with them. Interview them thoroughly after all you are employing them to assist in your healing. Remember someone might work well with your friend while you don't feel good about him or her or feel comfortable working with them at all. It is a good idea to make a list of questions before you call.

Some of the questions you might want to ask:

- What experience have you had treating my condition?
- How much time will you spend with me?
- Are you available by phone if I have any questions?
- How many treatments do you general require and what are the costs?
- Why should I want to work with you?

Ask enough questions so you really get a feel for the person. If they are too busy to answer your questions they certainly won't have time for you later. And if after a few visits you change your mind, talk to them about your concerns, and if you still have them move on. This is your life you deserve to be surrounded by loving, gentle people that will assist you in your process.

Homeopathy is Where the Cure is

Homeopathy is a system of medicine based on the principle that like cures like. The founder, a physician named Samuel Hahnemann took a large dose of quinine, which is used to treat malaria. He found had similar symptoms as people with malaria. Form that he concluded that diseases could be treated with dilute doses of the very things that caused the symptoms of the disease. He found that large doses of the medicine worsened symptoms and the efficiency of the medicine increased as the medicine is diluted.

The principle of like cures like or similia similbus curantur is found in the fifth century BC writings of the father of medicine, Hippocrates. Samuel Hahnemann, a German doctor rediscovered the principle in 1796. Homeopathy was a welcome relief to the treatments of the time. The public found it a relief and embraced over the practices of being

Clarity Corner

Homeopathy is a way of treating an illness by using dilute tinctures that cause symptoms similar to the disease. Dr. Samuel Hahnemann developed the theory behind homepathy when he accidentally took a large dose of quinine and found it produced the same symptoms as malaria, which it is normally used to treat. From this he concluded that diseases could be treated with minute doses of drugs that in a healthy person would produce symptoms similar to those of the disease.

bled, being forced to purge, leaches, or any other of the invasive techniques popular at the time. He took the name from the Greek homoios (same) and pathos (suffering).

His ideas quickly spread across Europe, North America, and Asia. In 1984 two American doctors who had furthered the theories of Dr. Hahnemann founded the American Institute of Homeopathy. Homeopathy ad all but disappeared by the 30's but reemerged in the 70's.

Today various remedies are readily available in health food stores. When you take a remedy it is important not to touch it with your fingers or your hand. The remedies should be placed on a clean spoon and placed under the tongue where they are allowed to dissolve slowly. There remedies came in the form of tablets, powder, pills, liquids, and granules. They are usually lactose based and taste somewhat sweet.

I've used homeopathic remedies for colds and the flu with good results as long as I took them as soon as my symptoms appeared. It is helpful to have a basic first aid kit of various remedies. Homeopathic remedies are also useful for reliving menopausal symptoms, insect bites, and life's general bumps and bruises.

Practitioners fall roughly into two categories, complex or classical. A classical practitioner by a process of elimination will find a single remedy to treat the illness based on the person's constitutional type and symptoms. Theoretically each constitutional type is more prone to certain diseases. Complex homeopathy rather than look at personality types treats 'sick organs' with dilute extracts often combined with herbs. There are between two and three thousand different remedies.

Get Back to Naturopathy

Naturopaths believe that the body's natural state is good health and that if something doesn't disrupt the body's balance it will naturally maintain good health or return to good health once the stress is removed. As with other holistic approaches naturopathy share the belief in the body's ability to heal itself. Many of the basic principles of naturopathy can be found in the writings of Hippocrates. His writings said that all cures should be as natural as possible and that the patient merely needed to have plenty of rest, natural, healthy, light food, plenty of fresh air, and exercise in moderation. The body's natural healing abilities would be triggered and balance would return.

Naturopaths use a lot of therapies to assist the bodies healing powers. They are all designed to improve the digestion, circulation, the elimination of toxins, and boosting the immune system. They proscribe a natural diet, herbal remedies, massage, osteopathy, and hydrotherapy.

Naturopaths believe a balance lifestyle is necessary to sustain health.

Clarity Corner

Dr. John Scheel of New York first used the term **naturopathy** in 1895. This system of health cures developed in the spas of Austria and Germany. They focused on hydrotherapy, fresh air, sunshine, exercise, and natural foods. Benedict Lust founded the American School of Naturopathy in New York in 1896. John Kellogg, the cereal man, popularized these methods by using them in his spa in Battle Creak, Michigan. Eventually the method lost favor in the 30's only to be revived again in the 60's.

> **Clarity Corner**
>
> **HYDROTHERAPY**
>
> The ancient Greeks believed water carried incredible healing properties, that it was the elixir of life. In hydrotherapy water is used both externally and internally in all of its forms including hot and cold, liquid, steam, and ice. It's used to cleanse and revitalize the body while restoring health. Today we have steam baths and whirlpools. Wraps using a variety of herbs and either hot or cold compresses are becoming extremely popular. At home you can take a hot bath with Epsom salts and sea salt. Take a small muslin bag and fill it with your favorite herb, light a candle, and sit back and relax.

> **Clarity Corner**
>
> **Osteopathy** comes from the Greek words osteon (bone) and pathos (disease). Dr. Andrew Still of Virginia prompted by the death of his wife and children developed osteopathy. In 1892 he founded the American School of Osteopathy. He ran into a great deal of opposition from the traditional medical establishment but when the mortality rate in his hospitals was shown to be significantly lower than in traditional hospitals his techniques grew in popularity.

They prescribe a healthy diet, plenty of exercise, fresh air, rest, sufficient sleep, relaxation, a life free of stress, a clean and pleasant environment, and a positive mental attitude. If any of those areas are out of balance it will reflect in your body. If you follow their prescription the quality of your life will certainly improve along with your health.

Dem Bones

Osteopathy is a holistic approach that emphasizes the relationship between the musculoskeletal structure and the functioning of internal organs. A Civil War doctor who was appalled at the treatment of soldiers during the war developed osteopathy as a reform movement.

Just as acupuncture is designed to get the qi in the body flowing more evenly an osteopath uses manipulation to free up blocked energy in the body. They believe that the bones, muscles, joints, and connective tissues not only support the organs but that they play a pivotal role in maintaining health. Their main is focus is soft tissue treatment to relax your muscles and bring mobility to your joints.

Since 1972 osteopaths have been licensed as conventional doctors. The education leading to a degree of doctor is similar to that for doctor of medicine. The four years of education covers the basic sciences with the main focus being body mechanics and their relationship to the function of health. Osteopaths are trained either in the United States or Great Britain.

Osteopaths gently manipulate the body to bring it back into alignment. Since joint, muscle, and bone pain register in the brain they cause the excretion of certain hormones that in turn effect the rest of the body. Perpetual tension in any area of the body will effect the well being of the entire system. Once the tension is released the body has an opportunity to heal itself.

An osteopath is also concerned with why the skeletal body is out of alignment. They will look for the underlying causes or the reasons behind the problem. A person's lifestyle and emotional or mental well-being are believed to be very important factors influencing physiological health.

Osteopathy is mainly used to treat joint pain, neck and back pain, arthritis, sport injuries, headaches, insomnia, depression, menstrual cramps, digestive disorders, and asthma. It is also useful when a patient s experiencing a great deal of stress or anything affecting the respiration, circulation, or nervous system. It differs from chiropractors because it focuses more on soft tissue while chiropractors focus mainly on misaligned joints.

The Old is New Again

Since the beginning of time herbs have been surrounded with myths, facts and fiction. Herbs were used as magic potions as well as healing potions. The ancient Chinese, Indians, Egyptians, Babylonians, Africans, and Native Americans were all excellent herbalists. Every region of the planet has herbs indigenous to that area and for millennia human beings have utilized them.

Shen Nung wrote the oldest known herbal text in 3000 BC. It was probably compiled from a much older oral work. The ancient Greeks and Romans used herbs on the battlefields to heal the wounded. In the Middle Ages herbalism was taught in the monasteries. Monks continued to copy the works of Hippocrates and other ancient healers thus maintaining their knowledge of the medicinal use of herbs.

Priests and holy men used herbs in ceremonies, incantations, magical rites, and worship. Even today many places of worship are filled with the smell of incense. Herbs were the first known medicine and they're still the source of many of our medicines. The rainforests are filled with healing plants just waiting to be discovered if we don't destroy them first.

Once societies became more centralized herbs were often only available to the rich because of their rarity. Today over 80% of the people of earth rely on herbal remedies. Originally herbs were specific to an area, herbalists rarely used herbs from other regions. That is no longer true as herbs from all over the world are regularly used to treat patients.

Chinese Herbs

Chinese herbalism is one element of traditional Chinese medicine. This method focuses on the pattern of symptoms rather than looking for a disease. Acupuncture and herbalism work hand in hand. The body is viewed holistically as a complex, balanced system dependent on the balance of Yin and Yang as well as the five elements.

The five elements are connected. Fire turns to ash or earth, the earth yields up metal, metal allows water to condense, water nourishes wood and wood feeds fire.

Smoke & Mirrors

Herbs are very powerful drugs—the main difference is they come from plants. They are just as powerful as any prescription drug and must be used with caution. Herbs can interact with each other and with other drugs. I highly recommend that you consult an experienced herbalist or ask your pharmacist or physician before prescribing herbs for yourself. It is easy to forget that the tea your are drinking could seriously harm you or a loved one if not used carefully.

Sage Advice

"Every flower knows it is unique as well as beautiful. The lessons that the flowers show their human sisters and brothers is one of love without comparison."
Jamie Sams

Here is a list of the elements and the things each one is related to:

- **Fire.** The season is summer; the taste bitter; emotion is joy; parts of the body are blood vessels, small intestine, heart, and tongue.
- **Earth.** The season is Indian summer; the taste is sweet; the emotion is worry; the parts of the body are muscles, mouth, stomach, and spleen.
- **Metal.** The season is autumn; the taste in pungent; the emotion grief; the parts of the body skin, large intestine, lungs, and nose.
- **Water.** The season is winter; the taste salty; the emotion fear; the parts of the body bones, hair, ears, kidneys, and bladder.
- **Wood.** The season is spring; the taste sour; the emotion anger; the parts of the body eyes, liver, gallbladder, and tendons.

A Chinese herbalist will look at your tongue and general state of health. They will listen to your voice and notice how your body and breath smells. They will ask you questions about your ancestors and lifestyle. Then they will read your pulses taken in various areas of your wrist. The herbal remedy will be prescribed based on your pattern of disharmony.

Herbs are seldom prescribed singly most remedies have ten to fifteen herbs in them. Generally you brew the herbs several times before you discard them. The herbalist will give you specific directions on the amount of water to add and the length of time to boil the herbs and how long to let them sit. My experience has been that they always taste rather nasty but they are very effective.

Western Herbalism

Herbal folklore was an oral tradition for centuries in Europe. Healers passed the tradition down to their apprentices. Mothers would tell their daughters what herbs to use to heal their children. With invention of the printing press herbalism really flourished until the 18th century. Europeans turned more toward traditional medicine while immigrants to North America held onto to their love of herbs. Herbal schools in America eventually revived interest in herbal remedies in Europe.

> **Sage Advice**
> "Every bladed of grass has its own angel that bends over it and whispers, Grow, grow."
> *The Talmud*

In Western herbalism remedies are designed to help the body heal itself, they are geared toward the patients rather than the symptoms. Herbs play a supporting role while diet, lifestyle, and other factors are also addressed. Herbs are a complex mixture of ingredients unlike traditional medicines. When all the ingredients are mixed together the sum of the parts is greater than the whole. That is why herbs are often more effective than pharmaceuticals based on the same plants.

Modern herbalism while still limited in the United States can be studied at British universities. It wasn't until 1994 that the U.S. relaxed some of its laws regarding the sale of herbs.

A western practitioners will check your heart and lungs with a stethoscope, feel your glands, and check your pulse. She will make her diagnosis based the various body systems, on your digestion, circulation, respiration, and elimination. The herbs that she prescribes will strengthen the weakened systems. Western herbal concoctions usually include licorice or other herbs to disguise the flavor but they are still pretty nasty tasting.

I use herbs frequently. I often focus on my sense of smell and use whatever herbs appeal to me. I find that often my body knows best what it needs. It is always beneficial to consult and expert but sometimes its fun just to play.

One of our strongest sense is our sense of smell. Herbs make wonderful potpourris and their smells can be very soothing and uplifting.

Herbs Here, There and Everywhere

Every place I've traveled has its own herbal practices. When I was in Peru the people that lived in the mountains used a variety of herbs to deal with the high altitudes. When I traveled in the Amazon basin the herbs were all together different and addressed issues like rashes from insect bites and snakebites. My guide had bitten by a very deadly, poisonous snake as a young boy. He survived because of the herbs given to him by the local shaman. When I was in Jamaica during the early 70's I came down with pneumonia while staying in a remote village. The local women treated me with herbs and poultices. To my amazement I fully recovered in no time at all. My friends at home were still suffering with the same bug long after I returned home.

Every are of this earth has herbs that are indigenous to that area and people have learned over the centuries how to use them. I have often wondered if particular herbs were in the area so we could use them or if we learned to use them because they were in the area. Just a thought. As a species we are very inventive. Each culture has found ways to use all the resources at their disposal.

Dash for the Doshas

Ayurveda is the healing modality of India made popular in this country by Deepak Chopra. It has been used in India since around 2500 BC. It was derived from the Vedas, ancient Hindu texts and has similarities to tradition Chinese medicine. It is an approach that heavily emphasizes the balance of mind, body, and spirit. Practitioners focus on balancing a patients three doshas or vital life energies. These doshas constantly fluctuate and are balanced using purification techniques, diet, yoga, massage, and remedies.

Ayurvedic practitioners believe that five great elements air, ether, water, fire, and earth make up the universe. They are constantly interacting and changing. They can be simplified into three doshas that also constantly change and interact. They must be in balance within a person's body if they are to maintain good health. Each person is a combination of doshas determined by their parent's energies at the time of their conception. A person's strengths and weakness, body type, and personality are determined by one, possible two dominant doshas. A practitioner's job is to keep the normal fluctuations of these doshas to a minimum.

The Three Doshas

Vata is a combination of air and ether. The season is autumn. The Vata dosha is characterized by the following traits:

- Tend to be hyper, tall or short and thin
- Energy centers in the colon
- Shares coldness with Kapha
- Pungent and bitter tastes increase Vata
- Raw foods should be avoided
- Sweet, sour, salty, and warming foods decrease Vata

Pitta is a combination of fire and water. The season is summer. The Pitta dosha is characterized by the following traits:

- Confident and slightly aggressive of moderate height and evenly proportioned
- Energy centers in the stomach and small intestine
- Shares lightness with Vata
- Sour and salty food increase Pitta
- Red meat should be avoided
- Sweet, bitter, and cooling foods decrease Pitta

Kapha is a combination of water and earth. The season is mid-winter. The Kapha dosha is characterized by the following traits:

- Heavy set and physically strong with a tendency to be possessive.
- Energy centers in the stomach and lungs
- Shares oiliness with Pitta
- Sweet and salty increases Kapha
- Dairy products should be avoided
- Pungent and bitter foods, and hot, spicy food decrease Kapha

During the first session the practitioner they will determine your doshas and note any imbalances. Your pulses will also be read. As with traditional Chinese medicine this is a very important diagnostic tool. They will also examine your tongue and palpitate your stomach.

Once the imbalances are diagnosed the practitioner will suggest dietary changes. They will recommend you eat or avoid certain foods as well they will have you eat at specific times of the day. The practitioner may also be suggested meditation and spending time outdoors during certain hours. Each of the doshas resonates with a certain time of the day so your practitioner will suggest certain sleep patterns and the best time of the day to do things. Certain herbs and minerals may also be prescribed. They may also pick a suitable mantra for you to repeat while you meditate. A mantra is a word that is repeated over and over again as you allow your mind to get quiet.

Once you are strong enough there are a variety of purification routines that can be prescribed. Some of them are fairly rigorous and uncomfortable. In India some of these purges will last over a month. These practices have been modified to accommodate our Western constitution and have been reduced to several days. There are spas where you can go and receive these treatments.

> **Smoke & Mirrors**
>
> It is important to listen to your body. Not everything a practitioner suggest will work for everyone. Some of the purifications used in Ayurveda can be very hard on a body not accustomed to them. In India people are very familiar with purges and various purifications. Radically changing your diet suddenly can cause a great deal of discomfort in your body. Be gently with yourself and ease into any changes in diet, sleep patterns or exercise.

The Eyes Have It

Iridology is used as a diagnosis tool by many holistic therapies especially in Europe. Practitioners look at the iris that includes thousands of nerve endings. Those nerve ends are believed to react to any imbalances in the body. Eye color is linked to body type. People with blue eyes are thought to be more prone to arthritis while brown-eyed people are more likely to have slow metabolisms and people with mixed colored eyes are prone to weak digestion.

Although Hippocrates may have used some form of iridology in the 5th century BC it wasn't until late in the 19th century the Hungarian doctor Ignatz von Peczely outlined the modern theories. As a young child as he was releasing a trapped owl its leg broke. He noticed the bird's eyes developed dark markings in his eyes. As his leg healed the marks turned to white. As a young doctor he dedicated himself to mapping diseases from markings in his patients eyes.

In the 1950's and American doctor Bernard Jensen developed the eye chart now used by iridologists. It breaks the eyes down into regions that correspond to parts of the body.

> **Clarity Corner**
>
> In Iridology, a practitioner reads the iris of your eye. Depending on the color of your eyes and the placement of any impurities or irregularities in your iris, a seasoned practitioner can tell you about the condition of your internal organs and your general overall health. Some practitioners take it a step farther and use it as a tool for predicting the future. Hungarian doctor Ignatz von Peczely developed iridology in the late 1800s.

When a practitioner studies the eyes it is believed they are really studying the brain. The eyes first develop in the human embryo by day 22. The eyes are made of brain tissue which is connected to the developing brain by a solid stalk that later becomes the optical nerve. This is why the eyes are believed to be so revealing.

White marks in the iris are believed to indicate inflammation in the organs while a dark rim around the iris reveals toxins in the body. It is believed that every organ in the body is linked to the nerve endings in the iris. Practitioners believe they are able to see past diseases as well as current ones. They also feel they can predict future weaknesses. Once a diagnosis is made treatment will depend on what holistic method they specialize in or you will be referred to someone else.

> ### *The Least You Need to Know*
>
> - There are a lot of alternative healing methods out there.
> - Some methods will appeal more to you than others.
> - Thoroughly interview anyone you are thinking about working with, this is your health and well-being we are talking about.
> - Holistic doesn't necessarily mean better.
> - Make sure you use all the tools at your disposal.

Chapter 6

Altered States

> ***In This Chapter***
>
> ➤ **You'll find out what an altered state can do.**
>
> ➤ **Be able to tell your mind from your brain.**
>
> ➤ **Learn how to hypnotize yourself.**
>
> ➤ **Find out how to float your troubles away.**

Altering our state of consciousness is a way to consciously choose how we are feeling physically, emotionally, and spiritually. Just as a car has different gears so does our mind. As we learn how to shift gears with our mind we can more easily harness the mind's ability to heal. With altered states we can learn to access our inner wisdom, to reduce stress, to heal our body, get rid of headaches, and the list goes on and on.

Beyond our every day waking consciousness there is another reality we aren't usually aware of. Behind the curtain, beyond the illusion of our perception exists a reality that is much closer to the truth. I often think of the scene in the Wizard of Oz where Toto the dog pulls back the curtain revealing the man behind the illusion of the Wizard. Altering our state of consciousness is a way for us to pull back the curtain and experience a clearer version of reality.

When we are focusing on our filter system instead of life we are in an altered state. When we drive down the highway and suddenly 'wake up' and wonder where we are we've been in an altered state. Our minds are magnificent machines that have the power to control every one of our bodily functions including things like blood pressure, metabolism, and our temperature. When we consciously learn how to alter our state of consciousness we can consciously control these bodily functions.

The Brain Meets the Mind

The brain is an incredible bio-computer that is far more efficient then anything we have been able to design. Scientists aren't exactly sure how the brain functions but they're still working on it. The brain makes up only 2% of the bodies weight yet it uses 20% of its energy. If the brain stops functioning we are dead.

> **Sage Advice**
> "The mind of which we are unaware is aware of us."
> R.D. Lang

In the early 1940's scientists developed the ability to read electrical impulses emanating from the brain. In the 60's scientists focused on the effect changing a person's brain waves had. Brain waves oscillate in a range between .5 cycles per second (cps) to 40+ cps. Changing our brain waves or cycles is much like shifting gears in a car. Each frequency range serves a different purpose and we can learn to consciously control our brain waves.

The brain has two hemispheres separated by a deep fissure. Generally the right hemisphere controls the left side of the body and the left hemisphere controls the right side of the body.

Brain waves range from the deepest sleep states to levels of hyper-awareness. They range from delta, to theta, to beta, to alpha, and to gamma.

- **Delta** (.5-3 cps). In this range a person is general soundly asleep.
- **Theta** (4-7 cps). With training a person can maintain awareness in this range. This state is associated with heightened creativity, accelerated learning, deep relaxation, vivid mental imagery, and increased feelings of pleasure.
- **Alpha** (8-12 cps). These waves are smooth and rhythmic and are generally associated with a light meditative state. A person will be more relaxed, stress is significantly reduced, will feel calm, and often have a pleasant sense of drifting.
- **Beta** (13-27). These waves are associated with external focus. We are alert and focused on external stimuli. A person is awake, focused, and actively thinking.
- **Gamma** (28-40+cps). These waves tend to be more random and less organized.

The mind isn't a physical organ it is our ability to be aware of ourselves, our surroundings, and that we exist. Our mind stores our filter system in our brain. Philosophers have spent countless hours debating what the mind is. The facts that the mind can think, has knowledge, has the ability to reflect or to be self-aware, and has purpose are common beliefs in all the popular theories about the mind. The mind is distinct from the body and it is separate from the brain. It is where our consciousness resides. Developing the ability to align our mind with our spirit is the most valuable step we can take on our journey of spiritual healing.

We can think of the brain as the hardware of our computer and the mind as the software. Our software is a bit out dated, has a few viruses and a lot of misinformation. But once we clean it up, life will be smooth sailing.

Whip That Brain into Shape

Meditation is an ancient form of mental discipline that many of the world religions practice in some form or another. It seems mysterious and is often misunderstood. It is a state of heightened awareness, of acute mental focus, combined with deep relaxation. You are generally aware of your surroundings and of thoughts passing though your mind but your attention isn't focused on them.

During meditation the brain produces intense alpha waves and both hemispheres tend to be synchronized. There is a definite sense of harmony and balance within the brain's structure. Meditation puts a person into an altered state of consciousness, one that with practice can be easily reproduced and harnessed.

> **Sage Advice**
> "Our life is what are thoughts make it."
> *Marcus Aurelius*

These are a few of the more common forms of meditation.

- **Rosary or prayer beads**. Prayers are repeated as your fingers move around the beads.
- **Prayer wheels.** The wheel is slowly rotated as prayers are said.
- **Mantra.** A word or phrase is repeated either out loud or silently.
- **Object meditation.** Your attention is focused on a suitable object such as a rock, a sculpture, a picture, or flower.
- **Candle.** Focusing on the flame is very relaxing.
- **Moving meditation.** T'ai chi, martial arts, walking, or any other rhythmic motion is used to focus the mind.
- **Mindfulness.** You are aware but detached from your environment.
- **Breath.** Focusing your mind on your breathing.

Spiritual Shortcuts

In the early 70's I was diagnosed with migraine headaches. The pain was unbearable, I got nauseous, and I was forced to retreat to a darkened room whenever I had one. I often had headaches several times a week. I went to doctors and we tried everything. Then I learned to meditate and to my amazement I was able to control my headaches with some relatively simple meditation techniques. I haven't had one in years. The power of the mind and our ability to harness that power is magnificent. Altered states allow us to do that.

There are as many forms of meditation as there are religions and mythologies. Usually during meditation we withdraw our focus from the external world and focus instead on our inner world. In some forms of Zen meditation the person focuses their attention on an object as a way of releasing their attachment to the physical universe.

Western religions have generally used prayer as their form of meditation. In the East meditation has been much more a part of their religions and their lives. The Harvard physician Herbert Benson popularized the "relaxation response" in the 60's. Medical science proved what mystics had known for centuries that meditation improves a person's health as well as the quality of their life.

Drugs

Sage Advice
"Let your life dance on the edges of Time like dew on the tip of a leaf."
Rabindranath Tagore

In the 60's the counterculture discovered psychedelic drugs. Native Americans had utilized hallucinogenic plants for thousands of years. The Aztecs called their sacred mushrooms the flesh of god. Apaches used peyote in many of their sacred ceremonies. Hallucinogens have been used throughout history to produce religious experiences or altered states of consciousness. Even today shamans in the Amazon do ceremonies with mind-altering drugs before they perform healings.

Drugs rapidly produce states of consciousness that might other wise take years of practice to achieve. The problem with drugs is besides being illegal they can damage your brain. You also have to have the drug to reproduce the results and even then you aren't guaranteed you'll get the same results every time.

I was fortunate to study with a shaman who didn't believe in the use of drugs. He felt it was important to learn how to alter our consciousness without them. The discipline it took to learn various mind-altering techniques was a major part of the experience. Fast food isn't exactly healthy for our bodies. Drugs in a sense are an unhealthy, fast food for the spirit.

You Thought You Already Knew How to Breathe

Perhaps one of the easiest ways to alter your consciousness is with your breath. It is something we do constantly yet we are seldom really conscious of it. For a moment notice your breath. Really notice how it feels to breath. Notice where you feel your breath in your body, do you feel it in your nose, your throat, your chest, or your stomach? Where exactly do you feel your breath as it enters your body? Do you feel it in the same place as it leaves your body?

Breathing deeply and openly has a profound effect on our health. Our skin and our breathing eliminate over 70% of our body's toxic by-products. When our blood is fully oxygenated virus and bacteria have a much more difficult time growing in our body. Most of the time we tend to breath tends to be very shallow and when we are under stress we often unconsciously hold our breath. Generally we only use 20% of our lungs full capacity.

By focusing your attention on your breath you automatically begin to quiet your mind. There are a variety of breathing techniques you can use. You can breathe rapidly or deepen your breath. You can count your breaths or hold your breath, anything you do to alter your breathing will help you focus your mind. One of the things I have my students do is breath in to the count of ten, hold their breath for ten counts, exhale for ten, and then hold their breath for ten counts. Breath like that at least three times.

Clarity Corner

The breath is defined as the air we inhale and exhale during respiration. It is our lifeline. Our bodies can live for days without food and water but without breathing our spirit rapidly leaves the body. Our breath is absolutely necessary to our life but we take it for granted. Mystics for centuries have believed the breath was the seat of the soul. In many traditions the spirit and the breath are considered to be one and the same. As you take your next breath imagine your spirit rising and falling with your chest. Allow yourself to really feel how your body and your spirit are connected through your breath.

Another very powerful breathing technique is to forcefully and loudly exhaling while completely emptying your lungs and then quickly and deeply inhaling. If you allow yourself to make noise while you are breathing it will help you release tension and blocked emotions. It also may make you feel foolish which is a good way to teach ourselves humility.

With any breathing techniques be careful you don't hyperventilate. Try these techniques and then return to your normal breathing. Do them while seated or lying down. When you get up, get up slowly in case you are light headed.

Three Part Breath

Believe it or not breathing properly takes practice. When you first do this exercise stand up, put your hands on you thighs to support your weight, and lean over slightly. Take a deep breath through your nose and imagine that your chest is like a huge balloon. Continue inhaling and fill your rib cage. Then breathe in a bit more and fill your upper chest. Gentle exhale and reverse the process. First empty your chest then the rib cage and finally your stomach. If you really concentrate on your breathing you will find you can inhale a lot more than you thought. When you exhale make sure you push every bit of air out. We seldom fully empty or fill our lungs. As you exhale really pull in the muscles of your abdomen. Breath like this for fifteen minutes every day and your energy will increase dramatically.

Bellows Breath

Sit with your back straight and imagine you are a huge bellows. Exhale sharply though your nose, imagining yourself blowing a huge bug out of your nose. Pull your stomach muscles in sharply as you do this. Relax and allow yourself to inhale naturally. Continue to breath out sharply until your stomach feels like a giant bellows or pump. Breath rhythmically and to the count of fifteen. Do three this three times.

Conscious Connected Breath

Conscious Connected Breath is a form of breathing used in rebirthing sessions and is good for releasing stress. Do this lying down and for no more than fifteen minutes. Make sure you give yourself a few minutes after the session to relax and get up very slowly afterwards.

Start by inhaling through the nose and without pausing exhale immediately through the mouth. Allow your breath to gush freely out of your body. Then inhale again without pausing between breaths. Make sure you allow your breath to be relaxed and easy.
Your breath becomes a continuous loop. Each breath is connected to each other with no separation or pause in between them.

Rebirthing Isn't as Painful as it Sounds

Rebirthing is a body-centered therapy that uses a powerful breathing technique that helps to activate and release stress, pain, and emotional trauma. The results are often profound because the breathing works

Smoke & Mirrors

With any breathing techniques, be careful you don't hyperventilate. Try the techniques and then return to your normal breathing. Do them while seated or lying down. When you get up, get up slowly in case you are light-headed. If you find your skin tingling or you are very light-headed, stop immediately. Allow your breath to return to normal, relax and sit quietly for a few minutes.

Sage Advice

"Death is not the greatest loss in life. The greatest loss is what dies inside of us while we live."
Norman Cousins

at the core of these issues and doesn't engage the mind. It is simple, easy, and effective. Leonard Orr and Sondra Ray developed rebirthing 22 years ago.

Rebirthing works with the breath and fills the body with a lot more oxygen and energy than we normally have. During a session you may fell heat, pressure, cold, tingle, "electrical currents", vibration and other body sensations. Emotions and memories can safely surface and be easily released. People frequently report significant changes on long standing issues. Rebirthing is done with the guidance of a trained rebirther. It is not a good idea to do it alone. Make sure you find someone you feel comfortable working with.

Using Your Head to Quiet the Noise

Biofeedback is a method of training your mind to control various body functions such as blood pressure using "biofeedback" instruments. Biofeedback equipment uses electrodes to measure subtle changes in your skins temperature or galvanic response, which is your skin's ability to conduct electricity. These devices are connected to audio or visual instruments so you can hear or see the results of relaxation techniques. By observing this feedback you can train your mind.

You can use breathing or muscle relaxation techniques to reduce your stress level. As your stress level lowers the beeps or lights will slow down relaxing your mind even further. With biofeedback machines you can actually see the results of your meditation or breathing or muscle relaxation so you know your doing it correctly. It takes the guessing out of the process so it makes it easier to quiet your mind.

Clarity Corner
Biofeedback is a method of training your mind to control various body functions, such as blood pressure. It allows you to see the results of your altered state of mind. You can feel your body relax and see or hear the results with the biofeedback machine. As you relax, the machine's beeping will slow down, the lights will flash slower, or the waves will deepen.

There are numerous computer programs that will assist you as well as devices you can merely slip on your fingers. Since the 60's the equipment has become much more sophisticated and is readily available. There are also clinics that will teach you a variety of techniques. Biofeedback is very effective in lowering blood pressure and in controlling headaches. As with any other of the altered state methods biofeedback takes practice.

Want to Quack Like a Duck?

Many people form their impression of hypnosis watching a stage hypnotist or watching a science fiction movie. You can't be made to do anything you don't want to do with hypnosis. Believe it or not people who get up on stage and make fools of themselves want to act that way. If you really watch a show you will notice the hypnotist first asks for volunteers to come up on stage. He watches the group and notices which ones comply first. He puts the group through a variety of "tests." He might ask them to raise their hands or turn around quickly. After each exercise he asks the slowest people to sit down. Eventually he weeds out the group until he has people left who have clearly communicated their desire play along with him.

Hypnosis is as ancient as sorcery and magic. Its scientific history begins with Frank Mesmer a Viennese doctor born in 1734. He believed hypnosis was part of the occult and thought 'animal magnetism' flowed through his patients helping them to heal. For a time hypnosis was called mesmerism after him. In the mid 1800's James Braid an English doctor became interested in it and coined the phrase hypnosis. By 1880's hypnosis attracted widespread interest. It was used during World War I and II to help treat soldiers with a variety of combat related problems.

Societies that rely upon shamans for healing are well aware of the power of the mind to hurt or to heal. Through a variety of drumming and chanting techniques shamans or healers induce trace like hypnotic states to assist the individual in healing.

Mind control as Hollywood portrays it just isn't so. No one quacks like a duck unless they want to. Brain washing isn't an everyday occurrence. When I first started my spiritual journey I was told my brain needed washing. After my initial shock I agreed. Your brain probably needs washing too. Hypnosis and self-hypnosis can help you wash your brain or at least begin to clean up the way you think.

Hypnosis and trance states aren't something we can readily measure so they remain clouded in mystery. Most people wonder what it feels like to be hypnotized. Even after a person has had a session they often wonder if they've been hypnotized.

Take a deep breath and imagine yourself walking down a flight of stairs, step by step. As you walk slowly down the stairs you come to a doorway. You open the door and walk in. There is another set of stairs so you walk down and down until you reach another door. You take a deep breath and walk through the door. Chances are as you read that passage you went into a light hypnotic state. A hypnotic state feels very much like being ordinary everyday waking consciousness but it isn't. It is a very powerful state of mind we can learn to use for our personal growth.

You're Feeling Very Sleepy

Hypnosis is a very valuable tool. It is a deeply relaxed state of mind in which the person is highly receptive to suggestions. Hypnotically induced trances are very useful in promoting healing, changing behaviors, and remove phobias. The person feels totally relaxed as if they were lost in a very pleasant daydream.

Clarity Corner

During **hypnosis** your brain waves slow down, your body relaxes, and your rational, linear, ego-based mind lets go. You go into a state of heightened awareness that feels very relaxed and dreamlike. Your mind is more open to suggestions, and your resistance to new ideas is greatly diminished. After a session many people feel like nothing happened, but to the hypnotist the person's relaxation was quite evident. The person's facial muscles relax, and the entire body goes limp.

Sage Advice

"Hold onto your dreams for if dreams die life is broken winged bird that cannot fly."
— Langston Hughes

In recent years hypnotherapy has been widely accepted by the general public as well as the medical profession. It has many applications. A hypnotherapist can assist you in achieving wonderful results in a number of areas. It is important to uncover the cause of your discomfort before replacing the behavior. If you don't uncover the root causes I've found that the behavior will manifest in our lives in some other form.

Hypnotherapy can assist you in:

- Building confidence and improving self-esteem.
- Breaking habits such as smoking.
- Relieving insomnia.
- Managing stress.
- Mastering public speaking and reduce stage fright.
- Alleviating anxiety, panic attack, fears, and phobias.
- Overcoming learning difficulties, improve study habits, and enhance memory and concentration.
- Improving sports performance and increase stamina.
- Increasing access to your creativity.
- Promoting good health.
- Controlling pain and aid in natural childbirth.
- Releasing emotional and physical trauma.

> **Clarity Corn**
>
> **Hypnotherapy** can be used to change your attitude, quit smoking, remember to floss your teeth, improve your self-esteem, remove phobias such as the fear of heights or flying, and improve the quality of your life in a myriad of ways. In a session the therapist talks to you about your goals, listens to your description of the problem, and then hypnotizes you. During the session, the therapist give you positive suggestions and reinforces your desire to change.

I'm Feeling Very Sleepy

Self-hypnosis is a way of inducing trace or hypnotic states by yourself. It takes practice but it can be used to achieve many of the same results achieved with hypnotherapy. Many hypnotherapists teach patients self-hypnosis so they can reinforce the techniques being used in their individual sessions.

The mind doesn't really know the difference between a suggested thought and reality when you are in an altered state. If you are in a hypnotic trace and your arm is touched with an ice cube but you were told it was a hot poker when you came out of the trace you would have a blister on your arm where you were 'burned.' When you make suggestions to yourself when you are in a self-induced trace the results can be remarkable.

It is important to clearly know what you want to work on and what you want to say to yourself. It is easy to become distracted and lose your focus when you are in an altered state. Self-hypnosis takes a great deal of practice to perfect. It is important to develop the ability to focus your mind while at the same time quieting it.

Practice Being Hyp

Be prepared to spend fifteen to twenty minutes every day practicing to become proficient at self-hypnosis. Find a place you won't be disturbed sit or lie down in a comfortable position. If your clothes are tight loosen them.

To induce a light trace you need to relax your mind yet remain focused. One way to do that is to mentally picture a relaxing scene. You can visualize walking along a peaceful path out in nature or sitting by the seashore watching the waves or even walking down a long flight of stairs. Another way is to count backwards.

Thoroughly picture the image you decide upon. If you are walking along a path really focus on the act of walking. Feel your feet you walk on the path, notice the sights, the sounds, and the smells around you. Really focus your mind on the experience. Relax your breathing and focus on your imaginary walk.

After you are fully relaxed repeat key phrases to yourself. Always make them positive. If you are dealing with a phobia don't say I am no longer afraid, your mind doesn't hear negatives. If you say I am no longer afraid your mind hears I am afraid. Instead say I feel confident, courageous, or relaxed. Remind yourself that each time you relax you will find yourself going deeper more easily and faster.

After you are done reverse the process to bring yourself back. If you walked down a path walk back up it or if you walked downstairs walk back up them. Before you open your eyes remind yourself that you feel fully refreshed, relaxed, and at peace. The more you do these techniques the easier they will become. The first time it helps to listen to a tape or have someone relax you. Once your mind knows what it feels like to be in a hypnotic trace it easier for you to get into an altered state of mind.

Smoke & Mirrors

Your mind doesn't hear negatives in your key phrases. If you say "I am no longer afraid," you mind hears "I am afraid." Instead, say "I feel confident, courageous, or relaxed." If you say to yourself, "I want" instead of "I have," your mind will stop once you have created the desire to have something rather than actually create having it. Remind yourself that each time your relax, your will find yourself going deeper faster and more easily.

Haven't We Met Before?

As hypnotherapists regressed patients to release childhood traumas they found some people spontaneously regressed into what seemed like earlier lives or existences. They would describe places they had never been to with uncanny accuracy. There are some cases where the historical facts supplied by the patient were later confirmed by research. These past life regressions seem to be some how related to current problems in the person's life. Very often the past life regression seems to help clear up these problems. People that experience drowning in a previous life release their fear of the water once they remember their death.

Whether these are actual memories of past lives or the mind's way of giving the person information really doesn't matter. These sessions seem to be effective in improving the quality of a person's life. I have done hundreds of past life regressions for people and have seen people's lives transformed by them. I am always very careful not to lead a person or impose my beliefs on them. I had done several past life regressions for one woman. The sessions all had the same theme. The woman believed she needed a relationship to be happy. Lifetime after lifetime she had lost herself in her relationships. I saw clearly what it was about but she didn't. The last session we did she popped into a future life and there was the same pattern. She had the chance to be a very successful musician and gave it up for a relationship. When I brought her back she was shocked. She realized the price she'd been paying for her relationships. She received some counseling and was able to form a successful relationship free of codependency.

Float Your Cares Away

Floatation tanks were first called sensory deprivation chambers and were used in the 50's to see how the brain reacted without any outside stimulation. They are soundproof tanks filled with water, salts, and minerals so you can float effortlessly. The water is kept at skin temperature and the tank is totally dark. Floatation tanks are often used to treat stress and addictions. The tanks are usually found in float centers or health clubs. The experience is incredibly relaxing. The brain releases endorphins that act as natural painkillers and can cause euphoria.

The tank itself is about eight feet long and four feet wide. The front of the tank is a door that easily opens so you won't feel trapped and can easily get in and out. Before entering the tank you take a shower and you generally float naked. The water is only about six inches deep and is so concentrated with salts that your body easily floats. The water is kept at 93.5 degrees. The door tank is soundproofed and lightproof. Some tanks have speakers installed so you can listen to music or subliminal tapes while you float.

The first time I ever floated in a tank I was on a health club located near Grand Central Station in New York City. I had floated for about an hour and I was feeling incredibly relaxed. Off in the distance I heard a faint rumbling, it sounded like the heart beat of the city. When I got out of the tank I felt totally connected to everything and everyone. It was an amazing experience, one I highly recommend. Most doctors accept the healing properties of floatation tanks because of the stress reducing hormones the body releases.

Out of Body, Out of Mind

Out of body experiences are brief but very interesting experiences in which a person's consciousness seems to leave their physical body. The person is then able to see the world from a totally different perspective.

Sage Advice

"We should be careful to get out of an experience only the wisdom that is in it – and stop there; least we be like the cat that sits on a hot stove lid. She will never sit on a hot lid again – and that is well; but she will also not sit down on a cold one anymore."

Mark Twain

Clarity Corn

Floatation Tanks are sound-proof tanks filled with water, salts, and minerals so you can float effortlessly. The water is kept at skin temperature, and the tank is totally dark. Floatation tanks are often used to treat stress and addictions. Laying in a small, dark chamber doesn't sound very inviting, but the experience is incredibly relaxing, loving , and nurturing. It is like being back in the womb again, all safe and warm.

They generally report seeing their body and a thin gold or white cord stretching toward them form their body. Often the person can see and hear things in other rooms or from various parts of the world. A person can often accurately describe a location they have never seen.

Out of body experience happen spontaneously although you can train yourself to have them through the use of hypnosis, meditation, and hallucinogenic drugs. Children frequently report out of body experiences. Studies have shown that roughly 14% of people in the United States have had an out of body experience at some point in their life. Most people who have had an out of body experience say they would like to experience one again.

Near death experiences are an example of an out of body experience. After people have one their fear of death is reduced and their belief in an afterlife is strengthened. Some people believe death is merely an out of body experience in which the person chooses not to come back.

Altered states are closely related to out of body experiences. In an altered state we perceive physical reality differently just as we do in an out of body experience. In the seventies I began to explore self-hypnosis. I had never heard of an out of body experience. One day I was lying on the couch practicing deep relaxation when I spontaneously found myself out of my body. I had no idea what was happening when I found myself floating on the ceiling. I was looking down at my body and there was a thin gold cord stretching from my body toward me.

Suddenly I took off and I found myself flying over the mountains near my home. It was early winter and we'd just had several feet on snow. The mountains were magnificent, the sun was shinning, and the sky was an incredibly blue. I flew around for what seemed like hours. Then just as suddenly I found myself hovering over my house. I went in and sat on the arm of the couch. I looked at my body but it seemed so confining I didn't really want to get back inside it. The next thing I knew I was staring up at the ceiling wondering what had happened.

It was an amazing experience that stayed with me for a long time. Over the years I have had other out of body experience and several near death experiences. I must admit I no longer wonder about the validity of anyone's spiritual experience. Altered states are very powerful and transformational. As a friend once told me once we know we can't not know.

The Least You Need to Know

- Your mind and your brain are two very different things.
- Altered states come in many shapes and sizes.
- You can use your mind to heal your body and your life.
- Relaxation techniques are the key to improving your life.
- You are definitely more than your body.

Chapter 7

Body Therapies

> **In This Chapter**
>
> ➤ Better understand the mind, body, and spirit connection.
>
> ➤ Learn about a variety of body therapies.
>
> ➤ Find out how you can smell to get well.
>
> ➤ Understand what flower can be used for beside centerpieces.
>
> ➤ Sound, light, and colors become tools for healing.

The mind, body, and spirit work together like an elaborately balanced ecosystem. If one is out of balance it effects the other two. The body houses both our mind and spirit so if it isn't healthy it is hard to focus on anything else. When we are in physical pain it becomes the focal point of everything we do.

There are literally hundreds of different types of body therapies. In this chapter we will explore quite a number of them. If you pursue one make sure you find someone you feel comfortable and confident working with. Also make sure you consult your doctor as well as your inner wisdom. Don't throw the baby out with the bath water. I have seen people die of curable diseases because they insisted on only using one method of healing.

Starting With the Spinal

Chiropractic diagnoses and treats imbalances in the central nervous system by manipulating and realigning the joints, spine, and muscles. When these systems are in balance it is much easier for the body to heal. The spine is a conduit connecting the brain to the rest of the body. When those signals are disrupted it affects other parts of the body.

In the 1960 the American Medical Association waged a legal battle declaring chiropractic an unscientific cult. They eventually lost their battle. It is now recognized as a complimentary treatment to Western medicine and is the most widely practiced of any.

Chiropractors treat the whole person and often address other issues such as diet and life style. There are numerous forms of treatment available other than just spinal manipulation. Neuro-Link, Biokinetics, and brain gym are just a few of the newer techniques. These address health from a perspective of the necessity of clearing up the communications between your brain and your body. Call around and see just what's available in your area.

Palmer Did it First

Each practitioner has their own style and particular way of manipulating a person's body. It is important to find someone who feels right to you. Palmer chiropractic is the original method and the most vigorous. Any misalignment of the spinal column may effect the way the entire body functions. Treatments are similar to the techniques used by Osteopaths.

The chiropractor will check your reflexes, the alignment of your spine and if necessary take X-rays to assess your condition. The doctor will take a complete medical history and your body will be checked for its ease of movement and flexibility. This technique uses much more force than other techniques.

Activator Chiropractic

The Activator method of adjustment was developed in the late 1960's. It is a low force method and is much easier on the body. An activator is a hand held rubber-tipped instrument designed to deliver a controlled, light thrusting movement that effectively manipulates a person's vertebrae.

Sage Advice

"Those who say it cannot be done should not interrupt the person doing it."

Chinese proverb

Clarity Corner

The term chiropractic comes from the Greek cheiro meaning hand and praktikos, which means doing. Chiropractic literally means doing by hand. An Iowan merchant Daniel Palmer developed chiropractic in 1895. He practiced his theories on a janitor who had been deaf since he injured his back when he was 17. He reportedly regained his hearing after Palmer worked with him for a while. In 1906 Palmer was arrested for practicing medicine without a license but his son continued practicing his methods.

The method became very popular in Canada, New Zealand, Australia, and in the US. In 1987 the AMA lost its legal battle and the methods are now recognized as a legitimate and effective form of healing.

This method is much more gentle. The activator is so quick there is no time for your muscles to resist so there is less pain and much safer.

Network Chiropractic

Dr. Donald Epstein developed this variation in 1979. It is a specific process using light and very subtle movements to align the vertebra in relationship to one another. Dr. Epstein believed that the spine is a conduit of an essential energy and constantly sends information to the entire body. When the spine is out of alignment the messages become scrambled and the body loses vitality.

> **Sage Advice**
> It takes courage to grow up and turn out to be how you really are.
> E. E. Cummings

The chiropractor uses a specialized system to evaluate your spine. There are twelve different techniques that are applied in a certain order and with specific timing. There are three levels of treatment that are delivered over a period of time.

Rubbing It Down

Massage is one of the simplest of the healing arts and the most ancient. Hippocrates considered massage to be of great benefit and suggested people take a scented bath daily as well as a daily massage with oil. Egyptians painted pictures of people being massaged on the walls of their tombs and ancient Chinese and Indian texts consider it an excellent treatment for disease. Western religion linked massages to sin so massage was not incorporated in Western healing arts until the late 1800's.

A Swedish gymnast brought massage to the attention of Western society and returned it to favor. During World War I massage was used to treat soldiers suffering from shell shock but at the same time brothels began to hide behind being massage parlors.

Over the centuries many forms of massage have been developed. All forms of massage help to improve the circulation and general over all well-being of the body. Massage can boost the immune system, improve muscle tone, lower the blood pressure, and improve digestion. And it feels good.

Shiatsu

Shiatsu massage, which literally means finger pressure, was developed in the early 20th century. It has its basis in Chinese medicine although it has been heavily influenced by Western medicine. The technique received official recognition from the Japanese government in 1964. As in traditional Chinese medicine the practitioner helps the energy in the body to circulate more freely by putting pressure along the body's meridians.

Shiatsu can be used to relieve many physical ailments. Pressure is applied to specific points in the body with the therapist's fingers, thumbs, feet, and elbows. Sometimes a small wooden stick will be used to create the necessary pressure. You remain clothed for the treatment although loose clothing is preferable. The patient lies on a mat on the floor so the proper amount of pressure can be applied. I find Shiatsu painful but very beneficial. At times you can feel worse before you feel better as the body releases toxins and heals.

Swedish Massage

Swedish massage is very gentle and utilizes mainly four movements or types of treatments. One is gentle stroking in long, slow movements. It aids circulation and helps the body to relax. Kneading the body like bread dough is another technique used to relax tense muscles. The massage therapist may also use friction, which is a steady pressure applied with the thumbs. The thumbs are moved in a circular motion generally on the back near the spine. Another type of movement is composed of small, short taps on the body with the side of the hands.

> **Sage Advice**
> "The lust for comfort, that stealthy thing that enters the house as a guest, then becomes host, and then master."
> *Kahlil Gibran*

> **Spiritual Shortcuts**
> Finding a massage therapist is a very personal thing. I have had hundreds of massages, and each therapist has their own style. Each massage is a unique experience. I find the massage room is almost as important as the therapist. I have had massages in a room with an annoying machine hum in the background and had a very hard time relaxing. I suggest you check out the office and get a general feel for the place. Talk to the massage therapist and see if you feel comfortable with him or her. He or she is going to be touching your body, and it is important the you feel safe and comfortable with the therapist.

Most massage therapists will use scented oils. I have found that massages vary greatly. I like the experience to be totally nurturing. Gentle soothing music and a pleasant environment are a must for me. As with any practitioner make sure you feel totally comfortable with them. Massages are very personal and I find Swedish massages the most gentle and nurturing. Having someone touch your body is a very personal thing so make sure you tell them exactly what you want.

Lomilomi

Lomilomi is a form of Hawaiian massage. It is a deeply spiritual experience. When you watch it looks like a rhythmic dance. The process starts out with an energy purification. Then the practitioner connects with their spiritual guidance and says a silent prayer. It is a full body massage starting at the head and systematically moving through the entire body. Various areas of the body are worked on more deeply depending on the person's inner guidance.

Lomilomi addresses the emotional and spiritual bodies as well the physical body. After the missionaries arrived in Hawaii the practice of this healing art was hidden. It is only recently that it is again be offered to the general public. There are several kapunas or elders who are teaching the ancient knowledge. A Lomilomi massage is an incredible experience it is very healing and nurturing.

Therapeutic Massage

All types of massage are really therapeutic. There are so many types and forms of massage. If you look in the Yellow Pages in most cities you will find hundreds of massage therapists listed. There are massages for relaxation and there are massages used strictly for physical therapy.

If you have a sports injury therapeutic massage can be highly beneficial. Some clinics have whirlpools and the combination of hot water and massage greatly accelerates the healing process.

Rolfing

Rolfing is a very powerful form of body realignment. Dr. Ida Rolf, an American biochemist, began developing Rolfing in the 1950's. She became interested in the concept of body realignment when she went to visit an osteopath for the pain she was having in her side. The doctor realigned one of her ribs and she felt better not only physically but mentally as well. Her digestion improved and she felt much better physically.

Dr. Rolf broke the body structure down into roughly seven 'bricks.' If these bricks are out of alignment the body is stressed and usually experiencing discomfort. Once the bricks are realigned properly gravity helps to reinforce the balance.

Clarity Corner

Dr. Rolf based the development of Rolfing on her knowledge of yoga, the effects of gravity, and physical therapy. Rolfing, also known as structural integration gained recognition in the 60's and has continued to grow in popularity ever since. A Rolfer considers themselves a sculpture, reshaping the body until it comes into perfect realignment.

Our muscles are all separated by a thin, connective tissue called fascia. Rolfers believe that emotional or physical stress will cause the fascia to loose its pliability, bunch-up and, harden. When this happens the body gradual adapts, physical movement becomes limited, and the body literally changes shape. Have you ever noticed an elderly person all stooped over and beaten down by life? We store the events of life in our bodies and they respond in the best way they can.

Rolfers work differently but generally they suggest you start out with a series of ten treatments spaced over a period of time. I have done the basic series as well as an advanced series and a few touch ups. I find the process uncomfortable but the changes in my body always amaze me. After the initial series the way I moved and the way I stood totally changed. I could breath better and my body felt more alive. Make sure you work with a well-trained Rolfer. In 1971 Dr. Rolf established an institute to train practitioners in Bolder, Colorado.

Other Therapies for That Body

There are hundreds of varieties of body therapies. Some are better known than others. I would feel remiss in my duties if I didn't at least mention a few more. It amazed me when I began exploring what was available to assist me in my growth. Once I asked the question methods seemed to come out of the woodwork. I eventually learned to rely on my own personal experience. I had a bunch of friends who were going to this one man who worked wonders according to them. I went and to me it felt like a bunch of smoke and mirrors. This type of work is so individual you really have to learn to trust yourself and beware of the snake oil salesman.

Tragerwork

Tragerwork is a gentle therapy designed to reintegrate the mind and the body. A boxer named Milton Trager found he could intuitively work with people and ease their pain developed Tragerwork. After he learned Transcendental Meditation he developed this approach. Sessions last for around 90 minutes and include instruction in movement therapy as well as bodywork.

The practitioner goes into an active form of mediation where they connect with the client. In that way they become intuitively aware of the patterns of tension in the person's body. Their goal is to instill a sense of freedom and lightness in the body. The effects are often subtle but they are cumulative.

Hellerwork

An American engineer developed Hellerwork in the 1970's. Joseph Heller had worked with Dr. Ida Rolf and agreed with many of her ideas. In his work he chose to emphasize the emotional aspect of the work. He believed our muscles locked up because of the stored traumas and it was necessary to acknowledge the emotional aspects in order to free up the body. He didn't believe restructuring the body would produce long term results unless the emotional aspect was addressed.

Hellerwork consists of 11 ninety-minute sessions that involve deep tissue work very similar to Rolfing. The major difference is the practitioner also guides the patient in dialoging about the emotional aspect of the bodywork. The patient is encouraged to feel and release repressed emotions.

Smoke & Mirrors

I had a bunch of friends who saw someone they though worked wonders. I went to him, and to me, it seemed like a bunch or smoke and mirrors. They spent a fortune going to see him because he kept dangling "the cure" in front of them. He claimed he could cure them, but of course he couldn't. They spent a lot of money on unnecessary herbs, vitamins and massages.

Feldenkrais Method

Moshe Feldenkrais founded the Feldenkrais Institute in Tel Aviv in 1962. His work was based on observations he made of the inherent grace of children, anatomy, psychology, neurology, and physiology. Practitioners prefer to think of themselves as teachers and call their clients students. Classes are held throughout the world.

The Feldenkrais method improves physical and mental health by repatterning movements using two approaches. The first is know as 'awareness through movement.' It helps the student develop increased body awareness and mobility but following the leaders instructions. The second approach is 'functional integration' which is done on a one-to-one basis that uses touch and gentle manipulation.

Alexander Technique

The Alexander technique is often connected with the performing arts. It started in the 1930's. This method is general taught on a one-to-one basis and is relatively easy to learn. The teacher will show you how to correctly move and be more graceful and flowing in your movements.

You will be reeducated on the efficient use of your muscles. The teacher will observe you and correct any awkward or stressful uses of your body. Students often realize how they use unnecessary pressure to open doors and turn on water faucets. A full course takes anywhere from 15-35 classes.

Bioenergetics

Bioenergetics is a body-oriented form of psychotherapy developed by Dr. Alexander Lowen. Unless we release them our body stores all of the mental and emotional stresses we experience in our lifetime. Emotions are really a form of energy in motion. When we aren't able to express them or release them in some way we store them. This stored up energy must be released in some way.

Dr. Lowen developed a large variety of movements adapted from Tai chi and other sources to assist the person in releasing this energy. Practitioners believe we each develop a unique way of dealing with our emotional trauma and it shows in our body. When the places we have stored the trauma are activated emotions are vented and we release the stress. The patient is shown how to 'ground' their bodies so they can stay more in touch with themselves and their inner life. For some people a short series of treatments can be life changing while other people continue for years.

Sage Advice

"If you wished to be loved, love."
Seneca

Sage Advice

"The foolish man seeks happiness in the distance; the wise man grows it under his feet."
James Oppenheim

Craniosacral Therapy

This is a healing approach that focuses on the alignment of the bones in our skull as well as our spine. It is a very gentle, non-intrusive therapy. It focuses on the movement of the fluid around the brain and spinal column. Dr. John Upledger developed this technique and believes the rhythmic impulses affects all areas of our body. By gently manipulating the plates in our heads and balancing the rhythms of the fluid the entire body can benefit.

I've gone to several practitioners and had wonderful results. I went to one man in San Diego who used the technique to do past life regressions. I found the sessions extremely profound, relaxing, and very helpful in my daily life. I felt totally relaxed after the sessions.

> **Spiritual Shortcuts**
>
> So many different body therapies and so little time. How do you know which one is right for you? One of the easiest ways to narrow down your choices is to see what's available in your area. Many practitioners have free or low-cost classes you can check out. Often you can talk to the person on the phone and ask about the benefits of working with her. Ask what symptoms the technique is most effective at alleviating. In a fairly short time, you can usually get a good feel for the person and decide whether you might want to work with him. As with everything else in life, follow your inner wisdom.

Reflexology

Egyptian Physician's Tombs built over 4000 years ago have pictures of people practicing some form of foot manipulation on the walls. Foot massage has been practiced for centuries. Reflexology is more aligned with acupressure than it is simple massage. Reflexologists believe ever organ and part of the body is has a corresponding point on the hands and the feet. If you stimulate the point in the feet it will in turn stimulate the corresponding place in the body. They claim over 100 ailments can be cured by reflexology.

If you feel the bottom of your feet you will notice areas that might be a bit tender. If you rub that area you will notice small grains of what feel like sand just under the surface. Reflexologists believe these grains are accumulated waste matter and toxins in the form of uric acid and calcium crystals. They will rub those spots in order to break down the particles so the energy of the body can flow more easily. They believe this will unlock blocked nerves and other energy pathways in the body thus restoring health.

Our feet have to carry us throughout our entire lives and frequently, unless they hurt we given them very little attention.

A good practice is to rub your feet every night before you go to bed. Many health food stores and new age bookstores sell wallet size reflexology charts. You can then understand what you are working on when you rub your feet. Even if you don't have one you can still do a deep foot massage. I guarantee you will find the places you need to work on.

Using a oil scented with lavender is most helpful. Slowly rub the bottom of your foot with your thumb making sure you use a firm pressure. When you feel particles rub them until you can feel them break up. Rub both the top and bottom of your foot as well as your ankles paying special attention to any place that feels at all sore.

Most cities have people that specialize in reflexology. Reflexology seems to work best for stress related disorders such as headaches, constipation, and tension. It is also good for imbalances in the internal organs.

Sage Advice
"In the world's audience hall, the simple blade of grass sits on the same carpet with sunbeams, and stars of midnight."
Rabindranath Tagore

Aromatherapy

Memories associated with smells affect us most profoundly. They did studies in large universities and found students tests grades were much lower when the test wasn't taken in their regular classroom. When exams were given in a different room the students had a much harder time remembering the information. Why? Their memories were keyed into the smell of the room. If you have to study for an exam peppermints are a wonderful tool. Peppermint increases your alertness and if you chew peppermints while you study and eat them during the exam your memory will be triggered by the smell.

Our olfactory receptors absorb scent molecules and allow us to smell things. Our olfactory centers are connected to the part of our brain most closely associated with our emotional mood. For centuries we have used scents for any number of purposes. Think of your own life. How does your house smell? Do you like and dislike certain perfumes? Have you ever ended a relationship and found yourself upset by the smell of the person's perfume? How about hospitals, do you like the way they smell?

Clarity Corner
A simple odor can cause us to remember a specific event in minute detail. Aromatherapy capitalizes on our mind's ability to remember and associate scents with specific memories. Each of us already has some smells wired up with old memories, and we can easily add to that repertoire. Certain scents illicit certain emotions such as relaxation, and you can use them to enhance your experiences in life.

This is only a partial list of oils and their uses.

- **Lavender** is wonderful for healing and purification, assists in connecting to your inner guidance
- **Chamomile** is gentle and very calming, great sleep aid, helps relieve depression, and enhances insight.
- **Sage** is a wonderful to enhance your dreams, brings balance and tranquility to your mind and body, helps boost confidence.

- **Eucalyptus** clears and opens the energy centers of the body, helps relieve cold and flu symptoms, speeds healing.
- **Peppermint** energizes, helps clear negative thinking, helps with digestion, and aids in concentration and memory.
- **Tea Tree oil**, known as miracle oil, great antiseptic, repeals bugs as well as stops itching from their bites.
- **Ylang Ylang** is sweet and sensual, an aphrodisiac, calms the heart and nerves and inspires creativity.
- **Rose** awakens and inspires the heart, soothing to children, helps with menstrual cramps, connects you with your divinity.

We can teach ourselves to associate certain smells with certain feelings. Chances are you already have you just didn't do it consciously. If you meditate on a regular basis use the same scent each time. Eventually your mind will associate the smell with mediation and automatically relax as soon as you smell it.

> **Spiritual Shortcuts**
> Different scents have different affects on our emotions and our body. Essential oils can be used on the body as well as in diffusers that scent the room. Placing 6 to 10 drops of oil in a hot bath can be very relaxing or invigorating depending upon the oils you use. Oils can help relieve cold systems, allergies, stomach upset, nervous tension, circulatory problems, as well as a host of other conditions. A good aromatherapist can blend oils specifically for you. Many stores sell essential oils and they are usually readily available.

Flower Essences

Flower essences were first used as a tool for healing by an English doctor named Edward Bach. By observing his patients he noticed that most physical diseases had emotional origins. He was certain that flowers could effect a person's emotional state. He was familiar with homeopathic theory so he developed his flower essences. He developed them intuitively by holding his hand over each flower and sensing its properties. There are 38 different Bach flower remedies.

Flower Essences include the following

- Rescue remedy is a composite and is a must in first aid kits, helps with trauma, upset, and bad news.
- Walnut helps you adjust to change and protects you from being overly sensitive.

- Olive helps you have faith in yourself and life.
- Cherry Plum gives you calm, quiet courage.
- Aspen promotes fearlessness.
- Mustard invokes inner serenity, stability, and joy.

A woman who did intuitive healing on animals first introduced me to Bach flower remedies. I had a dog that was afraid of her own shadow. Whenever someone would come into my house she would run, hide, and refuse to come out. Amy came over and gave me a small bottle of Bach flower remedies. I put a few drops in her water bowl everyday for ten days. To my utter amazement by the end of the ten days she was running out and greeting people.

> **Sage Advice**
> "The flower that follows the sun does so even on cloudy days."
> Robert Leighton

The theory is they work on the subtle energy body much as homeopathic cures. I have used them on and off with my clients, my animals, and myself for years and find they are very effective. Most heath food stores carry the Bach remedies. The new flower essences generally have to be mail ordered.

More recently flower essences have been developed from various areas of the world. Flower essences influence our relationship with our body, mind, spirit, and with nature. On an energy level they combine the ancient wisdoms with modern society. The very essence or soul of the planet is able to unite with us and assist us in releasing or harnessing energy in a totally different manner. Flower essence therapy is often referred to as the new alchemy of the soul; it is a form of communication that goes far beyond our conscious, rational, linear mind.

Finding a flower essence therapist may take a bit of research but it is well worth your time and effort. There are many fine books on the subject and several of them are listed in the appendix of this book.

Sound, Music, and Art therapy

Creativity is a powerful force in our lives. We so often suppress our creativity. We also forget the influence our environment has on our emotional and physical well-being.

Do You Hear What I Hear?

Drums have been used in battles to rally the troops for centuries. Buddhists monks and Indian yogis have used chanting to achieve altered states of consciousness. Native Americans use singing, chanting, and drumming in many of their healing ceremonies. Sound is a very powerful force that can be used to hurt or to heal.

Machines used for sound wave therapy were developed in the 50' and 60's. Children with autism or dyslexia often benefit from sound therapy. The children listen to filtered music that produces specific sounds and frequencies. Doctors have found that certain music increases circulation and mental clarity.

Clarity Corner

Om is said to be the sound of the universe. It is part of an ancient Hindu chant and is said to have the power to activate the body's energy centers. I find it very relaxing to chant it. I say the word slowly, allowing all the breath to leave my lungs while mouthing the word. Experiment with the sound, the pitch, and volume until you find a comfortable way to do it for yourself.

Sage Advice

"Except for hydrogen all atoms that make each of us up – were manufactured in red giant stars thousands of light years away in space and billions of years ago in time. We are, as I like to say, starstuff."

Carl Sagan

Specific machines are designed to project sound waves directly into the body. Different organs have different vibrations so the theory is that certain sound frequencies can assist organs in healing.

Chanting or toning is another way to use sound to heal. Chanting the word OM can be a wonderful exercise. Relax and sing OM as you slowly exhale. It will take a bit of practice to find your tone but when you do the sound just seems to float out of your body. Go up and down the scale as you chant and see how it feels in various parts of your body. It can be very relaxing.

A Joyful Noise

Music has the ability to stir the soul and generate emotions. Music therapy as a specific practice started after World War II. It was used to treat the emotional and psychological stress of returning combat veterans. A session usual starts with the therapist singing or playing a song. As you feel more confident you will be asked to create your own music and use it as a way to release trapped emotions. Playing the drums is a wonderful way to release anger.

Music itself can also be therapeutic. Baroque classical music is a wonderful study aid. Its very nature causes the person's mind to slip into an alpha state, which is most conducive to studying and retaining the information. Everyone reacts differently to different types of music. Understanding our reaction and capitalizing on them is very beneficial. I clean a whole lot better to some music and get very tired while listening to others. Find out what your cleaning music is a play it next time the house gets messy.

Coloring Within the Lines

Just playing freely with form and color can be very liberating. Some therapists specialize in art therapy using it to assist the patient in their healing process. It is something that is fun and you can do at home. Go to the art store and pick out a bunch of colors, brushes, and paper. Listen to your inner voice maybe you want to work in clay or origami. Wander around the art store until you find the right medium, then go home, and play. Art therapy isn't about the finished product – it is about the process and what it tells you about yourself later.

In my classes I have my students make masks. We all wear emotional masks in our lives and it is interesting and very healing to make the masks we wear and then choose to destroy them,

Color and Light therapy

Different colors have profound impact on our mood and emotional well-being. Different colors have different wavelengths and can be used to heal emotional based imbalances in the body. A practitioner will have you choose three colors from eight colored cards. Your choice provides clues about what is imbalanced in your life. Water left in the sun in a blue bottle can be used to treat insomnia. Wearing certain colored clothing or sitting under a certain colored light are also forms of color therapy. Red is used to treat procrastination, yellow helps you release unresolved issues, green relaxes you, blue helps treat insomnia, and violet helps relieve addictions.

Some people suffer from seasonal depression. Every winter, as the sun sinks lower and lower in the sky so do some people's spirits. Doctors have found that if these people spend several hours daily in front of full spectrum lights their depression disappears. Full spectrum light also helps us regulate our biological clock that regulates our sleep patterns and hormone output.

Natural sunlight in moderation is extremely beneficial to our minds, our hearts, and our bodies. We weren't meant to spend most of our time cooped up in buildings with stale air and artificial light. Nothing is more nurturing to your spirit and soul than taking a slow walk through a peaceful setting out in nature. Take the time to sit outside in a natural setting and watch the sunset or rise once a week and see what happens to your life.

> **Sage Advice**
>
> "A fool may be known by six things: anger without cause; speech without profit; change without progress; inquiry without object; putting trust in a stranger and mistaking friends for foes."
>
> *Arabian proverb*

> ### The Least You Need to Know
>
> - Chiropractors can help with a variety of ailments.
> - Massage can heal the body and sooth the soul.
> - Learning how to move our body differently can change the rest of your life too.
> - Your nose can relax and heal your entire body.
> - Feet are for more than just walking on.
> - Colors and creativity can be fun and profoundly healing

Chapter 8

Energy Work

In This Chapter

- You'll learn about a variety of healing techniques.
- Find out what Reiki is.
- Get in touch with your magnetic nature.
- Learn how to do healing yourself.
- Let rocks talk to you.

The human body is really a vast energy system. In Russia in 1939 Semyon Kirlian took the first photography of the human energy field. An electromagnetic field surrounds all living and inanimate things. Our general health, the level of stress in our lives, and environmental factors all affect that field. This energy has been recognized for centuries by many healing traditions. In Chinese medicine they call this energy chi or the life energy, in India they call it prana.

Energy work takes many forms and has many different names. Most religions include some form of faith healing or energy work. I have seen some healers cure the incurable and at other times seemingly do nothing for a person. The human system is incredibly complex and is affected by so many variables. Some people claim to feel the subtle effects in the environment like power lines. Energy work can be a very powerful influence in our life or do nothing. It can't ever hurt us and it is a wonderful opportunity to step

Hands-on-Healing

Hands-on-healing has many names and has probably been around since the beginning of time. When I moved to California I studied with a series of healers. They called it different things but it was all basically hands-on-healing or spiritual healing. There are many people who have chose to teach healing in a structured manner but it is still energy or spiritual or healing or hands-on-healing. A brownie is a brownie. Its taste depends upon the recipe but regardless it's still a brownie. Energy healing has different flavors too. The different techniques make it easier for our mind to grasp and to feel the subtle differences.

Hands-on-healing is a way of sharing our energy, love, and compassion with one another. I have seen mothers comfort their child by kissing the wound and the healing seems to be instantaneous. Energy healing is a wonderful adjunct to other forms of healing. If you have a serious illness is very important to treat illness physically as well energetically. Spiritual healing is not a substitute.

Therapeutic Touch

Dolores Krieger, a professor of nursing, developed therapeutic Touch in the early 1970's. Her mentor and teacher Dora Kunz had been a healer most of her life. They developed a method of teaching others these ancient techniques. Therapeutic touch is part of the resurgence of interest in ancient, non-invasive healing methods. Therapeutic Touch became part of a class called the Frontiers of Nursing. This was the first time hands-on-healing was taught as a full-time university course.

Therapeutic Touch stimulates the patient's natural healing response. The human body has the capacity to heal itself. Therapeutic Touch is based on the principles of energy exchange between people. As a society we have been taught to believe that the universe is inherently flawed and we fail to see its perfection. As we remember that everything in the universe is interconnected and whole we can tap into that universal energy to heal ourselves an others.

Healing Touch

A nurse Janet Mentgen developed Healing Touch in the early 80's. In the 90's Linda Smith joined her. Healing Touch is much more heavily based in spirituality. It is also based on the exchange of energy. They offer an in-depth training for all of their practitioners.

They extend the practice of hands-on-healing to animals as well as people. They have specific training geared toward working on animals. Vets have heartily embraced the system and find it very beneficial especially with horses.

Sage Advice

In a seed, the tree which may spring forth from it is hidden; it is in a condition of potential existence; is there; but it will not admit definition.

Samuel Mathers

Sage Advice

The miracle is not to fly in the air, or walk on water, but to walk on the earth.

Chinese Proverb

Hands of Light

Barbara Brennan has written several books on healing and has a highly focused four-year training for healers. Her work differs from the other in some of its approach. She firmly believes we must release traumas from our past in order to fully heal. She has developed very specific exercises and energy movements to assist in the healing process.

She feels that anything that depletes us energetically is due to resistance within us. As we clear out the resistance we are energized and our over all health improves.

> **Spiritual Shortcuts**
>
> **HANDS-ON-HEALING**
> We are all born healers we just aren't encouraged or reminded about our abilities. Here's a little exercise that will help you reawaken and feel that energy.
>
> Hold you hands a few inches apart and focus your attention on the space between them. Really focus your attention on the palms of your hand. Slowly move your hands in and out. Let yourself feel the space between your hands.
>
> If you allow yourself to relax and feel you will be able to sense your own energy field. Next rub your hands together for a few moments and then place them over your face. Breathe deeply and imagine a beautiful light emanating from the palm of your hands. Then slowly move your hand over your body.
>
> With a little bit of practice you will be able to feel the energy flowing from your hands into your body. This is a very simple form of healing. If you practice on your friends and don't listen to your mind's critical thoughts about the process you will develop your ability to heal very rapidly.

Reiki

Reiki is a Japanese word meaning guided universal life source. This is the same energy the Chinese refer to as chi. It was created by Tibetan monks over 2,500 years ago as a spiritual discipline for enlightenment. As the story goes a Christian minister Dr. Mikao Usui was asked by one of his students if he believed in miracle like Jesus had done. He replied yes. When the student asked if he knew how Jesus had done them he was forced to say no. This sent him on a journey of searching and learning.

Years later he found himself studying in a small Buddhist monastery. He found some ancient Sanskrit writings from Tibet. After studying them for some time he felt moved to go into the mountains and fast and meditate for twenty-one days. On the twentieth day he went to sleep and realized either he got something that night or not. In his sleep he had a profound dream in which he 'remembered' the symbols of Reiki. They were the same symbols he had been studying and he awoke with an understanding of the manuscripts he had been studying.

There are three levels of Reiki. The student is given attunements from a Reiki master to proceed from one level to the next. An attunement is a ceremony in which the master blows colors and symbols into the student's hands and head. The attunement creates the healer yet it does not actually give them anything new. It merely opens up and aligns what is already part of them.

Reiki treatments are gentle and very relaxing. A full treatment lasts from 60 to 90 minutes and treats all the major organs and energy systems of the body. Dr. Usui was very aware of the need for gratitude and compassion in our life. Reiki is a way of sharing love and compassion. As with any form of healing gratitude really accelerates the process.

Psychic or Absentee Healing

A psychic is a person who regular taps into their 'other' senses. Generally when we think of psychics we think of hotlines and predictions of the future. Everyone has psychic abilities. Everyone can tap into their inner knowing, into their energy being and do remarkable things. As children we all had the ability to see energy we forget how to do it. Psychics haven't.

Clarity Corner

SEEING

When we talk about meditations or psychics we often refer to a person's ability to see. When I lead guided meditations people often complain they can't see the images. Everyone 'sees' in his or her own way. Some people literally see pictures, other sense the presence, some people feel while others hear. If I suggest that you see a red fire truck, you will 'see' it or experience it in your own way. If I asked you to describe it I am sure you could even though it might feel like you were making it up. You really can 'see' it just might not be in three-dimensional, Technicolor pictures.

Many psychics are gifted healers and one of the ways they work is absentee healing. The healer works with a person who isn't physically present. Everyone has their own way of doing this but most often they first go into a deep meditative state and see the person.

Once they have connected with the person they send them healing energy. I had one woman describe it as holding a person in a brilliant white light and turning them around and around. Other people have told me they see themselves with the person sitting in front of them and they proceed with the healing as if the person was physically present. Other people heal through the use of prayer. They ask that God, the universal energy, the Great Spirit, or whatever else they connect with to heal the person.

Healing in whatever form it occurs is a very personal matter. No two people do it exactly alike. Some people work in their dreams. One of the women I studied with in San Diego was called Sister Sarita. She would get up every morning at 3:30 AM and do prayer work with all the people she had worked on. She would also work on people who had sent in their requests for healing. She would also spend time in prayer asking for healing for the planet and society as a whole.

As we do our individual healing we also help to heal the earth and society as a whole. It is important to remember you are part of a greater whole and the only way society can change and heal is if the individuals do.

Psychic Surgery

Psychic surgery originated in the Philippine Islands. It is a process in which the surgeon opens the patient's body with their hands and removes diseased tissue. It is preformed in the mind and the heart of the healer. Traditionally the surgeon has had some sort of a visionary experience in which he has been given the ability to heal. It is a deeply spiritual experience for the healer.

The healer goes into a semi-trance or meditative state and then views the patient's body. The healer detects which part of the body is diseased and injects spiritual energy into those parts of the body.

Energy projecting from the healer's hands actually opens the person's body and they are able to remove the unhealthy parts. Psychic surgery might be more accurately described as cleansing the human body. There may or may not be a faint line or mark where the surgery was performed.

Psychic surgery takes no more than a few minutes and is shrouded in controversy. Many people believe the surgeon or their assistant use chicken parts to simulate surgery. I am sure there are frauds out there. As with anything else knowing and being comfortable with your practitioner is very important.

I have had several experiences with psychic surgery. My first experience was when I lived in Vermont when I was at the very beginning of my healing path. A friend called and told me about this man that was in town doing healings and suggested I go. I wasn't sure what to think at the time. He removed spaghetti like substances form my brain and a tumor from my stomach.

Years later when I was studying with Sister Sarita and her son Don Miguel I slipped a disk in my back. I had done that several times before and knew how long it took to heal. This time I could get no relief from my chiropractor so I went to see Don Miguel. He operated on my back and told me I had to come back in five days to have the stitches removed. I got off the table very slowly still expect to be in pain. To my surprise I had no pain only a slight stiffness that disappeared when he removed the stitches. Sister Sarita taught a different form of psychic surgery. She said the need to 'see' things like blood and organs was just showboating. I saw that woman heal amazing ailments and never draw a drop of blood.

Smoke & Mirrors

BEWARE OF LOOKING FOR EXTERNAL CURES.

One of the best healers I knew in San Diego was a woman named Julie. One of her clients was having quite a few health problems. Julie worked very hard with the woman to get rid of them. After many months of hard work on Julie's part the woman was healed. That night Julie had a dream. The woman's spirit came to her and asked her if she was done. Julie answered in the affirmative and them woman's spirit said she was very glad. The spirit told Julie that maybe now the woman could learn how to take care of herself.

There is a part of me that has always wanted someone to fix me, to make my life and me all better. I had a tendency to look for healers and methods that would do that. Eventually I realized my healing was my job. I had come here to remember my own divinity and no one could do that for me. Be aware of the part of you that wants someone of something outside of yourself. We need support and guidance on our path but we need to do the walking ourselves.

When I perform psychic surgery it feels like a drop down into a place where I stand in the presence of God. I am filled with love and gratitude. When I begin working on the person I am almost unaware of my surroundings and feel a profound connection. Afterwards the person often experiences a deep emotional release followed by a sense of lightness and a feeling of connectedness. The whole process often takes several days or if the wounds are really deep it can take several weeks.

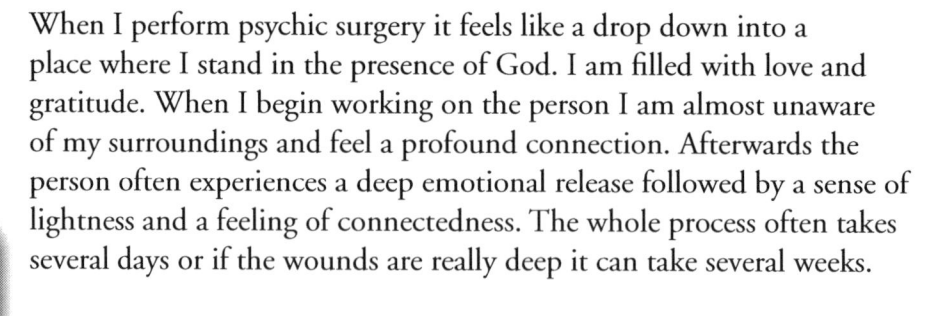

Magnets and Other Gadgets

Magnet therapy is just starting to get popular. It was frequently practiced in the ancient cultures of Egypt, China, and India. There are numerous theories on how magnets affect your body. Some scientists believe magnets interact with the iron in our red blood cells allowing oxygen to be carried more efficiently while others think they interact with our energy field. Some researchers believe that magnets stimulate the nerve endings.

Magnets are attributed with all sorts of uses. Some believe they can counteract electrical pollution in our lives created by microwaves, televisions, and power lines. Some people believe that the pollution in our environment upset our energy field and that magnets can correct the imbalance. Some feel that one of the causes of jet lag is being out of touch with the earth's magnetic field.

The north pole of magnets attracts energy so it is good at removing or pulling things out of our body or energy field. The south pole of a magnet repels and contact with it is said to be relaxing. In general magnets are used to relieve pain, accelerate healing, and boost a person's mental and physical energy.

> **Sage Advice**
> "Courage is not the towering oak that sees storms come and go; it is the fragile blossom that opens in the snow."
> Alice Mackenzie Swaim

> **Sage Advice**
> "We dance around a ring and suppose, But the Secret sits in the middle and knows."
> Robert Frost

To relieve a toothache you could place the north pole of a magnet against your check for 15 to 20 minutes. If you place the north pole of a magnet between your eyebrows for ten minutes at night it is said to help you sleep better. You can place a bottle of water on the north pole of a magnet for twenty-four hours to improve your digestion.

You can buy magnet insoles, mattress covers, and seat covers for your car. There are wraps that have magnets manufactured into them for almost every part of your body. They are said to relieve pain and help your body heal. For some people they work like a charm for others they don't do a thing. Next time you can't sleep or if you have an ache or pain you might want to try using magnets and see if they work for you.

Besides magnets there are a variety of other electrical devices that are said to accelerate healing. They go by many different names. The backs of magazines are full of advertisements for machines you hold, sit on, or sit in front of that are guaranteed to cure anything and everything. My acupuncturist uses a little gadget that sends a mild electrical pulse through the needles in your body and it seems to help. My feeling is that if it helps you, use it.

Crystal Therapy

Crystals are believed to possess inherent healing properties. Shamans have long believed that crystals are storehouses for the Great Spirit's life energy and aid or accelerate a person's healing. The can act like batteries or libraries and store energy or information.

There are many different types of crystals. This is a list of just a few of them and their healing properties. If you want to work with crystals I suggest you pick them out by for yourself using your inner guidance. When you walk into a crystal shop let the rocks 'talk' to you and you will always find the right one.

The ancient Hawaiians would always ask a rock if it wanted to move before they picked it up. If the rock agreed then they said they only had to carry the rock and not the weight of the rock. I always ask a rock if it wants to come home with me and surprisingly sometimes they do say no.

- Agate – strengthens the mind and body, imparts a sense of courage and strength, joy and oneness
- Amber – healing, soothing, and harmonizing, tends to help the intellect align with the spirit
- Amethyst – strengthens the immune system, cleanses the system, and helps to relieve addictions
- Aventurine – purifies mental thinking, aids in reducing fear and anxiety
- Hematite – cleans blood and enhances the will, courage, and personal magnetism
- Lapis – activates the thyroid gland, enhances psychic abilities and connection to spirit
- Malachite – reduces stress and tension, good for accelerating the healing wounds
- Obsidian – connects the mind and the emotions, grounds spiritual energy into the physical plane
- Quartz – amplifies thought forms, dispels negativity, and is excellent for meditation
- Tourmaline – aids in sleep, dispels fear and negativity

When I lived in Vermont I went to woman who did crystal energy balancing. Her house was amazing, full of both huge and small crystals. She would take you into the healing room and have you lie down on a table. The shelves of the room were lined with every imaginable kind of crystal. After saying a prayer she would stand at your feet for a few minutes. Then she would start placing crystals around and on you. I went the first time out of curiosity. I was amazed at how profoundly I affected me. An hour would pass and I would be totally aware of how much time had passed. I always felt relaxed and energized after one of her sessions. I haven't ever run across anyone who works with crystals in quite the same way.

Many people are attracted to crystals because of their beauty others because they believe they can do something for them. I believe they have whatever power we endow upon them. They are fun to work with and to wear. I often charge crystals at ceremonies for my students and give them to them as a reminder.

> **Spiritual Shortcuts**
>
> Crystals and rocks fascinate me; they each have a different feeling and seem to have a unique personality. Picking out a crystal is a very personal experience; each rock feels different to different people. Many cities have shops specializing in the ale of crystals. If not, you can usually find them in New Age gift shops. They are also available in catalogs, but I prefer to handle them before I buy one. Sometimes you can find rock and mineral shows where you can purchase crystals and rock specimens. If you live in certain ares of the country, such as Arkansas, you can did up your own crystals. Your local university can tell you what kinds of minerals are common in your area.

Spiritual Whammy Jammies

For years I called spiritual healing "*whooey phooey*" and never took it very serious. Even after my profession was teaching classes on spirituality I still made fun of it. Eventually I realized that was my mind's fear of what it couldn't see or control. Over the years I have had many remarkable experiences, seen people heal, seen their lives change, and seen them die.

If you look at all the events that were necessary for you to be sitting right where you are, reading this book it is absolutely mind-boggling and miraculous. Just for your body to exist hundreds and hundreds of men and women had to met, come together as a couple, and produce an off spring. Then you had to make millions of choices to be where you are right now at this time in this place. Then the same thing had to happen for me and then I had to write this book and you had to find it. When viewed from that perspective life is miraculous and there must be something to spiritual whammy jammies.

If you find yourself doubting and judging your spiritual journey you might ease up on yourself and let the miracles occur in your life, they will whether you judge them or not. Miracles can become a way of life if you allow yourself to be in alignment with your spiritual self.

> ***Spiritual Shortcuts***
>
> **ENERGIZING WATER**
>
> Water is a wonderful medium for healing. You can energize or charge the water for just about any purpose. They have taken photographs of holy water and the sign of the cross is visible in its energy field.
>
> To charge water for yourself take a glass of water and cradle it in your hand so your fingertips are barely touching. Take a few deep breaths and send energy or mental pictures into the water. Say you have a sore throat you could picture yourself drinking the water and your throat feeling soothed. Then imagine yourself later in the day talking to a friend telling them how good you feel. You can project pictures into the water or just energy. You can fill the water full of love.
>
> If your mind doubts that this sort of thing will work go out and buy two small plants that are exactly alike. Put them side-by-side on a windowsill. Charge two glasses of water. Charge on glass with the image of the plants growing, healthy, and happy. In the other see it as a weed remover. Imagine using it to rid your garden of unwanted plants. If you do this consistently for a month at the end of the month there will be a big difference in the two plants.
>
> You can also energize your food before you eat it. You can charge the water in your bath so it will energize you or put you to sleep. Our thoughts create our experience so use your thoughts to create a loving and supportive environment around yourself.

Spiritual Whammies

We forget just how powerful we really are. Our thoughts really do create our experience. When you walk into an old church if you let yourself you can feel something, an energy, or a presence. I used to go to an old mission in San Diego. When I walked in I could almost feel the spirits of all the people who had come there to worship over the centuries. They had left behind their love, reverence, and awe. For hundreds of years men and women had come to that building to pray and to worship. It didn't matter if their beliefs were different from mine, if their concept of God was different from mine. Energy is energy.

Many old churches are built over the sites of ancient temples or places of worship. There are spots on the earth that just feel holy and have a 'good' feeling. Frequently it has to do more with what we believe about the place than the place itself.

If you hate your job and your life every time you walk into your house you bringing that energy with you. When I began my spiritual journey someone suggested I put a hook outside the door and hang all my troubles there whenever I came home. They told me to imagine the door to my home was a magical portal where only loves dwell, where I would always feel safe and loved, and where magic and miracles happened. Doing that on a daily basis really changed my life. You could make your home a refuge that will greatly assist you in changing your life by doing the same thing.

Spiritual Jammies

Symbolism is a very powerful force in our lives. Madison Avenue has capitalized on that for years in its advertising campaigns. Look at how successful the tobacco industry has been at marketing cigarettes buy using them as a symbol. I really had to work at enjoying cigarettes as a kid but I was willing to work at it because f what I had been brainwashed into believing. Turning something into a symbol works. It goes beyond our rational, linear mind and grabs our attention.

> **Sage Advice**
> You did what you knew how to do and when you knew better–you did better!
> — Maya Angelo

What sort of things could you make symbols of in your life that would be beneficial? You could make your bathroom a temple of healing. When you take a shower imagine the water running through you and healing you. If you are worried about something create a cosmic answer box. I had a box in my bedroom that was my cosmic solution box. Whenever I put something in the box I let it go and knew that the universe was taking care of it for me. At times I had to pout the same thing in the box many times but I kept doing it until I was able to stop worrying about it. If I needed an answer to a problem I did the same thing. I would put it in the box and know the answer would come. It always did and often in very unusually ways.

Take some time and think about what you could do in your life. What could you create that would help you improve the quality of your life?

> ### The Least You Need to Know
>
> - The Least You Need to Know
> - We are all born healers.
> - You can use the symbols in your life as powerful transformational tools.
> - Crystals have lots of uses.
> - You can use magnets to relieve pain and help you heal as well as holding papers on the refrigerator.

Chapter 9

Spirit Stuff

> **In This Chapter**
>
> ➤ Learn how to meditate.
>
> ➤ Experience the power of prayer.
>
> ➤ Contemplate the meaning of life.
>
> ➤ Take a journey into shamanism.

We need to take care of our physical body and give it plenty of clean air, healthy food, and plenty of rest if we want to be healthy. Our spirit has needs too. If we want to have peace of mind, a rich inner life, and a sense of belonging we have to take care of our spirit. In our hectic lives our spiritual well-being often takes aback seat.

We are a spiritual being having a physical experience. Our spirit is the energy that keeps us alive. When our spirit leaves our body we die. If we aren't consciously aware of our connection to our spiritual essence the quality of our everyday life is diminished. Once you make that connection you will be amazed at how much more alive life becomes, the air is sweeter, the colors brighter, and life is more precious.

Care and Feeding of Your Spirit

From the beginning of time human kind has struggled trying to understand the universe and make sense of their place in the universe. Over the centuries we have tried to define god and explain the nature of the universe. Finding those answers for ourselves is a life long pursuit and well beyond the scope of this book. I hope to give you some guidance and enough fuel to sustain you on your quest. Feeding your soul is an important part of anyone's spiritual journey. Throughout this book you will find suggestions and a variety of exercises and methods. Try them and use the ones that work for you.

I have found that we are healthier and happier if we do something on a daily basis that feeds our soul. Most of us wouldn't think of not eating everyday but we are often too busy to take care of our spirit. Start taking the time. Feeding our soul can be as simple as taking a hot bath with candles or going for a walk and connecting with nature. You could light a candle and take a few moments to watch the flame. The possibilities are endless. Find o few things that work for you and do them – everyday.

Clarity Corner
What is *meditation* anyway? I think of meditation as standing on a train platform and watching the trains go by instead of getting on one and going for a ride. To meditate, all you have to do is think of your thoughts as trains and as much as possible just watch them go by.

Meditation

There are hundreds of forms of meditation. The best kind of meditation is one that you do on a regular basis. When I teach people how to meditate they usually think it's hard and requires a lot of discipline. The only discipline it requires is making time in your life to do it. It is only as hard as we make it. The word means to think or to contemplate. Meditation is really nothing more than sitting quietly with the intention to meditate.

Meditation is extremely beneficial to your body, your mental and physical well-being. Most religions practice some form of meditation. It is a wonderful way to feed you spirit and your soul. There are literally hundreds of different types of meditation. The most important thing is to make it easy enough so you'll do it on a regular basis.

How to Meditate

Everyone meditates for a different reason. Some people merely want the health benefits while others want to deepen their spiritual connection. Meditation is so easy but we tend to make it so hard. Whatever your reason here are some simple suggestions I have shared with others that seem to help. If you just practice these simple steps eventually you will find your mind quieting and your life improving.

The most important thing to remember is you can't do it wrong, unless you just don't do it. Even if your mind incessantly chatters you are doing just fine. Just keep doing it.

> **Start by creating a ritual for yourself.** Select a place to sit that is comfortable and where you won't be disturbed for ten to fifteen minutes. You might want to light a candle, burn incense, or play your

favorite meditation music. Do the same thing every time and it will help your mind know it is time to meditate.

➤ **Next get comfortable, gently close your eyes, and with your eyes closed look up towards the ceiling.** That will cause your mind to automatically produce alpha brain waves that are the type of brain waves that signify a meditative state.

➤ **Now focus your attention on your breath.** Notice where you feel your breath as it moves through your body. Now really focus your attention on feeling your breathing. Fully feel what your breath feels like as it goes in and out of your body.

Thoughts will come and go, that's fine, just keep gently bringing your attention back to your breathing. Do that for at least ten minutes. I suggest people meditate fifteen minutes every day but something is better than nothing.

There are many excellent books and classes on meditation. It is often nice to go to a meditation group or create one for yourself. I find meditating in a group much easier and more powerful than meditating alone.

> **Spiritual Shortcuts**
> If you really wan to reap the benefits of meditation, you have to do it on a regular basis. It is much like exercise; if you only do it once in a while, you won't really see any significant results. So shut off the phone, tell people not to interrupt you, and really give yourself the gift of time. It is okay to take time just for yourself. Make a ritual out of it; do it at the same time every day, light a candle with your favorite scent, and play some gentle music quietly in the background. You could even buy a special pillow to sit on do whatever it takes to make the time special, enjoyable, and relaxing.

New age bookstores, crystal shops, spiritual churches, and often Unity Churches will have bulletin boards listing classes. If you don't find a group in your area invite a bunch of your friends or put up flyers inviting people to come together and create a group.

There are also a number of excellent meditation books on the market. My meditations have taken on many forms over the years. I started meditating in the early 1970's by taking a class in Transcendental Meditation where a teacher gives you a mantra during a beautiful ceremony. For many years I meditated twice a day using my mantra. Then for a time I used visualization where I would picture certain outcomes happening in my life. At times my mind goes blank and I sit it the silence while at other times my mind chatters on endlessly about the events of the day.

My point is your meditations will change and that is all part of the process. Sometimes I start my mediation by reading a passage in a book and other times I just sit down. Play with your meditations, let them grow and evolve. The only way you can short change yourself is by not meditating at all. Read books on the subject, go to lectures, and talk to other people about their experiences. Allow your curiosity lead you and guide you. Our minds can't understand meditation our hearts and spirit can so have fun with the process. You don't have to do it perfectly because you can't do it wrong in the first place. Meditation can be fun if you let it. Give your mind a rest and see where your breath can take you.

Prayer

Prayer is another way we can connect with our spirit and feed our soul. Prayer can take on many shapes and forms. When you pray you can think of it as talking to a deity, to the universe, or just to your higher self. Many religions have beautiful prayers and at times I will read them to myself to out loud. Prayer is a time set aside to align yourself with your higher self, with a larger purpose. Pray takes you out of yourself and can assist you in seeing the world from a much broader perspective. When I first started on my journey I didn't believe in praying, it felt like I was begging God to do something I wanted. It felt like I was a child again asking my parent for permission and of course I knew God was going to say no.

Sage Advice
"There are only two ways to live your life. One is as though nothing is a miracle. The other is as if everything is."
Albert Einstein

At one point in my healing journey I was in a great deal of emotional pain. I wasn't sure about anything except that it hurt so much I wanted to die. I wasn't sure about spirituality, God, or any of the other stuff, the only thing I thought was real was my emotional pain. My mentor suggested I go someplace and pray. He found his connection to all things great and small sitting on the beach wall near his house. I'd always loved the ocean so one night, when I was in enough pain I walked down to the beach and prayed with an open heart.

I stood by the ocean, not sure if there was anything out there beside sand, wind, and water. My friend had told me to keep my prayer simple so I said, "Please love me." I immediately started to cry and I felt an incredibly loving energy surround me. I stood there and literally felt filled with love, acceptance, and understanding. I can do the same thing with a closed heart and the results will be very different. Prayer always works if we are willing to let it work; ultimately the only thing that gets in our way is ourselves.

Sage Advice
"How far that little candle throws its beams! So shines a good deed in a weary world."
Shakespeare

One of my favorite prayers was written centuries ago by St. Frances. And it goes something like this:

God, make me an instrument of thy peace
Where there is hatred let me bring love
Where there is wrong let me bring forgiveness

Where there is discord let me bring harmony
Where there is doubt let me bring faith
Where there is error, truth
Where there is despair, hope
Where there are shadows allow me to bring light
And where there is sadness let me bring joy.

This second part to me is the most important because it allows me to let go of my limited, little mind.

God, grant that I might seek to comfort rather than be comforted; understand than be understood; love rather than be loved. For in forgetting it is that we find and in dying that we learn to live. It is by forgiving that we are forgiven.

Some of the great prayers written over the centuries are always wonderful tools for learning about right thinking. When we are in our small, limited self we are fearful and unable to connect with the beauty and wonder of the universe. We live in fear so we make our choices based in fear. We are so busy trying to get that we forget to give.

In my practice I hear many people say they are recovering Catholics or Baptists or Jews. Try not to throw the baby out with the bath water, the good with the not so good. If you have had a hard time with religion in the past remember it isn't religion that's the problem. Religion is merely someone else's recipe for developing a connection with your own divinity. You probably just need to modify the recipe to fit your life.

Spiritual Shortcuts

Creating prayers of your own is simple. Prayers don't have to be elaborate or pretty just speak from your heart. If you are troubled about something start out by talking about your doubts or your pain. Pray as if you are speaking to an understanding, kind, and compassionate friend. Ask for help, ask the questions that have been troubling you and then wait around for the answers.

Prayer and meditation work well together. I often start my mediations out with a prayer. If I am troubled about something or need to make a decision I will open my meditation with a prayer to that effect and then open up to receiving guidance during the meditation. Sometimes I do but sometimes my answers don't come until much later but they always come.

Many of the world's religions have wonderful prayers. Explore them, find what parts of them work for you and leave what doesn't work behind. Emmet Fox wrote an interpretation of the Lord's Prayer that really opened up a whole world for me. I realized that what was important in the prayers of all the great religions was the meaning behind the words. I was able to release my judgments and let those words heal me. You might spend sometime revisiting the prayers of your childhood.

This is an example of a prayer of healing:

> *Oh, Great Spirit, hear your child. I have come to a turning point in my life. The way I have been doing things no longer serves me. Joy has left my life. I am afraid. I'm afraid I won't be able to pay the bills and that I'll never find love. I don't know what do to. Please help me find my way. Help me to hear your gentle voice in the wind. Help me to feel loved and protected. Help me to feel safe. Guide my way. Help my footing to be sure and my path to be broad. Help me to be gentle and loving to others and myself. Help me remember to reach out to those who come behind me.*
>
> *Grant me the willingness to be willing. Help me to have the willingness to whatever I need to do to heal. Help me to gracefully let go of the past and graciously move into the future.*
>
> *I give thanks for your love and your guidance.*
> *Namaste*

For a long time I wasn't sure what my relationship to the universe was so in my prayers I asked to be shown. Then I would walk along the beach with my mind and my heart open. Eventually the answers came. Walking mindfully is another form of meditation. You walk in silence while fully focusing your attention on the act of walking much as you focus on your breath when you are seated.

Prayers have an opening, middle, and a close. The opening can be something simple like "Oh, Great Spirit" or even "Hey Dude." Whatever you feel comfortable with. Then in the middle state your purpose. Then I suggest you close by giving thanks. Energetically the opening is like picking up the phone and dialing. The middle is the conversation and the close is saying good-bye before you hang up. They are as powerful as we allow them to be.

> **Sage Advice**
> "Life isn't a matter of milestones, but of moments."
> Rose Kennedy

Contemplation

When I think of contemplation I have a variety of mental pictures some humorous and some very serious ones but none of them seem inviting. Contemplation is very relaxing and can lead to profound insights and deep awareness about our world and ourselves. There is nothing really magical about it, we just have to take the time to sit quietly and think.

As with anything else in our life what's really important is the energy or our thoughts and beliefs that we put behind it. The more we focus our attention and act mindfully the more profound the results we achieve are. If we are fully present in the moment we are able to fully experience whatever is going on and receive the greatest benefit.

Imagine sitting down to a wonderful banquet. The dishes are lavishly displayed and prepared to perfection. The setting, the smells, the sounds are incredible rich and full. What would happen if you sat down to enjoy that meal and you weren't fully present? How much would you enjoy the experience if your best friend had just died? Now imagine what would happen if you really savored every moment and every bite of food? Life is an incredible banquet and often times we aren't present for the experience. We are watching a beautiful sunset worrying about whether we locked the car.

Sage Advice
"One can go back toward safety or forward toward growth."
Abraham Maslow

If you learn to live your life mindfully moment-by-moment how much richer our experience would be. Contemplation can give you that gift. Practice taking time to sit quietly and just be fully present to your experience. Sit and observe your breathing. What makes you decided when to inhale and when to exhale? How does your body feel? Do you feel any tightness any place in your body? Allow yourself to notice your surroundings. How do they feel? What are the colors and textures surrounding you? Before you sit down find a prayer or a passage in a book that is particularly meaningful to you. Read it over slowly a few times and then sit quietly with it. If a particular passage stands out read it over again, take a few deep breaths and let its words and meanings drift over your consciousness.

If you fully surrender yourself to the process of contemplation you will find it very relaxing and insightful. Of course that is true of anything we do in life. Brushing your teeth mindfully can be a very profound experience if you are fully present to it.

Spiritualism

Sage Advice
"A wise man, recognizing that the world is but an illusion, does not act as if it is real, so he escapes suffering."
Buddha

When I first started exploring my spiritualism I often got confused with religion. As a child I loved to watch the ceremonies but later I found the concept of original sin, the devil, and hell unsettling. I needed to feel loved not judged. Eventually I realized that religion was someone else's recipe for finding God. Spiritualism encouraged me to have my own experience and connection with God. I got to define God for myself instead of accepting someone else's definition.

Spiritualism is anything that assists you in experiencing your own divinity. It is a process of discovery rather than obedience and following someone else's path. Each person has their own unique path and no two are exactly the same. If we are lucky we will find people to share our path for a time but we can't expect anyone else's path to be exactly the same as ours.

Our spiritual path has a series of beginnings, middles, and ends. At times we don't want to move on, we want to stay where we are, and continue working with the people who have become familiar. When I started studying healing in San Diego an older man shared his process with me He said he had studied with a series of teachers, each time he thought he would be there forever, but when it was time to move on he knew. It is important to stay in one place long enough to move through issues. Some people move on just before they move through a core issue. If you are really honest you will know when it is time to move on. When I left because of fear I judged and criticized the group. When I left because I was finished I looked back with love and was able to go back and visit.

Spiritualism will mean something different to each of us. I believe we can be very spiritual and still follow religious practices. They aren't mutually exclusive. As a matter of fact our spirituality can enrich our religious experiences.

Channeling

My first introduction to personal growth came through a book called *"The Nature of Personal Reality"* by Jane Roberts. I don't even remember how I found the book or the book found me but to say that it profoundly changed my life would be a huge understatement. I couldn't read more than a few pages at once and spent many months reading the book. It was a book of channeled information or information received by Jane Roberts from an entity or spirit that resides beyond our physical plane. I once heard channeling describe as being a human telephone. The channel got out of the way and this other energy took over and spoke through him.

There are many wonderful books written by these other worldly beings. The information in them is amazing and written in such a loving and non-judgmental way it is easy to accept and understand. Everyone has the capacity to channel. When I allow myself to channel my spiritual self or I allow the energy of my true nature flow through me I am so much more loving and gentle. If we let the love of God flow or channel through us life is much easier and so much less stressful. The ability to heal is channeled. When I perform a healing on someone I don't really perform the healing I merely allow the healing energy to flow through me.

Smoke & Mirrors
CHANNELING

As with any thing else in life you have to be careful what you chose to believe and who you chose to listen to. I have seen many people channel over the years. Much of the information is very loving and helpful. I once went to a channel in the early 80's while living in Vermont who told me I would be writing books and working in a healing capacity with people. At the time I had no desire to leave Vermont or do anything other than run my retail store. I thought she was crazy but her I am doing exactly what she said I would be doing. And the suggestions she made about the necessity for me to do emotional healing were very accurate.

On the other hand there are people out there who will use a little truth and your vulnerability to steal your life savings. I had some friends who went to a well-known channel and lost their life savings by investing in land deals suggested by the channel. As the saying goes, "Trust in Allah but remember to tie your camel."

Channeling is really a matter of being sensitive to the energies that always surround us and choosing to let them flow through us. You have total control over everything that happens in your life, no one and nothing can affect you unless you let it. With channeling we decide to give permission and to open ourselves up to feeling and sensing energies beyond our ordinary realm of perception.

In a sense being in love is a form of channeling. We decide to open up to the possibility that love exists and to allow it to flow through us. When we are in love we are letting love flow through us and directing it toward another person. Where does love go after we break up with a person? It doesn't stop to exist we just stop channeling it for and toward that person. At times we feel unloved or unlovable because we refuse to channel it. So open up the floodgates and let all the wonders the world has to offer into your life. Do you want to be a channel of love or fear? Pain or joy? Freedom or limitation? Even though it may not seem that way the choice is always there and it depends on our beliefs and what we choose to think.

Shamanism

The word shaman originated in Siberia. It is a term that is now applied to most aboriginal healers. Traditionally a shaman was the healer of the village or an individual tribe. They would heal a person by clearing out their connection with their spirit and their connection to their divinity. In a sense the shaman was a channel who was able to release blockages and limitations the person might not even be aware of.

I define a shaman as a healer of relationships. Specifically a shaman helps heal the relationship a person has with themselves, with others, with their spirituality, and the energy we call God. Shamans use different means to achieve that depending on the tradition in which they were trained. The tradition was passed down orally to someone who seemed to have a gift for healing and was willing to spend years training as an apprentice.

> **Clarity Corner**
>
> JOURNEYING
>
> A shaman will go into an altered state or deep trance and travel into the spirit world for another person. This altered state is induced by a variety of methods depending upon the tradition. In some traditions drumming is used, in others singing and chanting, fasting and prayer, while some traditions use drugs.
>
> Once in an altered state the shaman travels into the realm of spirit to gather information or find the person's spirit. While in this altered state the shaman 'sees' the world in a totally different manner and is able to open doorways, go places, and see things that are well beyond our everyday awareness. They may be able to talk to spirits and ancestors bringing back information that is profoundly healing and beneficial t the person.
>
> A journey always has a specific purpose and is not something that is done lightly. It is a very sacred act of healing.

Shamanism is a wonderful way to learn how to access your divinity. Traditionally the shaman healed the person. They journeyed or traveled into the world of spirit for them rather than showing the person how to do it for themselves. Rather than trying to find someone to fix it for you seek out someone willing to teach you how to access the information yourself.

Shamanism is term similar to Christianity. Christian churches may vary in their practices and some of their beliefs but they all believe in Jesus. The same is true of shamanism. There are many different variations but

> **Clarity Corner**
>
> **SHAMANISM**
>
> Shamanism is based on direct communication with the earth. It is based on the teachings of the earth. Trees have voice when you know how to listen so do the clouds, and the rivers, and animals.
>
> Shamans give voice to a world we have begun to believe is inanimate. Shamans or Medicine people as they are called know the world is alive and act as translators of that ancient language.
>
> Next time you are out in nature listen, really listen to the world around you and feel its aliveness.

they all believe in the power of the spirit to heal and in the fact that we are an energy within the body. They have as many similarities as they have differences. Each branch or type calls to different people. Allow yourself to explore the various forms and if one calls to you follow that calling.

Native American

Each Native American tribe had its own beliefs, ceremonies, and traditions passed down orally form one generation to another. Their individual traditions are very rich and varied. I love studying their wisdoms and their perspective on life and their relationship to the universe. It is profoundly sad that the Europeans that came here failed to learn from their wisdom and grace. The world would certainly be a far different place if their traditions had been honored and incorporated rather than suppressed.

One of the common themes that weaves throughout Native American traditions is a deep sense of reverence and awe for nature. Native Americans believe everything has a spirit. Before they would kill an animal they would honor its spirit for its sacrifice. The land was also held as sacred and treated with a great deal of love and respect.

Mexican

I was trained in the tradition of southern Mexico called the Toltec Tradition. The Toltec believed that the universe is a complex energy system that accurately mirrors our beliefs. They were healers and were able to manipulate the laws of the physical universe. They believe we could understand the true nature of the universe by understanding our true nature. The more fully we connect with our godself the more fully we are able to express who and what we truly are.

This tradition is rich in tools designed to assist the individual in transforming their life. The goal or end result of this path is personal freedom. Personal freedom to me is the ability to act rather than react to the events in my life. The three masteries of the Toltec tradition are: Awareness, Transformation, and Intent. Awareness is an understanding of what is real and what is created by our mind. Transformation is the ability to change. Intent is the underlying energy or the decision to pursue our personal freedom.

South American

As in North America there are many traditions is South America. They have the same basic concepts about the land and nature as North American people do. The beliefs are as varied as the countryside. The Peruvians that live in the Andes are much connected to the mountains and the sky. The shamans in the

Amazon are connected to the rainforest. They use herbs in most of their ceremonies. As I have traveled the world I have found that each region has its own unique feeling, the spirit of the land seems to gentle enfold and embrace its people.

In the Amazon the shamans use a drug called Ayahuasca in their ceremonies. It is a powerful hallucinogenic that produces profound spiritual experiences. Traditionally it was used as part of their healing ceremonies. When a person is in need of guidance or healing they will go to the local shaman and request that he perform a ceremony for them. A variety of herbs are steeped into a very bitter brew.

When I was in the Amazon I participated in a Ayahuasca ceremony. We took a dug out canoe far into the jungle and met with a man. He was very tiny and had an infectious laugh. He came to our campsite the following night carrying a small metal pot. He had each of us drink some of the liquid. All that was audible was the sounds of the jungle. In the darkness he motioned for me to sit in front of him. He began to chant and fanned me with a bunch of herbs tied together in a bunch. After a few minutes I felt a profound connection to all things and myself. It was an amazing experience.

> **Smoke & Mirrors**
>
> In many native cultures, shamans regularly use hallucinogens, It is part of their culture, an integra; part of their belief system and their lives. DRUGS ARE DANGEROUS! It is easy to damage your mind and your body. The natives of these countries are accustomed to these drugs; we are not. Learning to achieve a deep spiritual connection without drugs will serve you for a lifetime. Indulging in drugs could ruin your life so be very, very careful!

There was a local couple there that had come for the shamans blessing and guidance. He talked to them for a long time and when they left their faces were filled with peace and joy.

Some people love the mountains while others are attracted to the desert or the ocean. The beliefs, the healing methods, even the myths are in alignment with the energy of the region. As you consider the various traditions you might notices what attracts you the most and follow your heart. In South America the traditions are so varied and rich. In Peru you have the mountain people with their love of colors and connection to the spirits of the mountains and the land. They work hard to harvest their crops and are used to the cool climate. In the Amazon basin you have a people used to heat and a land that easily provides all of their needs. In Brazil you have the festive music.

The music of the people tells you much about their spirituality and their inner world. Every continent is so rich in spiritual traditions. Give yourself the gift of exploring as many as possible.

European

When we think of Europe we tend to think more of traditional religions. But many shamanic traditions thrived in Europe. The Druids, Celtic, and Norse traditions are three of the most prominent. The Celtic were great storytellers. Their healers wove their magic in their tales. The Norse were fighters and relied heavily upon Odin. Their quest was to reach Valhalla. The Druids are most heavily associated with trees and the forest.

The stone circles such as Stonehenge are remnants of these traditions. Most of our direct knowledge of them has been lost over the centuries. Small groups all over Europe are reviving these traditions. If you allow yourself to stand in the presence of any of the great stones or mounds you can still feel the energy and the power generated by them.

African

In Africa each tribe has created stories that tie them directly to the gods they worship. Dance is an important part of most of their traditions. Many of the shamans in Africa were women. Their was as strong connection with the female aspect of God on this continent.

Rituals that guided a person from one stage of life to another played a prominent role. Birth, puberty, adulthood, marriage, having children, old age and death were all honored with a unique ritual.

> **Sage Advice**
>
> "Bless those who challenge us to grow, to stretch, to move beyond the knowable, to come back home to our elemental and essential nature. Bless those who challenge us for they remind us of the doors we have closed and the doors which have yet to open."
>
> *Navajo saying*

Voodoo

Voodoo is a merging of African, African-American, Native American, and European beliefs. It is a spiritual system that serves a large number of spirits or Loa. Practitioners have their own rituals and practices. Animal sacrifice is often part of the ritual.

A Loa is a spirit or a consciousness consisting of a immense number of sentient beings. The Loa is asked to speak through the priest or priestess and give guidance or direction. The word voodoo itself means mystery. Voodoo is a way of explaining the mysteries of existence. It is often referred to as a form of magic. I think of all forms of shamanism as magic.

Huna

Huna is a Hawaiian philosophy. It is based on the belief that each of us creates our own experience of life by our beliefs, perceptions, actions and reactions, by our thoughts and our feelings. It is deeply rooted in the concept of personal responsibility.

Huna believes that one of the most important things is the individual's initiative to take action on their own behalf. The Hawaiian traditions were almost lost because of the arrival of Europeans but as with many other traditions they went underground. It is only recently they are again being shared with others.

The Hawaiian system of healing is wonderful. Their chants are magical and their spirit is truly full of aloha.

The Least You Need to Know

- Meditation is an easy process.
- Prayers can be very personal as well as powerful.
- Contemplation isn't just for monks.
- Shamanism has many different shapes and forms.

Part 3
Making Your Mind Your Own

Right now your mind is full of information that has nothing to do with who you are or what you want to experience in your life. Our minds are like a computer that has been programmed for us without our permission. We never chose what we were going to believe or how we were going to react and feel about life. People made those decisions for us long before we had the capacity to think let alone chose.

As much as we rebel against society and our parents as a teenager our mind is full of their beliefs. Today 95% of your thoughts were the same as the ones you thought yesterday. It is time to make your mind your own. It's time to clean out all that useless information and fill your mind with your own thoughts and beliefs. From the first moment of our birth our minds are filled with sights and sounds, feelings and impressions. Advertisers tell us how to think and how to feel, use this product and you'll be happy. Be thin, be fit, be young and then it will be all right.

Knowing yourself, your own wants, needs, and desires is what will make you happy. I remember a friend of mine taking pre-med classes in college. It wasn't until after he graduated that he realized that was his parents dream not his. He wanted to be a writer. He is one of the lucky few. He realized in time to do something about it. This section will help you reclaim your thinking so you will know what really makes you happy, what really makes your heart sing.

Chapter 10

There is No "Out There"

> **In This Chapter**
>
> ➤ You'll get to see what's really happening.
>
> ➤ Start to see life from the inside out.
>
> ➤ Understand life as a big symbol.
>
> ➤ Everyone lives in their own separate reality.

If ten people witness an event there will be ten different versions of what happened. Even though you are reading the same words I wrote your understanding of those words might be very different from what I intended them to mean. I remember reading a passage from a book to a close friend. It had moved me deeply and after I read it to her she just looked at me blankly. When I asked her what she'd heard I was amazed. It was as if the two of us spoke entirely different languages.

No two people live in the same world. Believe it or not there is no such thing as the truth; there are as many variations of the truth as there are human beings. Our truth is relative to our perspective. Once we realize that we begin to experience a great deal more freedom in our lives. Everyone has his or her own point of view or perspective. One isn't better that the other they're just different. Once we accept our differences the world becomes a much more loving place. There is no out there. All that really exists is our belief about what's out there.

The World's a What?

In my classes when I begin talking about the fact that there is no out there people tend to get confused and upset, generally they get angry. For years I tried to improve the quality of my life by changing my relationships, where I lived, and what I did for a living. It didn't work. Where ever I went there I was. The world really is just a three-dimensional reflection of what's going on inside of us. The world is a very accurate, symbolic representation of our belief systems.

But this chair is real, the walls are solid, events happen, people are born and die – what do you mean this a reflection of my beliefs? Did I do something wrong? Is that why my mom died? Is the murder victim at fault for being murdered?

Sage Advice
"When the going gets rough, you are obviously in the wrong place."
Miss Piggy

That's where things get kind of sticky. Remember when I was talking about perspective? When we see the world from the perspective of what I call our little self it sure looks like the murder victim is dead and was a victim. But when we step back and see the world from the perspective of our spiritual self or our big self we realize the murder victim didn't really die and wasn't really a victim after all.

As we talk about this stuff just bear with me for a bit – humor me - I won't let you down or leave you in limbo. Yes physical reality is real but our perspective of it isn't. When we see someone die we think they're really dead but they're not. They've just stepped into the other room and we can no longer see them with our physical eyes. We tend not to see things from the bigger perspective. When I lost my home and my business I was very upset. I thought it was the worse possible thing that could've happened. I did everything possible to prevent it from happening. I didn't know what a truly wonderful event it really was. If that hadn't happened I wouldn't be living in Hawaii thoroughly enjoying myself and writing books.

How we experience the events in our life totally depends upon what we tell ourselves about them. If we think something is a good thing we will have one reaction, if we think it's a tragedy we'll act accordingly. Reality isn't really solid after all. Reality depends primarily in our inner dialog. So as we clear the sludge out of our minds our lives change. Someone who has never seen a chair would have no idea what it was for until you showed them.

Clarity Corner
Your experience of life is totally a matter of perspective. If you change your perspective or the filter you see life through, your entre experience of life will change. If you choose to see life through the eyes of your wounded or little self, it will look pretty bleak and hopeless. If you learn to see life through the eyes of love, you will be amazed at how it changes.

Now back to the murder victim. The person's body was assaulted the person's spirit wasn't. We have no idea why that person's spirit needed to experience being murdered or why they volunteered to play that part in the murder's life. "What!!" your mind says.

Another way to look at life is to think of it as a well-acted, beautifully directed and well written movie. You are the director, the leading character, and the scriptwriter. Long before you were born, you and a bunch of your closest spirits sat around drinking cosmic cappuccinos. You told them you wanted to learn more about freedom, love, and joy. You came up with a story line, some basic concepts, and asked your friends to play a variety of parts in your life. The people that were closest to you decided they'd be willing to play the villains in your life. Some of your acquaintances said they'd play the good guys, not as taxing a part after all.

Then you all grabbed a body, were born into a family, and started to improvise. Of course the minute you were born you forgot the plan but your spirit didn't. So your little self became a puppet, at times willing and at times resistant. The play came off well and in the end you all arrived on stage in each other's lives at just the right moment. After you all died you and your fellow spirits sat around and reviewed the play. You talked about the themes and how it all came off to the audience. You each realized you could have been a bit more loving at times and saw how fear affected your performance. You learned a lot and were closer than ever to remembering your own godlike nature.

Now, what would've happened to your performance if you remembered to take directions from your spirit? What if occasionally you'd checked in and asked for guidance? There certainly would've been a lot less fear and discomfort in your life.

> **Sage Advice**
> "A human being is part of a whole called, by us, universe. A part limited in time and space, he experiences himself, his thoughts, and his feelings as something separated from the rest. A kind of optical delusion of his consciousness. This delusion is a kind of prison for us restricting us to our personal desires and to affection for a few persons nearest to us. Our task must be to free ourselves from this prison by widening our circle of compassion, to embrace all living creatures and the whole nature in its beauty."
> *Albert Einstein*

The closest thing to the truth I've ever found is that life is very much like a movie. We all project our images up on the screen and then we interact in each other's movies.

> **Spiritual Shortcuts**
> So what's the theme of your movie? Get out your journal, find a comfortable place you won't be disturbed for a few minutes, sit back, close your eyes and relax. Take a few really deep breaths and imagine yourself sitting around drinking a cosmic cappuccino with some of your friends. Allow yourself to be gentle with the idea. Relax and remember this is a game of make-believe.
>
> Now gently open your eyes and begin to write. Make the story of what went on before you were born. What did you decide this life was going to be about? Let your imagination soar. Let this process be easy and fun. Do this exercise often and observe how the story changes.

It's an Inside Job

Well, if there is no out there then the only thing that really matters is going on right between your ears. You don't have to change your world in order to be happy. One of the most powerful shortcuts to happiness and personal growth is if you don't have what you want then want what you have.

I have found that whatever is in my life is there because at some level that's what I want. If something isn't in my life I either don't believe I can have it, or that I deserve it, or for some reason I don't really want it. So if I tell myself the truth that I already have what I want I can get on with the business of spiritual healing.

> **Sage Advice**
> "All that we are is the result of what we have thought: it is founded in our thought; it is made up of our thoughts. If a man speaks or acts with an evil thought, pain follows him, as the wheel follows the foot of the ox that draws the carriage."
> *The Dhammapada*

For example I say I want money but I never seem to have enough. So I admit to myself I really don't want to have enough money because that's what I have. I may whine and try to deny that but eventually I can say to myself lovingly and gently, without any judgment I don't really want to have any money. Then I ask myself how not having enough money serves me? What does not having enough money protect me from? What beliefs do I get to reaffirm by having bill collectors call? Do I get to prove mom or dad right by being a failure? Does it allow me to avoid taking responsibility for my choices?

Before I lost my businesses and for a time afterwards I never had enough money. Once I accepted that as my desired result I had some rather powerful insights. I didn't like setting boundaries with people; not having money assisted me in keeping that at a distance. I never had to say no to someone's request to borrow money. I also had an excuse not to do things, I couldn't afford it so I didn't have to decide if I wanted to go or not. So my lack of money took care of my boundary issues and allowed me to avoid making decisions. I found better ways of doing those things and was able to have a bit more money but still not enough. After some deeper explorations I realized I loved playing the role of the victim. Poor me, I have no money. Love me because I am needy. As I uncovered and changed more and more of my limiting beliefs my life continued to improve.

Life really is an inside job. After much soul searching a friend of mine declared bankruptcy but he never dealt with his internal issues around money. Once he was out from under all those bills he knew he'd be fine. Even after his debts were cleared a few months later he was in the same boat. The money isn't the issue, his beliefs were.

You really do have to look inside if you want your life to change permanently. If you fix a tire by putting a patch on the outside of the tire it won't last very long. The same is true of life change only the outside and the same issue will reappear.

Looking inside for our answers is hard. It sure looks like the problem is out there. If they were nicer to us, if they paid us more, or loved us better everything would be great. Remember what is in your life is there because that is what you really want; if it isn't in your life you really don't want it there.

When we go within ourselves it is often frightening and painful. We develop beliefs in order to avoid the pain. We explain the world in a way that makes us feel safe. As a child we couldn't have survived if we thought the big people in our life had anything wrong with them so we decided it must be us. At an early age we decided without much guidance how the world operated and what was true and just. We developed our sense of what was fair and what wasn't as well as how we could get what we wanted. If we found we couldn't get what we wanted we thought that was just the way it was. As an adult if we want something we make sure we don't get it because that's just the way it is.

If I sent a seven-year-old child over to your house and I told you it was going to be in charge of all of your decisions from now on how would you feel? Would you welcome the advice or question its accuracy? Well, most of your beliefs were firmly in place before you were seven so a child is making all your decisions. Scary though, isn't it?

> **Spiritual Shortcuts**
>
> Start observing your inner landscape. Every hour or so during the day stop and asked yourself, "Who said that?" Take the time to listen to your mind. Then ask yourself, "What am I feeling?" and "What do I need?"
>
> Your thoughts are in layers. The first layer is your thoughts. Our minds are constantly chattering. We are always thinking but thoughts aren't feelings. The next layer consists of our emotions. Beyond that layer lie our physical feelings. Once we are aware of our thoughts, emotions, and feelings we can make a clear decision about what we need at any given moment. When we aren't fully aware of what is going on internally our decisions are based on our thoughts. Our thoughts are generated by our childlike beliefs.
>
> So take sometime to observe. It will take a great deal of time and practice to unravel your internal landscape but it will be time very well spent.

I can't emphasize this enough. Be gentle with yourself especially as you start your inward journey. It took a long time to get where you are so changing will also take time. You are always right where you are and you can't be someplace else until you get there. Accept where you are as gently and lovingly as possible it will make it much easier for you to move on.

Mirror, Mirror on the Wall

If the world is a mirror and that angry person is in my face does that mean that I'm angry. Maybe you are and maybe you're not. When I first started to view the world as a mirror I drove myself crazy. Every time I saw something upsetting I judged myself. If someone was rude to me I started looking at myself wondering how I had been rude.

That's not quite how it works. If I am rude to someone the likelihood of them responding lovingly is diminished but it doesn't necessarily mean someone else is going to rude to me. I can be very loving to someone and they can still treat me poorly. How they are acting says a lot more about them than it does me but if I am upset by their actions that's my problem.

But you said there is no out there! Obviously other people do exist and there is a world out there but our answers aren't. Life acts like a mirror but not necessarily the way we think. It mirrors our gifts as well as our shortcomings. It is nice to bask in the glow of our loving creations as well as explore the creations that aren't as pleasing. And we often forget to honor the qualities about ourselves we enjoy. Too often we only focus on the areas we want to change.

> **Sage Advice**
>
> "Our deepest fear is not that we are inadequate. Our deepest fear beyond measure is that we are powerful beyond measure. It is our light not our darkness that frightens us most."
>
> Nelson Mandela

What I find most valuable is to observe what my reactions are to the world. If I find myself being upset by someone's rudeness I need to explore what within me is causing the upset rather than trying to get the person to be more polite. People will sometimes be rude but if I am able to remain loving and I'm not upset by their rudeness does it really matter?

What we really get to see in the mirror the world presents us is a clear picture of ourselves as well as our limited beliefs. My emotional upset is always an internal issue its root cause is never based in the external world. It certainly doesn't seem that way. It sure seems like someone else is making me angry or has disappointed me. The racism or prejudice or the economy is the issue not me. If my best friend steals money from me it wasn't my fault, they betrayed my trust. Yes, they stole your money but any feelings you have about their behavior is your creation.

Years ago I had a lot of beliefs about the world being an unsafe place and that people weren't trustworthy. I expected people to disappoint me and they did. I consistently picked people to be in my life that reaffirmed my limiting beliefs. I can look at the mirror and say yes I knew people weren't trustworthy or I can look within and say yes there is that limiting belief again. That is the most powerful choice we have. We can choose whether we are going to blame something outside of ourselves or look within and heal.

It is so important to use this choice to heal and not to hurt ourselves. When people were stealing from my retail store I judged myself very harshly. I felt like it was my fault. I didn't make those people steal, that was their choice. Yes I did need to improve my choice making but I was in no way at fault.

I've seen people who've been hurt in relationships begin to blame the intimacy. Eventually they avoid relationships all together. The sad part is relationships aren't the problem. For each person the real issue will be slightly different but the answer definitely lies in the person's belief system. It may be a question of feeling unworthy or a belief that love is unsafe or as simple as what our definition of love is.

Spiritual Shortcuts

What is your life telling you about your belief system? Take sometime and listen to what you are saying to yourself. What assumptions are you making about life, the events happening to you, and the people around you? What assumptions do you have about yourself? Do you see yourself as a victim? Are you a loving parent to yourself or do you judge yourself and your actions?

Take some time to sit down and write about whatever it is you want to change in your life. What are your beliefs about that issue? Is money, love, or success real? Or is it all based on your internal landscape?

The only power anything in our life has is whatever we endow it with. Money can just be a symbol of self-love and self-acceptance but it sure does seem to have the ability to affect the quality of our life. Take your power back and stop giving it away to the symbols in your life! Remember the events in your life say very little about you but your reactions speak volumes about your belief system. As you change your beliefs the mirror will reflect those changes as well.

The world very accurately mirrors our choice making capacity, which is dependent on our filter system. Our choices are constantly mirrored back to us. Our ability to choose is based on our ability to see our options and decide which one will be most beneficial. Years ago I remember my therapist spending months getting me to see that I had choices. Eventually I was willing to agree that I had two options. Now I realize that at any given point in time I have an infinite number of choices. My belief system dictates how many of them I am able to see. My filter system may only allow me to see a few of my choices and cause me to decide upon one that will cause me a great deal of emotion pain. We consistently make choices that will reaffirm our beliefs and not ones that will necessary create what we say we want.

Give yourself the gift of using the world to see your filter system. We assume it's the world but it's really a reflection of our filters. Once we realize that not only is it freeing but we can easily change what we are seeing. Our filter system isn't real once we change our mind the world seems to change with it. Remind yourself that your upset is caused by your belief system not the events in your life. And until you consciously choose what you're going to believe your beliefs aren't even yours other people told you what to believe.

Sage Advice

"A human thought is an actual existence, a force and power, capable of acting upon and controlling matter as well as mind."

Albert Pike

Do You Want to be Right or Do You Want to be Happy?

Smoke & Mirrors

More relationships have been killed by a person's need to be right than anything else. Think about a recent argument you've had with a lover or friend; wasn't it caused by each of you wanting to be right? If you want to improve the quality of your relationships, ask yourself frequently, *"Do I want to be right, or do I want to be happy?"*

We always have the choice to be right or to be happy. When I finally realized I could be happy and say the words 'I was mistaken' it was incredible freeing. We can spend years making ourselves miserable with our desire to be right. We don't hear what someone is really saying so we react to what we think they are saying. Someone can be saying I love you and we feel like we are being judged.

What a person says and what we hear are often two entirely different things. Even though we all speak the same language we often have different definitions for the same words. It is hard to listen to the words a person is speaking when we are having an emotional reaction to our internal filter system. Once we have an emotional reaction we are really listening to our mind and aren't really in tune with the outside world.

We all feel loved in different ways. When I work with couples the first thing I have them do is make a list of how they feel loved. I have them give it to their partner. The way I express love may seem thoughtless or uncaring to someone else. If I insist on saying I love you in my fashion I will get to be right but I will probably loose the relationship. Yet I have worked with couples that insist on being right even though they see how damaging it is to their relationship.

Our emotional wounds act like on/off buttons. If someone pushes on one we react. If we have an emotional wound that says we are inadequate it can be wired up to a variety of responses. We can respond in anger or by feeling pathetic, hopeless, and useless. Either way once it is pushed we stop reacting to the person and begin reacting to the wound.

Being Right

Take some time to really answer the following questions. Be as honest and thorough as possible.

- How does being right make you feel?
- What does being right really mean to you? Does it mean your okay, valid, or acceptable?
- What happens if you're wrong? What happens if you say I made a mistake?
- Is it necessary for someone to be wrong in order for you to be right?
- If there is a conflict of some sort can both people's opinions be valid? Can you easily agree to disagree?
- Is someone else's opinion important to you?
- Do you ever alter your actions based on someone else's opinion? Is it okay to do that?

Really explore the concept of being right. Look at the number of wars we have had and the number of people that have been killed because of our need to be right. Why do people need to be right? If we really love and accept ourselves we don't. Our need to be right arises out of our emotional wounds, out of our skewed thinking, our limiting beliefs, and our attempt to avoid the emotional pain caused by them. Giving up the need to be right is very healing and ultimately a very nurturing thing to do.

You are perfect just the way you are. My mind had a very hard time with that concept. For years I needed to do everything perfectly. If I made a mistake or didn't do everything just so there was something wrong with me. And no matter how hard I tried I couldn't be perfect. Someone would get angry with me or I wouldn't live up to someone's expectations so I had no value.

Eventually I realized being perfect was all wrapped up with my need to be right. And it was really all about an old emotional wound. As a child I tried to make my mom and dad happy all the time and of course I couldn't. I wasn't perfect so I assumed there was something wrong with me. So if I wasn't perfect at what I did I wasn't a useful, valid human being. I could believe I was imperfect and continue to try to act perfectly or I could realize I was perfect just the way I was.

Once I gave up trying to be perfect and realized I was perfect an incredible weight was lifted from me, I felt so much freer and happier it was amazing. I desired perfection because I already possessed perfection. A person totally devoid of compassion never strives to be compassionate. We already have to have the trait in order to desire it.

When aborigines are shown a photograph for the first time they only see a bunch of light and dark areas. They don't see an image because they've never seen a two-dimensional object before. Once the photograph is explained to them with a little practice they can see the image. In order for us to see compassion we must have experienced compassion we already know what it is. We already possess it to some degree.

If we believe we aren't compassionate we won't allow ourselves to be kind and caring. If we believe we are compassionate we will be. If you believe you already have what you want you'll have it. If you read books about manifesting what you want in your life they will tell you to already see it there.

> **Sage Advice**
> "Success is not counted by how high you have climbed but how many people you have brought with you."
> Wil Rose

Since the world is a mirror it can only mirror what is already there. So if you want more money know you already have it. But I don't have enough money so why should I lie to myself and tell myself I have money? Good question. Money is just a physical manifestation of an internal symbol. If money equals self-love in your personal mythology then fill yourself with self-love and the money will follow. If the world keeps reflecting no money back to you remind yourself constantly that money isn't real. It is an illusion. Then remind yourself that you have plenty of self-love and love yourself enough to allow in more of the illusion.

But what does any of this have to do with being right? We want our beliefs to be right. We constantly see our beliefs mirrored back to us so if we change our beliefs we change the world. Believe you are perfect and you will be. Believe your life is perfect and it will be. "But then I'll never change and grow," your mind says. That too is a belief. You can believe in yourself and your desire to experience your divinity, you can begin to move toward pleasure instead of away from pain.

Let Those Limits Go

Take a few minutes to relax. Find someplace you won't be disturbed for ten to fifteen minutes. You might want to take a few moments to set the stage. Light a candle, put some mellow, soft music on, or perhaps light some incense. When you do that consistently it will remind your mind that it is time to relax. As soon as you put on the music or light the candle your mind will automatically begin to relax.

> *Take a few deep breaths and relax. Focus your attention on your breathing. Really notice where you feel your breath as it moves in and out of your body. Focus your attention on that feeling. Notice what your breath feels like. Really notice what it feels like. Take a slow deep breath and relax.*
>
> *As you inhale totally fill your lungs. When you exhale push all the air out. Breath slowly and rhythmically. And relax.*
>
> *Imagine yourself floating in a huge inner tube. The water is warm and soft and very nurturing. You are totally safe and protected. You gently bob along in the inner tube looking up at the sky. You watch as the clouds drift slowly by. The sun is softly shinning and you feel loved, really loved. The water and the light have a magical, mystical quality.*
>
> *You find yourself drifting into another time and space. A time before time when you knew you were perfect, when you felt safe and all of your wants and needs were met. You find yourself drifting toward the shore. The inner tube lands on a sandy beach. There is a beautiful robe and slippers waiting for you. You stand up and walk toward the path just waiting for you. You walk through lush plants, the air smells fresh and clean.*
>
> *Up ahead there is a magnificent temple. On the steps an angelic figure is waiting for you. This being of light asks you if you are ready to be free, if you are ready to let go of all of your limitations and allow the universe to support you fully and lovingly. You take a deep breath and take a few moments to think about it.*
>
> *You decide you are ready so you say, "Yes I am ready to release all of my limiting beliefs. I am ready to let go of my limiting filters."*
>
> *With that the being of light reaches down a touches your head. You can feel energy surging through your mind. You are given the strength and the wisdom to see through your filters and let them go. You realize it is decision you have to make moment by moment and you know you can do it.*

For a moment in time you see the world through the eyes of the angel. You see a world filled with love and light and laughter. You see only beauty and wonder. The veil of fear is lifted and you see the world as it really is. You realize that only the love is real everything else is an illusion. You hold onto that vision and know, finally know the truth. Only the love is real.

You allow yourself to be filled with that, you allow the love to fill you. Take a few deep breaths and allow the love to fill you and flow through you. Only the love is real. Any pockets of fear left within you melt away in the presence of the love.

Take a few deep breaths and allow yourself to relax fully and completely in the knowing, in the love.

Whenever you are ready slowly and gently bring yourself back to this room. Get up very slowly and be gentle with yourself for a few minutes.

I always found mirrors very interesting. I use to own a stained glass studio. I loved looking at the reflection of my shop in one of the mirrors it looked all together different. One of the exercises I do with my students is to have them walk backwards while looking into a mirror. It is amazing how hard it is at first and how different the world looks once you do it for a while.

If you look yourself directly in the eyes in a mirror and talk to yourself it can be an amazing experience. We see ourselves in mirrors all the time but seldom acknowledge ourselves. We often judge the image we see; we aren't very loving to ourselves. If you look at yourself twice a day in the mirror and remind yourself how wonderful you are your life will change dramatically. Of course you have to allow yourself to believe it.

What would happen if you lived with someone who either ignored you or criticized you? You probably wouldn't like it very well. For years you have been living with your image in the mirror and have either ignored it or judged it. Try loving it instead, see what happens.

The Least You Need to Know

> My emotional reactions are based on my beliefs, not the events in my life.

> The world mirrors my filter system.

> I am perfect just the way I am. I don't need to do anything perfectly to be perfect.

> I don't have to be right.

Chapter 11

What Did I Just Say?

> **In This Chapter**
>
> ➤ You are not your mind or your thoughts.
>
> ➤ Assumptions have a heavy emotional price tag.
>
> ➤ Judgment doesn't make the world a better place.
>
> ➤ It's time to listen to what you're really saying.

When I first began my journey of spiritual healing I told a friend I wanted a magical tape recorder so I could hear what I really said. I would tell a friend something and then totally forget I'd said it until I was in a great deal of emotional pain. Then I'd remember my observation or thought and regret not acting upon it. At the time I couldn't really hear what I was saying even though I was saying it.

Luckily as we proceed on this wonderful adventure our ability to hear ourselves and others improves. A magical tape recorder would still be nice because when an emotional wound is surfacing we still can't hear what we are telling ourselves. I still can't see my beliefs when I'm in the middle of living them.

Making My Mind Behave

Left on its own your mind thinks, that's just what it does. And it thinks the same thoughts over and over again. My computer has certain programs installed on its hard drive and they operate in a predetermined way. I don't expect my computer to have new software or thought patterns unless I install them. The same is true of our minds. They won't think different thoughts unless we teach them.

> **Sage Advice**
> "Who you are screams so loudly in my face, I can't hear a word you are saying."
> Ralph Waldo Emerson

Your mind is an incredible bio-computer. You are not your mind or your thoughts. You are a spirit or energy that resides within your body. You can train your mind so it is your servant instead of your taskmaster. Your mind is a computer that has a wide variety of thought loops and those loops sometimes cause it to run amuck.

Your mind believes it's in charge. Imagine one day a young boy is hired to be in charge of a large mailroom in a major corporation. Everyday he makes his rounds and delivers the mail to all of the departments. For months he does his job and does it well. He listens well so he knows everyone and thinks he knows a lot about the company. Every time he goes into the CEO's office he notices that it's empty. The mail keeps pilling up.

> **Sage Advice**
> "For him who has conquered his mind, the mind is the best of friends; but for one who has failed to do so, his mind will be the greatest enemy."
> Bhagavad Gita

One day he sits down at the desk and takes charge. He thinks he knows about the company but not enough to make informed choices. He just makes choices based on what he's observed on his daily mail rounds, the gossip he's heard, and some assumptions he's made. The company begins to loose money and falter because he isn't really up to the job. He doesn't think to ask anyone what to do.

That is exactly what happened to your mind. Its real purpose is to gather information and deliver it to your spirit. Ideally your mind is an interface between you and the outside, physical world. It retains information but remains a neutral observer. It's your spirit's job to decide what actions to take and what value to place on the various events in your life. It's just that your spirit went to sleep or took an extended vacation and allowed your mind to take over. Now your life isn't working as well as it could.

I refer to making the shift from your mind to your spirit being in charge as waking up. Every so often the 'I' that is really, my spiritual self, goes to sleep and my mind takes over. When my life is in turmoil I can choose to wake up my spirit and let it take over or leave my mind in charge and let my life get really uncomfortable.

At first I felt like I was in a full-scale war with my mind. I fought my old beliefs and fought to change my thinking. I wanted desperately to have my spiritual-self guide my thinking. I didn't want to go to sleep anymore. I finally figured out that staying awake all the time meant I had to become an enlightened being.

A rather lofty goal and you can't become enlightened if you are still judging, resisting, or fighting anything. Enlightenment is synonymous with the concept of loving and embracing everything including our mind.

If I say to you, "Whatever you do don't think about a red fire truck," you have to think about one in order not to think about it. Negatives aren't very effective healing tools. Fighting with your mind and your beliefs doesn't work very well. If you want to be happy, focusing on what you want rather than on what you don't want will work much better.

As you become aware of some of your limiting thought patterns focus on what you would prefer to think. If you aren't happy focus on the things you enjoy doing. If you feel unloved take the time to love yourself and share your love with others. If you give what you want to receive to yourself first and then to others you will already have received what you desired.

It helps if you continually remind yourself that your thoughts aren't facts, they are just habitual thoughts that aren't necessarily even vaguely related to the truth. Our thoughts are created by our filter system and our filter system stops us from being fully alive and present in the moment. Train your mind gently and lovingly. Point out the flaws in its logic and teach it new ways of looking at life. The key words are always gently and lovingly.

Hearing Your Self-Talk

I had a client years ago that protested very heartily when I suggested he learn to hear his self-talk. He firmly told me he hadn't come to me to become a schizophrenic. When I began to separate my sense of self from the conversation in my mind I felt crazy. I had always believed what I said to myself, I certainly never thought to question my thoughts.

Spiritual Shortcuts

Who are you? Ask yourself several times an hour, "Who said that?" Then notice who asked the question. Really allow yourself to feel where the question came from.

Right now take a moment and go inside. Focus your attention on your inner world. Feel your thoughts, where do they come from? Let your mind do what it does best, just think, and notice where the thoughts originate. Consciously choose to ask yourself the question, "Who said that?" and notice where it came from. There is an energy within your body that is you. Your mind is not who you are. See if you can feel that energy, see if you can notice where the thoughts come from. I can feel thoughts in different parts of my brain.

Noticing the differences will take time and practice. As always, be gentle and loving with yourself.

Your self-talk is the foundation of your filter system. What your mind says to you is based on your beliefs, assumptions, and agreements. As you change your self-talk your filter system changes. Depending solely on what we tell ourselves we can view an event as a wonderful blessing or a horrible tragedy. The event or the story line is irrelevant. The only thing that really matters is our self-talk or what we tell ourselves about the event.

I tend to view all the events in my life and the lives of others as an opportunity to heal. No matter what happens we have an opportunity to see it through the eyes of love or fear. Once we step into fear our existence becomes our filter system.

> **Sage Advice**
> "The only real mistake is the one from which we learn nothing."
> John Enoch Powell

The holocaust and the atrocities committed by Hitler were abysmal. My Great Grandmother was killed by the Nazis. But there is another way to look at the events of World War II. For a moment suppose we look at the events as a tremendous gift or opportunity for humanity as a whole to heal. Hitler gave us a gift; he gave us the opportunity to see how destructive judgment and prejudice can be. He showed us what hate does.

What if we had looked at those events and instead of judging and hating the Nazis we had said as a society we can no longer hate. What if we realized we must never support judgment in any form again and that we must stop judging anyone or anything? What if we learned to love and embrace everyone and we fully realized that we must never judge anyone or anything again.

What if as a society we had collectively put all our efforts into freeing our thinking and our lives of judgment and the fear upon which judgment is always based? What if the entire world's community had decided to learn how to love and embrace all of our collective differences? What would the world be like now? It would certainly be a very different place free of violence, starvation, and war.

Changing our self-talk allows us to see things differently and make different decisions about what we need to do next. If we learn to free our thinking of fear life becomes miraculous and our decisions are very expansive and freeing. Imagine how different your life could be if your thinking was free of limitations, fear, and judgment or self-criticism. How would your decisions change? Would your ability to love change?

If I wasn't afraid of being hurt I would take a lot more risks, I would ask people more questions about how they feel, and I would take the risk of opening my heart fully and exposing myself. When we are free of fear we can take the risk of being ourselves and honestly showing others who that is.

If I wasn't afraid I would lose the friendship I would ask them why they had done something that in the past I might have felt was hurtful. I would take the risk and be vulnerable enough to really clear up my communications. Our relationships are with one another's filter systems not with one another's hearts or spirit.

Our self-talk creates our experience of reality. Once I realized how valuable changing it would be I was willing to take the time to really tune in and break free from it.

> **Spiritual Shortcuts**
>
> Take a few minutes and imagine how different your life would be if your inner voice was loving, powerful, supportive, nurturing, and in touch with your inner wisdom. What would change? How would you feel everyday if you knew everything in your life was perfect?
>
> An excellent way to start hearing your self-talk is to carry around a tape recorder. Every time you hear yourself say something judgmental or non-loving speak it into the tape recorder or write it down in a note book. It won't take long for you to separate yourself from that inner voice and begin to change it. Remember not to judge yourself or your mind. You are retraining the way you think. Be gentle and loving as you do it.

Don't Assume

Years ago someone told that assume was the best way of making an ass out of you and me. (Ass-u-me) Assumptions are the corner stone of our belief system and our self-talk. By definition when we assume something it means we are taking something for granted, without proof. Our assumptions are totally based on our perspective and having nothing to do with anyone or anything else. We assume our perspective is better or more accurate than everyone else's.

Assumptions are so destructive in our lives. Assumptions cause us to irreparable damage our relationships, loss jobs, and wage war. They seem so innocuous, so innocent and they are very powerful. Look at the history of humanity and all of the cruelty that happened over the centuries. Someone assumed they were right and defended their belief. Hitler assumed Jews were inferior and he proceeded to kill millions of them.

If I assume I know what is best for you and make you conform to my assumptions how will that affect our relationship? How did you feel when your parents told you what to do? Everyone of our beliefs is an assumption we've made about the nature of physical reality and we certainly didn't have all the facts when we made them!

If I assume your dangerous I will react to the danger not you. All prejudice is based in our assumptions. Many of our assumptions are based on our religious beliefs, on the beliefs of our parents, and of our society as a whole.

I can't emphasize enough what a powerful influence assumptions have on our lives. That influence can be positive when our assumptions are loving but an assumption is an assumption whether it's loving or not. They aren't based on fact; they are based on our assumption about the facts. If we admit to ourselves they are just an assumption and don't give them a great deal of power they don't present much of a problem.

In our relationships we often assume we know what our partner needs or wants. If we fail to check out our assumptions our relationship will suffer. My assumption about what you want or need is really based on what I want and need and has nothing to do with you.

No two people place exactly the same meaning or importance on words or actions. If I tell you I'm angry it might mean something entirely different than when you say you're angry. I might mean I'm upset and we need to talk while when you say you're angry you're ready to end the relationship. So if I tell you I'm angry your apt to assume the relationship is over and not want to talk at all.

Begin to notice when you're making assumptions. Notice how they affect your life. Assumptions save us the effort of having to think about things in our life. If we assume something we no longer have to give it much thought.

Once you notice your assumptions try changing them. Take your power back from them; don't let your assumptions rule your life. Decide what you want to do with them. Become the thinker in your life rather that being controlled by your thoughts. Direct your assumptions. Assume your mind doesn't necessarily know best. Assume your assumptions are usually limiting. Assume your life can be magnificent once your mind is no longer in control. Assume you can have a lot of money and all the love you want or need. Notice what happens to your life as you change your assumptions.

Staying Off The Train

When I teach people how to meditate I tell them to visualize a train station. If you're standing on the platform as a train comes into the station you have the choice to stand there and watch the train or you can get on it and go for a ride. When you have a thought you can also think of it as a train. You can watch it go by or get on it and go for a ride.

Our mind tends to get caught in thought loops especially when we are emotionally upset or stressed about something. We will think about something over and over again. And we will think the same thing about it. Watching our thoughts instead of getting emotionally involved with them is a very powerful way to begin changing the way we think.

Sage Advice
"Where fear is present, wisdom cannot be."
Lactantius

Staying off the train allows us to begin to develop the ability to be a neutral observer. As you begin to listen to your mind you will find that there isn't just one voice. There is a whole host of personalities that reside within our mind. The most valuable one we can develop is the voice of the observer. It is from this place of neutrality that we can most easily accomplish our emotional and spiritual healing.

As we develop the ability to observe our thoughts rather than immerse ourselves in them we can get in touch with all our parts. Here's where it feels very schizophrenic. As you begin to really listen to your self-talk you will begin to notice patterns of thinking. To personify those patterns I think of them as encapsulated parts of our psyche. As you observe your thought patterns you will find that they seem to have personalities. At times our thinking can be child-like or we can be self-critical and judgmental.

I have found that it's easier to change our thinking if we address the various thought patterns or parts and re-educate them one by one. When I ask myself the question, "Who said that?" if I know it is the child talking I know how to talk to her. As I proceeded on my path I became aware of a part I have come to call the pseudo-adult. It is a part of me that says I am the adult, I know what to do, and I can handle this. For a long time I believed that part. I really thought I was in touch with my spiritual-self but as I detached even further I realized the pseudo-adult is really a very wounded part that tries to feel safe by pretending it has the answers. Of all of the parts of my psyche this one is the most dangerous because it is so convincing.

> **Sage Advice**
> "Regret for the things we did can be tempered by time; it is regret for the things we didn't do that is inconsolable."
> Sydney Harris

When I find myself going for ride and am totally wrapped up in my thoughts, when I am assuming I know what's going on I remind myself to get back on the platform. As soon as I do that I'm once again in touch with the neutral observer. I can tell when I'm in touch with that part rather than my pseudo-adult because of my neutral perspective. I'm not judging myself I have compassion and understanding for my choices.

So when you find yourself caught up in your mind, believing your thoughts, and trapped in your emotions get off the train. Remind yourself lovingly and gently that you aren't your thoughts and that your thoughts aren't real. At times it is so hard not to believe our mind after all we know we're right and we need to be right in order to feel okay about ourselves and our decisions.

> **Spiritual Shortcuts**
>
> TThe first step is to realize you're on a train to begin with. Once you stop passively listening to your mind you can start asking yourself some in depth and thought provoking questions. What do I need right now? What do I want? What do I want to change, how would I like my life to be different? What do I need to do or what do I need to know if I really want to move forward in my life and heal? Am I willing to do whatever it takes to move forward? If I'm not what do I need to do to generate that willingness?
>
> Writing also helps us get back on the platform. Anything that interrupts our habitual thought patterns helps us awaken. After a while it feels better to wake up than it does to lie to ourselves.

Most people have had at least one failed relationship. Frequently when we end a relationship we feel like we did something wrong. In an attempt to avoid the pain of feeling like a failure we tell ourselves the other person was thoughtless or unfeeling or abusive. We invalidate the other person in an attempt to feel okay about ourselves.

We make up our version of reality in such a way that it supports our beliefs, our assumptions, and our version of the truth. We avoid the emotional pain the truth might bring by unconsciously making up a story. I have played the bad guy in many people's lives when their fear was greater than their desire to heal. I had to develop horns and become the devil incarnate so they could leave without feeling like they were running away from their issues.

We all do it. And what stops the process is to admit we are afraid, feel the fear, and go forward any way. Avoiding the emotional pain in our lives keep us stuck in the past, it stops us from healing. Deciding to feel the pain no matter what is the only thing that can set us free. Emotions are like a wave; they come, increase in intensity, crest, diminish, and then recede totally. They don't last for very long as long as we don't try to stop them.

When I first moved to Hawaii I decided to learn how to body board. After a few attempts I decided I was ready for the big time, I put my board on my moped and took the woman who was teaching me to a beach called Makapuu. It is known for its big waves. She chose to stay on shore; she said the waves were too big. I took my board into the surf and struggled to get through the surf. A big wave came up and I found myself kneeling on the sand looking up at this huge wave. I held the board up in front of me as the waved came crashing down. I was tossed and battered by the waves. I thought the last thing I was going to see in this life was white foamy water. Eventually the wave set me free and I staggered up onto shore coughing and sputtering.

Whenever see someone resisting their emotions I tell them my story about that wave. If I had allowed the wave to wash over me I would have been fine but I decided to resist it and almost died. If we allow our emotions to wash over us they will come and go fairly rapidly. If we resist them they will toss us about and nearly drown us. Our resistance has much more impact on our life then feeling them ever could.

Everyone's a Critic

Most people have a part of them that is critical. Everyone has an opinion about something. And it is important to get to the point that no ones opinion, including your own, matters.

Our opinions are based on our assumptions. Our fear often makes us critical of what we don't know or understand. One of my biggest struggles on my path has been to quiet my inner critic. My mind has an opinion about everything and its opinion keeps me separate from everyone else.

It doesn't matter whether your optimist or a pessimist our mind still keeps us separate from others. On my bulletin board I have a cartoon

> **Sage Advice**
> "The reason why all men honor love is because it looks up; and not down; aspires and doesn't despair."
> *Ralph Waldo Emerson*

of a man standing on a sand dune watching the sunset over the ocean. The little balloon over his head says, "I wonder if I locked my car." Our thoughts distance us from our experience of life. When we are thinking about life we aren't living it. When we are being critical we certainly aren't present in the moment.

When we think of being critical we tend to think of having a negative opinion. A criticism can be either positive or negative. All a criticism is really is an opinion but the problem is we believe most of the things we tell ourselves and we want others to believe it as well.

The biggest hurdle on our healing journey is convincing ourselves of the necessity of doing something. Once we realize we need to connect with our spirit we become willing to do things like pray and meditate. If we don't see the value in getting in touch with our spirit we won't do what we need to do. So step one in healing is always realize what we need to do in order to heal.

Start observing your inner critic. Notice how often the people closest to you are critical. Observe when you feel the need to be critical and how it serves you. Does it make you feel okay or justified in doing something? How does it keep you separate from true self and others? Explore the role of the critic until you realize the value of releasing it.

Notice how you feel when people are being critical of you or others. Do you join in when your friends are trashing someone or something? What roles do critics play in your life? Do you read reviews of movies before you go or do you choose on your own? We often use criticism to avoid being a free thinker. We avoid showing people our true self by unleashing our critic. We avoid the need to dig down and find out what we really believe by voicing our critical nature.

Judge Not

As the saying goes judge not least you be judged. For one thing judgment acts like cosmic super glue. Whatever you judge is stuck to you until you release the judgment and understand what your judgment is really about. Judgment is always based in fear. Whatever action we take based in fear is only going to generate more fear.

If we are judging someone else that person feels our judgment and reacts to it whether we verbalize it or not. Our reactions to life are based on not only what we tell ourselves but also on what we are feeling energetically. The reason it is so important to retrain our mind is we often base what we are feeling on our filter system. We can react to our belief that we are being judged when we aren't being judged at all.

Sage Advice
"We would rather be ruined than changed. We would rather die in our dread then climb the cross of the moment and let our illusions die."
W. H. Auden

Clarity Corner
When we judge ourselves or someone else, we come from a place of fear and a desire to feel safe by invalidating the person or ourselves. Our fear causes us to judge, or our judgement causes us to feel fear. It is a vicious cycle that does nothing but cause pain. Judgement causes a feeling of separation instead of a realization of oneness.

Whenever we judge something we have a predetermined opinion about it. The possibility of us seeing the event or person clearly is greatly diminished. Our judgment stands between the world and us.

One of the questions you might want to ask yourself is do you want to be in control of your experience of life or do you want your mind, programmed by others to be in control? We tend to be fiercely independent and rebel at anyone else telling us what to do. Yet we blindly listen to the opinions of our mind when we haven't even consciously decided what's stored there.

Do you have a judgment about your mind yet? That is how our minds work; it absorbs the information being feed it and judges accordingly. Your mind is a magnificent tool but it's a terrible master. Isn't it time you made it your tool? Isn't it time you fired it as your manager?

> **Sage Advice**
> "Whenever you see a fault in others, attribute it to yourself. That way you will get the benefit and will learn from other's mistake."
> Seventh Dalai Lama

But you can't do that if you judge it. Then how do you get to the point you're willing to change without judging what you are doing? That is often the struggle. How do we become willing to change and not judge ourselves, our mind, others or our behavior? Believe it or not it is as simple as making a decision. In order to change you have to find fault with what your already doing? If you do, make a new choice. Allow yourself to change just for the shear pleasure of changing or for no reason at all.

Begin to ask yourself questions that are positive and nonjudgmental. Ask yourself what you want rather than what you don't want. Ask yourself what makes you happy instead of listing what you don't like. Begin to think about life in terms of being the creator rather than being the victim. Embrace your creation; embrace everything and everyone in your life. Judge not.

We often believe we won't let go of something unless we judge it, we won't move on unless where we are is unpleasant. Those are beliefs and assumptions; you don't have to make your decisions based on them.

Ask yourself if you believe judgment serves you in any way. Explore your beliefs about judgment. What is your definition of the word? Really explore the role judgment plays in your life and find out what you need to do to release your need for it. Then set yourself free.

If we truly want to be happy and experience peace of mind being grateful for what we do have is the key. Whenever we are judging things we are coming from a place of fear but when we are grateful we are coming from a place of love. Whatever you focus your attention on you will get more of, if you focus on what you don't like you'll get more of what you don't like. If you are judging others and your life you will get more of what you are judging. If you are grateful for what you do have in your life you will get more of what you like.

The energy of judgment feels very different from the energy of gratitude. For a moment think about something you are grateful for, really allow your self to be filled with a feeling of gratitude. What does that feel like to you? It is hard to be afraid when you are grateful. Practice being grateful. Every night before you go to bed make a list of all the things in your life you are grateful for, make it a point to add at least one new thing a day. Then in the morning, before you start the day, read your list out loud to yourself. If you take the time to be grateful every time you feel afraid or judgmental your life will change very rapidly.

> ### *The Least You Need to Know*
>
> ➤ You are not your mind.
>
> ➤ Your mind is full of inaccurate assumptions and beliefs.
>
> ➤ You can choose what you say to yourself about everything.
>
> ➤ Whatever you judge is stuck to you like glue.

Chapter 12

My Emotions Made Me Do It

> **In This Chapter**
>
> ➤ Emotions and feelings aren't the same.
>
> ➤ You can get what you want.
>
> ➤ Words are as important as we make them.
>
> ➤ You can act instead of react.

When we are reacting emotionally we tend to make decisions based on our emotions rather than on what we want to achieve. We react to life instead of choosing how to act. We often regret our actions and the words we've spoken but once we react it is to late. We start off trying to say I love you and instead hurt someone's feelings by saying something they find upsetting.

Our emotions are generated by our thoughts. Our emotions are created by our mind. When we make decisions based on our mind our only choice is to react based on the past. When we learn how to make choices consciously we can choose to act instead of reacting. As we deepen our connection to our spiritual center we can make decisions based on what we want to achieve rather than repeating our past. For me the ability to act instead of reacting was one of the greatest gifts I received on my journey of spiritual healing.

Separating Your Emotions from Your Feelings

I find it useful to differentiate between my emotions and feelings. At times I use the words loosely but whenever I'm trying to figure out what's really going on inside of me I clearly differentiate between the two. Emotions are generated by our thoughts. Every event in life is emotionally neutral. No event has an emotion attached to it until we decide what emotion we're going to attach to the event with our thoughts. We all place different emotional values on the events and happenings in our lives.

Clarity Corner

Emotions are caused by the thoughts we think. Emotions have labels like anger, sadness, understanding and happiness. They are related to our thoughts, and we can talk about them in words. **Feelings** are related to what we are experiencing in our body. Our emotions can generate feelings in our body. Feelings are described by phrases like my chest feels tight, my stomach is churning or I feel a lightness in my body.

Feelings are sensations we experience in our bodies. Feelings can be generated by our emotions. If we are angry we do feel a certain way in our bodies. Once we label our feelings they become emotions, they move from the realm of our body into our mind. As soon as we name our feeling we stop feeling them in our bodies and start talking about them instead. When we talk about our emotions we don't get to feel them.

We can't heal what we can't feel. And much of our filter system is designed to avoid our feelings. As human beings we seem so much more comfortable talking about things rather than feelings things. No one taught us how to explore our inner world safely when we were children. Going there by ourselves was confusing, painful, and frightening.

Infants just feel things, they don't have any language skills, and at first they are very spontaneous. They can be screaming in fury one moment, suddenly notice their foot, and become totally engrossed in exploring this new found object while completely forgetting their anger.

Spiritual Shortcuts

Make a list of all of your emotions, the ones you have on a regular basis. Then describe how you feel internally when you are having each emotion. Describe exactly what happens in your body. Does your chest get tight or do you clench your jaw? Start at your head and review your entire body. List what happens in each part of your body. Then for a few days don't name your emotions. Concentrate on what you are feeling in your body. Stay with the feelings. Don't name them or talk to yourself about them, just notice what you are feeling in your body. After a while you will know what feelings your emotions generate.

But then they begin to learn. They notice if they cry hard enough someone will come and feed them or hold them. They are no longer alone. Their little brains begin to wire up action and reaction. Eventually much of their inner discomfort is erased by a bottle, or a by having their dippers changed, or by being held. As a child no one teaches us to go inside to see what we really want or need. By the time we are talking the family has a comfortable set of responses and the child learns to adapt.

> **Sage Advice**
> "Nothing has such power to broaden the mind as the ability to investigate systematically and truly all that comes under thy observation in life."
> *Marcus Aurelius*

Certain feelings and expression of emotions are acceptable others aren't. We are taught what our feelings mean and we aren't encouraged to find our own definitions. So, our feelings and our emotions become all wrapped up in our filter system and are no longer an accurate indication of what is going on internally. The conflict between what we think our emotions should be and what we are feeling isn't something we can resolve as a young child so we stop going inside. We learn how to react instead of learning to go inside, seeing what's going on, and then decide how to act based on our internal guidance.

As an adult it is important for us to develop the skill of knowing what we are feeling without automatically translating it into an emotion or a reaction. Once we know what we are feeling we can begin to ask ourselves what we want to create rather than simply going into reaction mode. Feelings are guideposts, they will gentle guide us and direct our attention to the areas of our psyche and our lives that we need to look at.

So How Do We Stop Reacting and Act Instead?

Learning to free ourselves from our habitual reactions and choosing how we are going to act is a process. It will take time and practice.

1. **Observe your "normal" reactions.** Start noticing what your knee-jerk reactions are to various events in your life. Notice how you react and what you are feeling when you react. You have to begin to understand your own inner symbols and what means what. Perhaps your stomach churning and your chest being tight means you need ask for something or set a boundary. Perhaps someone just asked you do to do something and you said yes when you wanted to say no and your anger is aboutnot setting a boundary not about their request. Only you can know for sure what your feelings mean.

2. **Ask yourself what you really want to create.** Now you know what you used to do. Now ask yourself what you'd like to do. Do you want to create loving, nurturing, and supportive relationships? If so, what actions do you need to wire up with certain feelings so you'll create that? Maybe if want to be able to pay your bills when your fear about finances comes up you need to be grateful for what you do have and balance your checkbook. It's your inner landscape, experiment. Try smiling when you want to frown or be loving when you want to yell.

3. **Practice**. It took you years to memorize your old reactions. Play with your new reactions. Rehearse your lines. Imagine yourself playing a new part in a play. You've changed characters. Ask yourself frequently how your new character would act. Play the new part as flamboyantly as possible.

4. **Ask for help.** Change is can be unsettling. Some of your old reactions cover up some very deep emotional wounds. You may need help sorting the issues involved. Don't hesitate to seek professional assistance, talk to your friends, or your spiritual adviser. You don't have to do this alone.

Your Emotions Aren't Facts

We tend to believe our emotions. If I feel angry obviously what you just did pissed me off. It has nothing to do with me it's all your fault. That's the most familiar and easiest way to view an event. It is also the least effective way to create happiness. If I'm angry and I take responsibility for the way I'm feeling I can heal that wound. If I blame you I don't have an opportunity to grow.

> **Sage Advice**
>
> "We live in deeds not years; in thoughts, not breaths; in feelings, not figures on the dial. We should count time by heartthrobs. He most lives who feels the nobeest and acts the berst."
>
> Bailey

If we are feeling anything other than peace and contentment we are not in alignment with our spiritual self and we are telling ourselves something that is fear-based. Sometimes emotional dramas can be fun and if we choose to create them consciously it's not a problem. It can be fun to get angry or sad; it feels good to yell or to cry sometimes. If we do it consciously we can still choose what we want to create. Anger is a very powerful emotion and at times I chose to use it consciously in order to hook someone's attention. Then it is a tool but when I get angry and react anger becomes my master. Emotions can be wonderful tools but they make terrible masters.

Once I realized my emotions weren't facts I was able to stop taking them so seriously. Millions of events happen all around us everyday but we only fully focus our attention on a few of them. We feel millions of sensations in our body everyday as well. Our mind does a wonderful job of filtering out all of those distractions. The problem is some of them aren't distractions at all. Some of they are very valuable messages we need to pay attention to and perhaps even act upon.

What are emotions anyway? One way I like to think about them is as energy in motion. They always have a beginning, middle, and end unless we keep them alive with our thoughts. Have you every done something you thought was wrong or foolish and spent days thinking about it? How many times did you punish yourself for doing it during your musings? What would happen if you learned to feel your emotions and then let them go instead?

Once we realize we tell ourselves something in order to generate an emotion we can choose to tell ourselves something different whenever we want. If we feel our actions were in some way inappropriate we can review what we did, forgive ourselves, and decide how we would rather act the next time. Instead of reliving the event over and over again and then doing the same thing next time we can decide to change. We can't do that until we realize we are responsible for how we feel.

What causes us to act in a certain way? We act that way because at some level we feel that's the way we are supposed to act. Our emotions hook our attention and we forget to think. We just act the way someone taught us to a long time ago. As a child we learned how to get our parents attention and the results varied. At times we got their attention and we were punished while at out times we were praised and loved.

At times our filter system won't allow us to experience the more subtle emotions. We can connect with our rage but not our joy. And if we put a cap on one emotion we put the same limitations on all of them. If we only allow ourselves to feel a fraction of our anger we can only feel a fraction of our joy. Since all of our emotions are self-generated we unconsciously dictate what we're willing to generate and what aren't.

So next time an emotion starts rising to the surface of your consciousness remind yourself it isn't a fact and ask yourself what's really going on. What choices do you need to make, what choices have you avoided, and what choices would allow you to create what you want n your life?

Is anything really real? What is reality, how do you define real for yourself? In many spiritual traditions they believe that only the love is real everything else is an illusion. How do you feel about that? Part of setting yourself free is learning how to think instead of merely repeating what you've already been taught.

Not Just Love is Blind

Two people's eyes meet across a crowded room and they feel a tremendous physical and emotional attraction. They know they are soul mates and almost immediately fall in love. They can only see how wonderful their partner is. Their friends look at one another and shake their heads. "Love sure is blind," they say.

What just really happened was when their eyes met they unconsciously said to themselves there's the perfect reflection of my filter system. We all play roles in each other's lives based on our filter system. A victim always needs a victimizer and even if the person isn't willing to play the role we can see them that way anyway.

Smoke & Mirrors

To find your happiness, you must master your emotions. Life is a series of choices and outcomes. If you don't like the outcome, you have to make a new choice. If your choices are based on your emotions, you can't make clear choices so your outcomes will never change. Learning to master your emotions will allow you to make your decisions based on the outome your want to achieve.

Sage Advice

"The basic principle of spiritual life is that our problems become the very place to discover wisdom and love."
Jack Kornfield

As long as we are seeing the world through our filter system we are blind, we can't see clearly what's going on. We project our filter system onto the world around us and see what we need to see to reaffirm our beliefs. Of course the minute we are willing to see our filter system it becomes visible. But most of the time even when we think we are willing we're not. Our fear stops us from seeing the world as it really is.

We are afraid of so many things. We are afraid of not being good enough, or being wrong, or we're just afraid of taking the risk of being vulnerable enough to be ourselves. Fear stops us from just being and instead we fill our lives up with doing things. As I was reminded years ago we are human beings not humans doing. For years I denied I even had any fear. I grew up as a tough, little street kid in New York City. I had no fear. Eventually I realized I was so terrified of my fear I wasn't even able to allow myself to acknowledge it.

Our emotions are layered one on top of another. The order of the layers varies from person to person but the categories are always the same. The major categories are anger, sadness, guilt, and fear. Within each category there is a whole host of other emotions that have a similar nature. If we allow ourselves to fully process through them we will get to a place of love and acceptance for what exists.

Getting to the point where we're able to embrace or accept life just as it is takes time and it's the only place we can truly heal from. Until we see our filter system clearly we certainly can't release it. Until we feel the other emotions and process the information contained in them we can't get to acceptance.

Spiritual Shortcuts

When an issue is kind enough to present itself in your life and you're ready to create something else it helps to write a series of letters. Sit down and write letter about your emotions. Start with whatever emotion you are most aware of and start writing, go through each emotion until you feel done, and then move onto the next one. Keep repeating the process until you get to a place of acceptance. You may have to write several letters about the same issue until the issue is finally resolved. Make sure you go through each category thoroughly in ever letter.

Sometimes it helps to write letters to the people as well as the events in your life. These aren't letters you'll ever send. You are writing these letters for yourself and they're not for anyone else but yourself to see.

After you're done writing a series of these letters you might want to create a ceremony to release them. The stuff we carry in our head doesn't hurt or limit anyone but ourselves. I like to burn my letters periodically. I light the fire with for the specific purpose of releasing anything I'm still holding onto. Sometimes I burn pictures along with the letters. Sometimes I have to grieve the death of an old part of myself before I can move on. Afterwards I always feel a sense of freedom.

I Never Agreed to That

Have you ever had a conversation with someone and felt like you weren't on the same page with the other person? Has it ever felt like you were both speaking a different language? Have you ever agreed to something and then found out the other person thinks you've agreed to something entirely different?

Emotions will blind-side us every time. When we are caught up in our emotions we are seeing the world through a very distorted filter. Words, actions, and expressions take on totally different meanings. If you stand behind a raging waterfall you can't see the outside word very accurately. So it is with our emotions, they distort our perspective.

> **Sage Advice**
> "Most of us remain strangers to ourselves, hiding who we are, and asking other strangers, hiding who they are, to love us.."
> Leo Buscaglia

And no two of us react the same way even when we are feeling the same emotion. My mother used to cry when she got angry. When you saw the tears it was time to run. Most people try to comfort people when they cry. That wasn't a good idea when my mother crying.

In relationships we all have un-negotiated agreements. They are non-verbal and totally based on our mutual filter systems. They are unconscious and operate silently in our lives until one of them starts to cause emotional discomfort either one of us. Since the agreements are un-negotiated neither party has consciously agreed to abide by the rules. Sometimes we have unwitting agreed to play a certain role in a relationship. We are supposed to be the victim while the other person plays victimizer, we're supposed to play the angry party, or be passive, or _____ fill in the blank.

Everything goes along fine for a time and then one day we decide to be ourselves or they do. Then all hell breaks loose. We may have agreed to play that part when we were feeling particularly needy or unlovable but when we start feeling better we decide to change how we've been acting.

Relationships are emotional by nature. We tend not to communicate very clearly, our fear stops us from speaking our truth. We want the other person to be a mind reader or at least have the same assumptions and agreements we do. We expect that or at least our filter system does. Just what have you agreed to in your life? What agreements do you need to renegotiate? What roles do you playing in your life that no longer serves you?

Retraining your mind is a matter of bringing all of your life into conscious awareness. We must become conscious of our emotions, our agreements, our assumptions, as well as our feelings and understand how we make our choices.

Life in the Freedom Lane: A Meditation

Find a place you won't be disturbed for at least fifteen minutes, shut off the phone, and go get your journal. If you've developed a personal ritual for your mediations get out the music, candle, incense, and whatever else you've decided to use. You can either read through this meditation, have someone read it to you, or read it into a tape recorder.

Get comfortable and take a few slow, deep breaths. Mentally give yourself permission to relax. Imagine yourself letting go and surrendering to the feeling of relaxation. Imagine a huge pink and green cloud swirling around you, gently caressing you, and filling you with a deep sense of peace and relaxation.

Take a few deep breaths, settle back, and relax. Notice your breath. Allow yourself to really feel your breath, really feel it as it effortlessly goes in and out of your body. Take a deep breath in through your nose then open your mouth and exhale with a soft ahhhhhh. Breathe in again and allow your breath to make a noise as you inhale. Then exhale loudly. Do this several times.

Now imagine yourself settling back into that cloud of pink and green light. Imagine yourself floating on that cloud. Feel yourself being supported and loved. Sink back into the cloud and allow yourself to relax totally and completely.

Imagine yourself standing in the middle of a field. You feel totally at peace and relaxed. The field is surrounded by mountains and is filled with beautiful flowers. The sun is shinning, the air is warm, and there's a gentle breeze blowing. You focus your attention on the wind. You feel it as it touches your body. Its touch comes and goes. The wind keeps moving no matter what it encounters. It doesn't fight it just flows, moving, constantly moving.

Now imagine your emotions moving through you like the wind. Imagine them just flowing and floating through you with no resistance. They come and go. Imagine yourself feeling very comfortable with all of your emotions. After all they're just a wind blowing through your life.

Imagine yourself letting them go and then asking yourself what you want to create at any given moment. Imagine yourself making your decisions clearly and with the image of what you want to create firmly in mind. Imagine your life with your spiritual-self in charge, guiding and directing your choices in a loving and gentle manner. Imagine yourself feeling safe, loved, and honored. See that feeling reflected in your life. What would that feel like? Let that feeling fill your entire being and know you can reconnect with that feeling at any point in your day.

To whatever degree you're willing and able decide to tap into that feeling before you make any of your choices. Peace is only a deep breath away.

Now take a few deep breaths and slowly and lovingly bring yourself back to your room. Whenever you're ready open your eyes. As you sit there practice feeling safe, loved, and honored. Take a few minutes to write about how you feel when you know you're safe, loved, and honored. Notice the words you use to generate those emotions within your body.

Get up slowly and give yourself a few minutes before steeping back into your regular activities. Repeat this mediation often.

Sage Advice

"God is a comic playing to an audience tha's afraid to laugh."

Voltaire

Them's Fighting Words

I have a close friend who will ask me if she can do something and when I say, "Sure, if you don't mind," she gets furious. She hates it when I say if you don't mind. She says, "I wouldn't have asked if I minded." To me saying "if you don't mind" is a matter of being polite but to her that phrase invalidates her offer. Even though we speak the same language our words have very different meanings. I was trained to say one thing while she hears something entirely different.

Our words are so important and there is no way to guarantee other people have the same meaning or place the same emotional value on the same word. So how the do we communicate? One thing we can do instead of reacting emotional to the words is ask the person what they really meant. Of course the only emotional reaction we can really do anything about is our own. When we find ourselves having an emotional reaction to a word or a phrase we can look inside to see what it's really about. What are we telling ourselves about the words we think we are hearing?

> **Clarity Corner**
>
> What are your *fighing words*? What can someone say that is guaranteed to make you angry? My friend gets furious when I say "If you don't mind doing it." Take a few minutes and write down some of your fighting words. then realize they are just words and you can change their meaning. Do you want to be right or happy?

I've seen fist fights occur because of words. Wars have been fought, people have died, and relationships have ended because of words. When we attach emotions to words we give them real power. What are your fighting words?

Feel Your Vocabulary

Spend a few minutes getting in touch with the emotional value you place on the following words and phrases. Notice how you feel and think of an occasion and write about how you reacted to the words.

Discipline	You're wrong
Commitment	How dare you?
Emotional Wound	Are you ever going to learn?
Passion	I'm very angry with you
Friendship	I'm afraid
Dedication	I made a mistake
Death	What's wrong with you?
Abandonment	What's wrong with you?
Love	I love you. *(What happens the first time someone says those words to you?)*
Opponents	

Spiritual Shortcuts

Over the next several weeks notice your reaction to people's words. Take note of any strong reactions you have and write about it. Is it the words themselves, the way the person spoke them, or what was already going on inside. Do you react differently to the same words at different times?

Really notice how you use your words. Do you choose your words carefully? Do you speak a lot or do you remain silent? Notice your style of communication. Do most of the people in your life have the same style? Notice how communications affect your life.

Learning how to Act Instead of React

Smoke & Mirrors

Beware of the words you use and the pictures you generate in your mind. For years I was terrified of going bankrupt. I thought it would be the worse possible thing that could happen. After focusing on that fear for more than 13 years, I finally created it. You get more of whatever gets your attention. Focus on love, and you will get more love; focus on fear, and you will get more fear.

How do you want to act? What areas of your life do you find yourself behaving in a counter-productive manner? In order to learn how to act you have to be aware of the emotional wounds surrounding the issue. Emotional wounds can act like land mines and explode when you least expect it.

Learning how to act is a process that will be facilitated by gentleness, love, and acceptance. Judging yourself or your process won't help one bit. If you ask yourself how you'd like to act and then act that way it sure helps.

Most of the time people tell me they want to be more loving and then they go on to judge themselves for not being loving. We can't treat someone else in a loving manner if we don't love ourselves. Since fear is one of our major hurdles perhaps we need to stop scaring ourselves.

One day I was taking my young niece for a walk. We went into an old shed and I told her a scary story just like I'd been told as young girl. As soon as I saw her fear I regretted speaking the words but it was too late. I apologized, gently reassured her, and told her my mom had always scared me that way. I really felt bad about scaring this precious little child.

Later that night she asked me if she could come with me on my walk. We were out in the middle of the desert and there weren't any streetlights. She was terrified of the dark and wanted us to take a flashlight. I wanted to watch the stars so I held her hand and talked to her about the magic of shadows. As we walked away from the house the porch light caused her to have a very long shadow. I talked to her about the stars and the sound of the coyotes. After we had walked along for a few minutes her fear was gone. She was as spell bound as I was by the magic of the desert at night.

I had given her a gift. She told me she was no longer afraid of the dark. Earlier in the day I had needlessly caused her to be afraid now I had removed one of her greatest fears. The only difference was the words I spoke and the outcome I wanted to achieve.

What would happen if you decided to stop scaring yourself with the words you speak? What would happen if you taught yourself the magic and the wonder of changing? How would this whole process be different? Next time you are about to tell yourself how hard it is or scary stop and tell yourself about the magic and freedom these changes will afford you instead. And remember it is a process, one you can enjoy or not. It's all up to you.

The Least You Need to Know

> ➤ Your emotions are created in the privacy of your own mind.

> ➤ Emotions cloud our ability to see life clearly.

> ➤ True freedom comes from choosing how to act rather than blindly reacting to life.

> ➤ Learning how to choose is a process that takes time.

Chapter 13

Dynamics of Change

> ### In This Chapter
>
> ➤ Find out what you really need to change.
>
> ➤ Stop believing in your beliefs.
>
> ➤ Learn that you're already perfect.
>
> ➤ Understand the process of change.

At times we seem to have a love-hate relationship with change. We want to change yet we resist the things we need to do in order to change. We try to control people, places, and things beyond our control so we'll feel safe. We fear change yet we crave it. We tend to be slaves to our routines, going to work the same way, eating the same foods, and repeating the same thoughts to ourselves over and over again. Remember today you will think 95% of the same thoughts you had yesterday.

If we're unhappy we try to change external circumstances. We unwittingly run away from the real issues only to bump into them again and again. Change must happen at several levels if we want it to be permanent and effective. They didn't have a course on how to change or on how to be happy in any of the schools I attended. Change is a skill anyone can master and apply in their lives. Read on and find out how.

Waking up to What's Really Real

Most of us sleep walk through our lives. One of the questions posed to me by one of my mentors was: How do you really know which is real? Are your dreams at night real or is what you define as physical reality real? Interesting thought, isn't it? How do you know what's really real? What if when you "go to sleep" at night you are really waking up?

Buddha and other great teachers talk about detachment as the path to inner happiness. Detachment is a way of viewing the world and the events in it from a different perspective. We can begin to see life from the perspective of our spiritual self rather than our fearful smaller self. I have found that when I'm attached to the form of my happiness it remains illusive. If I think love has to look a certain way and someone loves me in another way I won't feel loved. But what does all this have to do with change?

We think we know what we need to change. If we're lonely we need more friends or a relationship. If we don't have enough money to pay the bills we need more money. We look at the world, which is really a mirror, and try to change the mirror instead of ourselves. Would you brush the teeth you see in the mirror every morning and expect your mouth to feel cleaner? Yet we expect to change the external events in our life instead of addressing the real issue, which always resides in our internal landscape.

I like to think of life as a dream. There is a process called lucid dreaming. In a lucid dream you wake up in the dream while you remain asleep. Once awake in the dream you can do anything you want, you can change locations, manipulate the events in your dream, go places, create castles, lovers, or you can just ask the scary monsters to leave. You become a film marker controlling all of the events in your dream. With just a thought you can change anything. It is an exhilarating experience.

If you think of life as a dream you can wake up in your life and become lucid in the dream of your life. Once you really wake up you can change anything in your life with just a thought. It's waking up to what's really real in life that takes time.

Rounding the Bend

When you are driving along an unfamiliar road the view constantly changes. You may think you're approaching a large body of water but when you get around the corner you realize it just a small pond. So it is with our life. We may think the issue is lack of money when it is really an inability to love ourselves.

Sage Advice
"Reality is a collective hunch."
Lily Tomlin

Clarity Corner
Detachment makes change so much easier. When we are attached to an old way of thinking or a particular outcome, it is hard to take a different choice and get a different outcome. Detachment allows us to unplug ourselves and our thinking from the pas and move into the future free of our limitations.

If we want change to be permanent and effective it must occur at several levels. If lack of money is the issue we have to heal both our internal landscape and our external behaviors. If we constantly overdraw our checking account we need to learn how to balance our checking account as well as explore our beliefs.

Change is a balancing act in which we look inside, shift our internal thought process, then look at our external behaviors, and shift them. At times we shift our external behaviors and then wait to see what internal thought structures are affected. If we focus our attention solely on one or the other we won't really change.

You know you are about to round a corner with your car. Imagine trying to go around the corner without turning the steering wheel. You wouldn't be very successful. We must know where we are going but we also have to take the necessary action to get there. Our mind is like a magician focusing our attention in one area when we really need to look someplace else. Learning how to change will teach you where to look as well as what action to take.

> **Sage Advice**
> "Life is divided into three terms – that which was, which is, and that which will be. Let us learn from the past to profit by the present, and from the present to live a better future.."
> Wordsworth

Stranger Than The Truth

Change is a very simple process that is easy yet it is often the hardest thing we can do in life. Knowing what the real issue is can be confusing and very frustrating. If we knew what the issue was we could just change but 2 plus 2 doesn't always equal 4. In some areas of my life I've spent years believing something that had absolutely nothing to do with reality. I lived my life based on those beliefs and wondered why happiness alluded me.

When I begin working with my students they often believe there's something wrong with them. They begin looking at an issue, they modify their behaviors, and their thinking, but the underlying theme is still there. They subconsciously believe that there is something wrong with them. No matter what they changed they couldn't be truly happy because after all there's something wrong with them.

When I tell people they're perfect just the way they are they often look at me blankly, or they tell me they're trying to get over being a perfectionist, or they tell me what's wrong with them and their life. As long as we think there is something wrong with our life or ourselves we're going to continue to be unhappy.

But what you say! My life isn't prefect if it was perfect I'd be happy. Your life is what it is, you are where you are in your life, and where you are is perfect. And that isn't just a positive way of looking at things it's the truth. Where you are gives you an opportunity to see an area of your belief system you might want to modify. But you said I was prefect! You are perfect your filter system just creates limitations in your life, but it's perfect too. There is nothing wrong with anything. If you want to achieve different results in your life you do need to change your filter system and make different choices. Your filter system creates the results you are currently getting in your life, if you want different results you need to change your filter system.

Realizing everything is perfect just the way it is makes change so much easier. Whenever we judge anything we are in our small self, we are coming from fear and that makes change much more difficult. But we'll get back to this perfect thing again later in the chapter.

I Believe

"I believe" are two innocent, little words that cause so much pain and suffering in our world. Once you believe something that's what you'll experience. Your beliefs dictate your choices and your choices create the events in your life.

> **Sage Advice**
> "Loyalty to a petrified opinion never broke a chain or freed a human soul."
> Mark Twain

Beliefs cause separation, wars, and conflicts. We believe we are separate so that's what we experience. If we acted on the truth that we are all one instead of our beliefs that we're separate we could never hurt ourselves or anyone else. We would be truly happy.

It Ain't Necessarily So

What we think the problem is isn't necessarily what it really is about. We are seldom upset for the reasons that we think we are. The first and most important step in changing anything is to know what we need to change. Knowing what we need to change seems self-evident but the root cause of an issue is seldom obvious. First we need to know what's going on in our inner landscape. We need to know how we are feeling and what we are thinking before we react to the events around us.

Knowing what's really going on in your inner landscape is your first step toward successfully changing your life. We tend to be out of touch with our true inner wants and needs; we have learned to depend on the interpretation provided by our filter system. We believe we know what is going on rather than actually knowing what's going on.

Every half hour ask yourself the following questions until it becomes second nature:

➤ Who said that? (Observe what part of your belief system said that. Was it your small self or your spiritual self? Your inner critic or your inner child or . . .? You might want to give each of the different parts a name.

➤ What am I feeling?

➤ What am I saying to myself?

➤ Do I need something?

➤ Do I need to talk to someone or ask for help?

➤ Do I have any non-negotiated expectations about what's going on right now?

> Is my self-talk positive, loving, and nurturing or self-abusive?

> Am I being loving and gentle with myself?

Once you know where you are emotionally ask yourself if you want to stay there. Do you want to continue to feel the same way? Do you want to get different results in your life? If you want to change how you feel or the choices you are making change your inner dialog.

Once you know what you're feeling, what expectations you have, and what you believe is happening you'll be more fully aware of your filter system and see it for what it really is. You have to see it if you're going to change it.

Beauty is in Eye of the Beholder

Perspective is everything. Our experience in life has nothing to do with reality it is totally dependent on our perspective about reality. Once we are willing to detach from our need to be right, once we are willing to let go of our beliefs our perspective is the easiest thing to change. Once we change our perspective our experience changes and so do the choices we make. So the key to change is seeing our filter system and then changing it.

You must see the beauty in yourself. You must see the beauty in your life. It is much easier to change if you know where you're starting from and where you want to go. Hating where you are makes it harder to move forward. If you don't have what you want in your life try wanting what you have. If we hate our creation it is much harder to look at it truthfully. And only the truth can set you free.

There Is No The Truth

I spent years looking for the answer. I studied countless philosophies, religions, and metaphysical doctrines looking for the truth. I finally realized they were all belief systems developed by someone else. All of them were merely someone else's filter system. At first I found it upsetting but eventually I realized how freeing it really was. There is no such thing as the truth. I don't have to defend my beliefs because they aren't necessarily the truth.

Sage Advice
"Experience is not what happens to a man. It is what a man does with what happens to him."
Aldous Huxley

Everyone has his or her own truth and the truth is relative. There is no one truth. Truth is part of our perspective. Another word for the truth is a belief. Once we realize there is no 'the truth' we realize how things like right and wrong are relative. Once we let go of our need to find 'the truth' we are free to let go of many other limitations. We can stop searching for some ultimate yardstick against which to measure life and ourselves. We can begin to release our iron grip on our need to judge everything and everyone. We judge things so we can feel safe, so we feel like we are on the right side. If there is no 'the truth' we don't need to choose sides anymore either.

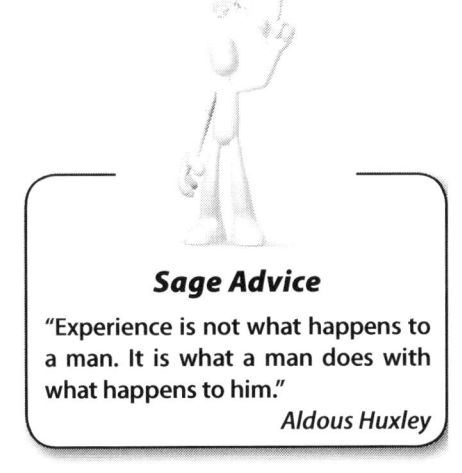

Giving up your quest for the truth will set you free. It will also allow you to see what your truth is for today and release your attachment to it. Defending yourself and your truth no longer prevents you from changing. Since there is no 'the truth' you can't be wrong. It becomes easier t accept the fact that you're perfect just the way you are.

Intent, the Wind Beneath My Wings

What is intent? It is the energy of creation. Say we want to be happy but at a core level we believe we will always be disappointed in life. We go about life trying to be happy but we always wind up feeling disappointed. Our underlying intent is to be disappointed so no matter what until we change our intent we will make choices that result in disappointment.

A railroad train can only go where the tracks take it. A switch can be thrown and the train will change directions but it still has to follow the tracks. Intent operates in much the same manner in our life. We create our life with our intent. Our life has no choice but to follow our intent. Once you start consciously using the energy of intent in your life it can be a very powerful force.

The Road to Hell

One of my mother's favorite sayings was, "The road to hell is paved with good intentions." I was always telling her I meant to do that and I did but my intent was to feel bad about myself so I forgot to follow through on my promises.

$$Intent + Attention = Intention$$

As a child I believed there was something wrong with me so my real intent was to feel bad about myself. No mater how hard I wanted to please my mother I couldn't because my attention was always distracted elsewhere. My attention would unconsciously be focused on upsetting my mother so she could tell me what a bad person I was. Becoming aware of your intent is a very important. You need what it is if you want to change anything.

So as you look at your life you begin to see your intent reflected there. Where do you focus your attention? Do you focus on what's wrong with you or what you love about yourself? How do your habitual thoughts make you feel most of the time? The answer to those questions will give you an indication of your intent. Are you going to judge yourself if you find out that your intent has been to feel disappointed or bad about yourself? If you do, that just indicates you need to change your intent.

> **Sage Advice**
> "The mind is restless, turbulent, obstinate, and very strong. To subdue it is more difficult than controlling the wind, but it is possible by constant practice and detachment. He who strives by right means is assured of success."
> *Bhagavad Gita*

> **Sage Advice**
> "We know accurately only a little, with knowledge doubt increases."
> *Goethe*

Freedom is a Choice

We aren't really free to choose until we are free to choose. If you choose freedom and continue to experience limitations you aren't free to choose freedom just yet. What do you mean I can't choose freedom yet? Until you are aware of your filter system and your intent you aren't free to choose anything. The only thing you are free to do is to make choices that are consistent with your intent and your filters. If it is your intent to remain the same no matter what you do, until you change that nothing will change.

I have had people study with me for years. They really seem to work hard. They came to class, asked lots of questions, explored, and stayed exactly the same. They rearranged their issues but nothing really changed. Their intent was to stay the same. A few of them were willing to see that and as soon as they changed their intent change happened very rapidly. Some weren't and they left feeling like the classes had failed them.

But How Do I Know?

How do you know what your intention is? Just look at your life. What kind of results are you getting in your life? Where do you focus most of your attention? If you are looking for what's wrong with you you don't really want to change. You want to find out what's wrong with you.

If you really want to change, if your intent is to change you will focus your attention on loving yourself or at least learning how to love yourself. You will make it your mission to accept yourself and your life as perfect just the way it is. You will make sure you talk to yourself in a gentle and loving manner. You will release any form of judgment you have about yourself or others. You will do whatever is necessary to connect with your spirituality. And you will keep moving in this direction. The moment you stop you'll know your intention has changed and you can again ask yourself, "Do I really want to change?" If the answer is yes you will change moment-by-moment where you focus your attention. And when you notice your attention has wavered gently refocus yourself.

You know what your intent is by looking at the results you are getting in your life. If you get angry a lot your intent to is to get angry. If you feel at peace most of the time and really love yourself your intent has been to be at peace and to love and accept yourself. Your life never lies. It will always show you exactly what you wanted to create. If you judge the creation you are part of the problem and not part of the solution.

There is no error in creating limitations. It is just an opportunity for you to create something else instead. If you don't like the creation change your focus and create something else. See your intent reflected in your life and change it. Fighting it, judging it, or pretending your intent isn't the creative energy in your life won't change anything. Blaming yourself or others in your life won't change a thing either but changing your intent will change it all.

Sage Advice

"You see things; and say, *Why?* But I dream things that never were: and I say, *Why not?*"

George Bernard Shaw

Choices and Outcomes

Life is merely a series of choices and outcomes woven together in a tale we call life. We make a choice and we get an outcome. We go to the store after it's been raining for days. We stand on the corner waiting for the light to change. We are lost in thought unaware of approaching cars. We are in a hurry so we are standing right at the edge of the road so we can cross as soon as the light changes. A car comes by, hits a huge puddle of muddy water, and we get soaked. We are furious how could that driver be so thoughtless!

If we explored a bit deeper we might find that you have a belief that people are thoughtless, hate rainy days, or dislike walking to the store. If we choose to stand in front of a huge puddle and not pay attention to oncoming traffic chances are we are going to get wet. But we don't consciously think of that when we choose to stand there. At some level we have a belief and in the context of that belief choosing to stand on that corner makes sense. Our beliefs caused us to get wet and feel angry.

Beginning to make our choices consciously with full awareness allows us to make our choices based on the outcomes we want to achieve. If we need to get wet we choose to take a shower or go for a swim. If some part of our filter system is triggered and we feel the need to get angry we can make a different choice. We can be aware of our filter system, the old need to get angry, and talk lovingly to the wounded part and find out what he or she really needs. We can also choose to be angry and enjoy doing it. The possibilities become limitless when we begin to consciously associate choices with outcomes.

Set Me Free Babe

Freedom is a very personal term. What one person sees as freedom another may experience as burdensome. When I studied with Don Miguel his teachings were designed to assist his students in achieving personal freedom. When I first began studying with him my definition of personal freedom was having a good paying job, a nice home, and enough money to go out and have fun. Over the years my definition of personal freedom has changed drastically. Today it has very little to do with external things like money, or homes. Today my freedom is based on things like peace of mind, inner tranquility, my ability to choose how I am feeling, and the ability to make choices that achieve the outcomes I desire.

Setting yourself free is ultimately a choice. The only thing that prevents you from being free right now is your attachment to your filter system.

But I Thought. . .

What do you think about change? Is it easy, hard, simple, complicated, or impossible? Really start noticing what you're thinking. Your choices are based on your thoughts, if you are unaware of your thoughts how are you going to change them? If the only thing you did was to stop judging yourself and others your life would change completely. But our filter system is totally contaminated with judgment. Your mind is in the habit of judging or observing everything in your life. (The term observing can be used as a friendly cover-up for judging.) Changing that pattern is a process that will yield tremendous benefits.

> **Spiritual Shortcuts**
>
> Over the Take a few minutes and write about attachment. What are you attached to? Are you attached to being right? Looking good? Youth? Money? Health? What thought patterns are you attached to? Do you have a judgment about your filter system? Do you have any resistance to accepting and loving yourself just the way you are? If you honestly looked at the events in your life what has your intent really been?
>
> If you judge yourself your intent is to judge yourself. If your intent is to heal yourself you must constantly focus your attention on self-love and self-acceptance. As soon as you find yourself judging anything, forgive yourself and focus on love instead.

But I thought we were going to talk about change! We have been we've been talking about some of the things that stop us from changing. This entire book is about change. As you read it your perspective will change and in the process so will your life. If you use the tools and actively participate in the process your ability to change will be greatly accelerated.

So love yourself, release judgment, and listen to your mind but don't believe what it tells you. Explore, experiment with new behaviors, play with this thing called change, and see what happens. If something works do it again, if it doesn't do something else. Observe your life and see what happens.

It's Simple but It's Not Easy

Change is simple and it takes a great deal of vigilance to change our thinking. Discipline and dedication can become two of your best friends and greatest assistants if you let them. Change is as simple as making different choices. That's all that's required.

> **Sage Advice**
>
> "The world is a looking glass. It gives back to every man a true reflection of his own thoughts.."
>
> *Thackery*

Keep change simple. Don't complicate it or make it harder than it has to be. Realize that all change basically comes down to learning how to love yourself. So simplify it, just focus on loving yourself and let everything else take care of itself.

How to Change Anything and Everything

Okay, so how specifically do we change things? Change is a process of uncovering, discovering, and discarding what no longer serves us in our life. Another way I describe the process of healing is first telling ourselves the truth, forgiving ourselves and others, and then filling ourselves with love.

- **Uncovering:** In this step we thoroughly explore all facets of the issue. You will need to observe the issue from as many different perspectives as possible. You might write, talk to trusted others, and do what ever it takes so you can tell yourself the truth about the issue. Is it really about money or self-abuse? You must uncover the answer to the question: What is the real issue?

- **Discovering:** Once you know what the issue is you need to discover how it has served you. Once you understand what a creative solution it was you can begin to forgive yourself and others. Everything we do serves us in some way, it may not assist us in achieving the results we want, but it does serve us. Often old behaviors allow us to avoid feeling the inherent pain in life. Living within our financial means is often emotionally painful; getting our body in shape takes work. Our old behaviors assist us in avoiding that discomfort.

- **Discarding:** In this step we let go of the old behaviors, beliefs, and situations that no longer serve us. Self-criticism, judgment, and abuse don't work. So in this part of the process we focus on loving ourselves and our old choices.

Healing with love

A woman and a group of people met with the Dalai Lama for several days. The meetings focused on dialoguing what they believed were the 5 most important questions to be considered moving into the new millennium. The group was asked to come up with five questions before meeting with the Dalai Lama. The questions were:

1. How do we address the widening gap between rich and poor?
2. How do we protect the earth?
3. How do we educate our children?
4. How do we help Tibet and other oppressed countries/peoples?
5. How do we bring spirituality - deep caring for each other – through all disciplines?

The Dalai Lama said all the questions fall under the last one. If we have true compassion our children will be educated, we will care for the earth, and for those who "have not." He asked the group: Do you think loving on the planet is increasing or staying the same? His own response was, "My experience leads me to believe that love is increasing."

He shared a practice with the group that will increase loving and compassion in the world, and asked everyone attending to go home and share it with as many people as possible.

- Spend 5 minutes at the beginning of each day remembering we all want the same thing (to be happy and loved) and we are all connected.
- Spend 5 minutes cherishing yourself and others. Let go of judgments. Breathe in cherishing yourself, and breathe out cherishing others. If the faces of people you are having difficulty with appear, cherish them as well.
- During the day extend that attitude to everyone you meet - we are all the same, and I cherish myself and you (do it with the grocery store clerk, the client, your family, coworkers, the person who cuts you off in traffic, the person who has more items than allowed in the check-out line, etc.).
- Stay in the practice, no matter what happens.

Just Make a New Choice

The only way to change anything is by making new choices. As long as we choose to see things the same way, think the same thoughts, or make the same choices nothing will change. We tend to be creatures of habit so making new choices requires effort. The emotional cost of that effort is often something our old behaviors assist us in hiding. Whenever you want to change anything take some time to get in touch with the emotional cost of making that change. If you take the time to feel the emotions you won't have to engage in old behaviors to avoid them.

For a week or two try changing all of your habits and routines. Go to work another way, eat different kinds of food, eat breakfast at night and dinner in the morning, get out of bed on the other side of the bed, everything you do habitually find a new way of doing it. Observe what happens. Do you feel uncomfortable; do you forget to do it after a day or two, what happens to you emotionally?

Forgiveness and Acceptance

This is such an important part of change. We seldom change things because we enjoy them we change things because we don't like something about them. When I work with people who are trying to break a habit like smoking one of the hardest things for them to do is accept the habit. We are almost afraid to do that because we're afraid that if we don't hate it we won't change it.

Any form of judgment acts like cosmic super glue. Anything you judge is yours to keep until you release the judgment. Once I realized that I was much more willing to release my judgments. Forgiveness and acceptance are really another way to say you've let go of your judgments. If you aren't judging something in the first place you won't have anything to forgive and you will have accepted it just the way it is. Life is what it is regardless of our judgments. Our opinion about people, places, and things doesn't affect anything except ourselves.

Smoke & Mirrors

Budda said anger is like picking up a hot coal and throwing it at someone else —we are the ones who get burned. When we are deeply hurt by someone, forgiveness seems impossible. We are free when we are able to forgive their actions. As long as we hold onto hurts from the past, we are limited by the past, and our happiness remains elusive.

There's no Such Thing as a Mistake

There really is no such thing as a mistake. Some results or outcomes are more pleasurable than others but there are never any mistakes. For years I would lament choices I had made, if I hadn't made that mistake my life would be just fine. I judged what happened, I judged my choices, and I judged the choices of those around me. The idea that anyone could make a mistake is a judgment in itself.

Viewing something as a mistake makes it much harder for us to see it or understand it with clarity. Judging something as a mistake says much more about our filter system than it does about the "mistake." If we look at the feelings we are having that make us want to call it a mistake we can clear a portion of our filter system. If we focus on the mistake we won't.

Embracing Everything is the Only Way to Let Go

Like I said if you judge something you're stuck with it. If on the other hand you embrace it changing it or letting it go is so much easier. One way to think of your life is to think of a large circle. Everything that's available to you is within that circle. Outside of that circle is everything that's beyond your belief system. Trying to push something out of the circle isn't a very effective way to change. Every time you push something out of the circle you circle gets a little bit smaller.

If you begin to embrace things your circle gets larger and larger. If you want to stop smoking trying to push the behavior out of your circle won't allow yourself to understand it so you can let it go. If you continue to judge smoking you won't be able to see the things like relaxation, contemplation, and moderate eating you have attached to it. If you push smoking out of your circle you also loose those behaviors attached to it. So invite it in, accept it, and love it. Smoking has a message for you. Once you hear it you can shift your behavior.

If you embrace your addiction you can dialog with it, you can understand how it has served you and find other ways to meet those needs. If you don't embrace it loving yourself becomes much harder and self-love is the foundation upon which to build your life. Just allow for the possibility that if you embrace anything you want to change it will be easier for you to change it. And isn't that really the point, making change easier?

The Least You Need to Know

> Self-love makes change so much easier.
> You have to accept where you are before you can move on.
> Change is a process and if you do each step success is guaranteed.
> You are perfect just the way you are.

Chapter 14

Journaling

> **In This Chapter**
>
> ➤ Realize what a valuable tool journaling really is.
>
> ➤ Begin to quiet your mind.
>
> ➤ See a way out of emotional turmoil.
>
> ➤ Get past your resistance.

When I first started doing my emotional and spiritual healing someone suggested I start journaling. If looks could kill they would've been very dead. And they were right, the most powerful tool I ever found is writing. As long as we think about things or talk about them we can get caught in thought loops. We can go round and round like a rat on one of those wheels.

Putting pen to paper is incredibly freeing and often our resistance to doing it is immense. As I was told, do whatever it takes to make yourself do it but just make sure you do it.

Write? . . . Yeah Right!

When I suggest people start writing on a daily basis most of them get a glazed look in their eyes. Until I realized what a valuable asset it was in my life I fought the idea of doing it vehemently. When I realized that I could actually change the way I thought, that I didn't have to continue thinking 95% of the same thoughts day after day I changed my mind.

At first I viewed journaling like a life long term paper, not a wonderful image. When I finally realized it was my ticket to freedom I tried it and found out how well it worked. The more resistance you have to the idea the more freeing it will be when you finally develop the habit of writing.

But I Don't Want To

For years I've been a Star Trek fan. One of the species, the Borg has a wonderful saying that is very applicable to journaling and many other things in life as well. "Resistance is futile." Our mind will generally resist the very thing that will set us free. I suggest that if you really want to heal you move toward your resistance instead of away from it.

If you have a great deal of resistance to writing make a list of all the reasons for and against. If you've never tried it you'll have to take my word for the fact that it works. Take a few minutes and write down why you're exploring spiritual healing in the first place. What improvements do you want to make in your life? What would it be like if you really loved yourself and your life unconditionally? That would show you some of the reasons you want to write. Writing will assist you in changing your life. Sneaky way to get you started writing isn't it?

Sage Advice
"When we accept tough jobs as a challenge to our ability and wade into them with joy and enthusiasm, miracles can happen."
Arland Gilbert

Thought Loops

When we think about a problem we tend to get caught in thought loops. We see the issue the same way, think the same things, and have the same conversations in our mind over and over again. Our thinking gets stuck in the same pattern and we go round and around the same issue and never get anywhere.

When we think about an issue it is very hard to see it from a different perspective. We are entrenched in our filter system seeing the issue through our filter system so clarity remains illusive. Writing helps us get beyond out thought loops. Seldom do we write the same thought endlessly. We can pick the issue up, turn it over, and perhaps see it from a different perspective.

Sage Advice
"We cling to our point of view, as though everything depends on it. Yet our opinions have no permanence; like autumn and winter, they gradually pass away."
Chuang Tzu

The Way Out

When we have resistance to anything the way to get beyond it is to embrace it. One of the ways I've found to do that is to begin by acknowledging I have resistance, look at the task, and then break it down into manageable pieces.

With writing I started by getting a notebook and putting it on my desk. Then I looked at it for a few days and just sat with my feelings about writing. I was careful not to judge my feelings, I felt them, and let them be. Then one day I decided I'd pick up the journal and write the date along with a few words about how I was feeling. I did that, put down the journal, and gave myself a lot of praise for following through. Gradually I increased my commitment to the process until I was able to sit and write everyday.

I found most people's resistance to writing is really due to a fear of judgment. No one need ever see your journal. If you are afraid someone might read it find a safe place for it or carry it with you. No one is going to judge your spelling, grammar, or content except you. And remember we are trying not to judge anything anymore. Be gentle with yourself. Writing is a very powerful tool and it will bring up some uncomfortable feelings and insights. But we can't heal what we don't know is there. The way out of emotional pain and turmoil is writing on a regular basis.

Stalking Yourself

As you've probably figured out by now if you want to improve the quality of your life you need to release your filter system or at least clear it out a little. In order to release your filter system first you have to find it. Our filter system is so much a part of us that it is almost impossible for us to see it. We believe our version of reality and seldom stop to think that maybe we aren't right in our assessment of the situation. Our mate could actually be saying I love you and not trying to pick a fight.

> **Sage Advice**
> "There is only one corner of the universe you can be certain of improving and that's your own self."
> Aldous Huxley

We all want the same thing, to be happy. Our filter system tells us how we are going to achieve happiness. I used to volunteer at the local prison teaching the inmates anger and stress management. One of the inmate's filter system told him that breaking into someone else's house was the way to relieve stress. As a young child his parents had severely beaten him so he ran away. After that they tied him to a tree when they beat him so he wouldn't run away. When his insides started to churn he got rid of the feeling by breaking into someone's home. His filter system chose his actions for him. If he changed his filter system his decisions would automatically change.

Stalking your filter system will allow you to see how it affects your life. Once you clearly see what it's creating in your life it's easier to let it go.

Finding the trail

Stalking yourself is like following a trail that leads to your true self. Our filter system causes a schism it separates us from ourselves. Writing is a wonderful way to find yourself. Have you ever watched a cat stalking its prey? It sits very quietly and watches. When it decides the time is right it pounces. The cat spends most of its youth learning how to hunt. As kittens they play, watch, and learn. They learn how to stalk their prey so they can be successful hunters as adults.

As children no one taught us how to stalk our mind. No one taught us how to listen to our mind without believing what it says. Stalking is doing just that. We stalk our filter system with full awareness that it's the problem not the events or people in our life.

Most of the time we point our finger at them out there and think they are the cause of our emotional turmoil. When we stalk ourselves we don't focus on external causes, we focus our attention on our mind and what we tell ourselves. We focus on finding our filter system and changing it. We decide we would rather be happy then right. Once we firmly focus our attention on our filter system we are at the beginning of the trail.

Spiritual Shortcuts

When an issue comes up set aside time to write about it. Find a place you won't be disturbed, turn off the phone, and don't answer the door. It is too easy to distract ourselves from this process. Sit down and begin writing.

Once we are beginning to feel emotions it's too late not to feel them so just write about them. As vividly as possible describe what you are feeling. Rant and rave about what they did to you if you feel that way. Get the feelings out of your system.

When you're done step back and look at the event or issue from another perspective. Without expressing any emotions or opinions write about the issue as neutrally as possible. Look at it symbolically, what did it mean to you?

After you have done that follow your feelings. Go back as far as you can in your memory and keep following the feeling. Keep going until you find the first time you felt that way. See it from the perspective of that small child. Now as an adult see the event. What did you decide so many years ago? How else could you look at it? If you saw the event through the eyes of love how would it look? If you realized that this event had the ability to help you remember your own divine nature what would you see? What part of your filter system was that event illuminating for you? We need to see our filters in order to let them go, every event in your life gives you the opportunity to see another part of your filter system if you let it. Write until you can see beyond the event and recognize your filter instead.

This process could take five minutes or days. Sometimes I have to write about the same issue over and over again until I can see my filters clearly and the issue is always about our filters.

Which Way Did I Go?

We lose ourselves to our filter system over the years. As a child we had an open heart, we were absolutely vulnerable, and trusting. Then we got hurt and we became a little more wary. Eventually we decided vulnerability wasn't safe and closed down bit by bit. We lost ourselves, we lost our true nature, and we become a puppet of our filter system.

Think of all the automatic reactions you have to life. We have so many triggers; a tone of voice, a smell, the way the light is, certain phrases, or our feelings. I saw a plaque that had a prayer on it thanking god for serenity, peace, and the ability to remain loving in the face of adversity. It went on to say that I'm about to get out of bed so I might need more help to continue doing that.

We decide we are going to be kind or more loving and before you know it we are angry again. Writing will assist you in finding the triggers and changing them. I had a student who was very uncomfortable in a grocery store that was being remodeled. She tracked it and realized that as a young girl she had almost drowned. The lighting in the store had the same quality so she felt uncomfortable.

Use you feelings as bridges as you write. Let your feelings act as a bridge between your filter system and you. Explore the bridge, write about it, describe it, and follow it back to its origin.

Now Where Do I Have to Go?

I remember the young idealist that was going to change the world. Before I started on my spiritual journey I had lost myself. Since then I have learned to redefine myself, to explore what really matters to me, and to make my decisions based on that information. One of the things I did along the way was define my own principles.

My mentor suggested I spend time examining my principles, what really mattered to me. I found that I didn't really know what mattered to me. I knew what my parents and society told me was important but I had never sat down and decided for myself. As I began stalking my filter system I saw that fear often caused me to abandon my values. I would take actions that flew in the face of everything that mattered to me if I were afraid. I would lash out in anger if you got to close because I was afraid of intimacy. Yet I said I wanted intimacy.

As you come to understand your filter system and explore your principles you'll begin to see the conflict. Defending our filter system prevents us from being true to ourselves. Until we make the conscious choice to clear out our filter system we will abandon the very things that matter the most.

Defining Your Principles

Defining my principles was a real struggle for me so I did some research. I read philosophy books on principles. The word "principle" stems from the Latin and Greek root that means beginning or foundation.

I began looking at my morals. The word "morals" had a negative connotation for me until I realized that a moral law was simply a fundamental principle of human conduct. I began defining my personal laws of conduct. I decided what was truly important to me. What's really important to you?

As you define your principles make sure they are your own personal values. Start by writing about who you really are. Write a short description of yourself as you want to be and distill your principles from that.

When I did this process for the first time in my life I decided what was really important to me. When I thought about cleanliness I realized personal hygiene had always been important to me but cleaning the house was a different matter. I'd always cleaned it because I felt I had to. After defining my principles I realized I really enjoyed having the house clean. I then began cleaning the house for myself and enjoying the process.

When I first defined my principles I came up with this list for myself: kind, giving, loving, loyal (to myself), reverent, thoughtful, intelligent, tenacious, truthful, harmonious, trustworthy, and considerate. I can now use these adjectives to review my actions. When I go against one of my principles I can see my filter system in action and begin to change it.

Take some time and define your principles. What is important to you? What sort of attributes do you admire in others? Do you like it when people are kind and gentle? Decide how you want to act in your life and define your principles to support that image of yourself.

Clarity Corner

Principles are an operating system. They are rules of conduct that govern our actions. Each culture has there own unique set of principles. Most often principles are set forth by society and embraced by the individual.

Developing a New Set of Antennas

Lobsters have two antennas they use to keep track of what's going on around them. In Hawaii moray eels live in holes in the coral and they love to eat lobsters. Lobsters frequently take up residency below a moray eel nest because they can eat the excess pieces of flesh the moray eels drops and because they are safe from other predators. They do have to focus their attention or their antennae on their protector though in case it decides to eat them. They keep one antennas facing up toward the moray eel and one toward the ocean in front of them.

Most human beings have their external antennas highly developed but they forget to go inside and see what's happening there. We forget to monitor our filter system. The eel is both the lobsters protector and potential destroyer. If the lobster isn't vigilant it could be the eels dinner. If we don't develop our internal antennae we could be destroyed by our filter system. We might not be literally destroyed but the quality of our life will be diminished.

Going inside and becoming aware of our inner landscape will assist us in developing our internal antennae. Remembering to ask yourself the questions in the last chapter will greatly assist you in developing that inner awareness. If the lobster loses focus and forgets to keep track of what the eel is doing he risks death. If you keep reacting to life the same way you've always done, what are you risking?

The Answer is Under Your Nose

Actually the answer is between your ears. And the question is always what am I telling myself about this that is causing my emotional upset. Stalking yourself is a process of constantly refocusing your attention. Something external happens in our lives and we get upset. It is too late not to be upset because we are already upset. That's just what is.

> **Smoke & Mirrors**
>
> Happiness is only ours when we learn to use both our internal and external antennas. When we are unaware of what is really going on inside, we make decisions based on our filter system instead of our desired outcome. If we aren't using our external antennas, we won't know what is going on around us, and we are apt to forget our rain jackets on a rainy day.

You didn't do anything wrong you just listened to your filter system so you got upset. Don't judge yourself for having emotions. Emotions are part of being human. Your emotional turmoil gives you an opportunity to see your beliefs and another piece of your filter system. You can use that information to heal or you can continue to upset yourself by telling yourselves all about what happened. You can get caught up in the story or you can choose to become part of the solution. Either way you'll learn about yourself and your reactions.

When we are feeling emotionally upset it is very hard to detach and hear what we are telling ourselves. Our mind wants to be right it certainly doesn't want to admit its belief structure has anything to do with our emotional turmoil. The other person or the outcome is what's upsetting us – it has nothing to do with anything except their thoughtlessness or the fact that they fired us or . . .. The story is the problem.

We can't detach from the person or event until we are able to detach. Sometimes it takes minutes and sometimes years. Write about the event as soon as you can. Writing about it will assist you in getting clear as rapidly as possible.

A man I knew hated a man for over twenty years. The man had stolen his reputation by lying about him. He spent years plotting and planning how he was going to get even with him. He wanted to destroy this man's reputation. One day he had a heart attack and he realized his hatred was only hurting himself. He wanted to forgive his former friend. Shortly after that he found out the man died eighteen years earlier. He had wasted eighteen years hating someone who was already dead. How much time have we all wasted blaming our upset on someone else instead of looking at the real cause is our filter system and freeing ourselves from our limitations?

> **Sage Advice**
>
> "Life can only be understood backwards; but it must be lived forward."
> *Kierkegaard*

Daily Pages

Spending a few minutes every morning and every evening journaling is incredibly freeing. I call them daily pages because you do them every day. Having a daily routine designed to facilitate your healing is a wonderful practice to develop. It sets the tone for the whole day and it will help remind you to stay focused on what's really important.

I set aside about a half an hour every morning to write, meditate, and get centered. When I need to be out of the house early I just get up a bit earlier. I find that half an hour makes the rest of the day flows and is much less stressful. If things get really rough I retreat to the bathroom, take a few deep breaths, and connect with my inner self.

There are times it feels like my mind is sitting on the edge of my bed waiting for me to wake up. The moment I start to stir it starts talking, sharing its version of life, how tough it is, how tired I'm going to be, how rough the day could be, and what a mess I've created in my life so far. It might have a huge list of things I should do that day or share conversations I might have with people in my life. Once, when I was feeling particularly good, my mind whispered to me, "What if you get cancer?" It was so out of context I laughed but the comment could have just as easily hooked my attention.

A Morning Ritual

Every morning before you eat or take a shower sit down and write. Get up, go to the bathroom, sit down, and write. Write at least three full size pages. Don't think about writing just write down any thing you are thinking. If your mind says I don't want to write – write that down. Just put all the rambling thoughts you have down on that blank piece of paper. Write until you fill up the three pages. Then if you have other morning practices such as meditating, yoga, or going for a walk do those.

After about a page and a half your mind begins to clear. You may notice thought loops or patterns. You might realize you need broccoli for breakfast. It is amazing what happens after you write three pages every morning for a period of time. You are taking out the mental trash. After you fill up a book you might want to take it outside and burn it – release all the stuff your mind hold onto so tightly.

When the Evening Winds Down

Sit down and write for ten to fifteen minutes. Briefly review the day. Were there any rough spots? Do you have any emotional turmoil lurking around? Do you need to stalk some old behavior or an event? Look at the high points as well. How did you share yourself with others? Were you loving? Give yourself a pat on the back for a job well done you lived through another day.

Before you finish writing write a list of at least ten things that you're grateful for. Finish your day with a feeling of gratitude.

Write Now

There is no time like the present to write. I carry a journal around with me and when I have a few spare moments I write. "Ah, but you're a writer," your mind says. "Of course you write!" But I wasn't always a writer. I hated journaling and writing. In school English was my worse subject but then I discovered the benefits and my resistance disappeared. That's not to say there aren't times I know I need to write that I don't. But when the emotional pain is great enough I start writing again.

Start off slowly. Find some time to get a journal you like and pen that is comfortable for you to write with. The first time you sit down to write just write the date and maybe a few lines about how you're feeling, how you don't want to write. Take things slowly but make writing on a regular basis non-negotiable.

Feeling Grateful All Over

When we are connected with our spiritual self we are living life from a place of love. When we are listening to our filter system our choices are all fear based. When we take the time to feel grateful we are automatically connecting with our spiritual self. Gratitude is amazing. It's like laughter, it keeps expanding, and it's contagious. The more gratitude you have the better life seems so you have more to be grateful for.

Whenever you have a spare moment think of all the things you're grateful for. When you're waiting in line or driving your car mentally make a gratitude list. When I was first started working with gratitude lists I was deeply in debt. Worrying about money only made matters worse so I decided to try gratitude. I took at my pile of bills and blessed each and everyone. I was grateful that I was able to incur those bills and I was grateful for the money I would use to pay them. I thought about people in underdeveloped places that were starving to death. I am sure they would be very grateful to be living my life, bills, and all. It didn't take very long before I was completely out of debt.

If you have health challenges or things about your life you hate try using gratitude. The amount of freedom I experience every time I release one of my limiting thought patterns is immense. While I am in the midst of the issue I am often experiencing emotional turmoil, I am not happy. If I am grateful for the unhappiness it is far easier to see the issue and deal with it. Be thankful for even you biggest challenges. Gratitude will help to set you free.

Every night before you go to bed take a few minutes to write a gratitude list. Add something new every day. If you wrote ten things yesterday write fifteen today. Make your list longer every day and watch your life change.

For What's it Worth

What is peace of mind worth to you? What is waking up every morning with a sense of excitement and joy worth? What would you be willing to give in order to love every moment of your life? What if you loved your body, had everything you needed, and could choose to be happy all the time? Would you like to have any or all of that?

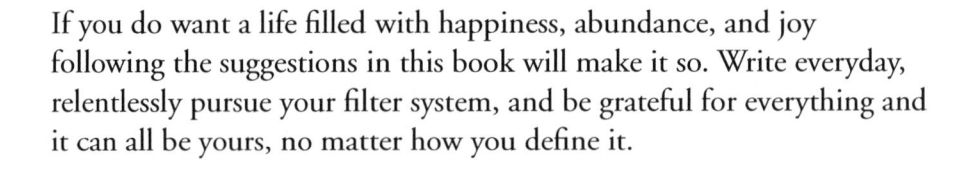

If you do want a life filled with happiness, abundance, and joy following the suggestions in this book will make it so. Write everyday, relentlessly pursue your filter system, and be grateful for everything and it can all be yours, no matter how you define it.

Stopping the Mind

The mind talks to you, it thinks that's its job. Imagine having a computer that talked to you. As soon as you walked into the room it would start nagging at you, telling you what to think, how to feel, and what to do next. You'd probably shut it off and take it to the repair shop.

Your mind is meant to be your tool not your taskmaster. It is an absolutely magnificent bio-computer that is far superior to anything we've developed. It is a computer and it wasn't designed to be in charge it is an interface between our spirit and the physical world.

Staying in the Station

The first step in quieting the mind is learning how to detach from it. For years I believed I was my thoughts, they defined me, and gave me my sense of identity. Now I know that my thoughts are just background noise that can distract me. If I choose to listen to them there is a strong probability that I will make my choices based in fear instead of love. When my mind is screaming at me it is hard to listen to the voice of my heart or spiritual center.

My mind always tries to convince me that it's right, it will plead, beg, yell, and if need be demand I believe its version of the truth. My spirit will quietly suggest that I might want to view things in another fashion or perhaps my greatest good lies this way. I have learned to listen to the quiet still voice of my spirit.

> **Sage Advice**
> "We should every night call ourselves to account: What infirmity have I mastered today? What passions opposed? What temptation resisted? What virtues acquired? Our vices will abate of themselves if they are brought every day to task."
> *Seneca*

> **Sage Advice**
> "Paradise is exactly like where you are right now, only much, much better."
> *William Seward Burroughs*

Detaching from you mind allows you to listen to your inner guidance and wisdom. One way to stop listening to thoughts is to think of your thoughts as trains. Imagine yourself standing at the station. Trains constantly come in and out of the station. You can choose to get on the train or stay at the station and watch it go by. If you find yourself going for ride on one of the trains just get off and get back to the station.

Whenever you find yourself caught up in your thoughts step back and observe them instead. Don't judge yourself, just notice that your attention has been hooked by your thoughts, and let go. As soon as you notice you're hooked step back and start observing your thoughts go by.

Where Are You Going With That?

Our minds do ramble. Once you start observing your thoughts you will be amazed at how your mind gets from a to z. My minds logic is often very illogical. Observing your mind will assist you in seeing your filter system with greater clarity.

Begin to track your thoughts. If you find yourself caught up in your thoughts follow then backwards. See how your mind hooked your attention. Let your mind wander and see where it takes you. Observe and allow yourself to begin to understand how your mind operates. Don't get attached or judge your mind just observe it.

As you write your daily pages and observe your thoughts you will come to understand how you think. Then it will be easier to change what you think. Imagine how much nicer your life would be if there were an inner voice encouraging you, telling you how wonderful you are, and guiding you lovingly.

Silence is Such a Relief

My computer has a sleep mode built into it. I can set it to shut off after a predetermined length of time. The screen goes blank and my computer sits there quietly. As soon as I touch a key the monitor comes back on and my computer is ready to serve me.

A quiet mind is an incredible gift. A quiet mind assists us in our internal explorations rather than distracting us. When our mind is quiet it is much easier to hear the quiet still voice of our spirit. When I am upset about something it is very hard for me to make a decision. But if I can quiet my mind it is much easier for me to see my options.

Several years ago I taught a class about connecting with your spiritual self. One of the assignments was to spend at least one day a month in silence. The idea was to make it a special day, a day of solitude, and reflection. Perhaps spend time out in nature, take long hot baths, nap, read, and write. Allow your environment to be silent. Sit with the silence and allow it to fill you. It is a very powerful experience of self-renewal.

The Least You Need to Know

- Journaling is your ticket to personal freedom.
- If you let gratitude fill your life your life will be full.
- Your answers always lie within yourself

Part 4
When Your Body Yells, Listen

Our body is constantly sending us signals but we seldom listen. I learned the hard way to pay attention to the signals my car sends me. When it starts acting funny I'd better have it looked at if I don't want to be stranded someplace. Whenever I ignore my cars early warning signs I wind up standing by the side of the road.

Our bodies have early warning signs. They tell us when we need more rest, reduce our stress level, get more exercise, eat more broccoli, or take a vacation. Most of us haven't been trained to listen to our bodies.

For years when I needed to slow down I would get a cold. Then I'd take a few days off, stay in bed, and relax. But after my few days of rest I'd still have the remnants of a cold and feel miserable for a week or two. Eventually I noticed the pattern and would take a day off, relax in bed, read, and nap before I got sick. That way I'd get my day off without another week or two of discomfort.

This next section is about paying attention to your body, learning to hear your subtle body's subtle signals. Our mind, body, and spirit are interconnected. If any part of the trinity is out of balance it affects the other two. Balance and harmony are necessary ingredients if you want to have a happy and healthy life.

Chapter 15

Mind/Body/Spirit Connection

> **In This Chapter**
>
> ➤ Realize the power of your mind.
>
> ➤ Find out about harmony and balance.
>
> ➤ Remember what a powerful being you really are.

The mind, body, spirit connection is very powerful. If anyone of the three is out of balance it is very hard to focus on either of the other two. If we are in physical pain it is hard to think or connect with our spirit. If we are out of balance with our spirit or our inner self it is hard to maintain our physical and mental well-being.

How we think and what we think about affects our physical body. If we focus all of our attention on our work and neglect our body eventually our health will suffer. Living a balanced life style allows us to achieve the best results. Listening to our mind, our body, and our spirit will create a rich life.

What do You Mean, It's All in My Head

Our experience in life is based on what we tell ourselves about the event rather than the event itself. And our mind doesn't know the difference between imagination and physical reality.

Imagine looking at a beautiful bright yellow lemon. Hold it in your hand and look at it closely. Notice the bumps on the skin, smell its clean sweet odor. Imagine slicing it open with a sharp knife and see the juices run out of it. Bring it close to your nose, smell it, and then take a big juicy bite of it. If you were really following the description your mouth probably salivated. Spend a few minutes imagining biting into a lemon and your mouth will react. Your mind doesn't know the difference between a real lemon and a lemon you conjure up in your mind.

Our thoughts constantly create pictures for our mind. If we are often afraid and worry constantly about getting sick or having no money we will automatically make choices that will create our fears. I have seen people who believed they'd get a cold if they got wet. Sure enough a few days later they'd be miserable with a cold.

Our mind is incredibly powerful. Our mind constantly monitors our body's functions. It controls our immune system, our blood pressure, and our temperature. It tells our body when to breath and automatically increases our respiration when we need more oxygen. And our thoughts affect what our mind tells our body to do.

When someone is in a deep hypnotic trance you can tell them you are about to touch them with a very hot poker. No matter what you touch them with their body will produce a blister at the point of contact.

I used to organize fire walks. I would build a huge bonfire and talk to the people as they watched the huge logs being consumed by the flames. Before they walked on the fire I talked about the power of the mind, spiritual energy, and raising the body's energy vibration so it wouldn't burn. Then I would rake out the coals and have people walk across a five or six feet of glowing hot coals. They would reach the other side and their feet would be untouched by the fire. It was a wonderful demonstration of the power of the mind and the spirit.

When we get sick our body is responding to some hidden messages it has received from our mind, perhaps for years. We don't make ourselves get sick because we are bad people or we are doing something wrong. We get sick because life is a mirror it is a cosmic movie with a hundreds of story lines. Since we are the writer, the director, and the main character in our movie we can choose how we are going to react to our story line. Other people in our lives have their own cosmic movies, sometimes our story lines overlap, and we play roles in each other's movies.

Sage Advice

"It is as painful to be awakened from a vision as to be born."
James James Augustine

Smoke & Mirrors

Beliefs aren't real, yet you use them to create your reality. If you focus a great deal of your attention on a fear, you greatly increase your likelihood of experiencing that fear. Rather than try to ignore your fears, play them out fully. Imagine all the gory details, and then ask yourself whether that is really what you want to experience. Tell yourself "I don't need to experience that." If the fear returns, remember your decision and focus on what you do want.

Being sick is really just another story line, not a very pleasant one, but a story line nonetheless. Our spirits can't get sick or die after all they're immortal. Our bodies can get sick, have intense physical pain, heal, or die. Physical reality is often very dramatic. Illness can totally consume our lives. Poverty, loneliness, incarceration, success, or any other story line can really hook our attention and make us believe its real.

We forget about what's really important in life. We get caught up in our little lives and loose our compassion. We think life revolves around us and we forget about society as a whole. We pollute the earth in the name of profit we mortgage our future to be happy today. We forget to love one another and take care of all creatures' great and small, including ourselves.

But life is really all in your head. Physical reality as we perceive it isn't real, it is a delusion of our filter system. The page you are reading is really made up of far more empty space than solid matter. But it sure does look solid. The paper this book is printed on is composed of atoms. Atoms are bits of matter rapidly moving around a solid core. There is a great deal of space between the tiny bits of matter but they are moving so fast we think they're solid.

If we were able to totally release our beliefs about matter being solid walking through walls or on water would be no problem. I have seen people put knitting needles through their arms and leave no mark on the skin when they were withdrawn. Mind over matter. If you learn how to harness the power of the mind, body, and spirit miracles are possible. They can become an every day occurrence if you're willing to let go of your old limiting beliefs.

As with anything else if you judge where you are it makes it much harder to get where you'd like to be. When I first ran across some of these concepts I judged myself terrible the first time I got a cold. What had I done wrong now, I was sick, and I knew it was all in my mind.

I hadn't done anything wrong. I just got a cold. Once I reviewed my actions prior to getting sick I realized I hadn't paid attention to my body. I hadn't gotten enough rest, I wasn't eating properly, and I wanted to take sometime off for myself. At that point I couldn't give myself permission to take a day off without a good reason so I got a cold.

Sage Advice
"Do not be too timid and squeamish about your actions. All life is an experiment. The more experiments you make the better. What if they are a little course, and you may get your coat soiled or torn? What if you do fail, and get fairly rolled in the dirt once or twice? Up again, you shall never be so afraid of a tumble."
Ralph Waldo Emerson

Once again understanding and releasing your filter system is your key to freedom and any sort of meaningful happiness.

Your Mind is Always Listening

In any given moment your mind is aware of hundreds of bits of information and it picks, and chooses which it thinks are important, and then filters out the unimportant ones. Your mind is aware of hundreds of things you aren't even consciously awareness of.

> **Spiritual Shortcuts**
>
> What really matters to you? If you had a magic wand and you could change anything, what would you change? Would you think only of your life or would you think of the greater whole?
>
> Take sometime and write about what matters to you now. What mattered to you as a child? What do you do on a daily basis to improve the quality of your life and those around you?
>
> Find some way to give back to your community. Give of yourself and your time. Often we'd rather give our money than give of ourselves. If you really love children, volunteer to hold crack-addicted babies, or share your love with homeless animals. You are the most valuable gift you have to give.

Years ago the government banned subliminal advertising because it was so effective. Years ago the movie industry experimented with it. They replaced a few frames in a movie and put in their place a suggestion to go buy soda and popcorn. The ad was so short it wasn't visible yet over half the people in the theater got up and bought snacks.

Most of our wants and needs are created in the same way. We see beautiful people smoking cigarettes, having fun, and living magical lives. The ads tell us that smoking will bring the same magic to our lives so we force ourselves to smoke. We ignore the coughing and the taste and before you know it we're hooked.

Our mind is constantly taking in hundreds of subtle pieces of information from ads, from other people's comments, from our environment, and from the thoughts we think. If we don't consciously choose what we want to believe or the thoughts we will act upon our mind decides for us.

Imagine someone suddenly appearing in your world with no prior knowledge of you or our society. They understood the language but other than that everything else was new. What do you think they think of your world? Would they think it was a fun place or fearful? If they saw the world through your eyes, heard your inner dialog, and were privy to your inner most thoughts what assumptions do you think they'd make about you? Do you think they would feel we were a loving and caring species?

Your mind is always listening to your thoughts and monitoring your feelings. When I was a teenager my favorite belief was a short life but a merry one. I told all my friends I would be dead before I reached twenty-five. Of course by the time I hit my twenties I forgot all about my high school prediction. The year I was twenty-four I was in and out of the hospital. I was diagnosed with migraines and ulcers. I had a variety of undiagnosed ailments. After several hospital visits I remembered how I had always said I was going to die before I was twenty-five. My mind had been listening. As soon as I remembered my prediction my illnesses stopped. Was it just a coincidence? Perhaps but whatever we place our focus on we create. Which would you rather create, a life that is based in fear or based in love?

Your mind is always listening so practice quieting your mind. If you are terrified of not having enough money you will probably experience a lack of abundance in your life. If you want to feel loved take the time to love others as well as yourself. The greatest gift we can give to ourselves is the one we freely give to others with no expectation of return. If we love in order to be loved it won't work but if we love just to love our hearts will be filled as we give to others.

A mind filled with fear and self-judgment can't love. A mind filled with love has enough of everything to share with everyone. Practice cherishing others and yourself as the Dalai Lama suggests and your mind will be filled with thoughts of love. Filling your mind with kindness and joy creates a beautiful reflection in your life. Fear and anger reflects pain and limitation, the choice is yours. If you choose your thoughts carefully your life will take care of itself.

So many people have judgments about their body. We don't pay attention to this vehicle, we don't treat it with kind and loving thoughts. What sort of a mental diet do we feed our bodies? I've heard people say, "I'm just getting old." We often believe old is synonymous with being infirm. Many companies require people to retire at a certain age like they magically become unable to work on a certain day. Each of has hundreds of beliefs about our physical health and well-being, about old age, and about the causes of disease. Doctors study diseases and people that are unhealthy. How many studies are there about people who are healthy? Do we study healthy, happy people who are leading fulfilling lives to see what they are doing? Do we know how to create health or are we more concerned with curing diseases?

Three for the Price of One

Al three aspects of ourselves must be in balance. If we favor any one the other two suffer. In this section of the book we are going to focus mainly on the body. But it is important to remember the mind and the spirit affect the body. The moment the spirit leaves the body it starts to decay. If our mind is in a constant state of agitation, the body will fall prey to stress related illnesses.

Sage Advice

"Everybody wants to be somebody; nobody wants to grow."
Goethe

Smoke & Mirrors

Some doctors believe 99 percent of all illnesses are psychosomatic in origin–that almost all illnesses have their origins in the mind. Depending on your personality type, lifestyle, and general mental attitude, you are more likely to have certain diseases.

Our body reacts energetically to all three aspects of the trinity. Physical reality is the most dense and slowest moving energetically of our mind, body, and soul. We can change our thoughts in a moment but it takes time to change our physical body. Our physical body reacts to things like exercise, the type, quality, and quantity of food, it also reacts to our thoughts, and our level of connection to our spirit.

In order to maintain optimum physical health we must attend to all aspects of our temple. Of all the trinities the most important one to attend to is thought, word, and action. Your body is always listening. If you think I am getting old your body will oblige. If you complain about aches and pains to your friends your body will agree with you. If you don't act loving toward your body your body won't act lovingly toward itself. Think of all the times you've had judgments about your body. Ask yourself what kind of messages you are feeding your body on a daily basis.

> **Clarity Corner**
>
> The **trinity** is a concept that appears over and over again in our religions and philosophies: Father, Son, and Holy Ghost; mind, body, and spirit; conscious, subconscious, and superconscious; id, ego, and super ego; thought, word, and action. Our concept of time and space is also divided into three parts; time has the past, present, and future while space has here, there, and the space in between.

Talking to Your Body

Your body responds to not only how you physically take care of your body it also responds to the thoughts you have about it. Put yourself on a thirty day mental diet. For the next thirty days spend ten to fifteen minutes loving your body. You'll be amazed what happens.

- Find a place you won't be disturbed and take a few minutes to relax and get centered. Remember you are here to love your body not judge it!

- Starting at your feet and mentally review every nook and cranny of your body. Find at least one part of your body you really like. It could be your little toe, your eyes, or any other part of your body. Allow yourself to connect with that feeling of love and acceptance.

- Now start with a part of your body you don't like. Talk lovingly to that part, ask it to forgive you for your thoughtlessness and your judgment. Talk gently and lovingly to that part and realize that it is part of your creation and your vehicle for this lifetime. Gradually expand the process until you can talk to every part of your body with love and respect.

- If you still have a judgment about your body find something about those parts you can accept and start with acceptance and move toward love. If you have any physical ailments spend extra time loving that part of your body, love even your pain, and physical limitations.

- Before you go to bed at might spend a few minutes thanking every part of your body for serving you all day. Surround each part of your body with love and light as you fall asleep.

Do You Know Your Own Power?

There is a great deal of power in the mind, body, and spirit connection. You do have the power to change anything, be anything, and have it all if you really put attention to your thoughts, your words, and the actions you take.

Everyone ages differently. I am often saddened when I see an elder person shuffling along unable to straighten up. They look like they've been beaten down by life. Yet you see other older people full of life, spry, and enjoying there lives to the fullest. Some of the aging process is controlled by genetics, if your family is longed lived and healthy you stand a much better chance to age gracefully. But a basic foundation of self-love, an open heart, and a generosity of spirit effects the overall quality of your life in a much more profound manner. Love has the power to heal almost anything while anger and fear hurts our body.

Your thoughts and words have the power to hurt or heal your body. Choice them well.

> **Spiritual Shortcuts**
>
> Your body is really made up of energy, a vast amount of energy.
>
> Hold your hands a few inches apart. Focus your attention on the area between your hands. Slowly move your hands in and out. Close your eyes and really feel the space between your hands. Vary the speed, gently touch your finger tips together, suddenly pull your hands apart, and then clap your hands.
>
> What did you feel? Some people say it felt lie they were playing with taffy, or something mildly sticky or thick, while others feel a tingling sensation. Allow yourself to relax and you will be able to feel the energy eventually.
>
> What you felt was your energy field, your life force. You can learn to channel and direct that energy. You already do that with you thoughts and actions.

Connect the Dots

What is the connection between your mind, body, and spirit? When I first began explore this connection I could understand how your body effects your mind, if you don't feel well it is hard to think about anything else but how can your thoughts affect your body?

When I used to go to bed I would look at the clock, decide how many hours sleep I would get, and then decide how tired I'd be in the morning. I was always right. Then when I learned about the power of my mind I would go to sleep, knowing I would only be able to sleep a few hours, and tell myself I was going to wake up fully refreshed. I was always right because my mind was listening and it obliged me, I said I'd feel fine and I did.

Sometimes the connection is less traceable or obvious. We judge our body and tell ourselves things like I'm getting older. Advertisers tell that if we want to be happy we need to be young. There is a definite connection between what you think and how you feel. Take sometime to notice what you're telling your body. Are you loving it or judging it?

The Effect of Thoughts and Words

Slowly read the following two quotes. Take a few moments to think about the words you've just read. See how the words and thoughts affect you. How do you feel after you read each of them?

> *"Spread love everywhere you go: first of all in your own house. Give love to your children, to your wife or husband, to a next door neighbor. Let no one ever come to you without leaving better and happier. Be the living expression of God's kindness; kindness in your face, kindness in your eyes, kindness in your smile, kindness in your warm greeting."*
>
> Mother Teresa

> *"Do not let your fire go out, spark by irreplaceable spark, in the hopeless swamps of the approximate, the not-quite, the not-yet, the not-at-all. Do not let the hero in your soul perish, in lonely frustration for the life you deserve, but have never been able to reach. Check the road and the nature of your battle.*
>
> *The world you desire can be won. It exists, it is real, it is possible, it is yours."*
>
> Ayn Rand

How do those words affect you? Do they speak to your mind or your heart? How do you want to live your life? What would happen if you embraced both of those philosophies? Notice how your body feels. How does your heart feel?

A Right Relationship With All Three

What activities make your heart sing? What kind of food does your body love? What type of physical activity makes your body feel really good? What does your spirit need to feel really whole and connected to the greater whole? How well do you understand your relationship with your mind, your body, and your spirit?

Developing a balanced relationship with your mind, body, and soul takes time and effort. It took me a great deal of time to find out what each part of my trinity needed. I watch my students struggle with this all the time. You are a trinity, a blend of all three types of energy. If one part of you is out of balance the entire system is.

Everyone's needs are different. What are yours? Take sometime and really think about the following questions.

Body

What does your body need to maintain optimal health? How much sleep do you really need? How much and what kind of exercise is best for your body? What kind of food is most nurturing to your body? What kinds of food provide emotional support but upset your nutritional balance? Do you need to be touched more? What exactly does your body need to feel fully alive, vibrant, and energetic?

Mind

What do you need to remain emotionally balanced? Do you need more mental stimulation? Do you need to go out to plays, movies, and poetry readings? Do you need to go on a mental diet? Do you need to fill your mind with more love and less worry? Do you need to unwire your old beliefs? What exactly does your mind need to be in harmony with the rest of the trinity?

Spirit

What does your spirit need? What type of behaviors feed your soul? Do you need to find a group of like-minded individuals? Do you need to find a place out in nature where you really feel your connection to your godself? Do you need to create a sacred space in your home or within yourself? Do you need to meditate on a regular basis? What exactly does your spirit need to remain in balance with your mind and your body?

Spiritual Shortcuts

Only you know what you really need. It is important for you to know specifically what you need in your life. What you, your closest friend, or even your brother or sister need is unique to each of you. One day your body might need too stretch, and the next day it might need to dance. Answering these questions about your body, mind and spirit will help you get in touch with yourself and greatly improve the quality of your life. Sometimes the most important thing for you to know you need today is a glass of water so you can avoid a bladder infection tomorrow. Answering these questions will help your develop that inner sensitivity.

Meditation

Set aside at least fifteen minutes when you won't be disturbed. If you are wearing any tight clothing loosen them and get comfortable.

Give yourself permission to relax totally and completely. Start to the top of you head and go throughout your entire body releasing and relaxing each and every muscle and each and every fiber in your entire being. (Pause)

Imagine a bright white light coming down through the top of your head filling your entire being with a deep feeling of peace and relaxation. Let it fill you. Let it wash over you. Feel it filling your heart with love removing any sadness, hurts, or emptiness. Now, imagine the white light washing though your mind, removing any cares or concerns. (Pause)

Take a deep breath and allow yourself to relax totally and completely. Imagine yourself walking down a flight of stairs step by step going deeper and deeper, more and more relaxed. Each flight of stairs takes you deeper. Each flight of stairs takes you closer and closer to your own inner wisdom. (Pause)

Smoke & Mirrors

If you listen only to your mind while you're doing a guided meditation, you severely limit your experience. If your mind keeps saying I don't see anything, and you focus on that instead of allowing yourself to be with the experience, you might feel as though you did something wrong at the end of the meditation. You can't do a guided meditation wrong; allow yourself to enjoy the experience, relax and just go along for the ride.

At the foot of the stairs there's a doorway. It's a magnificent door beautifully carved and covered with gold and silver. You reach out and it slowly swings open revealing a beautiful chamber deep within your inner knowing. You move around the room lovingly touching objects you had long forgotten. The room is warm and loving. You feel totally safe, at peace, and at one in this room. It feels so good to be home once again. (Pause)

In the center of the room is a large, comfortable chair. You sit down and it fits you perfectly. In one of the arms is a large consol with controls for a large movie screen. You also have access to an immense information center. Anything you could possible want or need is at your finger tips.

You sit back and ask yourself what your mind, body, and soul need to be in harmony, to work as a unit to create a life filled with abundance, joy, peace, and happiness. Slowly you have an inner knowing, images reveal themselves to you.

First a wise being comes forth and talks to you of your soul. This being reminds you what your soul needs. You feel and know deep within your being what your soul wants and needs. And you remember.

Next a wise being comes and talks to you of your mind. This being reminds you what your mind needs. You feel and know deep within your being what your mind wants and needs. And you remember.

Next a wise being comes and talks to you of your body. This being reminds you what your body needs. You feel and know deep within your being what your body wants and needs. And you remember.

And it feels so good to know exactly what you need to be whole again. Relax and go a little deeper.

Next a beautiful being of light comes and stands directly in front of you. The being reaches out and touches your heart. You feel warmth flowing through your body. The being reaches inside your heart, pulls out a little star, and places it over your head. The light from the star flows down over you. The star moves a little higher and shines its love over your entire life illuminating your way, guiding and directing you. The love fills you with a feeling of safety beyond anything you could have ever imagined. You know all is well in your world.

Take a few deep breaths and when you're done gentle bring yourself back to this room.

Repeat this meditation often, whenever you need guidance or want to connect with your inner wisdom. The star portion is a nice image to practice on a regular basis.

If you develop a balanced relationship within yourself it will be much easier to maintain a sense of balance in your life. Our lives move so fast it is often hard to find time for the things that really matter. When we take time for ourselves the rest of life goes so much easier. We seem to have more time and a lot less worry and stress.

> ### *The Least You Need to Know*
>
> ➤ Your thoughts affect your body.
>
> ➤ You need to balance your mind and your body and your spirit.
>
> ➤ The more time you spend loving and nurturing yourself the easier life is.
>
> ➤ Fear isn't fact, although believing it can make it so.

Chapter 16

But It Hurts So Good

> **In This Chapter**
>
> ➤ Understand the nature of addiction
>
> ➤ Learn how to successfully let them go
>
> ➤ Explore tools that will transform your life even if you don't have any addictions
>
> ➤ Experience personal freedom

Addictions start out as a temporary solution to an emotional problem but eventually the addictions wind up becoming the problem. Eventually most addictions diminish the quality of our lives. Addictions come in many shapes and sizes. We can be addicted to thought patterns, beliefs, behaviors, as well as substances. Anything can become an addiction if it is done to excess. Even healthy behaviors like exercise can become addictions.

Addictions are addictions and if they no longer serve us it is time to let them go, with love, and not from a place of judgment or fear. We are addicted to breathing but that's an addiction that adds to the quality of our life so it isn't a problem.

Me–Hurt Myself?

It doesn't make much sense but so many of our actions, a large percentage of our internal dialog, and our choices are abusive. We would never say some of the things to others that we say to ourselves. If we clearly saw the result of our choices before we made them we wouldn't make them. We choose a sedentary life style, have a heart attack, and wonder why. We smoke and pretend it won't hurt us. We drink alcohol, which poisons our mind and our body because it's a social custom to do so. Many of us overeat and abuse our body in so many subtle ways. Most of us wouldn't abuse our car every day and expect it to take us wherever we want to go yet we do that to our physical body.

When I suggest people create a daily practice for themselves of healing behaviors they look at me aghast. They don't have time to meditate or journal on a regular basis. If your car won't start do you have time to call a mechanic? If you're not joyously happy are you willing to take the time to change whatever is necessary in your life so you can be happy? We often wait until the emotional pain is almost overwhelming before we are willing to make a few simple changes.

We often base our decisions on what is expedient or most comfortable in the moment. We won't quit smoking or change our lifestyle until we have to and even then we resist change. I have seen pictures of people smoking through a hole in their throats rather than give up cigarettes. One of the questions you might want to ask yourself is: What is it going to take for you to be willing to change? Does your entire life have to go down in flames or do you just have to be slightly uncomfortable? How much do you have to abuse yourself and your body before you are willing to change?

Clarity Corner

Self-abuse comes in many shapes and sizes. It can be as simple as a negative thought or gesture we repeat to ourselves. Self-abuse can also manifest in our life choices; we can eat poorly, smoke, drink, drive carelessly, and make other choices that injure our body. Spiritual healing is a process of learning to release all forms of self-abuse and replace them with self-love instead.

You and Addiction–Face to Face

In this chapter will be exploring physical addictions. It is important to remember that some of our most debilitating addictions aren't physical they are mental and spiritual. I define an addiction as a behavior that controls our ability to choose rather than a behavior that we can choose to do or not do. Most addicts fool themselves into thinking they are at choice but if they are really honest with themselves they'll have to admit their ability to choose left a long time ago. That's why admitting that a behavior is an addiction is always the first step in overcoming it.

Sage Advice

"You can always pickup your needle and move to another groove."
Dr. Timothy Leary

Is It an Addiction?

If you aren't sure your behavior is an addiction or not ask yourself the following questions and be honest with yourself.

- Do you go out of your way to indulge in the behavior?
- Do you find yourself justifying your behavior to yourself or others?
- Does your behavior impact the quality of your life in any way?
- Has your behavior affected others in your life?
- Do you want to act one way and find yourself making choices not consistent with the way you want to act?
- Examples: You want to lose weight but continue to overeat; you hate being in debt but you keep buying things on credit; you go to a party, decide you don't want to get drunk, and by the end of the night you're loaded.
- Do you constantly think about the behavior or try to avoid thinking about it?
- Do you tell yourself you could easily give that up whenever you wanted to, you just don't want to?
- You've tried to alter your behavior but you can't?

Clarity Corner

Any **addiction** causes us to lose our ability to freely choose our behaviors. As soon as we become addicted to a substance, a person, or a thought pattern, we are under it's control. The last thing an addict wants to admit is that he is addicted; then, he might have to stop using. An addict is the last person to think he has a problem, so if you think you might have a problem, you probably do.

If you have people in your life you trust ask them if they think a behavior is a problem. If they say yes and you find yourself getting angry chances are it's an addiction. One of the strongest aspects of an addiction is denial; the addicted person will always say it isn't an addiction.

Once you admit a behavior is an addiction then you have to decide what you're going to do about it. Once you decide anything is a problem in your life you get to choose: Am I going to continue victimizing myself or am I going to change? Neither choice is better than the other. Life is just a series of choices and outcomes but sometimes we just like to pretend it isn't. In life we can remember our divinity and move on or not. It doesn't really matter, we'll always have another opportunity to bring love and light into a place of fear and darkness. Our choice is always love or fear. The sooner we choose love the happier we are.

Addictions are nothing to fool around with, they can kill you or at least ruin your life. If you have an addiction don't hesitate to ask for help. There are many 12 step programs that are wonderful and therapists that specialize in the treatment of addictions. Don't try to do it alone, reach out let others help you.

Drugs

All addictions are the same, only the object of our addiction changes. A substance abuse counselor once told me that the only difference between a drug addict and an alcoholic was that drug addicts tend to be sneakier because they have to find their drug of choice illegally the alcoholic just has to go to the store.

I was a child of the sixties so at one point drugs were very much a part of my life. My friends and I listened to all the public announcements about drug abuse we'd laugh about them until drugs almost ruined my life. I was one of the lucky ones, I handled my addictions before they killed me or totally ruined my life.

Drugs have a profound affect on all areas of our lives. Drugs affect not only your mind and body but they also affect your energy field. Some psychics say drugs put holes in your aura, which is the energy field that actually creates your physical body. All drugs affect your mind. The biochemistry of your mind is so delicate it isn't really something you want to mess around with.

When I was in the midst of my drug addiction I rationalized my drug use by saying it improved my performance, I was more creative. I had more profound meditations. I had a lot of excuses. Although the Toltec tradition, first popularized by Carlos Castaneda is filled with tales of the use of peyote, devil's weed, and other hallucinogenic drugs when I studied with Don Miguel he didn't believe in the use of drugs. He said it was important to know how to achieve altered states of consciousness consciously. If you use drugs to produce these states you need the drugs to reproduce the experience and drugs react differently every time.

Uppers, downers, prescription, mind altering, legally or illegally bought, drugs have ruined countless lives. Don't let them ruin yours. If you think you have a problem get help. Call Narcotics Anonymous or Alcoholics Anonymous, both numbers are listed in the white pages of your phone book.

> **Smoke & Mirrors**
>
> Addictions are nothing to fool around with; they can kill you or at least ruin your life. If you have an addiction, don't hesitate to ask for help. Many 12-step programs are wonderful, and some therapists specialize in the treatment of addictions. Don't try to do it alone; reach out and let others help you. One of the major components of an addiction is isolation. Don't listen to your addiction–get out into the world and get help.

Alcohol

Alcohol is an integral part of the social structure of our culture. Every ounce of alcohol you consume kills thousands of brain cells, if you drink to excess you will die yet we use alcohol in many of our celebrations, it is even used in holy sacraments. Many people can drink and it doesn't affect them or their lives but if you happen to be an alcoholic one drink is too many and a hundred aren't enough.

Only you can decide if alcohol is a problem in your life. If you are questioning whether it is or not in all likelihood it is. People who don't have a problem with drugs or alcohol don't question whether they do have a problem. As with drugs, if you do have a problem contact a treatment center or Alcoholic Anonymous whose number you'll find listed in the white pages of your phone book.

> **Sage Advice**
>
> "Life is a quarry, out of which we are to mold and chisel and complete a character."
> *Goethe*

Cigarettes

Nicotine is one of the most addictive substances known to mankind. Tobacco companies spend billions of dollars every year convincing people to smoke. Anyone who does smoke probably remembers their first few cigarettes. You really have to work at enjoying cigarettes. Your body reacts violently to the toxins in the cigarette, you cough, get nauseous, and feel terrible. Our body is so resilient is adjusts very rapidly to the poisons we are ingesting.

Sage Advice
"Quitting smoking is easy. I've done it thousands of time."
Mark Twain

Hundreds of people try to quit everyday and very few people succeed. When I quit smoking I realized what a powerful smoke screen it was, smoking allowed me to distance myself from my emotions. As with other addictions the reason they are so seductive is they allow us to ignore the pain and fear reality often causes. We abdicate our power of choice to a substance rather than face the necessity of making different choices in our life.

When I smoked I took it very personally when someone asked me not to smoke. Years after I had quit I contacted my friends in Vermont to let them know I was coming to visit. One friend asked if I minded if she smoked around me. I told her I would rather she didn't. She wrote me a rather angry letter telling me she wouldn't see me if she couldn't smoke around me. Small, white cylinders filled with a toxic mixture of chemicals and tobacco were more important to her than my friendship. I remember defending my right to smoke with equal vigor and in hindsight what a sad choice. Addictions cause us to choose substances over love.

Food

We don't tend to think of food as an addictive substance yet it is in many people's lives. For some people weight is not an issue but for millions of people their weight, body image, food, and the ability to control their intake of food consumes their lives. Eating disorders aren't just a women's issue, many men suffer with the same feelings of self-hate and hopelessness. Eating disorders can be just as deadly and debilitating as drugs and alcohol.

Sage Advice
"A bad habit cannot be simply thrown out the window, it must be coaxed down the stairs one at a time."
Mark Twain

Racism is no longer social acceptable by most individuals in our society yet weightism is still acceptable and very prevalent. Comedians poke fun at overweight people all the time, advertisers ignore their existence, manufacturers seldom make stylish clothing in larger sizes, and many people consider obesity a sign of laziness or a weakness of some sort. With most other addictive substances a person can avoid them but a person with a food addiction still has to eat on a daily basis. Eating disorders or food addictions are the hardest addictions to overcome.

If you've ever struggled with your weight you know the anguish it can cause in your life. Be gentle with yourself, judging yourself won't help you with your addiction. As with any other addiction learning how to make different choices and healing the emotional wounds of the past will set you free.

Sex

Sex creates a high unlike any other and it can be very addictive. I have lost friends to the AIDS epidemic that knew better but chose sex over their lives. Even after years of drilling safer sex into our heads how many people don't pay attention to the warnings. Sex is an extremely powerful force in our lives. Everyone has to decide their own personal code of conduct when it comes to sex, there is no right or wrong. Only you can define morality for yourself. External controls are ineffective especially if we don't personally agree with them.

Sex and love often get confused. Sex is used to sell everything from clothes to cereal. As with other addictions only you can decide if it's a problem in your life.

Gambling and Overspending

Although these are two different addictions they both involve the misuse of money. People that overspend are merely gambling with their future happiness. They are mortgaging their future in an attempt to be happy today. There is a certain thrill and rush involved in these two addictions. People who indulge in these behaviors live in a fantasy world where they think they can win at a game they'll never win.

The gambler always figures this time they'll make the big score. Overspenders rarely think of how they are going to pay for things. Neither person deals with their financial reality in a responsible manner. They live in a world of highs and lows. High when they have money, when they are winning, lows when they lose or get the bills and can't pay them.

Money issues destroy as many relationships as infidelity. Money is a wonderful way to avoid intimacy and to isolate or insulate yourself from other people. Money very often becomes a green-eyed monster in people's lives instead of the medium of exchange that it really is. If money is an issue in your life treat it as an addiction and see what happens.

Why Should I Stop?

There is no one reason to stop an addiction. My freedom to choose is very important to me and I don't like to abdicate it to anyone or anything. An addiction robs us of our ability to choose. It depletes our life force and causes us to make choices that go against our best interests.

But it stops our emotional pain and temporarily releases us from the constraints of physical reality. And addictions cause more problems than they serve. I find it helps to write a pro and con list but I suggest doing it the morning after rather than the night before.

Quitting Checklist - Am I really ready?

The first step in overcoming an addiction is admitting you have one. The next step is becoming willing to let it go. Developing the willingness to do whatever it takes to get rid of the addiction very often takes a great deal of time and effort.

If you're ready to handle your addictions great, but if you aren't here's how to get ready:

- Make a list of all the problems your addictions cause in your life. Look at how it affects your relationships, your work, and the over all quality of your life. Take time and really look at all the ramifications of your addiction.

- How would your life change if you never had to think about your addiction again? What would happen to you and your life if miraculously your addiction disappeared?

- For a week keep track of the amount of time you spend indulging in you're addiction, thinking about it, preparing for it, or avoiding it. Be honest; realize your mind will want to underestimate the time so write it down. Keep a time card for your addiction. If you're in doubt, add a few hours.

- How else could you use all those hours?

- See your life free of addictions. How would that freedom feel? What would it look like to be free? Be aware of the difference between being deprived of your addiction and free of it.

Spend some time writing about your addiction. See it for what it is and how it really affects your life. Make the mental picture of your addiction as clear as possible; freedom is always preferable to slavery. And make no mistake an addiction is slavery of the worst kind because it is self-imposed.

Your reason for stopping your addictions may be far different from someone else's. If you want to free yourself from an addiction you must do it for yourself. If you are doing it for your job, or your parents, or anyone other than yourself it won't work. The day will come when you are angry with that person and you'll get even by indulging in your addiction.

Take the time to look inside of yourself, look deep in your heart, and find out what really matters to you. Look deep inside and find our why you rely on an addiction and how it will serve you to let it go. Find out what really makes your heart sing and take the time to do it.

How Do I Stop Them, Once and For All

Addictions aren't something you can put on a shelf and forget. They will be with you for life. You can learn new behaviors so you no longer have to think about the addiction or indulge in them but they'll always be sitting at the edge of your reality waiting for you. If you stop smoking and you take a drag off someone's cigarette you'll be back smoking on a regular basis before you know it.

Addictions are based in our thought process. We avoid emotional distress by indulging in our addiction. An addiction is a learned behavior. We solved a problem by creating an even bigger problem. Part of releasing an addiction is understanding the purpose it serves in our life and finding a healthier way to meet that need. But ultimately we have to change our behavior regardless of the reasons for them.

Your willingness to do the work will fluctuate from day to day, some days it will just seem like too much, you will want to throw your hands up in disgust, and go back to your old behaviors. It is on those days you will have to dig deep within yourself and remind yourself your reasons for freeing yourself from your addictions. Being thorough with each step will assure your success.

Getting Ready To Let Go

It is important to set yourself up for success. We are all familiar with setting ourselves up for failure, especially if we are dealing with addictions. Now it is time to give yourself every opportunity to succeed by following the directions. I know I hate following directions and I seldom do. My mind generally thinks it knows a better way to do things and those shortcuts only shortchange me. My mind's shortcuts are based on my mind's best thinking and when it comes to addictions my thinking is the problem.

> **Sage Advice**
> "Only as high as I reach can I grow,
> Only as far as I seek can I go,
> Only as deep as I look can I see,
> Only as much as I dream can I be."
> Karen Ravn

Okay, so you've already decided you have a problem. I'm sure you'd rather have a magic wand to get rid of your addiction but that kind of thinking is part of the addiction. I'm not sure which comes first, the thinking or the addiction but it is important to remember that no one can do this work for you. There isn't anything or anyone who is going to make your life better except yourself. An addiction seemingly altered your life for years; it was an external solution that for a time worked.

Only you can change your thinking, you can change your behavior, and only you can free yourself from your limitations. Taking total responsibility for the choices we make in our lives in incredibly freeing and empowering, it is also one of the scariest things we can do. Once we step up and say this is my life and I am responsible for my thoughts and actions we don't have anyone left to blame. The great collective "they" didn't do it to you, the drugs, food, or whatever didn't ruin your life. You did. So gently tell yourself the truth, forgive yourself, and make new choices.

Once you can accept responsibility for your life you're ready to change, you can make new choices with conscious awareness of their ramifications. You can first ask yourself what you want and then make choices that will assist you in creating that. Life becomes a joyous experience once you learn to tell yourself the truth in a loving and gentle manner. You didn't make a mistake because there is no such thing as a mistake. You made a choice and you got a result or outcome. If you don't like the outcome you didn't make a mistake you just need to make a different choice.

The Process, Not a Magic Trick

Dealing with an addiction requires that you stay awake at all times. That means making conscious choices. In order to choose consciously you'll have to be aware of what causes you to check out in the first place. The addictive cycle is deeply ingrained and we aren't even consciously aware of most of the step.

The cycle looks something like this:

- Something causes us emotional discomfort
- We immediately ignore the discomfort – we numb out
- We start getting more and more uncomfortable
- The pressure builds until we are so uncomfortable we have to do something
- We use our addiction to neutralize the pressure
- We're comfortable being numb

What is consistent throughout the process is our lack of awareness of what's really going on. If we immediately recognized our emotional discomfort we could have taken appropriate actions. But as an addict what we do is numb ourselves to our feelings rather than honor them as signposts. An emotion is a call to action. The action that is required is totally dependent on the situation and the outcome we want to achieve.

In order to successfully release an addiction we have to become aware of emotions as they happen. At the beginning of the cycle if you'd been consciously aware of the emotional discomfort you could have stopped and explored what was going on for you. But instead we learned to numb ourselves first emotionally and then with a behavior or substance. Once we numb ourselves our behavior goes on automatic pilot and we react instead of choosing how to act.

First: Stop It!

Ideally the first step is to stop the behavior, which will force us to become aware of our emotions. Sometimes we can't stop the behavior so we have to work with the emotional aspect first. Either way we have to find a new way of dealing with our emotions. Ridding ourselves of an addiction is often a balancing act of trying to stop the behavior and dealing with the emotions.

Second: Tune In!

Start tuning in to your emotions on a regular basis. Throughout the day ask yourself: What am I feeling? If you're unfamiliar with your emotions the answer may often be nothing. But dig a little deeper, go past the habitual numbing. Ask yourself if you're angry, afraid, tense, nervous, happy, sad, joyful, hopeful, hopeless, guilty, secure, proud, lonely, sick, hungry, stuffed, loved, or insecure. You can experience many emotions simultaneously. I bought a watch with an alarm and set it to go off on the hour so I would remember to ask myself

---

Sage Advice
"The best way to make your dreams come true is to wake up.."
Paul Valery

Sage Advice
"Someone's sitting in the shade today because someone else planted a tree a long time ago."
Warren Buffett

Third: Ready, Set, Action!

Once you are aware of what emotions you're feeling translate them into actions. Based on what you are feeling ask yourself what you need. Meet that need consciously and not with an addictive behavior. It may take you a while to know what you need. If you're angry perhaps you need to write about your anger, scream into a pillow, beat your bed, go running, or do some physical exercise until you discharge the energy.

These two steps will allow you to break the addictive cycle but they are only the beginning of the work. Becoming fully aware of your emotions and the need associated with them opens up old emotional wounds we weren't even aware of. If you really want to free yourself from your addictions you'll have to dig out their roots and replace your old limited thinking. The stalking methods we talked about in Chapter 14 will be of great assistance in this process.

But understanding the reasons for your addictions don't matter unless you change your behavior. Our mind likes to look for excuses; I drink too much because I feel lonely. You can't stop there, once you realize loneliness is a problem drinking isn't the solution. Make new choices, reach out, and make new friends, volunteer, join a hiking club, do anything that will assist you in meeting new people.

Finally, Do It and Do It Again

Keep doing the first three steps until you are free of your addiction. Write, feel, stalk your behaviors, write all the letters in the following section, and then start all over again until you are free. Get support if you need it, join a 12 step program, find a therapist, get acupuncture, just do whatever you need to do to give yourself the gift of freedom.

The Letters to Nobody

Writing letters to clear out your emotions is a very powerful process. Whenever I find myself in emotional turmoil about anything and I need clarity I write a letter. I never send any of the letters I write them for myself.

Some of the letters may seem rather strange but just trust the process. You will be writing letters to yourself from your addictions. When you write those letters just sit down and write whatever comes to mind. You can't do it wrong, just imagine you're your addiction and write. You'll be amazed at the information you will get writing these letters.

It is important you take sufficient time to thoroughly write *free-form* letters. Don't skimp allow yourself plenty of time when you sit down to write these. After you finish writing the letters if other emotions

---

Sage Advice

"Education is an admirable thing, but it is well to remember from time to time that nothing worth knowing can be taught."
— Oscar Wilde

Clarity Corner

In **free-form letters**, you write anything that comes to mind about a particular subject. Make sure you have enough time to really finish writing the letter. You'll know when you're done because you will have nothing left to write. In a **structured letter**, you specifically explore your emotions. You go through your anger, move onto sadness, explore your fear, see if there is any guilt, and then move into a clearer understanding of the issue.

come up take the time to write another letter. These letters are a very necessary step in your emotional healing. It will be much easier to release your addictions if you aren't still carrying around a huge load of emotional garbage.

Write ...
- to your addictions.
- from your addictions to yourself.
- to each of your emotions.
- to your numbness.
- from your ability to be numb.
- to your life.
- to the significant people in your life: parents, partners, bosses, friends, etc.

Write *structured letters* whenever you're unsure about what's going on internally, you feel off balance, or you really want to indulge in your addiction. Systematically go through each of your emotions until you get to acceptance. Start writing about your anger then move on to your sadness then write about your fear finally explore any self-judgment, criticism or guilt you may have. Cycle through your emotions until you can accept the situation just as it is and understand what actions you need to take next.

> **Sage Advice**
> "Twenty years from now you will be more disappointed by the things you didn't do than by the ones you did do. So throw off the bowlines. Sail away from the safe harbor of your old thinking. Catch the trade winds in your sails. Explore. Dream. Discover."
> Mark Twain

Celebrating Freedom

Recognizing your emotions as they arise will allow you to make choices and take actions in the moment that are appropriate and assist you in creating what you really want. What a freedom that is. You no longer have to react to events in your life and regret the way you reacted. Being aware in the moment will give you time to think so you can choose how you want to act.

Whenever I react to life I am in fear and get results based in fear that are limited and limiting. When I am awake in the moment I can make choices based in love and get results that create a greater degree of freedom in my life. I feel a sense of peace, I feel safe when my choices are made from love. When I am reacting I never have that sense of inner peace.

Get a sense for yourself of how the difference feels to you. Imagine what the freedom from addictions and unconscious choices would feel like to you. Let yourself feel what the freedom to choose really feels like and celebrate that feeling. It can be yours. The most loving thing you can do for yourself is deciding to take care of your true wants and needs and to stop indulging yourself in self-destructive behaviors.

The Least You Need to Know

- Anything can be addictive if I use it to numb out emotionally.
- Releasing an addiction is a process.
- Emotions are a call to action.
- The first step in achieving freedom is admitting you're not free.

Chapter 17

Shake Your Booty

> **In This Chapter**
>
> ➤ Find out what your body needs.
>
> ➤ Get physical.
>
> ➤ Have a sense riot.
>
> ➤ Worship your temple.

Your body is a complex biological unit that needs proper rest, fresh air, healthy food, and exercise. I had a really hard time listening to my body and not my head when it came to exercise and movement. If you never change the oil in your car eventually the engine will get all gummed up and stop functioning as efficiently. If you don't pay attention to your body's needs it won't function as well either.

Just as with any other part of this process being gentle and loving with yourself will make the process much easier. In the past I've decided to get in shape physically and hurt myself because I didn't listen to my body's needs. Getting to know your body can be a fun part of this journey or a hellish experience, it depends on our choices.

Listening to What Your Body Needs

Learning to listen to your body is a wonderful skill. It very often takes time for us to develop this skill but we can all learn if we're willing to listen instead of constantly judging. Our bodies constantly tell us exactly what we need if we're willing to listen. Knowing you need to drink more water to avoid trouble in your urinary track is a very useful piece of information. Our body knows that, if we tune in so will we, and we'll know in time to act on the suggestion.

Our body is our vehicle for this journey we call life so we might want to treat it as lovingly as possible. If we don't like the size or shape of our body rather than unmercifully judging our body we might want to change how we treat it.

> **Spiritual Shortcuts**
>
> Take 10 or 15 minutes to totally scan your body. Sit quietly in a place you won't be disturbed. Take a few minutes to relax. Breath deeply and rhythmically. Relax and be gentle with your body. It is used to you judging it so sit quietly and with the eyes of love look at your body. To the best of your ability release any judgments you have about your body. If you're busy hating it you won't be able to hear what it needs.
>
> Start at your head or toes and go through each part of your body. Check in and see how each part is feeling. Does it feel relaxed or tense, heavy or light, fluid or constricted, healthy or in need of repair? Really connect with each part of your body and ask it how it's feeling, then listen. If you find an area in need of attention ask your body what it needs instead of assuming you already know. Get into the habit of doing this at least once a day.

Pain is a signal from our body that we need to pay attention. How often do we have an ache and rather than going inside and talking to our body about it we reach for a painkiller? We mask our body's symptoms with drugs rather than deal with the real issues. We drink coffee or another stimulant to wake up instead of getting more sleep. Our bodies can last for hundreds of years if we don't tax them with negative thinking, physical abuse, toxins, and lack of loving care. Start listening to your body, it is the only vehicle you will get this lifetime.

Work That Body

I have hated exercise almost as long as I can remember, until I started listening to my body. My body loves to move and stretch and play and have fun. When I do a little too much one-day the sore muscles feel good and remind me to lovingly stretch them. If you avoid exercise, hate sweating, and think sports are dumb I can guarantee you're listening to your head and not your body. Your body loves to move it is built to move. Even if you're physically challenged your body still likes to move in its own way.

Years ago I went to Sedona to do a book signing. I took two of my students with me. One of them was very athletic and Patti was a city girl at heart and wasn't fond of outdoor activities. I wanted to go see some of the sights, which entailed hiking. I hated hiking but didn't say anything, Patti did. I asked her if she liked walking and she said yes. I told her to think of hiking as a long walk over uneven terrain and at that moment I fell in love with hiking. I stopped listening to my head and listened to my body instead. Try different activities and listen to your body, change the way you think about them until both your head and your body agree. You may be surprised at what you wind up enjoying.

To keep your body in peak condition you will want o do a combination of aerobic exercise and weight training. That could occur in many ways you could go kayaking which does both, play tennis, or join a gym. What is most important is to find a combination of activities that you will do on a regular basis. It takes time for your body to adjust if you have been inactive for a while. Be gentle with yourself and experiment until you find a routine that works for you. As much as possible listen to your body and ignore your mind.

Aerobic

Any activity that raises your heart rate into the training zone is considered aerobic. When I think of aerobic exercise I think of skinny women in tights gracefully working out to music in a room full of mirrors. And believe me my mind has some rather negative thoughts about that image. Walking, running, swimming, cleaning house, and gardening can be aerobic activities. Any type of movement that raises your heart rate consistently above your training level is aerobic. Your heart rate depends upon your age and over all physical condition.

Aerobic exercise is a system of physical conditioning developed to increase the efficiency of the body's intake of oxygen. To be effective, aerobic training must include a minimum of three sessions per week. During each session the heart rate must be raised to the training level for at least 20 minutes. When you first begin exercising you tend to more tired and your appetite may increase. As soon as your body becomes accustomed to exercise you will begin to feel better, have much more energy, and your appetite will moderate.

Spiritual Shortcuts

If you subtract your age from 220 and then multiplying the result by .65 you can reliably estimate your heart rate for achieving your aerobic training level. 220 − 35 = 185 x .65 = 120.25. The aerobic training level for a 35 old person is 120 heartbeats per minute. If you just want to raise your metabolism, you can work out at a lower heart rate. The easiest way to tack your heart rate is to get a fancy gismo to do it for you, but you can do it the old-fashioned way by finding your pulse on your wrist, counting for 10 seconds, and then multiply the number by 6.

Weight Training

Weight training will improve muscle tone and improve bone density. It is very important for woman to assist in avoiding bone thinning. You can do simple exercises at home or in a gym. Many activities provide weight training. Running and walking strengthen the legs but do nothing for the upper body. Most women need to work on upper body strength. Activities like canoeing, tennis, rowing, or kayaking will help improve upper body strength.

Weight training needs to be done consistently. Carrying groceries works muscles but unless you do it everyday for a half hour it won't really keep your body in shape. Really look at your body as a beautiful vehicle, if we tune it up regularly and take good care of it our journey will be free from break downs and last a lot longer.

Smoke & Mirrors

Be careful not to overdo it when you first begin exercising. It is always a good idea to talk to your doctor before beginning any exercise program. It is much better to take your time and get into shape slowly, without injuries, thant it is to dive into the process and hurt yourself. An injury will delay the process a lot more than beginning slowly ever could.

Playing

We can make exercise fun. I live in Hawaii so I have summer almost all year. I can hike, swim, or kayak all year round. No matter where you live there are outdoor activities you can enjoy. When I lived in Vermont I loved to go skiing and snow shoe. Getting out in nature has the added benefit of giving you time to connect with the beauty and wonder of nature. A long hike in nature feeds the body and the soul.

Find physical activities you can do with your friends and loved ones. Find fun ways you can be physically active. Skip, jump, run, and have fun. In the fall rake leaves and then jump right in the middle of the pile. Make snow angels or snow forts, go sled riding, or help others shovel their drives. In the summer cut all your neighbors lawns one day when they aren't home. Combine physical activity with being of service, miracles can happen.

Bodies in Motion

When you really let go of your mind and just allow your body to move amazing things happen. Chanting, drumming, and dancing are all wonderful ways to achieve altered states of consciousness. The freedom to let your body move and the ability to move are such incredible gifts. So often our minds stop us from moving freely, we're afraid of looking foolish or not doing something well so we don't do it at all.

Take some time and go to a park where children are playing. Sit and watch them for a while, notice their bodies, witness the joy they find in using them. Some of them are still able to run, scream, and play with complete abandon. And sometimes you will see a child sitting off by itself watching. That child has already begun to listen to their mind, they have already lost their freedom. How much of your freedom have you given up? How many times do you stop yourself because you listen to your mind's opinion and believe it is fact instead of fiction?

Dance

Dance is a very powerful form of movement. Whether it is modern dance, ballroom dancing, or ethnic dancing they are all wonderfully rhythmic and freeing to the mind, body, and soul. I have a series of tapes about women's spirituality. In the background of each documentary there are scenes of a woman dancing with a scarf on hilltops, over cliffs, and out in the desert. The images are extremely moving stirring deep memories of freedom, inner wisdom, and power.

> **Spiritual Shortcuts**
>
> Get quiet for a few minutes. Close your eyes, take a few deep breaths, and allow yourself to relax. Imagine yourself standing in a clearing in the middle of a primordial forest. The clearing is bathed in moonlight and filled with the feelings of peace, safety, and love. It is a warm night and the air is heavy with the sweet scent of the earth. You take a few deep breaths and something deep within you begins to stir. You feel totally free perhaps of the first time in your life. An ancient rhythm starts to flow through your body. You can feel it in each and every cell of your body.
>
> You slowly begin to move around the clearing feeling your body. You become aware of each and every movement of your body. Love and self-acceptance begins to move through you. You find yourself moving more and more freely. Your body seems to have its own rhythm and inner grace. The ancient rhythm fills you and moves you. Just let yourself dance the dance of freedom in the beautiful moonlight. Relax into the experience and allow yourself to be one with it. Allow yourself to enjoy your body.

Power Moves

Power moves are specific movements designed to access energy and assist you in aligning with your spiritual self. Tai chi is an ancient version of power moves. They are invigorating to your body and they also assist with mental clarity and creativity. They are a wonderful way to rid your body of toxins and to promote a general feeling of well-being. Power moves are slow and deliberate movements following the flow of the energy through the body. It takes a bit of practice to feel the energy but once you do letting it flow through you and move your body is very freeing and energizing.

Sit comfortably in a chair and close your eyes. Pick up one of your feet and slowly move it in every widening circles. Make each movement slow and deliberate. Focus your attention on your leg and let it move. Let yourself feel the energy and let it move you. Then do the same thing with your other leg.

Relax your legs and focus your attention on your arms. Slowly lift your arms and focus your attention on the palm of your hands. Imagine yourself scooping up energy with your hands. Feel the energy flowing through your arms.

Once you can begin to feel the energy stand up and dance. Let yourself move around the room in a free and rhythmic movement. Dance as long as you can. When you're done take a few quiet moments to let the energy settle into your body. If you have any health challenges focus the energy on those areas.

If you want to create something scoop up a large ball of energy with your hands. Make the ball as large as you want to. When the ball of energy feels just right place the image of what you want to create inside it. Hold it in front of your heart and put your desire inside. Then hold it overhead for a few moments and then throw it up into the universe. Do this exercise as often as you think of it. Miracles will happen.

Stretching

Our body is meant to be flexible and fluid. If we habitually hold tension in our body it will tighten up and loose its ability to move. As we age our bodies tend to get more rigid and less flexible. If we stretch on a regular basis our body will remain more fluid and we are less likely to stiffen up.

When you stretch it is important to be very gentle and not bounce as we stretch. Check with your local YMCA or gym to see if they have any stretching classes. There are also many excellent videos that will teach you proper methods. As you start listening to your body you will begin to notice any areas of tightness. Learning some simple stretches will also help you to hear your body more clearly.

Clarity Corner

There are many variations of yoga. Some are more philosophical that physical. Some focus on the breath, others focus on nutriton, and others focus on the body. Check around and find out what is available in your area. There are also many wonderful books and DVD's, but nothing can replace personal instruction.

Yoga

Yoga is the Sanskrit word for union. Yoga is one of six systems of Indian philosophy. One of Yoga's basic principles is that spiritual freedom occurs when we free ourselves from the small self and align ourselves with our spiritual nature. Part of that process is a series of physical exercises or postures called Asana, which means seat in Sanskrit. These postures are help for a proscribed period of time. Pranayama or breath control is a series of exercises that encourage complete use of the breath and a deep sense of relaxation.

Hatha Yoga, which means union of forces, stresses mastery of the body as a way to attaining spiritual freedom. It is a wonderful form of exercise, stretching, and relaxation. It is important to do the various forms accurately so you receive the most benefit from them. Most cities have a variety of Yoga classes available. I find it is important to find a teacher you feel comfortable with if you want to begin practicing Yoga. Yoga teaches you so much more than mere body movements. Masters of these practices can control their body temperature, respiration, and digestive processes.

Marshal Arts

There are literally hundreds of variations of marshal arts. Years ago I took Judo lessons and enjoyed them immensely. Judo is a form of wrestling which definitely gets you in wonderful physical shape. Marshal arts are very personal. Each person resonates with not only the form but also the teacher or Sensei. Marshal arts are practices that include the mind, body, and spirit.

There are many types of martial arts classes offered in most areas. If you are interested in martial arts go and observe the classes and the instructor. I stopped enjoying Judo when the instructor changed. It became too combative for me and I was hurt several times.

Tai Chi

Tai Chi is a slow, graceful form of exercise derived from Chinese marshal arts. It is a low-intensity, low-impact form of exercise especially well suited if you're recovering from an injury; because it's a weight-bearing exercise it's also helpful in preventing the osteoporosis. Tai Chi increases strength and muscle tone, enhances range of motion and flexibility, and improves balance and coordination. It also has the ability to reduce blood pressure and heart rate. Many who practice tai chi also find that it improves concentration, an increases your sense of well-being, decreases feelings of stress, you'll have more energy, improved posture, and better circulation.

Tai chi exercises are graceful and rhythmic movements called forms. They have names like "Grasping the Bird's Tail" and "Wave Hands Like Clouds." Each form consists of a series of positions strung together into one continuous movement, including a set beginning and end. A single form may include up to 100 positions and may take as long as 20 minutes to complete. The forms can be performed anywhere at any time, but it is best if you do them at the same time every day. In China, tai chi is often performed in large groups as an early morning exercise.

Aikido

Aikido is a Japanese is a self-defense system that uses the force of the attacker to assist them in falling. It resembles the fighting methods jujitsu and judo because it uses twisting and throwing techniques. The word Aikido means the way of spiritual harmony. Aikido especially emphasizes the importance of achieving complete mental calm and control of one's own body to master an opponent's attack. The development of courtesy and respect is an integral part of Aikido training. Its aim of turning an attacker's strength and

---

Smoke & Mirrors

Make sure you really listen to your body. If it says "slow down," then slow down. If you push too far past your limits, you will only hurt yourself and slow down your process. When I first started getting in shape again, I was very tired at first. I took it easy and kept doing something every day. Before I knew it, I wasn't tired anymore. Listen to your body and your doctor. Make sure you find exercise that really nurtures your mind and your body.

Sage Advice

"Do not seek to follow in the footsteps of the men of old, seek what they sought."

Basho

momentum against him or herself along with the spiritual practices makes this form of martial art much gentler than the rest.

The basic skills of Aikido probably originated in Japan in about the 14th century. In the early 20th century they were formalized through the work of the Japanese martial-arts expert Ueshiba Morihei.

Karate

Karate means empty hand. It is a form of unarmed-combat employing kicking, striking, and defensive blocking with arms and legs. Timing, tactics, and spirit are considered as important as physical strength and the toughening of your hands and feet.

> **Sage Advice**
> "Everything you want in life is out there waiting for you to ask. Everything you want also wants you. But you have to take the action to get it."
> Jack Canfield

In sporting karate and sparring in training, blows and kicks are stopped short, preferably within an inch of contact. I took Karate lessons for a short time and found the process unsettling. Friends of mine love the thrill. As with other marshal arts the teacher and the other students play a huge role in your overall experience.

Karate evolved in the Orient over a period of centuries. Okinawa forbid people to carry weapons in the 17th century so it became a very popular martial art form. It was imported into Japan in the 1920s. There are several schools or forms of Karate and each one differs in their costume and general practices.

Qi Gong

Qi Gong means energy cultivation and refers to exercises that improve health and longevity as well as increase the sense of harmony within oneself and in the world. There are thousands of such exercises. Anything you do with the intention of increasing your energy or chi can be considered Qi Gong.

> **Sage Advice**
> "People are like stained-glass windows. They glow and sparkle when it is sunny, but when the sun goes down their true beauty is revealed only when there is light from within."
> Elizabeth Kubler-Ross

All Qi Gong contains common principles such as focusing the mind, eyes, various movements, and awareness of the breath. The practices themselves have little meaning in and of themselves but with practice you can a deep understanding of their significance.

The ultimate goal of all Qi Gong is harmonious existence and action in all situations. As you master these techniques you will find your life, heart and mind filled with curiosity, ease in action, clarity of focus and intention, perseverance, non-attachment, resilience, openness, creativity, responsiveness and fluid balance.

Although you may find books or teachers the power comes down to what you yourself are willing to practice and experience. As with any of the tools in this book only your use of them will change your life. Knowledge alone won't really change anything. The only way to change your life is to change the choices you make.

Anybody Home?

Even though we live inside our bodies a lot of the time the lights are on but there's nobody home. Learning to be present in our body has many powerful ramifications in our lives. The only point in time we have the power to change anything is in the present moment. You can't change the past or influence the future unless you make the choice in the present moment. You can't stop smoking tomorrow but you can choose moment-by-moment not to smoke right now. You can't choose for tomorrow but when tomorrow gets here it will be the present moment. Then you can choose what you're going to do in that moment.

Being present in your body is a skill anyone can learn. We get so busy in our lives that we forget to check in with ourselves. We forget to be present in our own bodies. There are many ways to remind ourselves, some are more pleasant than others. Whenever I'm not feeling well I am very aware of my body. You can set an alarm when it goes off refocus your attention, you can focus your attention on your breathing, or you can even put up notes around the house to remind yourself. Once you decide being present in your body has value you'll start remembering.

Grounding

Electricity can't flow unless it has a complete circuit it needs a ground to work properly. So do you. Grounding yourself means being solidly and practically in contact with physical reality. When we meditate, work with altered states of consciousness, or are out of touch with our body it is easy to spin out or lose contact with ourselves and our physicality.

When we do things like power moves, Tai Chi, or dance we can feel spacey and disconnected. I have seen people get totally disoriented. One way to ground yourself is to rub your wrist together. You can talk to yourself, rub your feet through the grass, or take a shower. One of the things I really like to do is take a bath in sea salts and add my favorite aroma or scent to the water. Taking a walk on the beach, lifting weights, eating a meal especially meat are other good ways to ground yourself.

Spiritual Shortcuts

This is a wonderful visualization to help ground yourself and make a spiritual connection simultaneously. Take a few deep breaths and imagine a beautiful gold cord going from the base of your spine down into the center of the earth. Feel the cord gently wrap itself around the earth's core and feel your energy flowing down the cord into the center of the loving earth. Feel the energy of the earth flowing up the cord into your heart.

Feel the energy making a complete circuit as it flows through your body going down to the center of the earth and up toward the heart at the center of the universe. Take a few deep breaths and feel the energy flow through you. Feel your connection to the earth, feel your connection to your spirit, and know you are one.

Centering

When I'm in my center I'm aware of my body, my emotions, my wants, my needs, and feel very connected to everyone and everything. Being in your center is very similar to finding your way home within yourself. Think of yourself as a big ball of energy. Deep within that ball of energy is your center. It is the place within yourself where you feel most balanced and whole. It isn't so much a place as it is a state of mind that has physical dimensions.

I know I'm not in my center when I start reacting to the events in my life. I start feeling edgy and uncomfortable. At that point I have to make a conscious choice and take some actions to get back in my center. I have to change what I'm telling myself, perhaps meditate and take a few very deep breaths. Each of us have to find our own way to get centered. Writing, meditating, breathing, power moves, or gentle, focused exercises like yoga and stretching sometimes help. Experiment and see what works best for you. The breathing techniques in Chapter 6 might be a good place to start.

Balancing

Think of a gymnast on the balancing beam, they have to move hundreds of muscles and really remain focused so they don't fall off. If we want to stay balanced in our lives we have to pay attention to the needs of our mind, body, and spirit. Some of the body therapies directly address and assist in maintaining this inner balance.

According to Indian tradition we have seven major charkas or energy centers in our body. This meditation is designed to help you balance them. It is a wonderful exercise to assist you in balancing your energies and helping you release blocked energy.

Your base chakra is located at the base of your spine and its color is red. Your second chakra is located a few inches below your navel and its color is orange. Your third chakra is located in your solar plexus the area just below your ribs cage and its color is yellow. Your fourth chakra is located in the middle of your chest parallel with your heart and its color is green. The color of your fifth chakra is blue and it is located in your throat. The sixth chakra is in your forehead, or third eye, and its color is indigo. Violet is the color of your seventh or crown chakra located at the top of your head.

> *Start with your root or base chakra and see a disk of red light spinning clockwise and getting bigger and bigger.*
>
> *Then move up to your next chakra and see an orange disk spinning clockwise getting bigger and bigger.*
>
> *Next see a yellow disk of light spinning over your solar plexus getting larger moment by moment.*
>
> *Now move up to your heart and see the green disk as is gets bigger with each revolution.*

Move up to your throat and see the blue disk getting larger as it spins clockwise.

At your forehead, where your third eye resides, see the indigo disk and on your crown chakra see the violet disk getting brighter and bigger as it spins clockwise.

Take a moment and see all the disk spinning larger and brighter as they all spin clockwise.

Then start at your crown chakra, see the disk change directions, and slowly close down as it gets smaller and smaller. Go through each of the chakras and gently close them until they are faint glow of brightly colored light.

Take a few minutes and focus your attention back on the room.

Your Senses

Our five senses are such a wonderful gift and they make navigating our physical universe much easier and more enjoyable. Our mind filters out most of the information received by our senses. We can tune out noises, ignore smells, walk by objects, and not even notice their existence.

I lived in Vermont for almost twenty years and I never really noticed spring. One day the trees were bare and suddenly they were covered with light green leaves. The year I began focusing on my spiritual healing I took the time to watch spring slowly unfold each day. I noticed the buds on the trees swell, watched in facination as the buds opened into tiny miniture leaves. As the leaves opened the air smelled fresh and clean. It was a wonderful smell very sweet and pungent. I asked a forester about it and he told me that the trees actually produce a gas when the leaves open and that was what I was smelling. For the first time in my life I saw spring and realized what I'd missed all my life by tuning out.

Here is a meditation to help turn up your senses:

Start by closing your eyes and taking a few deep breaths. Focus your attention on your hearing. Listen to all the sounds around you. Focus both inside your body and all around you.

Next focus your attention on you sense of smell. What smells can you smell. See if you can distinguish all the different odors around you.

Now breathe through your mouth and focus on your sense of taste. Just focus on your sense of taste and see how many things you can taste. Take a deep breath through your mouth and see what the air tastes like.

Now focus on your sense of touch. Focus on your skin– what do you feel? Feel your clothes as they touch your skin, notice where you are making contact with the chair or the bed. Feel the air, feel the hair on your body move as the air moves. Really notice you sense of touch. Touch your hands to your body, notice what it feels like to touch yourself or someone else.

Now just barely open your eyes. Keep your eyes partially closed and notice all the details around you, notice the colors, the shapes, and the textures.

Slowly repeat the process with each of your senses three more times.

The first time I did this I was amazed at how much richer my world had become when I went outside. Do this exercise on a regular basis and see what happens to your life.

Your Body As a Temple

Imagine yourself as the caretaker of a magnificent temple. The temple is in need of constant care and upkeep. When you make up in the morning you look forward to taking care of your temple. You clean it and lovingly clear away any liter. You water the plants, feed them, and trim their leaves. You do everything to make sure everything in the temple is perfect. You show visitors how to love this temple as much as you do. You polish everything, walk lovingly on the floors you have cleaned. They are so full of love they have a warm glow. The altar is full of flowers and is absolutely gorgeous.

Your body is your temple. Imagine treating yourself with as much love and respect. It would make a huge difference in your life if you did. Practice treating your body with the love and respect it deserves. Remind yourself that your body is a temple and you are its caretaker.

The Least You Need to Know

- ➤ Your body has its own inner wisdom and its important for you to listen to it.
- ➤ Your body needs movement to remain healthy.
- ➤ Exercise comes in many forms and can be fun.
- ➤ Life can become very rich when you fully engage your senses.

Chapter 18

Eating Mindfully

> **In This Chapter**
>
> ➤ Food has many functions in our lives.
>
> ➤ Eating consciously can change your life.
>
> ➤ Your body is the one that needs food.
>
> ➤ Eating can become a sacred act.

Eating is at the center of many of our social interactions. In many families mealtime is the only time of the day they get together and have time to talk. Restaurants, food courts, and supermarkets are major industries in our culture.

My Mom's life revolved around meals, eating them, serving them, and planning them. Yet how much do we enjoy our food, how often do we eat on the run, or eat while we are doing something else? This chapter is about relating to food in a more soulful manner.

There's More To Eat In Life Than Chocolate

Food is fuel for our body and it has so many more meanings and associations. As an infant we cry and someone brings us food and we feel satiated and loved. Our love affair with food begins. Very few people choose what they want to eat based on their body's needs. How do you choose what to eat? Do eat what's most convenient, or smells good, or is on your diet? How often do you go inside and ask your body what it wants or needs?

Separating out the other roles food plays and making eating be an enjoyable, nurturing experience enriches the quality of your life. Once we remove food and eating from the realm of our limiting filter system it can become a life enriching, sensual, and loving experience. Eating can be fun and healthy without being a struggle. If you're overweight you can learn to eat and lose weight. Food and eating can stop being an opponent and become a loving tool designed to sustain good health.

No matter what kind of relationship you have with food you can improve it and make it more mindful and nurturing.

> **Spiritual Shortcuts**
> Write a letter to yourself about food. What does it mean to you? How often to you think about it? Do you take time to prepare nice meals for yourself if you're all alone? Write a letter to food and let food write a letter back to you. Write about your relationship to food, what does it mean to you? Is it your friend or your foe? Do you think about it often or not at all? Next, let your body write a letter to you about your eating habits and choice of food. You'll find the experience very enlightening, and your answers may surprise you.

Food as a Tranquilizer

Most people have comfort foods which are often favorite foods from their childhood that make them feel better. Eating large amounts of food makes us feel sluggish. If you eat large amounts of carbohydrates your body produces tryptophan, which causes the brain to produce greater amounts of the neurotransmitter serotonin that acts like a tranquilizer by calming and relaxing us.

If you take the time to catalog your favorite foods you will find they all have an emotional value attached to them. You might want potato chips when you're angry and mashed potatoes when you need comforting. To some people warm bread and butter equals mom's love.

Food as a Friend

Especially people who have eating disorders often feel food is the only friend that won't leave them. People feel that way about the object of their addiction. Unfortunately food, when it isn't viewed as fuel for the body winds up hurting us. And if you view a substance as your friend you won't take the risk and make real friends. The unresolved emotional issues will still be there and you'll remain trapped in the endless cycle of an addiction.

Eating disorders usually go undiagnosed and are one of the most emotionally painful of all the addictions. If you struggle with your weight, eat and purge, or have an unrealistic body image seek professional help. You don't need to suffer; you can redefine your relationship with food and your body. Laurel Mellin runs one of the most successful programs I have ever found. She has written a book called The Solution and the name of her organization is the Institute of Health Solutions.

Spiritual Shortcuts

Make a list of your favorite foods and the food you hate. Write about why you like or dislike the various foods. Do you base your likes and dislikes on how a food makes your body feel? I have seen people put foods they have a severe allergic reaction to on their list of favorites. While you're writing about food ask your body what it likes best.

After you compile your list of favorites, notice when you crave them. What is happening around you? What are you feeling or trying to avoid feeling? Review the list of foods you don't like. Why don't you like them? Did you have to eat them as a child? Did you have a negative experience with them? Have you tasted them recently to find out if you really don't like them? Now find other ways to meet your emotional needs. Learn to feed your emotional body instead of your stomach.

Food as Fuel

We don't spend a great deal of time dressing up bowls of gasoline, floating flowers in it, coloring it, and adding spices. We do manufacture different octane levels and different brands of gas put in different additives but when you come down to it gas is pretty much gas. We just put the gas in our car and drive. We may have a preference when it comes to brands or the location of the gas station but when my gas tank is empty I fill it up. When it is already full I don't add more gas because I'm feeling lonely, sad, or anxious. Gas is fuel for my car and it has very little emotional attachment for me. I suppose if you've been burned by gasoline it might have an emotional charge but I doubt if you'd stop driving your car because of it.

Food really is just fuel for our body. Eating is a very sensual experience. It is a big part of our social structure. Food plays a major role in many of our celebrations and our religious practices. Separating the emotional component from food and focusing on food as fuel for our body is very freeing. Once you have unwired food from anything else in our mind we can really enjoy our experience of eating. We can be free to eat and enjoy each and every bite while we are nourishing our body.

> **Sage Advice**
> "Paradise is always where love dwells."
> Richter

Seeing the Sun in Every Bite

Food is beautiful. The shapes and colors, fragrances, textures, and tastes are so varied. There is no denying that food and eating is a very sensual experience. Look in your cabinet and grab a package of anything. Lets say you grabbed a package of crackers. For you to be holding that package in your hand someone had to buy it and bring it home. For that package to be in your local store a person had to order the crackers, the stock person had to put the packages on the shelf, and someone had to build the shelves and the store.

The box for the crackers had to be designed, printed, made, and trucked to the cracker factory. The cracker itself had to be baked after the recipe was developed. Someone had to order the wheat and other ingredients. Each ingredient had to be planted, tended, harvested, driven to market, sold and stored. The seeds for the ingredient had to be grown, stored, packaged, and bought by the farmer. While the crop was in the field the sun, the rain, the moon, the wind, the earth and the stars shared their energy with the growing plants. After the growing season was over if the conditions were favorable the crop could be harvested.

If you look closely you can see the moon and the stars in everything you eat. Think of how many people it took for you to be able to eat that single cracker; it took farmers, truckers, bakers, grocery store managers, stock clerks, as well as your ability to earn money, the people who designed and printed the money, bankers, seed growers, and the nurturing support of mother earth.

Take a few minutes and sit with a piece of food. See the stars, wind, and every one who made that piece of food possible. You are eating stardust and moonlight every time you eat.

Exploring What Food Really Is

If you tried to eat mindfully you know food is more than fuel. It has so many emotional, physical, and spiritual components. There is no error in eating because you need nurturing. If you eat for emotional needs consistently and it becomes a habit you'll never solve the real problem. We all eat in a habitual way. Some of us eat rapidly, some people eat very slowly, and some of us eat when we are starving, while others eat when we're not hungry at all.

Food plays a very big role in most of our lives. As long as we consciously choose those roles we can get the results we want in out life. But when our emotions or a part of our filter system makes those choices for us food becomes our master instead of our servant.

> **Spiritual Shortcuts**
>
> If you want to eat an entire meal mindfully make sure you set aside at least a half hour. Fill up your plate and sit down quietly. Take a few minutes to look at each item on your plate. Look at the texture, the color, and the presentation. Now smell all of the aromas as they blend together. Smell your food. Really allow yourself to experience your food fully with all of your senses.
>
> Take a small bite and slowly chew it. Feel the texture, notice how it tastes as it touches the various taste buds in your mouth. Savor the bite completely before you swallow. Think of all the people who made this food possible and silently thank each and everyone of them as you slowly eat your meal. Between bites put your eating utensil down and look at your plate. Smell, look, and listen to the food. If you have a partner take turns feeding one another.
>
> When you are finished eating take a few minutes to write about the experience.

Use your curiosity to explore the various roles food plays in your life. Watch your friends and family, see what role food plays in those relationships. Notice advertising, see what role food plays even in ads that aren't about food.

Once you start focusing on the role food plays in your life you'll be amazed. It plays a big role in diplomacy. Food was given as an offering to healers and spiritual leaders. Explore the many roles food plays in your life and in our society as a whole. Then decide what role you want it to play in your life, do you want it to be friend or foe?

Listening to What Your Body Really Wants

What does your body need? Your nutritional needs vary every day. Some days you'll need more calories than others. One day you may need more calcium while another day you need extra zinc. Your body knows what it needs. Your thirst tells you how much liquid you need but by the time you are thirsty you are already dehydrated. Before you feel thirsty your body has more subtle signals we unconsciously ignore.

I had a car I was particularly fond of as a teenager. I could tell when everything wasn't running perfectly. When I'd take it to the mechanics he'd say it was fine because he didn't know the sound of the engine as well as I did. Your body constantly tells you what it needs. You have to learn how to listen.

> **Sage Advice**
>
> "To love your body is to learn its song–the song that's in its heart, and sing that song and meet its needs when you might just as easily have forgotten."
>
> Dr. Susan Gregg

It is important to go beyond the surface desire, to ask yourself what you really need. Do you need a doughnut or a nap? Do you need to go for a walk along a stream or write in your journal instead of going to a fast food restaurant? What does your body need? If you ask that question often enough and wait around for the answer you'll begin to know what you really need at any given moment.

True freedom is having the ability to meet your real needs and not settling for a poor substitute. When we don't know what we need we can't satisfy ourselves. If your body really wants broccoli and for emotional reasons you eat an ice cream sundae everyone looses. Your body's needs aren't met and your emotional issues aren't addressed either. If you deal with your emotional issues and listen to your body you can eat the broccoli and have a small sundae. Everyone has their needs met and your body doesn't have to suffer because you use it as a toxic waste dump for the life issues you don't deal with directly.

Smoke & Mirrors

Don't use your body as a toxic waste dump for the life issues you don't deal with directly. If your body really wants broccoli and for emotional reasons you eat an ice cream sundae instead, everyone loses. Your body's needs aren't met, and your emotional issues aren't addressed either. If you deal with your emotional issues and listen to your body, you can eat the broccoli and have a small sundae.

Listening to Your Body: A Meditation

Repeat the following meditation on a regular basis until you really know what your body wants and needs and you are regularly taking care of those needs:

Start by focusing your attention on your breathing. Really notice your breath. Notice how it feels as it comes in through your nose and how it feels as your lungs expand and contract. Take a few moments to really notice your breathing and while you are doing that, mentally give yourself permission to relax. As you continue to observe your breathing, notice how your chest relaxes. With each breath really allow your chest to relax. Let out a few heavy sighs, take a few really deep breaths, and really let yourself relax. (Long pause)

Settle back into your spirit; settle back into your body. Just follow your breath and let it flow into a gentle rhythm. Follow that rhythm; become that rhythm. Just let your breath relax you. Take some time to notice how good it feels to relax, and sink into that feeling of relaxation. (Pause)

If your mind wanders just allow that to relax you even more. Gently bring your attention back to your breathing and relax.
Focus your attention on your breathing. Really notice where you feel your breath. Do you feel it in your nose, your chest, or your stomach? Where do you feel your breath? Focus your attention on that part of your body and really notice your breathing. Follow your breath as it goes in and out. (Long Pause)

Imagine yourself sitting at a table, across from you is your body. In front of you is a pad of paper and you have a pen in hand so you can take notes. You welcome your body and thank it for coming. You apologize to it for all the years you failed to listen to its wants and needs. You tell it you are here to listen.

If your body is angry let it vent its feelings of neglect and abandonment. Encourage your body to say whatever it needs to say and you just listen. Don't defend yourself just listen, and agree.

Then ask your body what it needs. Ask it what kind of exercise it enjoys and how much. How does it like to move? What does it like to do? What does it like to eat? How much and how often? Be specific ask your body what it really needs to be happy. If you here things that are unhealthy realize then it is probably your mind speaking and not your body. Your body wants to feel healthy.

Take some time to write about your insights. Perhaps read a few books on nutrition and the general care and feeding of your body.

Eating as a Sacred Act

A sacred act is something that is done with full awareness and with a deep sense of reverence and awe for our connection to that which is most holy. We can make almost anything a sacred act. When we make eating a sacred act it becomes a sacrament instead of a mindless act of consuming food.

When you think of a sacred act what do you picture in your mind? Do you see priests in robes or people in loin clothes? What is your mental image of sacred acts? Now put yourself in that picture, how can you create a sacred act for yourself?

A sacred act is more of a state of mind than anything. While in that state of mind you do perform certain actions but the actions aren't half as important as your state of mind. Sacredness is an internal matter. You can feel more sacred in the shower than you do in the largest cathedral, sacredness depends on what you are telling yourself; it totally depends on your state of mind.

How could you make eating a sacred act for yourself? What would you have to do or not do? Take some time and really picture how that would look for you.

Making a Ceremony out of Eating

Imagine making eating a sacred ceremony for yourself. You could start before you prepare the meal in the grocery store. Get centered and say a silent prayer of thanks and ask for guidance. Then as you pick out the ingredients for the meal you thank everyone that made this food possible. You lovingly pick out each piece of produce. You hold the cans and containers for a moment before you pick just the right one.

You carry the food home filled with a feeling of deep reverence and awe for the bountiful gifts the earth has provided. You unpack each item lovingly and gently place it in the spot prepared for it. Before you get ready to cook you clean the area and prepare yourself. You might want to take a shower or a bath and then put on some special clothing.

With a silent prayer you place all the ingredients on the counter. Perhaps you light a candle and play soft music. Then will a sense of sacredness and focus you chop all the ingredients and fill each morsel of the food with love. You cook it and tend it mindfully. Whatever you do you do it with love in your heart and a blessing on your lips.

Before you eat you take the time to set the table placing each object with a quiet prayer. You treat the table as if it is a beautiful altar. When you sit down you give thanks and eat each bite slowly and deliberately. You allow yourself to feel the spirit of the food you eat and you give thanks.

Imagine how food prepared and eaten in that fashion would taste. Now compare that experience with going to a drive through and eating your food while your driving. No comparison is there?

Being in the Moment

The only way to do anything mindfully is to be fully present in the moment. We waste between 80 and 90% of our lives by not being in the moment. We are thinking about the experience rather than experiencing it. How often are you fully awake and aware? How often do you choose to act consciously rather than reacting to the event in your lives? How often do you know the reasons for the choices you are making?

We are seldom in the moment. Eating mindful is a wonderful practice to remind us to be in the moment. Stop missing most of your life, be right here right now, and be fully alive. Tomorrow will never get here because by the time it does it's already today and you can't change yesterday because it's already gone.

Spiritual Shortcuts

In a Japanese tea ceremony the spiritual aspect is most important. The basic principles are harmony, respect, purity, and tranquillity. Harmony can be created between persons, between objects, between a person and all matter of things in the world. The tea ceremony teaches us we should respect everyone and everything without distinction of status or rank. Spiritual purity is essential. Tranquillity can only be achieved when we make harmony, respect, and purity our own.

During the tea ceremony the guest sits quietly as the tea master prepares the tea. The ceremony is beautiful to watch. The tea masters movements are deliberate, rhythmic, and precise. The quest and the master communicate spiritually rather than physically. It is an art that shows you how special and holy any occasion can be.

Your Body Really Need More

You are a multidimensional being. You consist of a mind, a body, and a spirit. Your body has hundreds of cells. Your body is a complete universe. Imagine you are a cell in your liver. It looks out and sees billions of stars (other atoms and molecules) and galaxies (clusters of cells). That liver cell feels like it's all-alone, it believes it's unique, that it's an individual. It is totally unaware that it is part of a system called your body and that the whole depends upon each of its parts.

Now imagine yourself standing outside looking up at the stars. You are a cell of the organism called universe. What you do affects the whole and the whole affects you.

In that context what does your body really need? Your body needs proper rest, fresh air, exercise, good food, love, respect, and affection. It needs to be nurtured, treated with care, love, gentleness, and full awareness of its unique needs.

Take some time and ask yourself what your body needs. Then ask yourself if you're willing to meet those needs. If you aren't it is time to work some more on your self-love and acceptance.

Remember this is the only vehicle you will receive for your journey though life. Much of your experience will depend on how well you treat that vehicle. And the length of your stay could be dramatically shortened if you don't take the time to maintain your body.

The Least You Need to Know

- Food has many different purposes in your life.
- Eating mindfully can be a very powerful and sacred act.
- Food means many things to people and it is different for everyone.

Part 5
The Spirit That Moves You

You are a spiritual being having a physical experience and not a body trying to have a spiritual experience. You are a spiritual energy that resides inside that beautiful temple you call a body. What an incredible gift, to wake up every morning and be alive in a human body regardless of how it looks or feels. It is the spirit that keeps you alive. Sometimes from our limited physical perspective we wonder why we are here and what we are doing. It is important to remember that we can't see very clearly from that perspective. From our spirit's perspective everything makes perfect sense.

In this section we are going to talk about things that will help you become more aware of your spiritual nature. Some of the suggestions may seem a bit odd to your mind. The more your mind resists them the more likely they will help you. Your spirit knows you exist, after all it creates you. You're the one that needs to wake up. So wake up and smell the coffee!

Chapter 19

Prayer, Connection, and Inner Guidance

> **In This Chapter**
>
> ➤ **You'll learn to listen to your inner voice.**
>
> ➤ **Develop a meaningful connection to your divinity.**
>
> ➤ **Find out where your safety lies.**
>
> ➤ **Understand discernment.**

I was very confused about this whole prayer thing when I started pursuing my spiritual healing. People talked about guides, intuition, and prayer and I had visions of people sitting in the clouds yelling out orders with megaphones. At times it would be nice if the inner guidance was a bit clearer. I just wanted God to leave a note on my night table telling me what to do, when to do it, and how. I didn't want much.

Any path of self-exploration ultimately leads to the desire to make your own choices and be responsible of your own life. As we begin to heal we stop playing the role of victim in our lives, even to God.

Feeling Safe

When we don't feel safe obviously we are in fear. As soon as we make any decisions based on fear we are reacting instead of acting. We aren't really deciding at all, we're just replaying some memory from the past and making our choices based on it. So, if we really want to be free to choose, we must feel safe enough to do that. One way to feel safe is to have a conscious connection to our spirit, to god, to the universal energy, or however you feel most comfortable phrasing it.

> **Sage Advice**
> "To get to heaven we must take it with us."
> Henry Drummond

The key to feeling safe is that conscious connection and the belief that you are safe. The most important decision you can make for yourself is if this is a safe or hostile universe. If you really believe this is a hostile universe you will never be able to feel completely safe. You'll constantly have to find new ways of defending yourself from the perceived threat. That is the way most people lead their lives.

The physical universe isn't safe, your body can be injured and even killed, but you aren't your body. Your spirit is infinite and eternal, it is invincible, and it cannot be destroyed!! A man and his wife came to one of my lectures. I was talking about safety and how it was an inside job. The man sold security systems and talked about using the proper locks, alarms, and security systems. He wanted to arm the exterior of the house so people would feel safe inside. If we have to live behind bars, alarms, and locks how safe do we feel? I never lock my doors. I figure if someone really wants to break in they will anyway and I'm not afraid of that. When I volunteered at the local men's prison I asked the guys how they picked out the house they were going to break into. They said it was a feeling, a certain house just felt right. Fear makes it feel right.

Feeling safe is an inside job. We must each do whatever is necessary to feel safe, but we have to start from the inside out. Of course we don't needlessly place ourselves in harms way. As the saying goes, "Trust Allah but tie up your camel."

How do you feel safe spiritually? Some people feel safe within the context of an organized religion. Others prefer to find their own path or connection to that universal energy. Whichever path you choose you need to do something on a regular basis so you develop and maintain that connection. Just as we feed our body we must feed our soul. No two foods are just right for everyone and the same is true of spiritual practices. What works for me may not work for you or it might. The only way you'll know what works for you is to experiment.

Developing a Conscious Connection

In order to feel safe, really safe deep down inside we must make a conscious connection with our spiritual self. Knowing we are spirit intellectually doesn't give us that feeling of safety. Physically and mentally feeling that we are spiritual energy inside a body does. Consciously feeling that connection does take time, patience, and practice. And it is a conscious feeling, not just a concept. Once we have that conscious feeling we can tap into it whenever we feel fearful and the fear will dissipate.

There are a myriad of ways to make that contact. We've already talked about a few of them. Meditation can be an excellent way for some people for some it is too hard to quiet their minds. Focusing your attention on feeling the energy between your hands also helps. Hold your hand slightly apart and feel the space between them as you move them slowly in and out. After a while you will be able to feel your energy or your life force.

> **Spiritual Shortcuts**
>
> Go outside on a sunny day and find a place sheltered from the wind. Feel the warmth of the sun on your face, and let yourself focus on feeling it as it warms your skin. Do you have any trouble feeling the warmth of the sun? Know that the warmth of your spiritual connection is just as real, much more profound, and will be with you for eternity.
>
> Find somewhere in nature where you feel at peace and ask for your spirit to reveal itself to you. As you move through your days, ask your spirit for assistance, ask to feel its loving presence, ask to know and understand the nature of your relationship to it. Just keep practicing and eventually you will feel your spiritual energy.

Find somewhere out in nature where you feel at peace and ask for your spirit to reveal itself to you. As you move through your days ask your spirit for assistance, ask to feel its loving presence, ask to know and understand the nature of your relationship. Just keep practicing and eventually you will feel it. In class there is always someone who just can't feel energy and then one day they come in all excited because they felt it. You will too if you keep practicing.

I enjoy going to old churches and feeling the energy in them. When I lived in San Diego I enjoyed going to an old mission there. For centuries people had gone to that church to worship. Even though don't have the same beliefs the energy is still the same. Do some research in the library or talk to people who have lived in your area for a long time, find out if there are any ancient sacred sites in the area. Explore and find places that feel sacred to you and then spend time there.

Another way to feel safe is to redefine the nature of your relationship to the energy, the universe, and to God or whatever you choose to call that energy. We'll do some exercises in chapter 22 that will help you do just that. You are safe, fear and the feelings of being unsafe are all part of your filter system.

Your Inner Voice

We have so many voices in our head. We have the voice of the judge, the victim, the optimist, the pessimist, the angry teenager, the whinny little kid, and the list goes on and on. Amongst the symphony of voices there is also the voice of our spirit, our inner voice. The voice of our inner wisdom is a quiet, still voice. It isn't raucous like the rest of them. Our other voices will demand our attention, bargain with us, judge us, berate us, and do whatever it takes to get us to agree with them.

The voice of our inner wisdom will quietly and lovingly make a suggestion. It won't do a sales pitch on its idea or keep bugging you about its suggestion. Our inner wisdom or our spirit respects us too much to do that. Learning to hear and listen to our inner voice is one of the most valuable and life-changing things we can do for ourselves.

In the 1980's I owned a retail store. A friend of mine also owned a store and one day I went in and ordered a present for my mother. I "knew" in that instant that her employee was stealing from her. As a child I had learned to ignore my inner voice so I immediately forgot what I knew. Through a series of misadventures several years later my friend's employee came to work for me. She managed to embezzle over ten thousand dollars from my business. After I fired her I remembered knowing she was a thief. This was before I started doing any of my emotional and spiritual healing so I was furious with myself, judged myself, and generally made my life miserable.

After several more blatant reminders I started to value the information I received from my inner voice. Once I was willing to listen to my inner voice I had to learn how to tell it from the other voices clamoring for my attention. It was actually quite humorous. I'd be driving along and get a feeling to go another way, I'd be crazed trying to decide if it was my inner voice or not. I successfully learned discernment or the ability to know the difference though trail and error. My theory is it is better to error on the side of caution. I'd rather listen than not. Whenever I failed to listen to my inner voice I always regretted the decision.

Clarity Corner

Listening to your **inner voice**, or your intuition, is a skill worth developing. Take a few minutes each day, sit quietly, and listen for your inner voice. It feels different from the normal chatter; it has a quiet, still, and strong feeling to it. I first started using my inner voice to find things I had misplaced; not it is my best guidance.

Sage Advice

"Endurance is one of the most difficult disciplines, but it is to the one who endures that the final victory comes."

Buddha

Your inner voice won't suggest you go out and buy expensive computers, cameras, or clothing if you can't afford it. Your inner voice will give you insights and information you may not have access to otherwise but you still have to make your own decisions. It will just give you one more piece of information to weigh as you consciously make your choice.

As you clear out your filter system the multitude of voices will begin to quiet and you will be left with a loving, supportive inner voice. That inner voice will encourage you, assist you to tune in, and let you know when you need to make a different choice. Whether you tap into your intuition or not it is important to talk to yourself in a loving, gentle, and supportive manner. That quiet, still voice within you only has kind and caring messages for you, if you learn to listen to that voice you'll certainly feel a lot safer.

Remember your safety always comes from within. If you look for external sources of safety they won't last. Even the strongest fort decays eventually. But once you connect with your inner knowing and that inner feeling of safety and love - people, places, and things no longer control you. Fears of being abandoned won't affect you, you won't be worried about not having enough, and you won't have to look for external solutions for your internal feelings.

Develop that connection with your inner voice and you will be amazed at how much better you feel. As soon as we remove fear as the basis of our decisions the quality of our choices improves, and we begin making choices that create a greater sense of ease and happiness in our lives. Whenever you hear the voice of fear change the channel and remind yourself that you are safe, that all is well in your world.

If you're standing in front of an oncoming car and fear tells you to move by all means move as fast as you can. Fear in the context of physical reality is very useful. Dogs do bite, cars and guns can kill us, and you don't walk down alleys filled with muggers. Fear isn't very useful in the realm of our emotions and the choices we make based on them, in those areas it only causes us limitations, pain, and suffering. Your inner voice will always know the difference, it will tell you to run when its time to run.

I Knew That

As soon as we say, "I know that" we close the door on any new knowledge or information. As human beings we seem most comfortable when we understand things, when we know. Spirituality is an area where we know very little. I recently did a memorial service for a man who had died of a heart attack. While I was speaking I talked about death. I have many beliefs about the afterlife and spirit but do any of us really know. I have had near death experiences and I know I believe what I experienced but did it really happen that way.

I know when I pray or meditate I feel a very profound connection to an energy that feels loving and supportive but if I know what that energy is I limit my experience of it. If I know what my relationship is to that energy I limit the possibilities that are available to me. The phrase "I know" limits us so as much as possible I try to avoid using it. When I do say I know I also know that everything in my knowledge is subject to change and revision at any moment.

Non-attachment is the way to peace of mind and serenity according to Buddha. Non-attachment to your mind, your beliefs, your thoughts, and your feelings is also the way to personal growth and freedom.

Sage Advice

"The only thing we can never get enough of is love. And the only thing we can never give enough of is love."
Henry Miller

Sage Advice

"When you judge another, you do not define them, you define yourself."
Wayne Dyer

Clarity Corner

Non-attachment is an attitude that will allow you to be free. Our mind, our limited, small self, gets attached to everything. When we release our attachments, we are free to see things differently and to make choices that are expansive. We are free as soon as we truly develop an attitude of non-attachment and live by it.

> **Sage Advice**
>
> "Life is a magic vase filled to the brim; so made that you cannot dip into it nor draw from it; but it overflows into the hand that drops treasures into it - drop in malice and it overflows hate; drop in charity and it overflows love."
>
> John Ruskin

Don't limit yourself by believing that you know the answers. That knowing leads not only to limitations but also to things like prejudice and hatred. A friend of mine and I were putting together a workshop on prejudice for high school students. We were targeting emotionally charged prejudices like homosexuality and group identification. I suggested we have students choose a piece of colored cloth from a basket. Each color would represent a different group. Reds would hate blues and purple would be accepting of both groups. Each student would have an opportunity to hate, to be hated, and to see the results of hatred. Our hope was that once they saw the result of prejudice they would be less likely to participate in it.

What causes us to judge a person based on their race, looks, or sexual preference? It isn't based on them it is totally based on what we know or believe about them in general. Once we know homosexuality is wrong or that fat people are lazy we can't get to know them as a person. We judge them before we have that opportunity.

Those words, "I know" have caused a tremendous amount of pain in this world. Often when we are acting because we "know" something we're unaware that is why we're making those choices. We are acting because that's just the way it is. Hatred never makes any sense and it is always based on beliefs we know to be facts. There are no facts, there is no such thing as the truth, and the truth is relative. The beauty about spirituality is being open to experiencing the energy of love and allowing it to unfold, grow, and expand. Let go of your belief that you know anything and just allow the energy to teach you, make no assumptions, just remain open, and continue to grow. Love and be loving.

Love is an act of giving. If you give in order to receive something, you're really trading you're not giving at all. So if you love in order to get something or you only give your love if you've received something you aren't loving, you aren't giving at all. Don't trade your love give it freely.

The Right Prayer Just Left Me

Prayer is defined as a form of spiritual communion or supplication with God or to another object of worship. Prayer is often viewed as a petition or entreaty. When I was a kid I got the impression that if you begged enough, were extremely humble, and had been good, God might answer your prayers if you were lucky. I really had a skewed idea about prayer. I was fortunate enough to meet a woman named Patty who was incredibly spiritual, she had a profound connection to her divinity, and she kept it very simple.

We spent many hours talking about spirituality and how to connect with our divine nature. One of the things I learned is there really is no right or wrong way to pray. It helps if you don't beg or feel inferior to whoever or whatever you are praying to. It is best to think of praying as having a conversation with your best friend.

> ### Spiritual Shortcuts
>
> A prayer starts out with a salutation or greeting, the conversation or request, followed by the closing. I find the best attitude with which to approach prayer and life for that matter is with a profound sense of gratitude.
>
> Great Spirit, god, goddess, all there is I give thanks for this opportunity. I give thanks for all the gifts and blessings in my life. I give thanks for your presence in my life. I wish to know the nature of my relationship to you. I need the courage, the wisdom, the discipline, and the dedication to pursue my spiritual healing. I ask for your guidance, help, and your assistance. I give thanks for your help. In love and light I give thanks.
>
> There is no right or wrong way to pray. Allow yourself to talk lovingly and openly to whatever your concept of divinity is. Open your heart and allow yourself to connect fully and openly to that concept of divinity.

Patty told me that prayer was a time to connect with my concept of divinity, if I asked a question she told me to be available to receive the answer. One of the most important things I learned was to know I already had whatever I was asking for. I was also told to keep my prayers simple and that the energy wasn't an employment agency, dating service, or a real-estate agent.

I find prayer most helpful when I just open my heart and talk. I ask for things like courage, wisdom, serenity, and to feel the love. When I first started to pray I would go to the beach and just ask the energy to love me. I would use prayers to assist me in opening up my heart and connecting to the universal energy of love.

There are also many wonderful prayers written by others. There are many wonderful books available. Check out a few of them, it will help give you some ideas. The most important thing is that you feel comfortable and get the results you want.

Row, Row, Row Your Boat

As the lyrics of the childhood rhyme says life is but a dream. In the dream of your life what kind of a relationship do you want to have with your divinity? That is one of the many choices you have. I know some people who believe they have to act in a certain way, do certain things, and believe in a certain way and then God will love them. I gave up that sort of a relationship years ago. My concept of that universal energy doesn't require me to perform in order to be loved or to get the goodies in life.

> ### Sage Advice
> "Man is never helped in his suffering by what he thinks for himself, but only by revelation of a wisdom greater than his own. It is this which lifts him out of his distress."
>
> C. G. Jung

If I am open and willing to connect to that energy I am able to tap into a vast storehouse of wisdom, understanding, and love. And what a relief it is to know that the universe is safe, that you are loved, and there is help available all you have to do is ask.

So ask yourself what kind of a dream you want to create. Do you want to let in the help and the love? Are you willing to ask for help and then allow someone to help you? Help seldom comes in the shape or in the manner we expect. We just have to remain open, willing, and available.

> **Sage Advice**
>
> "There is a spirit who is awake in our sleep and creates the wonder of dreams. He is the spirit of light, who in truth is called immortal. All the world rest on that spirit and beyond him no one can go."
>
> Upanishads

When you think of a dream does it seem very solid, does it have much substance? If we don't write down our dreams or in some way decide to remember them, we forget them a few minutes after we get up in the morning if we even remember them at all. What if you gave your life as much consideration? What if you didn't take the events in your life very seriously? What if you just decided to make up your spiritual connection?

> **Spiritual Shortcuts**
>
> Take a few minutes and write a myth, a powerful and haunting story of a person on a spiritual quest. Write a myth in which the gods look kindly upon that person's quest and lovingly help them out. Write a story that describes how you would like your life to be in relationship to your spirituality. Write about your relationship to your divinity. Make it as loving and supportive as possible.
>
> Then make it so in your life. Make your dream as grand and glorious as possible and then give yourself permission to live it. The ability to live your dream really just takes a decision and the courage to follow through.

Following the Energy

When we begin to listen to our inner wisdom and guidance we also have to learn how to follow the energy or the guidance. When I first started following the energy it made little or no sense to my rational, linear mind. The easiest way to explain following the energy is that you do the next indicated step. It probably won't make sense but you do it anyway.

Before I moved to California a friend of mine in Vermont gave me the name, address, and time of a spiritualist church she was affiliated with. I loved her dearly so I wanted to check it out. The Saturday after I arrive in California I bought the paper and looked in the church section. There was a spiritualist church meeting at the same address at a different time and it had a different name. I went anyway because I felt it was the next indicated step, it was what I needed to do. The woman who ran the church welcomed me with open arms and introduced me to everyone like I was her long lost daughter. Through her I met Don Miguel the man I spent years studying with. Going to a church with a different name made very little sense but I did it.

> **Sage Advice**
> "Behold the turtle. He makes progress only when he sticks his neck out."
> James Conant

One of my students was browsing in a bookstore when a book fell off the shelf. Against the advice of her mind she bought the book. It was a book on forgiveness. She really needed to forgive herself although she didn't know it. And as a bonus the author was speaking at a local Unity Church a few weeks later.

Your mind is definitely not your best guide but your spirit is. Following the energy will always get you where you need to be in plenty of time. It is a subtle inner feeling, a knowing. How do you pick which book you are going to read? Often it is our inner knowing that leads us to just the right book at the right time.

Following the energy requires us to take risks. It requires us to go beyond our habitual thought and behavior patterns. If you've ever watched a dog sniff and follow the invisible trail left behind you know on an intuitive level what it means to follow the energy. Your mind may say it doesn't know what it means but you do, if you'll let go of your mind for a minute and drop down into your heart you know. It means doing things like letting go of a relationship because you know it's holding you back. It means staying in a relationship even though it scares you to death because you know it's your fear of intimacy that is holding you back.

Following the energy often means doing the very thing that scares you most or not doing the thing you crave most to do. Following the energy usually means going in the opposite direction your mind is telling you to go. It means staying when you want to run more than anything and leaving when you really want to stay. But you stay or go from a place deep inside where you make your decisions based on love rather than fear.

Fear tells us to stay when we need to leave and leave when we need to stay. Following the energy requires us to plunge head long into our fears so we can reach the freedom that awaits us just on the other side. Following the energy takes courage at first but once you see the results you get it is the only logical choice there is.

Following the Energy

At first following the energy is a very conscious and deliberate act. When you are about to make a decision take a few minutes to focus on your decision and get clear about it. After you run through this process a few times it becomes almost second nature. The more emotional charged a decision is the more thoroughly you'll have to examine your motives and emotional attachments. At first I find you need to write out the answers but once you're acquainted with your inner workings the writing won't be as necessary.

Ask yourself the following questions and be very clear and honest with your answers. Remember the easiest person for you to lie to and the only one you can really fool is yourself.

> What does this issue really mean to me? What is its symbolism in my life?
> What are my feelings both pro and con?
> Which is the safer and more logical thing to do?
> What attachment do I have if any to either outcome or choice?
> What would fear tell me to do right now?
> What would love have me do?
> What decision would I normally make?
> What decision feels right?

Sage Advice
"Experience is not what happens to a person. It is what a person does with what happens."
Aldous Huxley

Once you get a real sense of your answers to these questions you'll know how to follow the energy. Your inner guidance is a quiet still voice. If you really, really, really want to do a particular thing chances are its your filter system but only you can really know what decision is following the energy and which is not. Go inside, get clear, and you will always know. If you fool yourself remember how it feels to fool yourself so you won't be able to do it as easily in the future. There are no mistakes, just outcomes you like better than others. If you don't like the outcome learn how to make a different choice.

Knowing the Difference

Discernment is a very important tool in any ones life. The best snake oil salesperson in the world couldn't do a better job of conning us than we could do for ourselves. We can do a better and more believable sales pitch on ourselves than anyone else ever could. We know what we'll buy and what we won't.

When are we listening to our mind, our emotional wounds, or our inner guidance? No one can tell us that but ourselves and at times we aren't very accurate. There have been times I was absolutely certain I was following my inner guidance and it was really the emotional desires of my wounded self masquerading as my inner guidance. I couldn't or wouldn't tell myself the difference, when I saw the results the truth was very evident.

Practice will really help you develop discernment. Deciding there is immense value to listening to your inner voice also helps a great deal. It isn't that my inner voice intrudes upon my life constantly it only seems to make suggestions at pivotal points in my life. And after a while I noticed that every time I failed to listen, I regretted my choice. After numerous self-induced traumas learning to hear that voice became a priority for me.

Look at your own life. Has there ever been a time or times you had a hunch or a feeling you needed to do something and ignored the feeling? Did you regret your decision? If it hasn't happened yet I can guarantee it will.

Knowing the difference between your inner guidance and one of the other parts of your psyche is very similar to learning how to follow the energy. It is a feeling, an internal knowing, and only you can know the absolute truth for yourself. Others in your life may know when you're lying to yourself but their opinions only count if you give them a vote in your life.

As I learned these new behaviors I found it did help to have people in your life that I call trusted others. They are people you know love you, respect you, and in no way want to control you. They are friends or a counselor that really cares about you and don't want to see you hurt yourself. They are also people who have done or are in the process of doing their emotional and spiritual healing. Trusted others are definitely not allies, they will call you on your stuff in a loving way when you give them permission to.

Smoke & Mirrors

When we first get in touch with our inner guidance we can easily go overboard. It was exciting when I first started listening to my inner voice. I'm sure I drove my friends crazy saying my little voice told me to do this and it told me to do that. It became another way to avoid taking responsibility for my choices.

In the 1970's, comedian Flip Wilson had a hysterical routine called "The Devil Made Me Do It." If we're not careful we'll start saying the same thing about our inner voice and believe me it won't be much of a comedy act.

Use your inner voice as guidance, don't make what it said gospel. Ultimately you are responsible for all of the choices and outcomes in your life. Your inner voice is just another source of information, granted important and valuable information. But it is just information, you still have to make the choices.

The Least You Need to Know

- Prayer is a way of talking to a dear friend who is willing and able to help you.
- Discernment is a very valuable tool.
- Learning how to listen to your inner voice will save you a lot of pain and trouble.
- Life is just a dream.

Chapter 20

I Give Up, I Surrender

> **In This Chapter**
>
> ➤ Understand surrender as a path to freedom.
>
> ➤ Realize the difference between giving up and letting go.
>
> ➤ Find an easier way to change.
>
> ➤ Learn about dominion and domination.

Surrendering and giving up are two entirely different things yet they can mean the same thing. Your mind says, "What did you just say?" You're saying they're entirely different but they're exactly the same. Well they are, it just depends upon how you look at them.

If we give up because of fear or discouragement then it isn't surrender it's giving up. But if we give up an old behavior because we love ourselves that's freeing, not limiting. And surrender can be very freeing or not, the difference lies in our underlying motive.

Surrender Doesn't Mean Giving Up

Surrendering is one of the most powerful and freeing things you can do. I used to think surrendering meant giving up and giving in to hopelessness and at times in my life it did. Surrendering is giving up your habitual way of thinking and feeling about life. It is giving up doing things your way and allowing for the possibility there is a far better way to do things.

If you continue to hold onto your issues you can't change. I have seen people hold onto an issue and refuse to let go of it for years. They'd modify the issue, rationalize the behavior, and try to deny its existence but it was still there, it still affected the quality of their life. Often we want the outcomes in our life to change but we don't want to change our behavior. We continue to overspend but we want to have money, or overeat and we want to be thin.

Surrendering means getting to a place where we can be reasonable and be persuaded to change our behavior. A friend of mine is fond of saying she has never let go of anything that wasn't covered with claw marks from her taking it back. Life really is so much easier once we finally surrender it is only then that we can learn a different way of doing things. Until we let go we doom ourselves to repeating the same behavior over and over again.

At times we're very creative, it may look like we've let go but we're really still holding on just as tightly as ever. Hold a pen or pencil in your hands with the palm of your hand facing upwards. You can let go of the pen or pencil but there it is still sitting in the palm of your hand. It isn't until you turn your hand over that you've truly surrendered the object. So it is in life we can let go of things in such a way that we still really have them.

Clarity Corner
Surrendering definitely does not mean giving up. Surrendering means letting go of your small, wounded, fear-based self and aligning yourself with your loving, spiritual self. What you are really surrendering is your limitations, your fear, and your misery. Surrendering is all about setting yourself free.

Sage Advice
"You must do the thing you think you cannot do."
Eleanor Roosevelt

Only you can decide if you're really ready to surrender something. Sometimes we let go, pick it up, let go, and then pick it up again. Surrender is a process and as with any process it takes time. You may not be able to fully let go of a behavior, thought pattern, or issue all at once. You may have to let go of it piece by piece.

I'll Never Give Up

I have watched addicts and alcoholics vehemently defend their addictions. I have seen people in immense emotional pain say I'll never give up drugs or alcohol even though to everyone except themselves it is evident they are creating huge problems in their lives. I had one student who constantly wanted to blame me rather than look at her own issues. She never felt part of the group and was often very hurt by what she perceived as my attempt to exclude her from the group. I talked to her many times about her filter system coloring her perception. It was sad to see her in emotional pain unwilling and unable to let go of the way she saw things.

Our turmoil always originates in our filter system, which in turn dictates how we react to the events in our life. Our mind is often quite adamant and it won't give up the way it thinks. The sad thing is we believe what our mind is telling us so we hold onto the very thing we need to let go of. There is very good chance that the very thing you are holding onto most tenaciously is the thing you most need to let go of.

> **Sage Advice**
> "The greatest griefs are those we cause ourselves."
> *Sophocles*

How do we know what to hold onto and what to let go of? We know, deep inside of ourselves we know, and it's often a real struggle getting ourselves to acknowledge the truth. A large part of our spiritual healing is creating an accurate map of our inner feelings. It feels a certain way when we are lying to ourselves. It feels a certain way when we are trying to convince ourselves of something that isn't the truth. One thing I have found consistently across the board is the quicker we want to deny something and avoid it the more important it is to our healing journey.

One day I was talking to a close friend about a drama that was unfolding in my life. It wasn't the first time I had created this particular drama. As we talked about it I offhandedly said I hate children. As soon as it was out of my mouth I started saying I don't really hate children and rationalizing and denying my words. Once I was off the phone I started thinking about my feelings toward children and how they would affect my life and the way I treated others and myself. The affects were tremendous in my life that inner feeling colored most of my choices and to a large degree affected the way I felt about myself.

I was shocked. I had no idea I felt that way but once I did it was so healing and freeing. It took quiet a while to uncover all the beliefs that stemmed from that feeling. After a time that knowledge changed almost every area of my life. The only reason I explored it in the first place was because I wanted to deny it so strongly. That denial told me it was an important piece of information.

Observe yourself. Notice how it feels deep inside when you feel the need to defend yourself. Often we defend ourselves when we know we aren't in alignment with our spiritual self. How does it feel when you plant both feet and say no never, I won't do this? Map your emotions; review your past especially times when you later realized you should have moved on instead of holding on. Notice what it felt like when you lied to yourself or denied something you later realized was true.

Knowing What's Really What

Only you can decide for yourself what your beliefs are, where you're in denial, and what you need to surrender and what you need to keep. Others can help you by listening to you but you have to find the truth within yourself. And that takes incredible courage when you're approaching your core issues. The deeper you explore your filter system the more defenses you have, the landmines are better hidden, and the more frightening and unsettling it gets.

When I fail to let go of something I need to surrender, the toll it takes on my life is immense. Once I really understood the importance of knowing when I need to let go, I became much more vigilant and willing to look at areas in my life I would much rather have ignored.

Your spiritual healing, your ability to be gloriously happy, and your right to have a healthy and successful life depends on your willingness to look deep within yourself. The irony is once you surrender and let go the process of healing becomes so much easier.

The easiest way to know where to look is to look where you don't want to look. Follow your resistance it will lead you to your freedom. Catalog your feelings, find the areas of your life that don't work, and tell yourself the truth.

What are you holding onto? Find that feeling inside you and uncover the words that cause it. Then shout those words over and over again loudly until they begin to transform. Then shout those words until you know you're at the core level. Then let go and tell yourself something less limiting and more loving. Keep reviewing your inner words until they are loving and supportive, until you can believe that you are perfect just the way you are.

Sometimes when we start hitting the bedrock or core of our issues we need the assistance of a good counselor or spiritual adviser to get us to the other side. When we are in the middle of one of those issues it is hard to remember we're lovable, it is hard to love ourselves when we're faced with beliefs that say we aren't. And that is a perfect time to say I surrender, help me to love myself, show me how to heal. When we finally realize our old beliefs and ways of doing things aren't working we become more willing to let go and learn a new way that does.

Well Maybe

I think of getting to the place where I am willing to say well maybe as being reasonably teachable. I once had a near death experience, my heart had stopped, and I experienced myself being on the other side. I did not want to come back, not at all. I was talking to my mother and several other people. They were trying to convince me that I wasn't done and I needed to go back. I wasn't willing to come back. This discussion seemed to go on for an eternity. I was getting very tired of arguing. Finally I tried to appease them by saying I'll think about it. I no sooner spoke the words than I felt myself slamming back into my body. At the time I was really angry, I felt betrayed, like I'd been tricked back into my body.

I now realize that what happened was I became willing, I was willing to learn how to live my life differently. I wasn't happy about it for a long time but now I am so grateful and often harness that power. The moment I let go even though it was just for a second everything changed. I was alive again.

If you just open the door a little your spirit will gladly help you. The universe is really an abundant place. There is more than enough of everything. We unwittingly have to work very hard at creating limitations in our life. As soon as we let go and surrender to the universal goodness all the things we have been holding at bay come rushing into our lives.

Literally our filter system acts like a huge dam preventing all the things we desire from entering our lives. Our beliefs in lack and limitation hold back the money and the love. Having them would dispel those limiting beliefs. It is amazing at the miracles that become every day occurrences once we remove those blockages. Once we surrender life becomes so much easier.

Your mind and your small self will have a hard time understanding the idea of surrender. Your mind will make it hard, you will resist letting go, and you will make yourself suffer needlessly. Just getting to the point that you are somewhat willing to maybe, perhaps let go is incredible freeing. There is nothing in your life worth holding onto. Now wait a minute your mind says. The less attachment you have to anything in your life the more freedom and happiness you will have. It is our attachment that causes most of our discomfort so if we wear life loosely and realize there is nothing worth holding onto surrender becomes easy and almost second nature.

> **Sage Advice**
> "When the heart weeps for what it has lost, the spirit laughs for what it has found."
> *Sufi Aphorism*

Phew!

All your life you've been surrendering to something, most of the time you've just been surrendering to your filter system and your small self. Once you realize how powerful surrender is and how easily you can do it, your sense of relief will be immense. When you surrender to your spiritual self you surrender to your greater good, you release your small self and move beyond your self-imposed limitations. Once you start surrender to your spiritual self instead of surrendering to your mind the results you're getting as well as your life changes very rapidly.

Let's look at an addiction. An addiction is definitely a form of surrender. You surrender to your addiction, the addiction takes over, and you've given up, you've surrendered the freedom to choose your behaviors. You have doomed yourself to indulge in your addiction. The thought patterns, your choices, how you act, and how you react get all wrapped up in the addiction. The addiction becomes bigger and more pervasive.

Once you surrender your attachment to the addiction, changing your behavior is so much easier. Once you realize the power lies not in the addiction itself but in your need and desire to surrender to it, change is possible. Then you just have to understand your needs and desires and surrender the belief that your addiction is the only way to meet them.

> **Sage Advice**
> "Two birds, inseparable companions, perch on the same tree. One eats fruit the other looks on. he first bird is the individual self, feeding on the pleasures and pains of this world. The other is the universal self, silently witnessing all."
> *Mundaya Upanishad*

Surrender, wanting to hold on, letting go, and deciding what we need to surrender can be very confusing and frustrating. At times if feels like your chasing your shadow on a cloudy day, it's allusive at best. Once you get a feeling inside for what I'm talking about it all suddenly makes sense. Confusion lifts and you know exactly what you need to do.

Life makes a wonderful barometer. If you've tried to change something in your life and you've succeeded you must have surrendered and dealt with all the necessary issues. If you can't shift a behavior or you continue to react in an undesirable manner to events in your life or have the same feelings or create similar situations then you have to look deeper. Looking deeper means surrendering knowledge hidden deep within your mind that you've spent years protecting yourself from.

> **Sage Advice**
> "Two birds, inseparable companions, perch on the same tree. One eats fruit the other looks on. he first bird is the individual self, feeding on the pleasures and pains of this world. The other is the universal self, silently witnessing all."
> *Mundaya Upanishad*

The very things we think we're protecting ourselves from are really the things that limit our experience in life and create much of our emotional pain. Let go of it all and be free. When we surrender to our spiritual self, life gets so much easier, we are much freer, and happier.

Now You Get To Win

How do you define winning? Your answer to that question will influence a great deal of your experience in life. If winning is something you achieve externally you'll have a hard time allowing yourself to just be happy, you'll find it necessary to achieve and do things in order to win. If you define winning as an internal feeling it will be much easier for you to relax and enjoy life. You won't have to accomplish anything in order to feel good about yourself.

Take sometime to answer these questions for yourself:

- How do you define winning?
- Is winning important to you in your life?
- What would your life look like if you were a winner?
- What would it look life if you were a loser?
- Does there have to be a loser in order for there to be a winner?
- How can you live your life so everyone is a winner?

Winning and losing are heads and tails of the same coin. As long as you think in terms of winners and losers, surrender, support, and vulnerability become undesirable and unavailable in your life. The world is based on the paradigm of domination. When you view life through the eyes of domination there is always someone better than you and someone less than you. Life is a competition and cooperation isn't available.

Surrender is a sign of weakness. The symbol for domination is a line. Sayings like "climbing the corporate ladder" fit into the worldview of domination. Right and wrong, good and bad, judgment of any kind is all part of looking at the world through the eyes of domination.

It's Not About Winning

There is another way to look at the world. It is called dominion. In dominion we are all part of the whole, better than and less than doesn't play a role in dominion. In dominion things are different but there isn't a value judgment placed on that difference. The symbol of dominion is a sphere. Everyone in life is just standing on a different place on the sphere so their view is different.

Winning when you look at life through the eyes of dominion doesn't require a loser. When you're living life in dominion everyone wins. Instead of climbing over other people on the way to the top everyone walks to the top together. Life becomes about cooperation. Surrender makes sense, it's the obvious choice if we really want to be happy and it's no longer frightening.

Mentally experiment with the ideas of domination and dominion. Our minds have been trained to think in terms of domination so it takes time to think in terms of dominion. Dominion leads naturally to the spiritual truth that we're all one. Play with the idea. When you're upset with someone or something imagine that they're part of you and that you're part of them. See how your perspective changes.

Imagine what life would be like if everyone lived their lives based on dominion. There would be no need for rules or regulations. When we live our life from a place of dominion all of our decisions are based on love. When our decisions are based on love we can't make decisions that will hurt ourselves or anyone else. This would certainly be a different world if it were no longer based on domination.

> **Clarity Corner**
>
> Being in **dominion** means being part of a whole. I think of dominion as standing on the surface of a huge sphere. Everyone is still a part of the sphere, and everyone has her own unique perspective depending upon where she is standing. If the sphere represents infinity, everyone and everything are within that sphere. so there is no such thing as being separate from the whole.

> **Sage Advice**
>
> "Shoot for the moon. Even if you miss it you will land among the stars."
>
> Les Brown

A Story of Wisdom

The following story is what I call a teaching story. A teaching story gives us information at many different levels. We don't have to dissect the story, we only have to read it and allow its subtle messages to slowly sink in. This is one of my favorites I hope you enjoy it.

Many centuries ago in a village high in the mountains a woman lived very happily with her family. One day a warlord carried her husband off to war. The woman was deeply saddened by her husband's absence. After many years she gave up hope that he was even alive. All she could do was pray for his soul.

One day he returned to the village and she cried with joy. After a time she realized he had changed, he was no longer a loving and playful husband. He was often mean and angry. She then cried with sadness.

The woman went to the wise-woman of the village and asked her what to do. The old woman told her that there was a very special, magic potion that could cure anything but the woman would have to gather the ingredients herself. First she told the woman to gather several herbs that only grew by the river far away. It was a long journey but the woman gladly went.

When she returned the old woman told her she needed one last ingredient, the whisker from a live tiger. Even though the woman knew there was a tiger living high in the mountains above the village she felt hopeless. She knew she would never be able to get a whisker from a live tiger.

That night she awoke to a voice saying, "Go to the mountain and take a bowl of meat with you. Then be patient and watch." She climbed to the top of the mountain carrying a bowl of meat. She left it in front of the tiger's cave and waited. After a time the tiger appeared and looked all around. He could not see her because she hid behind the jagged rocks, downwind from the cave. After smelling the air to make sure it was safe, he ate the meat and went back to sleep. She collected her bowl and ran back to her warm bed.

The woman continued to feed the tiger every evening for weeks, moving a little bit closer each night. Eventually she could stand a few feet away from the tiger as he ate. One night, when she knew the time was right, she lunged forward pulling out a whisker. Joyously, she ran all the way home.

The next day she went to the healer's hut and proudly handed her the whisker. The old woman took the whisker and threw it into the fire. The woman stood there in shock as she watched the fire consume her hard won prize. The old woman smiled and said, "The tiger has taught you much, my child. With your patience, discipline, and dedication you got the whisker, by overcoming the tiger you learned many lessons. You also overcame your fear and your hopelessness. With the knowledge you've gained you can change anything."

Learning from a place of dominion is much easier, gentler, and more loving. Instead of struggling with knowledge we allow it to become a part of our life and a part of the way we act, think, and live. Much like a teaching story the paradigm of dominion infiltrates our thinking and our lives. It is a subtle difference but an extremely powerful one.

Dominion also makes it so much easier to connect with our spiritual self. Dominion is how our spirit or god operates. Domination is the way of the rational, linear, limited mind and small self.

There Is An Easier Way

This chapter is not about giving up it's about surrendering. The easiest way to live life is to be in alignment with our spiritual self. Life is seductive, we get so caught up in physical reality that we start to think it's real, and we hold onto it as tightly as possible. We forget we're a spiritual energy inside a body and start thinking we're the body. My body sure seems real. When my Mom died I sure missed her presence in my life. But when I let go of my mind and tap into my essence I know my mother never left, she's still here with me.

When I let go of the part of my mind that tells me I'm separate from you and everyone else, I can feel the love of the universe all around me so I can never feel alone. When I allow myself to be in dominion with the universe, everything else is so much easier. Change can become a fun filled adventure of exploration instead of something done in desperation in hopes that we can stop the pain.

Surrendering our sense of separation is a process that is very freeing. I'm sure enlightened beings like Buddha, Lao Tse, and Jesus still had to take care of their physical bodies but they weren't attached to them and they certainly knew they were a spiritual being. They enjoyed life, lived it to its fullest, yet they remained unattached.

> **Sage Advice**
> "There is hunger for ordinary bread and there is hunger for love, for kindness, for thoughtfulness, and this is the greater poverty that makes people suffer so much."
> Mother Teresa

The easiest way to fully enjoy life is to let go of your attachment to it. Surrender your life to the service of your spiritual self and its amazing how much fun you can have. When I was attached to my life looking a certain way I missed out on a lot of opportunities. If you think love can only come from a certain person or money can only come to you through your job or you need x, y, and z in order to be happy you've really short changed yourself.

The thought of surrendering my life to my spirit, giving up my goals, and just following where the energy leads me scared me a lot. After all I know what makes me happy, I know what I want, and where I want to go. What I really know is how to limit myself and my happiness. What

> **Sage Advice**
> "If you understand, things are just as they are. If you do not understand, things are just as they are."
> Zen Koan

my spirit self knows is how to lead me to greater joy than I ever thought possible. But hearing that voice and listening and then following the directions is one of the hardest things I've ever done.

My contentment and my happiness are directly proportional to the degree I've surrendered. I know beyond a shadow of a doubt that if I'm in emotional turmoil I'm holding onto a limiting belief or something else I need to let go of. Does that make me let go? Not necessarily. We are a stubborn lot us humans, sometimes it takes a lot of emotional pain before I let go, sometimes it takes none at all. It all depends on how attached I am to it in the first place.

My attachment, my willingness, and my acceptance of things as they are help me a great deal. As long as I remind myself that surrender is always my key to freedom I remember to let go. As soon as I start listening to the fears of my mind I want to hold on again. As long as I believe my happiness lies beyond myself, as soon as I start thinking in terms of them out there, I'm lost. I am back in the world of external solutions and a happiness that always lies just beyond my grasp.

There is no out there. Surrender to the fact that the cause of your emotional turmoil always resides in your filter system and freedom will be yours. Look outside and you'll have to keep on looking.

The Power of Silence

Beyond words there is a universe free of limitations. As soon as we name something we limit it and ourselves. I once did an exercise in which I didn't name my emotions I let them remain nameless feelings. It was a very powerful experience. One day I was feeling something, if I'd named it I would have called it anxiety but by the end of the day I realized it was excitement. They feel very much the same but I certainly would have responded very differently to them.

Words have real power. Remember the old saying sticks and stones may break my bones but words will never hurt me? Nothing could be further from the truth. We imbue words with a tremendous amount of power. Words can ignite riots and cause incredible violence. Words can hurt us or they can heal us. Think of the small child who is told by their parent that they have a terrible voice. The stronger the parent's reaction is to that child's singing the less likely that child is to enjoy singing as an adult. On the other hand words of love and encouragement can help us overcome other wise insurmountable obstacles.

When I teach students about the Toltec tradition, one of the things I talk about is shadows. In that tradition shadows are thought to be doorways to alternate universes. I know they are definitely doorways to a deeper understanding of ourselves and our world. Shadows allow us to be able to see. Without the contrast between light and dark everything would look the same. Watching shadows can be a very interesting and informative pastime.

> **Sage Advice**
> "One never loves enough."
> Aldous Huxley

Just as there are shadows in the light there are also shadows in the sounds. The shadows in the sounds are the spaces between the noises, they are the silences between the sounds. When I was studying with don Miguel he had me practice hearing the shadows in the sounds. The first time I did, it was magical and it remains that way, I love hearing the shadows in the sounds.

I was taking my dog for a walk one morning before sunrise. The sky was just turning colors and as I walked by a Yucca tree a bird sounded her first note of the day. I heard the spaces between her notes and it felt like I found an entire universe in the silence. It took my breath away. Silence is a very powerful force. It holds the sound so we can hear them.

Years later I began to think about silence. We are seldom silent, if we are spending time with a friend we talk, we fill up the silences. As I proceeded with my training I found I was quiet more and more of the time. People were often uncomfortable with my silence, they'd often assume I was upset with them. I just enjoyed the stillness.

Talk less, listen more. We use a lot of energy trying to fill up the silence. Look at how many devices we have invented that make noises, or allow us to communicate with others. But how often do we spend time alone and in silence communicating with the godself that lives within? Silence is so powerful, silence is golden.

> **Spiritual Shortcuts**
>
> Decide to spend one day a month in silence for a year. Most people resist the idea of it but once they try it they realize how powerful it is. Set aside a specific day and honor yourself with a day of silence. Make it a day designed to be loving and nurturing. Turn off the phone, tell your family you are going to be silent, and spend the day with yourself. Don't watch TV or listen to music. Be in the silence and be silent. Eat healthy and nurturing food, take a long hot bath, journal, read spiritual or inspirational literature, go out in nature and just be quietly with yourself. Make sure you set yourself up for success. If you go out in public carry a note with you that you can hand someone so if they talk to you they'll understand your silence. After you try it, even if only for part of a day you'll realize how much energy we waste talking.

The Least You Need to Know

- Surrender will set you free.
- You're always surrendering anyway, the choice is what you're going to surrender to.
- Dominion allows you to be part of everything and everyone.

Chapter 21

Nature as Healer

> **In This Chapter**
>
> ➤ Learn how to listen to nature.
>
> ➤ Find your element.
>
> ➤ Connect with yourself at a deeper level.
>
> ➤ Feel the peace.

I find being out in nature very healing. Most people find it very easy to connect with their spirituality in nature as well. I once had an old medicine man tell me to go talk to a tree. He told me to come back after I had. At the time I thought he was a bit odd but he wasn't. It was a very profound experience.

Unwittingly as a little girl growing up in New York City I used to climb trees and sneak off to the cemetery, it was peaceful and full of trees, birds, and beautiful plants. I tried to ignore the dead people although they used to scare me some. Nature has all the information you'll ever need and it will help you heal if you let it.

Go Tell it to the Mountain

Learning to connect with nature allows us to connect with our essence in a totally different way. We can feel the elements, we can feel the energy, and we can feel the very stuff we're made of. Feeling nature, connecting with the elements takes us beyond the chatter of our mind into the realm of pure energy. Our mind can chatter to us about the fact that we don't feel anything but we can't go out into the silence of nature and come back unchanged. If you throw an ice cube in hot cup of tea is has no other choice, it has to melt. When we spend time in nature we are changed by the experience.

Clarity Corner

Feeling nature does generally require you to be in nature, but being in nature doesn't mean your are feeling it. Feeling nature means really dropping down into your body and feeling the elements: Feel the wind on your skin, smell the earth, feel the warmth of the sun, and let the sounds around you fill your being. Allow yourself to feel the presence of nature as it surrounds you.

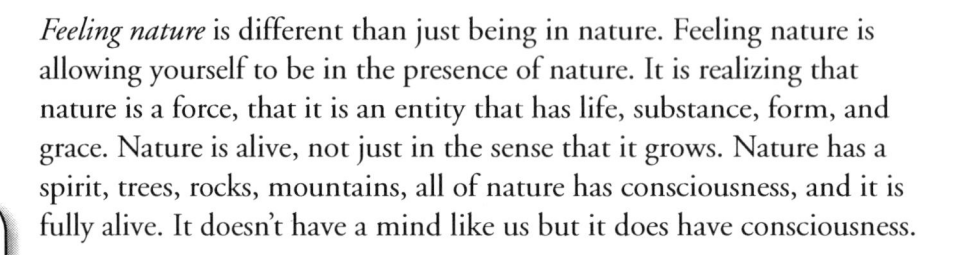

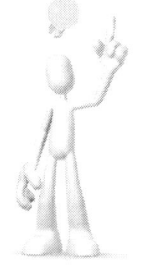

Sage Advice

"Walk on the rainbow trail; walk on a trail, and all about you will be beauty. There is a way out of every dark mist, over a rainbow trail."
Navajo Song

Feeling nature is different than just being in nature. Feeling nature is allowing yourself to be in the presence of nature. It is realizing that nature is a force, that it is an entity that has life, substance, form, and grace. Nature is alive, not just in the sense that it grows. Nature has a spirit, trees, rocks, mountains, all of nature has consciousness, and it is fully alive. It doesn't have a mind like us but it does have consciousness.

Before I started my journey of healing I enjoyed standing in the quiet of the forest, I felt something but I never really gave it much thought. Once I started studying with don Miguel nature took on a totally new meaning. As I explored myself as an energy being suddenly I saw life and energy everywhere I looked. Nature is one of the most powerful teachers we can have if we're wiling to take the time to learn how to listen.

We can only listen to the wisdom nature has to offer if we drop down inside ourselves and go beyond the chatter of our minds. Once we do it's amazing what we can see, hear, feel, and learn during a simple walk on nature. Walking in silence through the woods can be an incredible experience. You can hear the wind approach and it can talk to you. Once you become acquainted with the wind you can feel its moods, at times it is impatient, while at other times it is soft and loving. The wind was one of my most powerful teachers and it still is. It can remind me to be still, or nudge me into action.

There is a place within us that we can access our inner knowing and our ability to connect with our spiritual essence. When I access that place it feels like I am dropping down into my heart or my center. It literally feels like my consciousness goes from my mind down into the center of my being. It feels different to everybody. But it is a process in which you connect with the stillness of your spirit. Allow yourself to find that connection within yourself and allow it to feel however it feels for you. We are all unique and if we try to do it the same way as someone else it may not work for us. Ultimately we all have to find our own path. Luckily there are certain techniques that will point the way, you just have to take it from there.

> **Spiritual Shortcuts**
>
> Sit quietly and focus you attention on your breath. If you need to move around to get comfortable do so but don't let your body needlessly distract you. If your nose itches scratch it and then refocus your attention on your breathing. Breathe very deeply and rhythmically. Really allow yourself to relax and imagine yourself connecting with your spiritual essence. Breathe, relax, and connect. Keep doing that until you feel yourself dropping down into your center. At first you may only stay there for a second but with practice you can stay longer. You can tell when you've connected because it feels different, like your mind just shifted gears. Practice, be gentle with yourself, and remember it's a process so it will take time. You can do it as long as you ignore your mind's opinion that you can't.

The Majesty of Mountains

All of nature is wonderful but mountains are so majestic and ancient. Mountains rise up from the land and stand as silent guardians of an ancient wisdom. Every mountain has its own beauty, a feeling uniquely its own, it is magical and wonderful. Here in Hawaii the mountains are like no other place I've lived. They are the remnants of old volcanic craters eroded over the centuries by the gentle trade winds. They look like they've been sculpted out of primordial clay by the gods. They are full of deep crevasses that fill with waterfalls during times of heavy rains. The trees are scanty on the windward side where the winds always blow. As you crest the mountains the leeward sides are full of trees ranging from pale green to a deep forest green. As you approach the leeward coast the hills become arid and desert like. Rainbows and mists often fill the valleys.

In Vermont the Greenmountains beckon you to come and play with them while the Rockies dare you to try and enter their domain. The mountains outside San Diego are barren and a gateway to the magnificent Anza-Borrego desert. They are made of huge boulders exposed by centuries of exposure to the Santa Ana winds. Mount McKinley in Alaska glows as the sun reflects off its snow capped peaks. Each mountain has its own spirit, its own special quality, and feeling. When you stand in the shadow of a mountain let it speak to you, open your heart, and see what you feel. Mount Fuji seems to stand tall and proud inviting pilgrims to come and journey there. Think about some of the mountains you've seen personally or in pictures, what kind of feelings do they invoke in you?

Go out and walk in the foothills, find a path that leads you to the top of a hill. Stand out in nature, stand out in the elements, and listen. I hated hiking until I hiked in the hills around Sedona in Arizona. I went out and hiked up to a stone arch. I stood under that arch and I was in awe. There was this massive bridge carved out by nature. I stood in its shadow and chanted. Then magically up out of the valley came the sound of a flute, echoing melodically. I couldn't help but laugh, the sun, the warmth, the wind, and the flute made the surrounding surreal. Ever since that day I have loved hiking.

In some areas they have full moon hikes, parks or botanical gardens where they give guided tours on the night of the full moon. When the moon is full you could drive to the beach or anywhere out in the country on a clear night and let yourself bask in its light. Let yourself dance, sing, and play. Set your spirit free in the moonlight.

Go out and find a place you can watch a mountain or hill for the day. Take your lunch, sit, meditate, read, write, and just let yourself feel. During a single day a mountain change so much. I used to love to watch the shadows of the clouds as they passed over the mountains. If you can go out before the sun rises, watch it set, and wait for the stars to come out. Let yourself get to know the mountain. Take the time to watch a mountain progress through the seasons, watch winter embrace the land, spring return, summer unfold, and fall put the land back to sleep again.

> **Sage Advice**
>
> "Come to the edge
> He said. They said:
> We are afraid.
> Come to the edge
> He said. They came.
> He pushed them, and
> They flew..."
> — Guillaume Apollinaire

Sit and watch the landscape change. Each of us has a time of day that is special to us. For me it's the early morning when the sun has first risen, the shadows are still long, and the grass is fresh with the dew. I have more energy in the morning, I connect more easily with the land and myself. For some people it is evening, or midday, some people feel fully alive at high noon. Pay attention to how you feel throughout the day, when do you feel the strongest, which light do you like the best, what time of day calls to your soul.

Find a place out in nature and go there often. Go there at your time of day, sit and listen. Even if you're not an artist sketch, write, draw, play with the dirt, collect rocks, twigs, and look for feathers. Let yourself become reacquainted with nature. Talk to the hillsides, talk to the mountains, and then listen to what they have to say. Be playful, experiment, and be open to experiencing nature in a totally different manner.

Talking to the Trees

Trees are wonderful. Without the air they provide we'd all be dead. They provide us with wood for shelter and to warm our homes, paper to write on, moisture, and air. They also have a wealth of information. There are so many different kinds of trees and each one not only looks and smells differently they also feel different energetically. When is the last time you climbed a tree if ever?

> **Sage Advice**
>
> "A tree trunk the size of a man grows from a blade as thin as a hair. A tower nine stories high is built from a small heap of earth. A journey of a thousand miles starts in front of your feet. Whosoever acts spoils it. Whosoever keeps loses it."
> — Lao Tse

When I was studying one-day don Miguel suggested I climb a tree and watch the shadows on the water, and then he walked away and left me up in the tree. It took me a while to get comfortable but when I finally did I started to notice the leaves as they moved in the wind. I leaned back against the tree trunk and relaxed. I imagined the sap rising in the tree carrying nutrients to the leaves. As I lay there I could feel a gentle humming. I watched the sun set and felt a tremendous amount of peace.

A few weeks later I started going to a park with a small manmade lake surrounded by Eucalyptus trees. I would stand in front of a tree and lean my back against it. I would call on the four directions, north, south, east, and west and ask the tree to clear my energy. I would relax and continue leaning against the tree. After a few minutes I would feel my body begin to gently rock back and forth. I would stand there nestled against the tree until the rocking stopped. I would thank the tree and go about my day. I always found it very relaxing and centering.

I often tell my students to go talk to a tree. I tell them to find a tree that feels friendly and tell the tree all their problems out loud. I tell them to sit there until the tree answers. After they get over their feeling foolish they usually find it quite helpful. It is amazing what kind of answers you get. The answers probably have more to do with your being relaxed than they do with the tree but regardless it is a wonderful exercise.

Remember none of the exercises in this book will work unless you actually do them. And not just think about them but actually get out there and do them. Thinking about talking out loud to a tree is not the same as standing there talking to one. Try it you'll be amazed by the results you get. Just ignore your cynical mind.

> **Spiritual Shortcuts**
>
> Find an old tree that appeals to you and is somewhat private. Let the tree cradle you. Stand on its roots and lean your back against it. Breathe deeply and allow yourself to merge with the tree. Imagine yourself becoming one with the tree. Feel your body melt into the tree. Imagine yourself standing there as the tree. Feel your roots as they go deep into the earth. Focus your attention on your branches as they reach toward the sky. Feel the sun and the wind on your leaves. Imagine the seasons going by, feel the creatures that live in your braches. Feel the sap rising inside your body. Relax and stay with the feeling until you are the tree.
>
> Now look around at the world. Experience life as a tree, notice your surroundings, and notice how differently you see time. Feel the immense knowledge you can pull up through your roots. Be that tree.

The first time I really became a tree I was amazed. I saw people as blurs moving around aimlessly. I knew all about the earth and humanity. I was connected to all the other trees through my roots. I felt so peaceful and free of fear. I was part of a great ecosystem. I wasn't alone I was really part of the greater whole. I experienced through the tree that which I sought on my spiritual journey.

Another fun exercise is to pick up a pinecone that is still full of its seeds or acorn and hold it in your hand. Feel the energy that is stored within this tiny package. Then think about a mature tree and realize that a huge tree exists inside this tiny seed. If you planted that seed, nurtured it, gave it plenty of sun, and helped it grow, someday you could sit in its shade. The universe is a giant seed filled with potential energy just waiting for you to plant the seeds of your imagination and reap the rewards.

Babble at the Brook

When I was in college I got a work-study job at the local public broadcasting station. I was the receptionist at night and had to sit next to a huge fish tank. At first I tried to ignore its bubbling noises but after a very short time I found myself totally enthralled with the noises and by watching the fish. Water has a very healing influence in our lives. Fountains, aquariums, and babbling brooks all have distinctive sounds that are very soothing and relaxing.

When I was nine or ten my parents started taking me to Vermont for the summers. It was a huge change from New York. I remember the first time I walked along a mountain stream. It was so still, as if time had stopped, the air was moist and there was a bit of a chill to the air even though it was a warm day. The sunlight flickering through the canopy of trees created dancing sparkles of light on the surface of the water. I felt like I'd died and gone to heaven. My mother had to yell at me several times in order to get my attention. The water was so clean and clear; you could still drink the water back then. Imagine at one point in the history of mankind all the water was clean enough to drink.

Water is so healing for many reasons. One of the reasons is moving water creates negative ions in the air, that's why the air smells so fresh. Negative ions have been touted to have miraculous healing powers. I just know they make the air smell good and I feel better in their presence.

> **Sage Advice**
> "Insomuch as love grows in you so in you beauty grows. For love is the beauty of the soul."
> —St. Augustine

Water is also very fluid and absorbs energy very easily. Taking a shower mindfully can be a very healing thing. If you stand in the shower and imagine the water washing away any cares and concerns it will. If you let the water wash over a sore spot in your body, imagine the water going deep into the muscle, and feel it washing away the soreness it will. Taking a bath in sea salt and your favorite herbs can be a wonderfully relaxing and healing experience. Your spirit as well as your body is really soothed, nurtured, and restored in the presence of water.

Water lends itself well to many different forms of healing exercises. The ancient Greeks and Romans were strong believers in the restorative nature of baths. They built buildings and spas dedicated to the healing powers of water. You don't have to go any further than your bathroom to experience the healing powers of water but the ocean, hot springs, lakes, rivers, and brooks all have their own unique properties.

Sitting by a brook on a warm summer's day can be magical. I used to like to go and sit beside the rapids of the river in the middle of winter. The banks would be covered with snow and the edges of the river would be frozen. Icicles would hang from the ice ledges and the sun would make them seem alive. It doesn't matter what time of year it is, running water can be magical. If the waters in your area are polluted get involved with an environmental group and work to clean them up. Getting out of ourselves and be of service is also a very powerful healing balm.

Find a stream, lake, or beach near you where you can go swimming. Spend time in the water. Let the water support you. Floating is a wonderful way to remind ourselves that we are supported by the universe. In Hawaii we have hundreds of waterfalls. I often hike into the valleys with my students and do energy work under the waterfalls. Most of the waterfalls here are gentle trickles and you can stand under them and let their water cleanse you. The pools beneath them are fairly calm and it is easy to float in them.

> **Spiritual Shortcuts**
> This exercise is best done with a least four or five people. Find a place where you can stand in the water and it is at least up to your middle of your chest. Get a plastic float, either a small inflatable raft, a body board, or a large inner tube. Take turns floating on it. One person floats while the other people stabilize the object and talk lovingly and gently to the person in the center. Say things like, "You're lovable, you're loved, and you are safe or I am honored to be in your presence." Basically tell the person how wonderful and loved they are. The person lying down needs to breathe deeply and let the words in. Let each person take a turn both giving love and receiving love.

Let your imagination go, find a body of water someplace near your home, and go play in it. Sit by its edge and feel the energy. Sit quietly there and greet the water. Talk to it, feel it, allow your spirit to communicate with it, then gentle place your hand in it and feel the water on your skin. As you start to enter it feel the water, feel its fluid nature, its temperature. Really allow yourself to feel yourself getting wet. Feel what wet feels like. We've all been wet hundreds of time but how often do we pay attention to the process of getting wet? How often do we really allow ourselves to feel what wet feels like?

The rain is also wonderful. Take a long walk in the rain. Watch the reflections on the sidewalks and in the streets. Smell the air just after the rain starts. Splash in the puddles, run naked in the rain, play, and let yourself be free. In the winter if it snows where you live make snow angels, let a snow flake melt on your tongue, get a magnifying glass, and look at snowflakes. No two are exactly alike, sort of like people.

Rock on

One of the exercises I often suggest to my students is to adopt a rock. I have them go out and find a rock. Not just any rock but the perfect rock, and the rock has to want to come with them. Once they adopt the rock they have to love it, nurture it, and provide for all its needs. Of course they always ask me what the rocks needs are. I tell them to ask the rock and find out. It is a very interesting exercise, one that pushes the limits with your mind.

Since I was a little girl I have always collected rocks. I like the way they look and the way they feel. I use large rocks as paperweights and doorstops. I used to carry a smooth one as a worry stone. When I was uncomfortable or feeling out of sorts I'd rub on it. It was very comforting.

Rocks come in all sizes. When I go out to Joshua Tree there are large rock formations. I like to find one, sit in the midst of the boulders, and meditate. In some areas of the world the rock formations are incredible but all rocks have a very solid energy. Rocks are wonderful tools for grounding. When I go to sacred sites around the world I am always attracted to the rocks. The surviving ruins of earlier civilizations are all made out of huge rocks. When you stand in the presence of the pyramids or walk through the deserted stone cities of Mexico or Peru you can feel the ancient energy, the sacredness, and the power.

To have any sort of significant experience with rocks or anything else you have to ignore the protests of your mind. Your mind can stop you from feeling the energy. God could come and sit down beside us and we wouldn't notice if our mind didn't want us to. Our cynical nature is useful, we don't want to get lost in space, or give up our power of choice to someone else. But we do want to be able to choose to feel the energy or connect with love when we want to.

Go out and connect with some rocks. Go for a walk and let the rocks talk to you and talk to the rocks. Sit among some rocks and see what you feel. Find just the right rock and adopt it. Go out in nature, drop down, and see what you feel. Let nature guide you, follow your heart, and see where it takes you.

You're Home

For such a long time so many of us have lived in artificial environments, closed off, and separated from nature. We are so often out of touch with our environment. We have allowed the earth that supports us to be polluted, maimed, and destroyed. We talk about saving the earth when the earth will be fine we're the ones in danger.

Sage Advice

"Happiness is not in our circumstances, but in ourselves. It is not something we see, like a rainbow, or feel, like the heat of a fire. Happiness is something we are."
John Sheerin

Make nature your home. Reacquaint yourself with nature. Allow yourself to connect with nature at a profound level. I grew up in New York City so nature was very foreign to me. The first time I saw a horse laying down I thought it was dead. Bugs and spiders sent me running. But as I learned to spend time in nature I found it could touch me at a level nothing else could. There is something about watching a sunset and being fully present with the experience that can't be duplicated.

Get up early one morning and go someplace and watch the sunrise. Get up at least two hours before sunrise and find a place to sit where you know you can see the sunrise. Then watch nature slowly wake up.

Watch the subtle changes, see the sky slowly brighten, hear the wind, feel the air, and listen to the birds. The world wakes up slowly and methodically. Dawn unfolds so gently upon the land. Spend an entire day sitting in the same place, in silence. Watch the sun move through the sky, watch the clouds, and the shadows upon the land, and then watch the sunset. After it is totally dark go home and walk mindfully into your home, see how if it feels different to you.

Everyday you are given the gift of an entirely new day. You can fill that day with anything you want, love, fear, joy, or sadness. The choice is really yours. Everyday you have a new beginning and we usually choose to make today the same as yesterday. We remember all of our limiting beliefs and relive them.

> **Sage Advice**
> "One should count each day a separate life."
> *Seneca*

Make a commitment to yourself to spend at least a few hours every week out in nature. If you live in the city and can't get out into the country go to a park, buy some plants and create a window garden. Do something that will allow you to connect with the environment it is your home. Even in the middle of the city you can watch the sunrise and set.

Each person connects differently with nature. We all have our favorite element. Some people love the water, some love the wind and the air while others connect with the earth or the sun. Spend some time with each of the elements and find out which one is your favorite. Play with each of them. I am very fair skinned and sunburn very easily. I used to hate the sun but with the advent of waterproof sun blocks I have learned to love the sun. I love to feel its warmth on my skin. Years ago as soon as I felt the sun I got uncomfortable because I was afraid I'd get burned but now I can enjoy its warmth in moderation.

My mother always hated the wind. She would insist that the winds be closed and she went out of her way to avoid the wind. I felt the same way for a time until I let myself really connect with the wind. Remember your feelings about nature are created by your filter system until you make choices based on your actual experience in the present. So go out and make nature your home.

Rather than think about nature or some of the exercises I have suggested go out and try them. Actually walk in the sun, feel its warmth, let the wind tousle your hair, walk in the rain and let it wash over you, and rub your feet on the earth. Then do it all again and again until you can hear the voice of the earth speaking to your soul. Your body is of the earth and will return to the earth when you die. A body is a gift. Buddha once said having a body is as likely as a sea turtle surfacing inside a small six-inch ring afloat on the surface of the world's great oceans. Let yourself fully enjoy the gift of your sense and your magnificent body.

Finding a Peace That Lasts

Peace of mind is a precious gift that money alone can't buy. We can do certain things that allow us to feel peace, that assist us in quieting our minds. Sometimes we know what those things are and we fail to do them because we get too busy with life. What a state of affairs when we get too busy to do the very things that add to the quality of our life. We spend more hours a day providing for our food and housing then we did when we were hunters and gathers. What does that tell you?

Perhaps as a society we have lost touch with what really matters. Find ways to bring peace to your life. Care for an animal, call a loved one, go for a walk, find out what brings you inner peace, and do it. Find an outside activity that you enjoy and do it. Seriously consider spending some time out in nature. Maybe plan an outward-bound type vacation next year. Do something outrageous for yourself. If you've never been camping rent a tent and get away for the weekend.

Find out where you feel peaceful and spend time there. While you're there notice what you tell yourself and tell yourself the same thing when you're at work or in the middle of a stressful situation. Nature is a wonderful place to connect but it isn't nature itself that makes us feel good, it is our open heart, our connection, and our vulnerability that makes us feel good. But nature is a good place to begin.

When we are in nature time can take on a different meaning. Things seem to slow down, we seem to slow down, our mind gets quieter and it is easier to feel at peace. In nature the concept of divinity and perfection makes much more sense. I never judge the clouds, or the sunset, or a fuzzy little animal but I certainly have no trouble judging myself and my choices.

Become one with nature and see what happens in your life.

> **Sage Advice**
>
> "To everything there is a season, a time and a purpose under heaven: A time to be born, and a time to die. A time to plant, and a time to pluck what is planted; A time to kill, and a time to heal; a time to break down, and a time the build up; A time to weep, and a time to laugh; a time to mourn, and a time to dance; A time to cast way stones, and a time to gather stones; A time to embrace, and a time to refrain from embracing; A time to gain, and a time to lose; a time to keep, and a time to throw away; A time to tear, and a time to sew; A time to keep silence, and a time to speak; A time to love, and a time to hate; a time of war, and a time of peace."
>
> *Ecclesiastes 3; 1-8*

The Least You Need to Know

- You can connect with nature and allow it to heal you.
- You can wash away your cares.
- Trees, rocks, mountains, and all of nature has a spirit.

Chapter 22

Love, Compassion, Judgment, and God

> **In This Chapter**
>
> ➢ Define your concept of God.
>
> ➢ Connect with your compassionate self.
>
> ➢ Let go of judgment.
>
> ➢ Explore the idea of a spiritual awakening.

A big part of our spiritual healing is deciding what we really believe in. Do we believe this is a friendly place or a hostile universe that we have to protect ourselves against? Is God an old man with a white beard and a big book keeping score and if the bad outweighs the good do we go to hell? Are we going to continue to lead our lives based on fear or are we going to learn how to be loving and compassionate?

Answering those questions for ourselves will allow us to make better choices in our lives, or at least allow us to make conscious choices. Our answers to those questions will affect every aspect of our life.

God Who?

Who or what is God? That is a question that has been debated for centuries; millions of people have died in holy wars defending their version of God. And we still don't have one answer that everyone can agree upon. But you can decide for yourself what you believe, what you feel, and you can develop a conscious contact with that energy for yourself. You can connect with that energy for yourself and together you can define the nature of your relationship.

When I was a young girl every Sunday my parents would send me to church by myself. At first I loved going. The church I went to had a beautiful rosette stained glass window behind the altar and the sun would shine through it. I loved watching the colored rays fill the church and hearing the chorus sing. In hindsight what I was doing was connecting with the energy.

One Sunday the minister preached a hell fire and brimstone sermon and I knew I was going to hell. I went home crying and when my father asked why, I told him God was going to send me to hell. His own father was a very religious man and had just died a very painful death. My father was bitter over his father's death so he told me if God was such a nasty old man that he would send a little girl to hell he wasn't worth believing in.

Nearly twenty years later I found it necessary to find a God that worked for me. One of my mentors told me I needed to find a god I could do business with. At first I was appalled, I didn't feel comfortable thinking about God no less having the nerve to create my own definition of one. God is a funny thing; he or she will be whatever you want it to be. Eventually I realized that God is. As human beings we limit that energy with our definitions. If we believe in a vengeful god so be it, if we don't believe in god that's fine with god too. If we want to have a personal relationship with that energy God is right there in whatever shape or form we desire.

Sage Advice

"The soul is indestructible and its activity will continue through eternity. It is like the sun, which, to our eyes, seems to set at night; but it has in reality only gone to diffuse its light elsewhere."

Goethe

After years of explorations I finally realized God is a lot like electricity, it is silent, there behind the scenes available for our use. We can plug in some woodworking tools and build a masterpiece, cut off our fingers, cook food, or build an electric chair to execute people in. Electricity doesn't care if we use it or how we use it, we don't have to believe in it, it doesn't care. It is just there.

When I spend time in the presence of that energy I experience it as loving but beyond what I define as loving, its love is huge, unconditional, and expansive. Whatever words I use to describe that energy many of us call God limits that energy. If I call it loving it is limited to my definition of loving. That energy totally respects me so it never interferes with my choices or my beliefs. It lovingly holds up a mirror so I can see what I am projecting with my thoughts. My concept of God is fluid, it changes, grows, expands as I do. I have learned to allow my definition of God to be organic and not static, that way I don't limit my experience of that energy.

Finding Your God

God is a personal experience. I can tell you about my experience but until you have one of your own you won't know for yourself. If your religion allows you to have an unfiltered, uncolored, uncontaminated, and direct experience of God for yourself that is wonderful. Until we develop a personal relationship with that energy we are like fish out of the water. At the level of spirit you are God so without that direct relationship you aren't connected to yourself.

Start by writing about God, your old definitions, and how you'd like it to be. Do you want to be accepted just the way you are? Do you want God to be your friend? Write about your fears, doubts, hopes, and dreams.

Then start going someplace you really feel connected with the energy. (Use some of the exercises from the last chapter to help you find that place) I used to go to the beach and at times I go to old churches. Just find a place that works for you, spend as much time there as possible, and ask that energy to teach you about the nature of your relationship. Ask God to love you. Ask God what to do. Then hang around long enough to hear the answer.

It took quiet a bit of time for me to really feel the connection but once I did I felt an immense amount of love and unconditional acceptance. After I felt safe with that connection I began to ask that energy what the nature of our relationship was. One day I heard, "I am your creator and I am well pleased with my creation." When I stop to remember that voice all of my judgments dissolve. That energy or God only wants me to be happy and God uses my definition of happy. I don't have to do anything or act in a certain way, I don't have to go to church, or be prefect, that energy loves me no matter what. But when I align my purpose with that energy miracles happen and I am truly happy from the depth of my being.

Spend time and develop your own personal relationship with that energy. Don't take anyone else's word for it. Take the time to find your own path and your own way of connecting to that energy. It is well worth the time and effort.

God will be whatever you want God to be. Try not to limit God with your mind instead let that energy lead you to a way of being and believing that is beyond limitations. Surrender to your concept of God and let it teach you and lead you into a life far beyond what you could ever imagine.

What Do I Believe

What do you believe about yourself, life, and your role in your life? What do you believe about God and the nature of your relationship? As you believe so it will be. The power of your beliefs is immense. The less aware we are of our beliefs the more they run our lives and create untold misery. We don't see our beliefs as something we've chosen to believe we believe that they're true. Beliefs and the truth aren't even in the same ballpark. It really saddens me when I think of the millions of people that have been killed, maimed, imprisoned, and tortured because of other people's beliefs.

Sage Advice
"Imagination is the eye of the soul.."
Joubert

Take some time and really think about it. How do you want your spirituality to affect your life? Do you really want to connect with your true nature or do you just want your life to get better?

What do you believe? What do believe about having a personal relationship with this energy we call God? Really look deep into your heart and be honest with yourself. Is even thinking that way sacrilegious or is that only available to a chosen few? In your heart of hearts what do you think about spirituality, God, religion, and surrender?

I have a very dear friend who is an independent contractor. Whenever she needs money the phone starts ringing and she has more than enough work and as soon as she has enough money the phone stops ringing. I've watched this happen numerous times over the years. One day I asked her how she did that. She said she knows what she does has value, that she always does the best job she can, that her customers are always pleased, and they get their money's worth. She said when she knows she needs money she acknowledges her need but thinks more about what she can do for others. She doesn't do what she does to get something she just does it and in the process she makes money.

> **Sage Advice**
>
> "The eternal is empty (like a bowl); It may be used but its capacity is never exhausted. It is bottomless, perhaps the ancestor of all things. t is blunt in its sharpness; It unties its tangles; It softens its light. It becomes one with the dusty world. Deep and still, it appears to exist forever. I do not know whose son it is. It seems to have existed before all else."
>
> Lao Tse

She has the need, puts the need out there, and then lets it go. When she is working for someone she focuses on doing the best job she possible can, it's not about making money. If she focused on the money it wouldn't work. The same is true of our spiritual quest. If we do it to get something our results will be less effective. If you develop a personal relationship with God and your spirit your life will improve dramatically. But if you try to develop that relationship so your life will improve it won't work as well. If you're doing your emotional and spiritual healing for any other reason than just doing it you are short changing yourself.

So what do you believe? Do you believe you deserve to be happy? Do you believe this work has value for you even if nothing else in your life changes? Our actions and choices aren't nearly as important as our motives for doing them. Take sometime to really look inside and tell yourself the truth.

Loving The Self

If you don't love yourself it won't matter if everybody else on the earth bows down and declares their undying love for you, you won't be able to accept it or really feel it. If you're unable to feel loved you won't be able to let God in either. It's like the age old debate, "Which came first the chicken or the egg?" And willingness and truthfulness are the two things that will break the deadlock.

If you admit you don't love yourself and are willing to learn how to love yourself; if you are willing to let this energy you can't really see teach you about love and you are truly willing to let that happen all sorts of things will start to magically happen.

> **Spiritual Shortcuts**
>
> Get some crayons, watercolors, or paints of some kind. Let go of your mind's opinion of your talents as an artist. Draw a picture of you and your relationship with God as it is now and as you'd like it to be. Hang them on your wall or mirror and look at them for a while. Observe what kind of feelings come up for you. If need be, redo the picture of the way you want your relationship to be until you capture the essence of that relationship. When it feels just right put it in an envelope addressed to God, don't use a return address, put a stamp on it, and mail it. It's a great symbolic way to let it go.

Love is such a funny thing, we crave it yet we run away from it. We say we want intimacy and then as soon as we're in a relationship we do everything in our power to avoid it. All the walls come up, we engage all of our emotional defenses and then when the relationship ends we say, "See, I knew intimacy wasn't safe."

Is it a risk to love ourselves unconditionally which means exactly like we are? What if we do, does that mean we won't ever be able to change? Does acceptance mean we doom ourselves to remain the same? That may be what our minds think but it isn't true.

The willingness and the ability to love ourselves is at the core of our ability to change or to achieve a sense of happiness and inner peace. Without self-love we can't experience either of those. Can you love another freely and without fear if you don't love yourself? I think not. As long as we fear love we won't be able to see it as the healing elixir it truly is and we'll continue to avoid it and keep it out of our lives. That is why truthfulness is so important. We must be able to look inside ourselves and acknowledge that fear of love so we can stop living our lives based on it. We must be able to be truthful with ourselves and admit our fear.

Love is a scary proposition. If we let some one love us they may hurt us, leave us, or see the truth about us. They may come to know us and we may see ourselves reflected in their eyes. Take a few moments right now to go look in the mirror, look deep into your eyes and love the image you see. Love yourself, realize that the person you see in the mirror is an incredible gift in your life, and at least be willing to start loving yourself.

Look into your eyes and tell yourself the truth as you know it today. How much of yourself do you really love, how many judgments do you have about yourself, how often do you think unkind thoughts about yourself? The first step in healing is the truth. The next is forgiveness. Forgive yourself for judging, for the imperfections you think you have, for being less than loving to yourself. Forgive yourself and ask for forgiveness and then let the love in because the finally step in healing is to bathe the wound in love.

Love yourself as if your life depends on it, your happiness surely does. Love yourself, then call upon your conscious contact with your creator, and let that energy love you too. The words sound so simple but you have to remember it is a process and it will take time, discipline, and dedication. Be gentle with yourself and it will be much easier.

Being Gentle Is Not Always Easy

Some people have difficulty with the idea of being gentle with themselves. They are afraid that if they're gentle with themselves that somehow they will lose something, they won't change, or they won't get what they want. If you are having a hard time with the idea of being gentle, translate the concept into being kind to yourself.

> **Sage Advice**
> "He who does not attempt to make peace When small discords arise. Is like the bee's hive which leaks drops of honey Soon, the whole hive collapses."
> Nagarjuna

Nurturing yourself is an active way of being loving to yourself; it is treating yourself with kindness, gentleness, respect, and dignity. Nurturing is an act not a concept. We may nurture ourselves by the way we talk to ourselves, by how we act toward ourselves, and by how well we meet out wants and needs. We are all well acquainted with ignoring our basic needs, or creating situations that aren't very supportive or loving.

My students tell me all the time they were too busy today to eat, or get enough sleep, exercise, or attend a gathering they find supportive and nurturing. We are so used to putting the demands of the world first, thinking of our job instead of our family, and putting other people's needs first. Nurturing ourselves is learning to put ourselves first.

We've talked about nurturing in other sections of this book. The thing I can't emphasize enough is that nurturing yourself requires you to take actions, to make loving choices, and to not abandon yourself. So may of us are afraid of being abandoned and yet we do that to ourselves all the time.

What has nurturing got to do with connecting to God or our spirit? In a sense it has nothing do with it and everything to do with our ability to connect. If we aren't able to love or nurture ourselves we won't be able to connect in a healthy manner with our inner wisdom or with anyone else for that matter. The difference between living in heaven or living in hell is in the way we see things. Our limited thinking stops us from seeing some of the other possibilities. I once heard this story about a man who died and was shown the difference.

> **Sage Advice**
> "If spring came but once in a century, instead of once a year, or burst forth with the sound of an earthquake, and not in silence, what wonder and expectations there would be in all the heart to behold the miraculous change!"
> Longfellow

A man died and passed over into the afterlife. An angel greeted him and took him first to a room where everyone was sitting at a lavishly supplied banquet table filled with every delicacy imaginable. Everyone had spoons with two-foot handles attached to both of their hands. They were emaciated, starving in the presence of abundance as they tried desperately to feed themselves. The handle on the spoon was too long so the food fell onto the table untouched by their lips.

Next the angel took him to a room where everyone was laughing and having a wonderful time. They too sat at a banquet table with the same spoons attached to both hands but they were feeding each other. The angel looked at the man and told him that being able to love and share was the difference between living in heaven or existing in hell. The man realized they had both been given the same gifts the only difference was the how they had chosen to use those gifts.

What choices have you made about the gifts you've been given?

The Compassionate Heart

When I think about compassion I think of people like Mother Teresa, the Dalai Lama, Thich Nhat Hanh, and Gandhi. I think of people who had big hearts and gave freely of their love and of themselves. Compassion allows us to be loving, gentle, and to speak the truth with kindness.

One of my favorite stories about Gandhi is about a woman who brought her young daughter to see him. The woman was concerned about her daughter because she ate so much sugar. The woman asked Gandhi to talk to her about it, he told her to come back next week. When they arrived Gandhi looked solemnly at the girl and told her sugar wasn't good for her. Then he told her not to eat it. The woman was a bit annoyed and asked him why he couldn't have said that last week. He replied, "Last week I was still eating sugar."

Compassion is a deep sympathy for another's suffering combined with a desire to assist in alleviating the pain or removing its cause. The compassionate heart applies not just to others but to ourselves as well. A

Spiritual Shortcuts

Take sometime and write about compassion. How would your life be different if you were surrounded by compassionate people? How would you feel if all your thoughts toward yourself and others were compassionate? How do you think your life would change if you bathed it in the light of compassion?

Write a short story about your life, leave all the facts the same except add a character to your life. Add a person who is always there for you with love, encouragement, and compassion. Look at the pivotal events in your life, how would this person's presence have changed your life?

heart filled with compassion is one filled with love and understanding. And with love and understanding anything is possible.

How could you be more compassionate toward others and yourself? What would you have to change in your life if you wanted to be more compassionate, what different kind of thoughts, and actions could you choose? Where do you fail to be compassionate? If you think about nurturing yourself and being compassionate with yourself how does that feel?

Judgment Hurts

How many times a day do you judge yourself, someone else, or something? Society is filled with judgments, prejudices, and opinions about almost everything and so are we. Judgments hurt, if you've ever been the but of someone's joke you know how it feels to be judged or laughed at in public. As a species we can be very cruel. We hurt one another emotionally and physically, we even kill one another. Words can really hurt, once they are spoken they can never be withdrawn.

How often do you judge yourself? What do you think those words do to your ability to love yourself and treat yourself with compassion? Can you connect with your godself through the veil of judgment?

Smoke & Mirrors

Judgement keeps us feeling separated and apart. We can't heal the wounds of the past when we are constantly re-wounding ourselves. Whoever said "Sticks and stones can break my bones but words can never hurt me" was totally out of touch with his inner self. Words can cut us to the soul; physical wounds can't.

Moment by moment ask yourself if your thinking is positive and loving. If your thoughts aren't positive and loving change what you're saying to yourself. Our first thought is spontaneous but we can choose what we think next. Get into the habit of monitoring your thoughts. Get an alarm wrist watch and set the alarm to go off every hour, when it goes off focus on what you've been thinking, if your thoughts aren't loving change them.

Waking up is a large part of our spiritual healing. Our thoughts tend to be habitual and our habitual thoughts stop us from connecting with God and our divinity. Waking up or choosing our thoughts allow us to feel loved and safe no matter what is happening around us.

Whose gift is it?

Sage Advice

"If you create an act, you create a habit. If you create a habit, you create a character. If you create a character, you create a destiny."
Andre Maurois

A man had been studying with Buddha for sometime and really loved his teachings. He was excited to share his teacher with his best friend. The next time Buddha was giving a class he took his friend with him. His friend sat in silence for a while and then began asking questions that made it very clear he didn't think much of Buddha's teachings. His friend was very embarrassed by his friend's behavior. The Buddha answered all his questions with love and patience.

The friend finally said, "I think you are a fraud and your teachings are of very little value. These fools sit here and watch you smile and say they feel your love. What they should feel is how much time they waste listening to your drivel. Love and compassion are fine for you, you are the son of a wealthy lord. We must fight for everything we get."

Finally the man jumped up he could stand it no more. He looked at his friend and yelled at him, asking how he could show such disrespect to such a great man. The Buddha smiled and held up his hand.

He looked directly at the man's friend and asked him, "If someone gives you a gift and you refuse to take it, then who does it belong to?" The man thought for a few moments and then replied, "I guess it still belongs to the person giving the gift."

Buddha looked deeply into the man's eyes and said, "Thank you for your gift but I choose not to take it."

Whenever you judge yourself or feel judged remember it is a gift you don't have to accept. You don't have to accept other people's opinions, judgments, or advice. The gift belongs to the other person unless you agree to accept it.

It is so easy to forget why we are doing all this work. We start to feel better and then we slip back into our old habitual thought patterns. It doesn't take long before we feel disconnected and miserable again. Developing a spiritual connection requires a lot more work than maintaining one does. Judgment in no way assists in creating or maintaining that connection. If you judge your process or yourself it won't accelerate your growth it will only slow it.

Give yourself a chance to have a life beyond your wildest imaginings. Be kind to yourself, love yourself, and fill your life with compassion.

Spiritual Awakening

Once we learn to see life through they eyes of our spirit instead of our mind life changes. It can never be the same. A spiritual awakening can happen in an instant but for most people it is a gradual process.

There are many accounts of people who have had a near death experience, afterwards their lives are totally changed. The things that used to matter to them in life no longer do. Their friends report that they are more loving, open, and compassionate. People who were scoundrels suddenly become altruistic. People who were confirmed atheists have a faith and understanding of the nature of the universe that surpasses people who have studied theology for years.

Clarity Corner

A **spiritual awakening** sounds profound. I expected lights, angels and a voice from heaven. What I got was a gradual shift in my perception. Day by day I could feel the prescence of love around me stornger and stonger until one day I knew I was safe no matter what. I awoke to my own true nature as a spirit in a physical body.

For most of us its not that easy. We have to work at it and it is often slow arduous work. A burning bush is nice but most of us are so practical we would run over and put it out before it had a chance to deliver its message.

I remember wondering why I would want to have a spiritual awakening in the first place. And then I was upset because I had a near death experience and it hadn't changed my life. So maybe spiritual awakenings weren't all they were cracked up to be. But as my life continued its tailspin I began to think maybe there was something to it after all.

Over the years I have observed that people who have really surrendered to their spiritual self and maintain their connection have lives that are filled with magic. And people who insist on living their life based on the whims of their mind have much more trauma and drama in their lives. They don't seem to have the same inner peace and serenity that their spiritually connected counter parts do.

A spiritual awaken is the result of letting go of your filter system and connecting to your divinity. First you must decide for yourself that it is worth the effort and then you must ask yourself if you're willing to do whatever it takes to achieve one. It makes the process much easier of your answer is yes to both those questions.

Meeting Your Spirit

Set aside a few minutes, shut off the phone, put up the do not disturb sign, and get comfortable.

> *Take a few deep breaths and mentally give yourself permission to relax. Really focus your full attention on your breath and as you inhale breathe in relaxation and as you exhale release anything unlike relaxation. Allow yourself to fully experience your breath as it moves in and out of your body. As your breath fills your body with life sustaining air relax the muscles in your chest and let go. Let the feeling of relaxation flow into your stomach and let go of anything unlike relaxation in your chest or your stomach. (Pause)*
>
> *Relax your jaw and all the muscles in your face. Breathe in through your mouth and out through your nose, slowly, deeply, and rhythmically. Relax your shoulders and your neck, allow yourself to feel totally relaxed. Allow your consciousness to drift gently moving you into a place of total relaxation.*
>
> *Imagine yourself standing in the center of an ancient cathedral. You are standing on a huge disk or polished marble, there is a shaft of light flooding the cathedral causing the slab of marble to glow with an inner beauty. As you stand there you are filled with an immense feeling of love and acceptance.*
>
> *You ask to understand the energy of compassion. An inner knowing begins to fill you, you see*

images, feel emotions, and hear thoughts that all teach you about compassion. You stand there with a willingness and a curiosity. You truly want to understand compassion and you do.

Then you ask to understand the nature of a spiritual awakening. As you stand there the marble begins to resonate. You feel an energy begin to surround you and you begin to think what a spiritual awakening would mean to you. How it would affect your life and what it would look like for you to have a deep spiritual connection.

You find yourself standing in the presence of your spirit. You look deeply into its eyes and you can feel its love and acceptance. You feel whole in the presence of your spirit. You feel at peace. You ask your spirit for its help, for its support, and its guidance. You take a deep breath and allow yourself to connect, you allow yourself to be one. Allow the connection to deepen and grow.

When you are ready bring yourself gently back to your room and open your eyes. Take your time getting up. Take a few minutes to write about your experience.

> ### *The Least You Need to Know*
>
> ➤ Compassion is a healing balm for most of our emotional wounds.
>
> ➤ You can change the way you think.
>
> ➤ A spiritual awakening can happen in an instant but it usually takes time and effort.

Part 6
Putting It All Together

Okay we've looked at the three components of the trinity – the body, mind, and spirit. Now we'll look at how to blend the three of them so you can get your life as a whole working. You've made it this far in your life, now you can learn how to really make your life wonderful.

We all learned how to survive but very few of us learned how to be deliriously happy. Most of us learned how to walk but only a few of us became Olympic gold medallist in tack and field. The same is true in life, we've all learned how to live. If you'd like your life to improve dramatically read on.

Chapter 23

Coming Up with a Formula

> **In This Chapter**
> - **What you need to do.**
> - **How you need to do it.**
> - **Decide if you're really ready.**
> - **Give meaning to your life.**

Each one of us has our own process and our own unique way of changing. If you find out what works best for you it sure makes life a lot easier. If you do what works for your best friend it may not work for you. But if you pinpoint exactly what you need and figure out the best way to get it, your spiritual journey will be a lot smoother.

When I first started my journey I could ask myself what I needed endlessly but I was clueless. I was so out of touch with my wants and needs that half of my journey was dedicated to finding out what they were. If you already have an answer to those questions you're half way there. By now you probably have a pretty good idea about what you need to change and now you're going to find out the easiest way to let it go.

Figuring Out What You Need to Do

We all have habitual behaviors. We are predictable, at least to our friends we are we often fail to see our own predictability. So if you want to release your filter system and heal, you need to change your behavior. No news there, if you want different results in your life make different choices. But first you have to know what your "normal" response is to events in your life.

If something is upsetting do you worry in silence? Do you talk to people and ask their opinion? Do you look for a solution? Do you try to get people to choose sides? What exactly do you do when you're upset? Do you avoid your feelings, wallow in them, or use something or someone to ignore them? Do you get numb? Do you get angry? Do you get fearful? Or do you get busy?

Clarity Corner

Habitual behaviors are things we do over and over and over again withou really giving them much thought. They can be actual behaviors such as being late, overeating, or overspending, or they can be thought patterns such as thinking that your gong to fail, that you're not good enough, or that life is hard.

If you tend to isolate then you need to learn how to reach out. If you automatically look for external solutions you have to learn how to go within. Whatever you normally do you have to learn to do something that is more effective. Our survival skills were developed long ago when we had very limited internal resources. Now we must learn to objectively evaluate what we do and learn how to do something else that actually allows us to achieve the results we desire.

Take time to answer the following questions thoroughly and write down your responses.

Something major and very emotionally upsetting happens in your life such as a death in the family, an ended relationship, or a serious health problem.

- What is the first thing you do? Do you fall apart, get quiet, and get very emotional? What exactly do you do?
- After your initial reaction what do you do? Do you call friends, do you make a conscious decision about what needs to be done next, do you numb out?
- What kind of things do you think? Do your thoughts seem overwhelming or do you immediately see the light at the end of the tunnel?
- How rapidly do you move toward resolution?

Something minor but annoying happens such as a flat tire or you got lost.

- What is your first response?
- Do you ask for help or take care of it yourself?
- Is your thinking positive and supportive or doom and gloom?
- How long does it take you to find a solution or take the appropriate actions?

If you want to get different results you have to make different choices. The solution is obvious but usually not to ourselves. If you change the habitual way you do things your life will change automatically. If you're messy all the time, be neat. If you overspend, be thrifty. If you want someone to take care of you and you feel like a victim most of the time take back your power and take care of yourself. And if was that simple. If you could just start being neat and your life would change there wouldn't be a need for books like this.

You have to take different actions. You have to make the effort and do the actually work, no one else can. Thinking about it won't do it, writing about it won't do it, and talking about it won't change it. The only thing that will assist you in changing is for you to wake up every day and make different choices. By the end of this chapter you will hopefully have a good idea what those choices are. If you want your life to be different you will have to take the necessary action.

Years ago a client came to me and on the first visit told me she had a whole wall covered with bookshelves filled with self-help books she'd read. Yet there she sat, and her life still wasn't working. I asked her if she had done any of the exercises and she told me she had thought about them. You can join a gym but if you don't go regularly and actually exercise you won't get in shape. The same is true of your life. Action is a must.

Sage Advice
"Like bubbles on the sea of matter borne, they rise, they break, and to the sea return.."
Pope

Sage Advice
"Success unexpected in common hours. If you have built castles in the air, your work need not be lost; now put the foundation under them."
Henry David Thoreau

Is it My Mind or My Body or My Spirit?

You are a trinity so none of your issues exist in a vacuum. Right off the top of your head, without giving it a lot of thought answer the following question.

Take a few deep breaths and then ask yourself: When do I think of my life and the way it's going? If I had to guess where the problem originates where does it start? Even if weight or health issues are your main focus the problem may not be in your body, it may be your mind or your spiritual connection. Don't second-guess yourself. Just write down whatever figures come to mind.

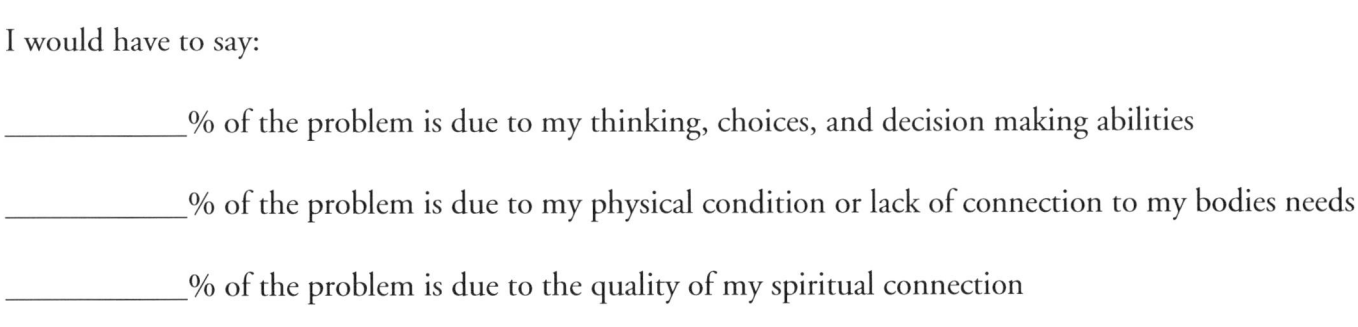

I would have to say:

_____% of the problem is due to my thinking, choices, and decision making abilities

_____% of the problem is due to my physical condition or lack of connection to my bodies needs

_____% of the problem is due to the quality of my spiritual connection

Once you've established the percentages you know what percentage of your time you need to spend addressing each of those areas. Life is a mirror, if our trinity is out of balance so is our life. If we want the quality of our life to improve we need to get back in balance.

If your mind, body, and spirit are in balance your life reflects that balance. Your environment is pleasant. Your life is balanced between work and time for yourself. Your social activity is has a balance of time for yourself as well as for your friends. You eat well and take care of your bodies needs and your finances are in order. Your life is pleasing, and balanced. Stress, turmoil, and drama are not a regular part of your life, you are generally happy and at peace.

And I Asked Myself

What do I need to do for my mind, my body, and my spirit? Over the years I've realized that some of the very things I rebelled against are the most valuable things I can do for myself as I travel my path toward wholeness. Ridiculous things like cleaning my room really can make a positive difference in my life.

> **Sage Advice**
> "The learning and knowledge that we have, is, at most, but little compared with that of which we are ignorant."
> *Plato*

Now you need to decide what you've been rebelling against that you really need to do. If the answers in the preceding section showed you that 30% of your focus needs to be on your thinking, 40% on your body, and 30% on your spiritual connection then you need to divide your attention accordingly.

Our mind will usually tell us to go in the opposite direction, it will resist most vehemently the thing we most need to do. If we need to get more exercise our mind will try to convince us that exercise has nothing to do with it. With that in mind ask yourself if you were really honest when you decided on the percentages. Change them if you really need to.

Suppose your thinking is part of the problem.

- ➤ Do you tend to think negatively?
- ➤ Are you overly optimistic and avoid dealing with reality by ignoring what's going on?
- ➤ Are you overly emotional or unaware of your emotions?
- ➤ Do you have good problem solving skills?
- ➤ Do you react emotionally to life?
- ➤ Do you think about life rather than living it?
- ➤ Exactly what role does your mind play in your problems?

Answer these questions to find out what role your body plays with your problems.

- Does your health stop you from doing things?
- Do you eat properly?
- Do exercise enough, not at all, or too much?
- Do you take care of your physical needs?
- Do you get enough rest?
- Do you provide for yourself, do you have enough money, a nice place to live, work you enjoy?

Answer these questions to find out what role your spirituality plays with your problems.

- Do you have a conscious contact with your spirit?
- Are you comfortable with your concept of god and your connection?
- Do you take enough time to connect with your spirituality?

And I Answered

So what do you think you need to do in response to your answers to these questions? What actions do you think you need to take? Obviously if meditate six hours a day you don't need to meditate more maybe you need to move your body.

Now is the time for you to take some action. Take a cold, hard look at your answers to the questions, the percentages, and make some choices. You need to create a treatment plan for yourself. You need to decide what you most need to do to change your life.

As a human being we all have certain needs. We all need food, clothing, and shelter. We need to feel safe and loved. We need to know how to take care of ourselves as well as what our wants and needs are. Only you can decide how you are going to do that.

If you're a big meat eater obviously a vegetarian diet won't be your first choice. There are no absolutes, you have to go inside and find out what really matters to you.

There are certain things that are consistent to a well-balanced life. Nothing to excess and no deprivation are keys to balance. Balance implies just that balance.

There are some things you can do to bring your life back into balance. Here's a list of a few of them:

- Clean your house
- Eat balanced and nutritional meals
- Get rid of any excess in your life
- Balance your checkbook
- Get plenty of rest
- Spend sometime every day connecting with your spirit
- Exercise moderately at least three times a week
- Write a daily gratitude list
- Treat yourself lovingly
- Be kind to others

Add to this list as you find other things that help you stay balanced.

You must take the time to figure out what you need to do if you want your life to really change. Give yourself that gift. So few of us are willing to do that. We want someone else to tell us exactly what to do so we can ignore their advice or do it halfheartedly and then blame them when it doesn't work.

The question is what do you need to do if you want to be happy? And your answer is? Write about, right now and right here.

_____

_____

_____

_____

_____

_____

_____

How to Apply It All

There is a lot of information in this book. There are lots of suggestions about things to do and not do to improve your life. Now it's time for you to take action for yourself.

Design a daily routine for yourself. Every morning when you wake up, decide what the most important thing you can do today to improve the quality of your life. Make a list of what you could do each day for your mind, body, and spirit and then do it. Experiment, if you find what your doing isn't working modify what your doing. The most important thing is to take the action to do it.

> **Spiritual Shortcuts**
>
> As you design your ritual constantly ask yourself if your thinking is loving, positive, and supportive. Take sometime and decide what you are going to do each day. Make sure your routine is manageable, don't decide to do more than you can realistically do.
>
> What do you need to do everyday for your mind? Check in on your feelings throughout the day. Ask yourself what you need. Make sure your thinking is loving, positive, and supportive. Write every morning. Do positive affirmations in the mirror. What do you need to do for your body? Eat well. Exercise. Talk lovingly to your body. Go for a walk. Get some fresh air. Stretch. What are you going to do for your spirit? Meditate. Pray. Read spiritually uplifting material. Get out in nature. Spend time in silence

Apply the percentages when you create your daily routine. Remember, what you tell yourself about what you're doing will be almost as important as what you're doing. If you know you need to move your body more and hate every minute of it you won't continue doing it for very long. If you decide to do it, and decide to enjoy doing it, you will. If you want to enjoy moving your body one way is to allow yourself to feel your body moving and enjoy the gift of movement. You can enjoy anything just by changing what you're telling yourself. If you hate cleaning your house and it's a cluttered mess you could allow yourself to enjoy the process. Do whatever you need to do to enjoy it, break it down into manageable pieces, play loud music, sing, be foolish, and play at cleaning.

As you create your daily routine, as you decide what you need to change about your life think big. You can have it all however you define all for yourself. Sometimes we have to keep praying for the willingness and the guidance to find out what we need to do. With some of my issues I have had to try many times and many different approaches until I got the results I wanted.

Sage Advice

"Do not say, "I follow the one true path of the spirit," but rather, "I have found the spirit walking on my path," for spirit walks on all paths."
Khalil Gibran

Smoke & Mirrors

We often resist doing the very things that will help us the most. When I suggest people take the time to develop a treatment plan, they often say "But I just want to be happy." Change of any kind requires concrete action. If you aren't willing to take the actions, don't be surprised when your life doesn't change.

No matter what you do don't give up on yourself. Don't give up on creating happiness. I smoked for years. I quit many times and always went back to smoking. I tried hypnosis, acupuncture, nicotine gum, cold turkey, you name it I tried it. I took several stop smoking programs, nothing seemed to work but I kept trying. I finally took a stop smoking program and really looked at the roots of my addiction and I have been smoke free for over a decade. I didn't keep doing the same thing, I kept exploring the nature of my addiction at a deeper and deeper level until I was able and willing to let it go.

Going the Extra Mile

Are you willing to do whatever it takes to change? Whenever you want to change anything in your life start out by ask yourself that question. If the answer is yes, go for it. If the answer is no, be truthful with yourself and take the time to do whatever you have to in order to get willing. Until you are willing to go the extra mile there is no sense in pretending. Without that willingness the likelihood of success is minimal. Rather than fooling yourself take the time to get willing.

If you're not willing to take the time to create a plan for your healing what will it take for you to get willing? If you're not willing to spend the time it will take for you to heal there is no sense whining about wanting to be happy. There have been many times in my life I've said I wanted my life to be different but I wouldn't take the time to make that happen. I made myself miserable. Once I accepted the fact that I wasn't ready to change I had the choice of enjoying where I was or if that wasn't possible doing whatever it took to get willing to change.

Change really takes going that extra mile for ourselves. What would going the extra mile look like in your life? Would it look like cleaning out your closet, writing everyday, or loving and accepting yourself just the way you are? What do you have to for yourself to heal? What do you have to change, accept, or do? If you know what you need to do and you can't seem to get yourself to do it then what you do you need to get willing to do?

Change is merely a matter of taking new actions. Once you know what actions you need to take, take them. Willingness is absolutely essential if you really want to successfully change anything.

Am I Really Ready?

Sometimes getting to the point that we're willing and ready to change is well over half the battle. You can use a lack of willingness as an excuse not to change or you can use your lack of willingness as a guidepost showing you what you need to work on first.

When I wanted to stop smoking I had to be willing to stay stopped no matter what. When I reviewed my prior attempts to stop smoking I found that I had a variety of excuses that enabled me to resume smoking. Until I decided that no matter what happened I wouldn't resume smoking I continued to create excuses in my life. We can always find an excuse to stay the same. I can always find an excuse to do or not do something, the question is what do I really want to do? The excuses are irrelevant, they are just excuses. Do I want to change or not?

When I quit smoking I had to get willing to not smoke no matter how uncomfortable I got. I had to make my desired outcome, the freedom from smoking out weigh my desire to smoke no matter what. When our desired outcome is greater than our desire for the old behavior we are finally ready to change. And sometimes it takes a great deal of time, self-knowledge, and understanding to get to that point. We need to set ourselves up for success.

> **Sage Advice**
> "Silence is a great help to the seeker after truth. In the attitude of silence, the soul finds the path in a clearer light, and what is elusive and deceptive resolves itself into crystal clearness. Our life is a long and arduous quest after truth, and the soul requires inward restfulness to attain its full height."
> *Gandhi*

So when you want to change anything make sure your mental picture of what you want to create is clear, positively charged emotionally, and highly desirable. Your mind doesn't work in negatives, if you want to stop smoking get a clear picture of what being smoke free would look like to you. Make it emotionally desirable and be prepared for the discomfort change causes.

If you're not ready yet ask yourself what it will take for you to be ready and then do it! And if you're not ready to do that, back up another step until you are ready, and then move forward again.

It's My Life

Is it really your life or is your life ruled by your past? Do you make choices about your behavior or do you just react to life? Part of your healing journey is reclaiming your life. In order to make it really your own you have to be able to choose what actions you are going to take. If you are still in the midst of an addiction your freedom belongs to your addiction. If you're still reacting to life your life still belongs to your filter system.

So I pose the question, what do you need to do to make it your life? If it is to be your life you need to figure out how to make it so. Do you need to clean the house, clean up your thinking, deepen your spiritual connection, or get out and go jogging? What do you need to do?

I remember spending years reading books, listening to lectures, and going to seminars. 90% of people who attend seminars never use the information they receive. People told me what I needed to do for years through their words but in order for me to change I had to decide what I needed to do for myself. I had to be willing to take responsibility for my personal growth and for taking the actions that would create the change. Granted I needed to read those words and hear the concepts but I had to take the actions.

> **Sage Advice**
>
> "If a man only does what is required of him, he is a slave. If a man does more than is required of him, he is a free man."
>
> Chinese Proverb

Years ago if someone had asked me what I needed to do I probably would have gotten angry and with a few stronger words said, "Why the hell do you think I'm reading this book? That's what your suppose to tell me."

Well to a large extent I already have. The rest of this book has some more information to help you clear out your filter system but if you keep making the same choices what good will all the knowledge in all the books in the world make? None. This chapter is about coming up with a formula that will let you heal your life.

You have to understand what that formula is for yourself. What do you need? What do you want? If you haven't already looked at your definitions of happiness, love, support, nurturing, joy, peace, contentment, and freedom. One of the most valuable exercises I ever did was to define for myself what personal freedom meant to me, what it was, how it would feel, and how I would know if I had achieved it. That definition has changed many times over the years and it has always acted like a beacon guiding me on my journey home.

Once I had a definition of personal freedom I could look at whatever was preventing from feeling like I had it. My definition assisted me in bringing to my attention anything unlike freedom in my life. After a time instead of being annoyed or feeling like a victim I became more willing to embrace my limitations as an indication I was getting closer to achieving my freedom. As soon as I embraced my limitations it became easier to actually do the next indicated step; it became easier for me to take action.

> **Sage Advice**
>
> "Everything here, but the soul of man, is a passing shadow. The only enduring substance is within.
>
> Channing

So what do you need to do? What prevents you from honestly being able to say this is my life and I am at choice in my life at all times? What stops you from experiencing personal freedom in your life at all times? Once you have an answer to that question, ask yourself what you have to do in order to be willing to embrace that limitation?

At the beginning of my process I was told that if I was willing to move a muscle and change a thought I could change anything, freedom would be mine. Taking action is what it takes. What actions are you going to take?

What is My Process

Each of us has our own process. Some of us dive right into action, some of us take time to look around and decide what to do, and some of us like to watch others. At some point in your life you have successfully changed something in your life. If you think about how you changed it you will begin to understand your process. Systematically review exactly what you did. Then all you have to do is repeat the process.

What has made you decide to change in the past? Did it take a big blow up or major trauma? How uncomfortable do you have to be before you are willing to change? Spend sometime writing about your process. Realistically what does it look like? How do you make choices in your life? Do you choose by not choosing, do you think about it, or do you choose based on your emotions? What are your decisions based on?

Once you know how you make your choices you can use that knowledge to help you make different choices. Say you decide you want to change your behavior around money. In the past you've spent money you didn't really have. If your purchases are emotionally based you need to make the choice not to overspend as emotionally inviting as possible. Create the image of not overspending and fill that image with strong emotions. See yourself choosing not to buy something and see yourself being so excited and pleased with yourself and your decision. Reward yourself emotionally with a lot of praise and joy and happiness when you make your new choice.

If you make your choices intellectually make your new choices intellectually rewarding. Figure out your mental process and then use it to your benefit when you decide to change something. Frequently we work against ourselves. We make our decisions emotionally and then we decide to change because intellectually we know the results will be beneficial. And then we wonder why we can't seem to change our behavior.

Strong emotions drive all of us, even if we think we're thinkers. The more desirable you feel the outcome is the more likely you are to take the necessary actions. If you absolutely knew you would receive a million dollars if you answered all the questions in the chapter, how long would it take you to answer them? The freedom you will achieve in your life if you do all the exercises in this book is priceless. So how long is it going to take for you to do them? If you knew what I know you'd be doing them all right now. Imagine the grandest life you could possibly imagine and know it could even be better.

Take sometime and create a vision of your life that's worth working for. Make it as vivid as possible and then ask yourself if it's worth figuring out what your process is. If it isn't worth the effort make the vision grander until you are willing to do whatever it takes. You're worth it.

> **Sage Advice**
> "As purpose is emptied the heart is filled."
> *Victor Hugo*

The Least You Need to Know

- Change is a matter of willingness.
- Sometimes the best thing you can do is get willing.
- You can make your life your own if you really want to.
- Your life can be absolutely glorious if you're willing to do what it takes to make it that way.

Chapter 24

Relationships

> **In This Chapter**
>
> ➤ Define Intimacy.
>
> ➤ Revamp your ideas about relationships.
>
> ➤ Clear up communications.
>
> ➤ Embrace the people who drive you nuts.

Life is really just one big relationship. We have a relationship with ourselves, with our world, with other people, and with the universe. The quality of our relationships dictates to a large degree the quality of our lives. If we have successful relationships our lives tend to be easier and we tend to be happier. If we don't have very good relationship skills life tends to be more problematic.

If you look at your life you'll see that it's composed of a variety of relationships and relationships are all based on communications. Relationships aren't necessarily about living happily ever after. They are an opportunity to polish some of the rough spots in our psyche and for them to be successful they often require work. They are the greatest gift we can give to ourselves and within their context we learn about the nature of reality and ourselves.

Intimacy (Into-me-see)

The thing we crave most as human beings is intimacy yet the thing we fear the most is being seen. Having someone see all of us not just the façade we hold up for the world terrifies most of us. We try so hard to avoid letting other people see our inner self, our hidden nature. We avoid looking at our darker side or our shadow self. And then when someone gets close, all of our walls instinctively come up, and we wonder why the relationship doesn't work as well as we'd like it to.

Sage Advice
"We have opportunity to live in joy. Do not postpone happiness until the debts are settled and relationships rearranged. Joy doesn't exist out in the world somewhere; we find it inside."
— Rev. Mary Manin Morrissey

Clarity Corner
Intimacy is defined as a close, familiar, loving, and warm personal relationship. It is also defined as a detailed knowledge or understanding of a subject, place, person, or thing. Words used to describe intimacy are deep, innermost, essential nature, and intrinsic. Intrinsic means associated with the very nature. Intimacy is in a sense part of our very nature.

Ultimately your spiritual healing depends upon your having a deep, loving, and intensely intimate relationship with yourself, your spirit, and the universal energy whatever you choose to call it. Of course, until we can be intimate with ourselves we can't really be intimate with other people but we have to start somewhere.

What is your definition of intimacy? I think of intimacy as an ability to be genuinely myself, to be open and giving, available to receive, to be present in the moment, and feel safe enough to be authentic at all times. It is the ability to speak my truth candidly and openly, to be heard, and to be willing to hear the other person's truth as well.

I used to think intimacy meant having sex. That may be part of the intimacy but I have intimacy with many people and sex isn't part of it. One of the gifts intimacy provides is a deep sense of relaxation. When you are free to be intimate you don't have to feel guarded and be wary all the time. You can just relax and enjoy being yourself.

Intimacy doesn't depend on the other person, you can be vulnerable, open, and receptive regardless of how the other person is acting. Remember there is no "out there." As human beings we often trade love rather than actually love. Loving is an act of giving. If you have to receive love in order to give love you aren't loving you are trading. An open heart is free to love and is safe from harm.

Think of love as an energy flowing out of your heart. If water is rapidly flowing out of a faucet nothing can flow back into the faucet. The pressure of the water flowing out keeps the faucet from letting anything back in, the water is constantly flushing out the faucet. So it is with your heart, if you are really just giving love and not trading it nothing and no one can hurt you. It is only when we are letting love out in exchange for letting love in that we can be emotionally wounded or hurt.

Intimacy is really a lot safer than being cautious or protecting ourselves. The world is a mirror, if we think love isn't safe it won't be. If we love just for the sheer pleasure of loving the world will mirror that love.

> ***Spiritual Shortcuts***
>
> Take a few minutes and write about intimacy.
>
> - What are you current beliefs about intimacy?
> - What are your thoughts about loving for the sake of loving rather than because someone loves you?
> - How could you change your beliefs about intimacy in light of what you just read?
>
> Love is a gift and if it has strings attached to it then it isn't love at all. Does your love have strings attached to it? What would it take for you to get rid of those strings?

Love Without Strings

What would love without strings look like? Society is pretty much based on trades, you do this, and I'll do that. Unfortunately most of our trades are unspoken agreements and when one of the parties fails to come through the other person gets to feel hurt or betrayed.

What if we redefined our concept of relationship? What if we decided relationships are really a divine appointment? What if we viewed each relationship in our life as an opportunity to deepen our understanding of our true nature and in the process release another part of our limiting filter system? It would certainly be easier to release those strings and get rid of some of our unrealistic expectations.

> ***Sage Advice***
> "We are each of us in this world an angel with one wing. In order to fly we must embrace each other."
> *Gordon*

I know used to expect all my relationships to all have fairy tale endings. I didn't know how to communicate clearly so as soon as issues surfaced in a relationship I thought I had done something wrong, would try desperately to fix it, and really just made matters worse. I alternated between thinking it was entirely my fault or completely their fault. I had no idea we were both giving one another an incredible gift. When a relationship causes us to feel emotionally upset we have each touched upon an emotional wound. We each have an opportunity to look at our emotional wounds and heal them or we could try to get the other person to change, which never really works.

Until we shift our perspective on relationships we will continue to have a series of relationships with different people but the issues are the same. I think of it as changing the exterior but keeping the interior the same. People are consistent unless they make a conscious effort to change. Our issues remain the same unless we make a concentrated effort to change them. Our relationships will remain the same until we look at the root causes, until we look at our emotional wounds.

But They Drive Me Crazy

Petty tyrants are the bane of our existence until we realize what an incredible gift they are. Petty tyrants come in many shapes and sizes. They can be our boss, parents, lover, best friend, coworker, the person who lives next door, or the guy who just cut us off in traffic. Petty tyrants are people in our life that seem to have the power to upset us. We no sooner seem to get rid of one and another one shows up until we heal the emotional wound they push on.

> **Sage Advice**
> "A raindrop, dripping from a cloud, was ashamed when it saw the sea. "Who am I where there is a sea?" it said. When it saw itself with the eye of humility, A shell nurtured it in its embrace.."
> *Saadi of Shiraz*

Rude people used to be one of my petty tyrants. The world seemed to be full of them. I hated it when I'd say hello to someone and they'd just look at me. One day a new neighbor moved in. I didn't know rude people still bothered me because I hadn't been around any for a long time. When I'd say hello to her she'd just give me a cold stare. One day I was walking down the driveway to get the mail just as she drove up. I said hi, she starred at me, and asked me what I wanted. I told her I was going to get the mail. At that moment I realized why rude people had always upset me. I was taking it personally when people wouldn't say hi and I liked to be liked. I realized this woman was very angry, defensive, and quite wounded, it was her not me. After that I was able to look at the part of my filter system that wanted people to like me, heal it, and let rude people just be people. They no longer upset me.

Once we look at ourselves instead of thinking their behavior is the source of our emotional upset we can heal the real problem, our emotional wound. The more someone upsets us the greater opportunity we have to heal ourselves. And to me that's what relationships are all about, healing and loving.

Relationships give depth to our lives. We are born alone and we will die alone but we can improve the quality of the time in between by filling our lives with love. I believe one of the major things we came here to do is remember how to love unconditionally and to do that we have to practice with other people. Relationships are one of our keys to personal freedom.

> **Sage Advice**
> "Listen within yourself and look into the infinitude of space and time. There can be heard the songs of the constellations, the voices of the numbers, and the harmonies of the spheres.."
> *The Divine Pymander*

What's Love Got To Do With It?

What does it mean to you when you say, "I love you" to someone? Does that mean they have to act in a specific manner? How do you decide when you are going to say I love you? Does love necessarily play a part in intimacy? These are all questions you need to answer for yourself.

No two people have the same definition of what it means to love one another. We show people we love them by doing what we consider loving and thoughtful. What you think of as being loving may seem rude or intrusive to the other person. And they may show their love toward you in a way that you don't understand or enjoy. Relationships often fail because we don't have the same definitions and we don't communicate clearly with one another.

The truth is in most of our relationships our internal rules, definitions, and expectations have a whole lot more to do with it then love. If you want your relationships to be about freely sharing love, having fun, and enjoying life you must clear out that pesky filter system. And relationships are the very place to do it. Actually without relationships we wouldn't even be aware of our filters, we'd just sail through life immersed in our limitations unaware of their existence. The biggest gift relationships bring to us is an opportunity to experience our limitless nature but first we have to let go of our limitations.

> **Spiritual Shortcuts**
> Take some time and write about your rules and definitions. How are people supposed to act? Write about a variety of scenarios. You say "I love you," how are they supposed to respond? When you say hi what are they supposed to do? How long does someone have to return your phone call? Really look at your code of conduct and your definitions in the area of relationships. What does the phrase, "I love you" mean? How do you feel loved by another person? What do they need to do, how do they need to act for you to feel loved? How do you show people you love them? If love is a pure act of giving with no expectation of a reward how often do you really simply love in your life?

Relationships as Reflections

Relationships are a perfect mirror. I had a dog that was very territorial. He loved people but hated all other dogs. If he saw a dog go by he would jump through windows to attack it, luckily we lived in the country, and other dogs seldom went by. One day I was hanging up a large mirror and leaned it against the wall while I went to answer the phone. A moment later I heard growling and barking followed by the sound of glass breaking. I ran into the room thinking Nikki had jumped out another window but there he stood, the mirror was shattered, and he looked rather confused. Nikki had attacked his own image in the mirror. Something we do on a regular basis in our own lives except we don't see a shattered mirror, we damage the relationships in our lives instead.

What would happen if the next time you started to get angry with your closest friend you stopped and noticed what you were telling yourself instead? If you went inside instead of attacking the mirror you would have the opportunity to let go of a large piece of emotional garbage. Our rules are outdated, they are based on fear, cause pain and suffering in our lives, and the lives of the people we care about. Are they really worth defending?

I know when someone pushes on one of my emotional wounds I want to react to them not to the wound. But when I do look at the wound I can heal it, I can get rid of another obstacle to my divinity and move one step closer to releasing my feelings of separation.

Behind the Mask

We all tend to unconsciously or consciously be on our best behavior when we first meet someone or start dating. We all wear a variety of masks in our lives. Some of us wear a happy face most of the time; we smile no matter how we are feeling. We can wear the mask of the scholar, the fool, the nurturer, or the controller. The list is endless. We each have a mask for every occasion and behind all those masks lies the truth.

True intimacy is allowing someone to see beyond the masks into our inner self. Until we clear out our filter system we don't even know what lies beyond our masks. We are so used to wearing mask we aren't even aware of their existence. When someone strips off our mask and sees our real self we are often terrified or furious. Remember our mind would rather be right than be happy. Our mind would rather hide behind our masks than be real. Until we are authentically ourselves our chances for true happiness are greatly diminished.

If deep within our being we know we are only pretending to be something how safe do we feel? And so often we are what we are pretending to be. I am a softy at heart but for years I cultivated a rough, gruff exterior for protection, or so I thought. The only people willing to overcome my rough exterior were the very people I was trying to defend myself from. My open, soft, nurturing exterior attracts like-minded people so I have no need to defend myself.

We are safest when we are being totally authentic and completely vulnerable. What! Your mind says. We spend most of our lives avoiding being vulnerable and yet that is a position of strength. Being defensive is a position of weakness. When we are vulnerable we can give and receive love, love is real and expansive. When we feel the need to be defensive we are fearful, fear is an illusion, and it contracts, it makes us feel smaller and less powerful.

Sage Advice

"The willow which bends to the tempest, often escapes better than the oak which resists it; and so in great calamities, it sometimes happens that light and frivolous spirits recover their elasticity and presence of mind sooner than those of loftier character."

Walter Scott

Smoke & Mirrors

The fear of being hurt actually makes it much easier for us to be hurt. Intimacy isn't the problem, but our lack of intimacy is. If we take the time to be truly intimate with ourselves, knowing our true wants and needs, we can be vulnerable enough to love. When we love without attachments, we realize people will come and go in our lives. We will be sad when they leave, but we won't be devastated.

Taking off the mask is the most empowering and loving thing you can do for yourself. And it is a major part of this journey of spiritual healing.

What You Heard is Not What I Said

Have you ever played that game where you sit in a circle and whisper a story into the ear of the person next to you? The story goes around the room, from person to person, and by the time it gets to the last person it barely resembles the original story. Even though we speak the same language we all hear different things. No two of us have exactly the same definitions even though we use the same vocabulary.

Frequently when we are talking we aren't really talking about the same thing. I once had a conversation with a student about broccoli and she heard me talking about herself worth. You can talk to your roommate about the bathroom being messy but they may assume you are talking about their worth as a human being. We react to what we think we hear rather than what is actually being said.

Active listening is a good way to avoid that sort of confusion. After each person speaks the other person says I just heard you say. Then the first person can say yes or no what I actually said was, if you go back and forth long enough each person can begin to hear what is actually being said. It takes a great deal of time, practice, and a willingness on the part of both parties to be honest about their emotions. And sometimes we don't really know what they are.

Control – the Big No-no

Trying to get someone else to act differently so you feel better entirely misses the point. When we try to control someone else we are focusing our attention in the wrong direction. Whenever we are upset about anything we have to first look inside, that is where our emotional turmoil always originates. In the early example where rude people upset me, the solution was for me to heal the part of myself that wanted to be liked. Once I did that rude people no longer upset me. Does that mean I have to allow people to be rude to me? Well, I can't control how other people act. If someone wants to be rude that is their choice. My choice is if I choose to be around that person.

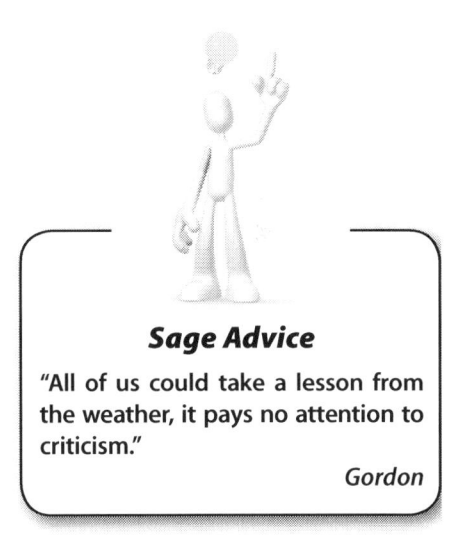

> **Sage Advice**
> "All of us could take a lesson from the weather, it pays no attention to criticism."
> *Gordon*

It is a waste of energy trying to get someone else to change. It also isn't very loving to expect someone to change his or her behavior. If you can't love them as they are then you don't really love them. You can negotiate behaviors and expectations but you can't demand them.

There is a big difference between negotiated and non-negotiated expectations. But we are so used to using control and manipulation in an attempt to get what we want that we don't think to take the risk of clearly asking for what we want and taking the risk of someone saying no. Instead we try to manipulate someone into changing or doing what we want by withholding our love or using our anger or sadness.

Sometime relationships become a battle field where we try to wrestle our happiness from another person. It is much easier to create our own happiness and then share that happiness with another person. When we are whole we are less likely to get enmeshed in an unhealthy relationship.

That's Just the Way It Is

We all define love differently, we all feel loved, or know someone loves us differently. Knowing what we want and need and communicating that clearly makes our relationships much more fulfilling and less stressful. It doesn't matter if it's a relationship with a coworker, friend, lover, or relative. We train people how to treat us, if we settle for less than we want that's the best we'll get.

> **Spiritual Shortcuts**
> What is important to you in a relationship? List the qualities you want in a partner. How do you want them to treat you? What do you want their voice to sound like? How much time do you want to spend together? How do you like to be touched? How do you feel loved? Do you like cards and unexpected phone calls or do you need plenty of private time? What really matters to you? Make a list of all the ways you feel loved. If you're in a relationship ask your partner to make a similar list and exchange lists.

If you look around you'll see how you've trained people to treat you. Are you happy with the results? I have had dogs most of my life and have trained them all. Shortly after I got a puppy I was feeling very frustrated with her unruliness. I was watching TV late one night and saw a commercial for some dog training tapes. I ordered them and learned a new approach to dog training. It made my life so much easier. If you don't like the results of your training methods try some new ones. Know clearly what you want and ask for it.

Love Means Saying You're Sorry and Meaning It

A friend of mine used to get furious when I would say I was sorry. He would say I don't want to hear about your sorrow I want you to change your behavior. When we love, when we just give love our relationship becomes a series of negotiations. We say "I'm sorry" and mean it.

When a pilot flies from one location to another they are off course more than they are on course. The automatic pilot keeps adjusting the course so they do get to right place. Sometimes in relationships we are off course, saying I'm sorry, meaning it, adjusting the relationship, and moving on is a major part of the process.

People seldom set out to hurt one another. We just do what we do and when we have different definitions and operating rules we unwittingly hurt one another. Acceptance, forgiveness, and negotiation are the key to a healthy and happy relationship. In order to really deepen our relationship with ourselves and handle our core issues we need to be in a long term, intimate relationship with someone. If we make our relationships disposable we will get to the same issue and end the relationship rather than deal with it.

If you are really lucky you will find someone willing to work through their issues with you. It doesn't necessarily have to be a lover it can be a very close friend. Give yourself that gift, let someone get close enough to really know you, and for you to know them. When you bump into one another issues love one another enough to work through them. Say I'm sorry, look deep within yourself to see what your issues are, heal them, and then move on.

> **Smoke & Mirrors**
>
> Forgiveness isn't for the other person; we really do it for ourselves. When we say, "I'm sorry," we free ourselves. When we hold onto anger, we enslave ourselves. Anger only hurts the person holding onto it. Forgiveness heals all wounds. Use forgiveness generously in your life–toward yourself and others.

Negotiating a Love That Lasts

Non-negotiated expectations are what cause most of the problems in our relationships. They key to healthier and happier relationships is to have clear negotiations about any of our expectations. If we assume anything we are on slippery ground. As the saying goes when I make an assumption I make an ass out of you and me.

The primary thing you have to negotiate is the basic nature of the relationship. Are you going to stay around when things get tough or are you going to bail out? Disagreements are part of any ongoing relationship, negotiating how to handle those disagreements is also very important.

> **Sage Advice**
>
> "Great thoughts speak only to the thoughtful mind, but great actions speak to all of mankind."
>
> *Emily Bissell*

When you are at the beginning of a relationship the last thing we think of is setting ground rules and that is one of the most important things we can do.

What does the concept of negotiation mean to you? Does it mean there has to be a winner and a loser? Make sure your concept of negotiation includes the possibility that you both win. When you are negotiating terms of a relationship that is what usually happens. You both win because the quality of your relationship will be vastly improved.

Our relationships as well as society are based on domination. From the perspective of domination negotiations do require a winner and a loser. But if you infuse your relationships with the concept of dominion everything about them becomes easier, more supportive, and loving. When you stand in a place

> **Spiritual Shortcuts**
>
> Write about your last several relationships. What were the major issues in each of your relationship? What would you like to have changed? What did you enjoy about each relationship? Is there anything you could have changed? What would have happened if you'd negotiated some of the basic first? What do you think you need to negotiated about your future relationships?

of dominion you realize that everyone occupies a different place and has a slightly different perspective. It is much easier to accept people and to negotiate your wants and needs.

As soon as we feel judged we are much more likely to dig in our heels, when we feel judged we usually feel the need to defend ourselves and want to be right. In dominion there is no right and wrong, there is just a different perspective. When we negotiate from a place of dominion we are less likely to feel judged or to judge the other person. It is much easier to see that everyone has slightly different needs. It is easier for us to compromise and come to a mutually satisfactory conclusion.

The key to happy relationships is mutual respect, the willingness to compromise without losing yourself, and the ability to give freely of our love. Relationships are a gateway to greater understanding and personal freedom.

Let's Talk

Volumes have been written about communications. The more efficiently and clearly we communicate the easier our lives will be. It is important to remember that we communicate at many different levels simultaneously. Only a small percentage of our communications are verbal, most of them occur on nonverbal or energy levels.

Have you ever experienced someone telling you something and you know they didn't mean it? Have you ever told someone they looked nice or some other white lie and were really thinking critical or judgmental thoughts? We can always tell when someone is doing that, we may prefer to lie to ourselves and pretend to believe them but we know. We read the energy all the time, we just aren't consciously aware of the fact that we're doing it.

When you want to communicate something clearly learn to be congruent. By that I mean let your insides and your outsides match. If you want to tell someone something that may be emotionally challenging take a few minutes to decide what you really want to communicate. If you've been withholding your feelings from a person for a long time they will spill out every time you talk to them. That is why people often react to us, they hear our unspoken words, they feel our thoughts, and react to them.

So, if there is a lot of old, uncommunicated words between you and the person you need to talk to I find it helpful to write a letter to them, one you do not intend to give to them. In that letter write all those words, write all your pent up feelings, and write until you feel done. By the time you're finished you will have a much better idea what you really want to communicate and be able to do it with much greater clarity.

If someone talks to you about something and you have that feeling, that inner knowing that there is a lot more being left unsaid have the courage to ask. Ask them if there is something else going on. They may not be ready to talk about it yet and you have to respect their choice but at least you've opened the door.

> **Sage Advice**
> "In seeking wisdom, the first stage is silence, the second listening, the third remembering, the fourth practicing, and the fifth teaching."
> *Solomon Ibn Gabirol*

I find it useful to set aside a set amount of time each week to talk with my partner and other people close to me. I always have the willingness and the desire to clear up communications with people in my life. I have learned over the years how important it is to ask those uncomfortable questions and speak the words I fear the most. I know if they are left unsaid they will act like a corrosive acid slowly eating away at the very heart of the relationship.

When I speak I try to have love in my heart and speak as truthfully as possible. At times it is hard, there are times I want to be right instead of happy. But if I ask myself before I speak what it is I really want to communicate and then focus on that my communications are much smoother.

> ### The Least You Need to Know
>
> ➤ Relationships are a wonderful place to learn and grow.
>
> ➤ When you step into dominion with your relationships they work a whole lot better.
>
> ➤ The people that drive you crazy can help you heal your deepest emotional wounds.
>
> ➤ Communications occur at several levels simultaneously.

Chapter 25

Who Am I and What Do I Want To Do?

> **In This Chapter**
>
> ➤ Explore who you really are.
>
> ➤ Write your eulogy.
>
> ➤ Change your personal myth.
>
> ➤ Redefine work.

I remember standing in the shower, I was twenty-two, and I asked myself the question, "Who am I?" My life was never the same after that, for a long time it felt like I had opened Pandora's box, and let out the furies of hell. Now I know I would never have enjoyed my life as much if I hadn't asked that question and searched for an answer. Looking for the answer to that question has lead me on an amazing journey of self-discovery and on a spiritual quest.

You wouldn't have picked up this book if you hadn't asked yourself that question in some form and at some point in your life. Our journey toward spiritual wholeness or holiness always starts with a question. Our journey begins with a question but along the way, if we're lucky, we realize there is no destination and we begin to focus on enjoying the journey.

What's Behind the Curtain?

One of my favorite scenes in the Wizard of Oz is when Toto pulls the curtain back and reveals the real wizard. Dorothy and everyone else is shocked that the wizard is really a mortal man just like them instead of the flashy guy up on the screen. Everyone really wants the same thing and is made of the same stuff. We aren't less than anyone nor are we better than anyone we are all the same.

Our inner definition of ourselves is so important. Most of us have no idea who or what is behind the curtain in our lives. Unfortunately we aren't very frequently encouraged to define ourselves. Society isn't designed for individuals; it is based on people following not leading. What if we all woke up one day and decided we were going to decide for ourselves what rules governed our lives? There would be chaos. An organized society depends upon our willingness as individuals to abide by the rules. And that is partially what keeps us trapped in our filter system; it is what stops us from having or seeking our own spiritual awakening. We depend too heavily on other people's rules and regulations instead of creating our own.

It is easier for us not to think about things like who we are, what really matters to us, and what we want to create or experience in lives. Society encourages us to be victims in our own lives instead of the writer and director of our own play. Society is fear based that is why it's based on controlling the masses. If we make all of our decisions based on love we have no need for external controls, rules or regulations. If our decisions are based on love we won't make a choice that will hurt someone else. Pure love does no harm. Fear is the only thing that makes us believe we need rules of conduct. Love knows better.

> **Sage Advice**
> "Life is the soul's nursery – its place for the destinies of eternity."
> *Thackery*

> **Clarity Corner**
> Our **inner definition** of ourselves is one of the cornerstones of our life. If we believe there is something wrong with us, happiness will elude us. If we believe we were meant to suffer, suffer we will. We all have an inner definition of ourselves, but until we consciously decide to define ourselves, that definition generally limits our experience of life.

God, the creator, the universal energy, or whatever else you want to call that unconditionally loving spirit it has no judgment so it has no need to control anyone or anything. It exists in dominion so it just loves. That energy knows there is no such thing as duality, that right and wrong are creations of our limited mind. Duality, right and wrong, good and bad, godliness and evil are all part of the concept of dominion. They are all fear based and are an attempt to explain reality from the limited perspective of our filter system, which is impossible.

Behind the curtain of our filter system lies freedom, happiness, joy, abundance, unconditional love, and everything and anything we could ever possibly desire. We just have to have the courage to let go of our filter system and it has been our lifeline and our protector for our entire life. So letting go can be frightening but take a deep breath and do it anyway.

When something 'tragic' happens in someone's life I frequently hear people ask how God could have let this happen. I know I was very angry with God when my mother was killed in a car accident. Tragic and death aren't real they are part of our filter system they are created by our definitions and not by reality itself.

I don't like to see people suffer, I don't like to see children starve to death in a famine, I don't like cruelty to animals, and they are all relative. A spirit can't die and suffering is optional. From the limited perspective of my filter system they sure seem real but they aren't. I have no idea why a spirit needs to experience cruelty, starvation, or death but it certainly isn't my job to judge it or call it wrong.

You're Not Your Body or Your Actions

You aren't your body, your actions, or what your filter system tells you are. You are a spirit inside a body; you are infinite, eternal, and immortal. You are made up of an energy that is pure, unconditional love. If you remember that when you're afraid and start believing it your world won't be the same. Fear can't rule your mind and when you make your choices based on love they are much more expansive.

When we realize we aren't this body we begin to realize that there is a divine order to the universe. It is very tiring to swim against the river's current but rather effortless to float down a river. So it is with life swimming up stream is hard but once you get in alignment with your spirit things get a whole lot easier.

You are responsible for taking care of your body and for the choices you make. You are responsible for your actions but you aren't them. If we make a choice that causes anyone emotional pain we often judge ourselves. If we don't like our actions we often translate that into not liking ourselves. You are not your actions and you can choose to take different actions.

When someone upsets us it is so easy to say you make me so angry. There are two problems with that statement. First of all we upset ourselves and secondly we aren't upset with the person but with their choices and behaviors.

What Really Matters?

My first long-term relationship was filled with turmoil. We used to fight about cleaning the house, paying the bills, the toothpaste, and whether or not the other person used the last piece of toilet paper and didn't replace the roll. When it was over I realized we had both wasted the gift of love by focusing on a lot of meaningless details. I no longer let things like that upset me love is too precious a gift to throw away over things that really don't matter.

Does that mean that I'm a door mat and let people walk all over me? No, but it does mean I have taken the time to define what really matters to me. Today I know things like respect are non-negotiable. If someone doesn't respect me they have no business being in my life. If they forget to replace the toilet paper I don't translate that into a lack of love or respect. I realize they just didn't replace the toilet paper.

Our filter system translates reality into something it isn't. I tend to be forgetful, some people think that means I don't care, and they can't feel

> **Sage Advice**
> "Know that the life of this world is but a game and a pastime and show and boast among you; and multiplying riches and children is like rain, whose vegetation delighteth the infidels – then they wither away, and thou seest them all yellow, and they become chaff."
> *Koran*

the love I have for them. Other people realize I'm forgetful and don't let their minds translate that into not caring. They get to experience the love and respect I have for them while they realize I'm forgetful.

What really matters is what is important to you. Maybe a full toilet paper holder really matters to you, there is no error in that but is that really important to you or was it important to your mother? There was a woman who always cut a few inches off the roast before she put it in the oven. When her husband asked her why she did that she said her mother always had. The man went and asked his mother-in-law and she replied her mother had always done that. Now he was really curious so he called up his wife's grandmother and she said she had always cut a few inches off the roast because otherwise it wouldn't fit in the oven. For years two women had been cutting off slices of meat because their predecessor had a small roasting pan.

So when you ask yourself if something is important to you make sure it really is important to you and not just a family tradition.

Your Personal Myth

We all have a story we tell ourselves. Often, we will gladly repeat the history of our life to anyone who will listen. The problem is it isn't really history, it is just our version of the past as seen threw our filter system. And it has a predictable outcome based on our beliefs, expectations, and agreements.

When I tell people suffering is optional in life they tend to look at me rather oddly. Most people want to argue for their right to be miserable and explain to my why I'm wrong. Many of us believe life is full of suffering and that is just the way life is. Beliefs like that are all part of your personal myth. Your filter system is what defines the parameters of your mythology.

Mythology is an important part of a societies definition of itself. Our mythology creates our choices. A study of comparative and ancient religions shows us how society changes with its mythology. And no

Spiritual Shortcuts

Write your personal myth; what is the story you tell yourself and others? Now rewrite it from a different perspective. Create a story based on a heroic character who is on a spiritual quest to find their truth, to understand their limitations, and to let them go. How would your childhood and your life until this point in time be changed? How would it look different? Now write a new ending. What is your life going to look like from now on? What kind of adventures do you want in your life? How will the other characters in your life act? Will your life be filled with love and abundance, pain and suffering? Remember to rewrite your story as often as you'd like.

society thinks its mythology is just a myth, they believe it. Zeus was just as real to the Greeks as Jesus is to a Christian. Now if someone is a devote Christian they would probably take offence at that statement because they believe their myth is real. We all do. And there is no "the truth," our myths are just valiant attempts to understand reality from our limited perspective.

Did a man named Jesus walk this earth? Did Buddha? Lao Tse? I don't know but I think they probably did and they cleared out their filter system, set their spirits free and left behind some suggestions for us to do the same. But each of us must find our own path home. No one can walk the road for us. They can point us in the general direction but you must choose to pick up your feet and walk. Take the time to look at your personal myth and see where it holds you back. You can rewrite your mythology whenever you want and however you want.

Clarity Corner
Besides the **mythology** of our society as a whole, we each have our own personal mythology. We all have a story or mythology we tell ourselves about our life, our loves, and the role we play on the stage called life. Unless you decide to play a different role, you will continue to get the same results in life.

Now, Who Do You Want To Be?

In light of all you've learned now what do you want to be? You really can choose to be anything, limitations only exist in your mind. Every morning we wake up and remember who we think we are, how we think we're supposed to act, and then go on about our day accordingly. Do you want to keep doing that or would you like to be someone else? I used to be very fearful even though I was unaware of my fear, I used to be closed down emotionally, and very self-centered in a negative way. I thought only of my needs, and myself. I worried about what I'd get if I'd do something.

I decided I didn't like being that way so I changed. The first thing I did was become aware of how fearful I was. Then I slowly cleared out my filter system and my choices changed and so did I. I used to call people who liked to hug touchy feely people and I had a very big judgment about them. Now I am a touchy feely person and it feels good. I love to love. Fear and anger cause my heart to contract and that hurts. I don't think there is anything wrong with them its just that love allows my heart to expand and that feels good.

Sage Advice
"The most beautiful thing we can experience is the mysterious. It is the source of all art and science. He to whom this emotion is a stranger, who can no longer pause to wonder and stand rapt in awe, is as good as dead; his eyes are closed."
Einstein

What do you want to be? Who are you and what really matters to you? Your answers to those questions are very important to you. They are questions you need to answer for yourself and no one else. When people first meet and you ask them about themselves often they start off by telling you where they are from and what they do for a living. That isn't who you are anymore than your body is.

If you had a magic wand and you could be anything or do anything what would it be? How would you act? How would you like to be described?

Your Eulogy

When my mother died I arranged a memorial service. I only expected a few people to show up. To my surprise the church was full. People came up to me later and told me amazing stories about my mother. She was always a stoic woman and I never thought she had much to do with people outside the family. Numerous people told me about incredible acts of kindness she had performed. I was deeply touched and confused, I'd never seen that side of my mother.

A year later her mother died. My grandmother was a very cold and angry woman. She lived alone and never reached out in love to anyone. She was very fearful and was constantly afraid of being taken advantage of. Her funeral was a sad contrast. There were only a few people there and no one had a single nice thing to say about her.

I thought a lot about that as I began my spiritual quest. I didn't want to die alone, forgotten, and unloved. I wanted to fill my life with love, I wanted to give freely, and I wanted to surround myself with loving people. Egyptian Pharaohs started building their tombs as soon as they assumed the role of leader. The moment they died all work on their tombs stopped. The hieroglyphics on their tombs told the story of their lives. In a sense they lived to die. I believe we need to live each day to the fullest and if we do that from a place of love our life will be a glorious experience and we'll have a great funeral.

After one of my near death experiences I saw my funeral. It was very strange standing there hearing people talk about me, I had no idea how people really felt about me. Several years ago a close friend of mine died suddenly. One of the things I realized at the time was how important it is to tell people how much we care about them. When one of my student's mother died she was grateful she had no regrets, all the words had been said. Live each moment as if its your last, live fully, with gusto, and make sure you don't leave unsaid your words of love.

Spiritual Shortcuts

This is an incredibly powerful exercise. Write your eulogy. What do you want people to say about you after you die? Imagine you're watching your own funeral, all your friends are there, and everyone has an opportunity to stand up and say something about you. What do you want them to say? How many people do you want to be there? Now ask yourself if you're leading your life that way? If not, what do you need to change?

After you wrtie your eulogy, have someone read it out loud to you or read it yourself to a group of friends. This is a very powerful and life-changing exercise to do in a group.

Work Can Actually Be Fun

So what do you want to be when you grow up? I had owned a retail store for over thirteen years when I lost if because of some very bad business decisions. I had no idea what I wanted to do. I went to a career counselor and I was feeling rather hopeless, I had always worked for myself, and I couldn't imagine doing anything else. One day I went to see my counselor and she gave me a definition of work that included it being fun. I was amazed at the thought. She told me work could be something that was fulfilling, fun, enriched the quality of your life, and supported you financially.

> **Sage Advice**
> "Success is a result, not a goal."
> *Gustave Flaubert*

If you didn't need the money would you still work at your current job? Do you wake up in the morning excited about going to work? If you had unlimited financial resources what would you do everyday? I love what I do and it hasn't always been that way. I was once told that if you don't have what you want, want what you have. When I had my own stained glass studio I loved what I did but I turned it into work and didn't let myself enjoy it.

When I first moved to Hawaii I waited on tables. When I waited on tables in college I hated it, I quit one of my jobs in the middle of the dinner when were incredible busy. Later, when I waited on tables I loved it, I viewed it as an opportunity to be of service, I enjoyed talking to the people, and I had fun. The restaurant I worked at was on the beach and every night I watched the sunset. I was relaxed and managed to give everyone excellent service. The other people I worked with ran around like crazy and felt very stressed by the end of the night. We had very different experiences even though we worked in the same place.

When we got a new manager at the restaurant she wanted to know how I did it. I tried to explain to her that I stayed in the moment, allowed myself to enjoy what I was doing, let it be fun, and playful. She looked at me rather curiously and asked me again now really, tell me how you do it. When we aren't stressing ourselves out by what we tell ourselves we can get a lot more done in a lot less time.

As with anything else in life our experience of it depends on what we tell ourselves about it. Work can be fun if we let it be.

Doing What You Love and Making Money

Sometimes we think making money and having fun are antonyms of one another. I know I used to believe they were mutually exclusive. They aren't. Actually if you love what you are doing it is a lot easier to make money at it. Money is a symbol, it is really a medium of exchange but many of us have turned it into a monster that controls our lives and our happiness.

> **Sage Advice**
> "The biggest mistake people make in life is not trying to make a living at doing what they most enjoy."
> *Malcomb Forbes*

When our work is fulfilling getting up for it everyday sure is a lot easier. What do you love doing more than anything else in the world?

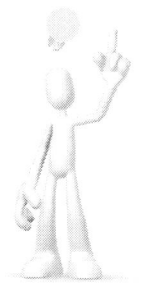

Figure that out, figure out how to make money doing it, and then do it. I have had students tell me all they enjoy doing is relaxing, they hate work. If you feel that way try changing your definition of work and relaxation.

Chances are your filter system may make it impossible to enjoy working. Writing a book like this is hard work. It takes a lot of time, effort, and a willingness to delve deep into your belief system. I could focus on it being hard or I could allow myself to enjoy the process. Thousands and thousands of people try unsuccessfully to get their books published every year.

When I tried to get my first book published I received over one hundred and fifty rejection letters. I could have stopped at anytime. My friends were amazed every time I would send out another round of query letters. I never did get that book published but I didn't stop there. I love writing so I kept on going until I found a publisher and an agent that believed in me. I had to believe in myself and in what I was doing.

You're the only one who can allow yourself or stop yourself from doing what you love for a living. Work doesn't have to be hard, a drudgery or take up a lot of your time. We have made work overwhelming in our society. We work many more hours earning our daily bread today than we did when we were hunters and gatherers.

It is time for you to make work manageable in your life. Define it in such a way that you can enjoy it. Allow it to be a positive part of your life, a part you enjoy, and look forward to rather than something you have to dread. How many people work all their lives just waiting for their retirement only to die a few years later? Whatever you are doing you have the power to enjoy it. You can be as happy as you make your mind up to be.

Sage Advice

"The human's progress is that of one who has been given a sealed book, written before he was born. He carries it inside himself until he 'dies.' While a man is subject to time, he does not know the contents of that sealed book."

Hakim Sanai

Having it All

You can have it all as soon as you define what all is to you. And believe me most people have a different definition of all. You really do have the power to make the choices necessary to have exactly what you want. Unfortunately we don't make most of our choices consciously.

When I had my retail store I made a series of terrible business decisions that caused me to lose two business as well as my home. I certainly didn't wake up one day and decide to do that. I made my decisions based on my fear, I was afraid of going bankrupt and I did. I remember clearly telling the manager of the mall that when I settled my mother's estate I was going to sell my business and travel for a while. I didn't do that consciously instead I did close my business but I certainly didn't sell it. I did travel but on a very limited budget and only on the way to my new home.

If I had listened to myself I might have gotten to travel to exotic places like India and Bali as well as other places I wanted to visit. Instead I just traveled by car cross country on my way to California in search of a job. So its the same story define what you want and then make conscious choices based on your desires.

If You Have To Be a Street Sweeper

When I was a little girl my grandfather told me if I was going to be a street sweeper be the best street sweeper you can possible be. At the time I thought he was just a crazy old man. I now know how important that really is. Not just because it's important to do your best but because if you don't you'll never get a chance to enjoy what you're doing.

There are times in life we have to do things we don't really want to do. If we focus on not wanting to do it we'll never have the possibility of enjoying it. I used to hate cleaning the house but I liked it after it was all neat and clean. If I focused on how much I hated cleaning I'd still hate cleaning the house. I realized I hated cleaning the house because I just wanted it to be done. Instead I began to focus on the process and after a bit of practice I began to enjoy cleaning. I enjoyed making things shinny and putting things in order rather than focusing on them being shinny and neat. For a time I even cleaned houses for a living and really enjoyed it.

Do whatever you are doing well, be in the moment with it, and enjoy the process. If you do that moment-by-moment at the end of every day you will put your head down on your pillow with a feeling of accomplishment and joy. We can do anything for a moment and enjoy it. The only thing you do have to do for the rest of your life is breathe.

Do I Have a Life's Purpose?

Does your life have to have a purpose for it to have meaning for you? If it does and you need your life to have meaning in order to be happy you'd better come up with a purpose. When people first start coming to my classes they are often unhappy with what they do for a living and they wonder what their life's purpose is.

What if the moment we die that's it, we're dead, gone, finished? Would it really matter? Our memory will continue as long as someone remembers us, and maybe it's as simple as that and maybe it's not. What is going to happen tomorrow, what we are here for, what's the purpose of life is really irrelevant. Thoughts like that keep our mind busy; contemplating things like that assists our filter system in remaining intact.

> **Sage Advice**
>
> "There is a difference between happiness and wisdom that he that thinks himself the happiest man really is; but he that thinks himself the wisest is generally the greatest fool.."
>
> *Colton*

We can't understand God, we can experience that energy, but we will never fully understand it. Our life may very well have a purpose and if we stay focused in the moment, make conscious choices based on love we will fulfill that purpose even if we never become consciously aware of it.

The moment you utter the words "I know" you have stopped the flow of knowledge. Once you know your life's purpose you won't ever get a chance to live it. I am writing books, leading workshops, and teaching classes right now. If I say that's my life's purpose what happens if next year I need to go to India and spend a year in a cave fasting, praying, and meditating? I won't be able to hear my inner voice suggesting that's what I need to do.

If I was going to suggest any definition for my life's purpose it would be to be in the moment, be aware of my inner guidance, follow my heart, and live in the most loving and giving manner possible. That sounds very spiritual but even as expansive as that sounds I could limit myself if that's all I thought I had to do.

I have watched people wander off into Never-never Land by listening to their inner voice. Look at members of a cult. They believe they are listening to their inner guidance and that their life's purpose is to follow their spiritual leader or spiritual self. Minds are funny things they can make mountains out of molehills and twist the facts to fit into even the most peculiar set of beliefs.

Stay grounded, remain focused, but surrender the will of your small self to the guidance of your highest good. Any spiritual path is full of paradoxes. We surrender to win. We must be in the moment to follow our life's purpose and we can only live our life's purpose if we don't say we know our life's purpose.

> **Sage Advice**
>
> "Perfect wisdom has four parts: Wisdom, the principle of doing things aright. Justice, the principle of doing things equally in public and in private. Fortitude, the principle of not fleeing danger, but meeting it. Temperance, the principle of subduing desires and living moderately."
>
> *Plato*

In dominion goals are no longer externally oriented and limiting. When we are in dominion we embrace all of life so the journey not the destination becomes our focus. In dominion you may still want to get your college degree but the focus would be on the knowledge you gained rather than the degree. The actions would be very much the same but your focus and motives would be very different. You won't be focusing on needing x number of credits, instead you would decide what knowledge you'd like to acquire.

In life if you're in dominion and thought about a concept like your life's purpose you would be more likely to define it as an inner feeling rather than some external accomplishment. Your life's purpose might be something like experiencing a profound sense of connection to a loving source at all times. Once you had achieved that you might expand it to include sharing that feeling with others.

You could judge yourself for a lack of connection. Instead you would stay in the moment and make choices that would deepen your feelings of connection. You might remind yourself that your breath is your connection to that energy and start out by focusing your attention on your breath on a regular basis.

Thinking about something like your life's purpose can either deepen your connection with yourself or totally distract you. I used to think I was here to leave the world a better place for my presence here. One day I realized that was a judgment on my part. I viewed the world as flawed. I realized I was seeing the world through the eyes of fear. Most of my life I had thought that was my whole reason for living and realizing that was a fear-based egotistical assumption was very unsettling for quite a while.

Maybe it's simply that we're here to have fun and remember how to love. Remembering how to love is a wonderful gift to yourself and to the world for that matter. The world already has more than enough fear. An old medicine man once asked me what I was leaving behind in my footsteps. I looked at him and

> **Spiritual Shortcuts**
>
> Take some time and write about your concept of a life's purpose. Imagine what you're here for, if you think you are here for a reason write about it. As you write about your perceived life's purpose see if there is any fear involved or ego. Really take time to look at your motives. Why do you want to do what you think you're here to do? A useful guideline is to notice if a behavior, thought pattern, or mental exploration helps you be more or less focused in the moment. If thinking about something regularly leaves you confused and frustrated it could be an emotional wound or your mind's way of distracting you. Knowing the difference is where your developing sense of discernment comes in.

he explained every time we place our foot down on the earth we leave a small piece of our energy in our footsteps. Are you leaving love, fear, hatred, prejudice, joy, or acceptance behind in your footsteps? Perhaps our life's purpose can be as simple as leaving love behind in every footstep.

> **The Least You Need to Know**
>
> - The Least You Need to Know
> - Work can be fun.
> - You can be as happy as you make up your mind to be.
> - Myths are real only if you believe them.
> - Our life's purpose can be as simple as being loving.

Chapter 26

Finding a Happiness That Lasts

> **In This Chapter**
>
> ➤ Define happiness for yourself.
>
> ➤ Find a deep sense of inner peace.
>
> ➤ You are the answer to your own prayers.
>
> ➤ Life has got it covered.

Happiness is such a personal thing. I might be overjoyed by an event or happening while the same thing might bore you to death. Happiness is relative and it is definitely an inside job. The dictionary uses words like pleased, delighted, glad, and having good fortune to define the word happy. Someone may be happy about having a full stomach after a wonderful meal while another person may be horrified and feel the need to purge.

The same event can make one person happy and another person sad. Happiness is relative. Finding out what makes you happy and then doing it on a regular basis is a simple way to improve the quality of your life.

You Can Be Happy, No Matter What

The same event can make us happy, anxious, sad, or angry. The truth is our happiness isn't caused by the event. It is created by what we're telling ourselves about the event. Happiness is only a thought away yet it can be one of the most elusive things there is. What were you told about happiness as a child? I had a belief that happiness was fleeting, and was always followed by some sort of tragedy.

> **Sage Advice**
> "Life is raw materials. We are artisans. We can sculpt our existence into something beautiful, or debase it into ugliness. It's in our hands."
> Cathy Better

When we are feeling depressed, hopeless or angry it is hard to remember we can be happy just by changing our thoughts. Often we really believe we aren't happy and that's just the way it is, we forget that all of our emotions, all of our feelings are created by our thoughts, change what we're thinking and the emotions change.

Once we start feeling something it is too late not to feel it. If we're angry, we're angry! But we don't have to act based on our anger. Emotions are like waves in the ocean they rise, peak, and then fall; they come and they go. So it is with our emotions, they come and they go but we get attached to them. If we are feeling angry or sad we continue to tell ourselves thoughts that cause us to stay angry or sad.

It's funny how we'll often wonder why we are feeling angry. We will explore it, resist it, judge it, blame it on someone else, and fight against it. But when we are happy we hold onto it so tightly we choke it out before it has a chance to fully arrive.

Judge Not

> **Sage Advice**
> "There is no calamity greater than lavish desires. There is no greater guilt than discontentment. And there is no greater disaster than greed. He who is content with contentment is always content."
> Lao Tse

We judge our feelings; we have positive and negative emotions, good ones, and bad ones. We like to feel good and try to avoid feeling bad. Emotions are energy in motion, there're just passing through if we let them. We can let them float through our lives like clouds across the sky. And we can choose to feel happy as we watch them pass through or we can dive in and become the clouds.

The choice is ours, we can watch the clouds, be fully present in the moment, and let the moment pass. Just because a cloud passes overhead and we are in the shade right now doesn't mean in thirty seconds we can't be in the sun again. Let your emotions be clouds passing through your life. If you want to be happy be happy.

If you have a long list of things that are necessary for you to have before you're happy it will probably take a long time for you to be happy. If you decide to be happy and you're not, notice what you are telling yourself. Happiness is only illusive because we have been taught to believe it is. Advertisements tell us we won't be happy unless we have their product. Society tells us we have to have a certain lifestyle and looks a certain way and then we'll be happy.

We can have all those things and still not be happy until we decide to be happy. I remember chasing the great American dream and the goal post would move just before I got there. I bought a house and then I worried about the mortgage. I lost weight but then I was afraid of getting fat. I did a lot of things in my life and happiness remained just out of reach until I simply decided to be happy.

Happiness Now, Not Later

I watch my students scramble for happiness. They look at the students that have been around a little longer and figure they'll be happy then. If you postpone your happiness for anything or anyone it will elude your grasp. Happiness is more a state of mind than it is a feeling.

Listen to any arguments your mind might have to the contrary. Is it saying it's easy for her to say she's happy she doesn't have my problems! One reviewer said my earlier book would have been more useful if I'd had the responsibilities of a relationship, bills, and had to work for a living. She assumed I had the luxury of just working on my spirituality and writing. She couldn't have been more wrong. At the time I was living paycheck to paycheck when I had a paycheck and frequently didn't have enough money for food.

I'm not happy because I have an idyllic life and I have nothing to be unhappy about. When I decided to be happy no matter what then my life became richer. I still have dramas in my life I just don't take then very seriously. People come and go, my pets die, and I have to pay the bills. Life happens I just chose to be happy sometimes because of it and at other times in spite of it.

Happiness is relative. In the seventies I went to Jamaica, I had a plane ticket, my backpack, and two hundred dollars. I traveled around the country and stayed in small villages. The local people thought I was rich because I came from the United States. I spent two weeks in a fishing village renting a small house for $10 a week including meals. I was worried about how I was going to pay my bills when I got back home. I felt poor because although I was able to travel I couldn't stay in nice hotels I had to share my house with a goat and a chicken. I wasn't able to see how lucky I was to travel in that way. In hindsight I realize it was such a gift, to know the people and their ways rather than stay in some stuffy hotel.

There is always going to be someone richer or poorer than you, fatter or thinner, have a nicer house or have what you want. Want what you have, be grateful for your life, and you won't have to change a thing in order to be happy. Stop moving the goal post on yourself. Let yourself be happy right here and right now

> **Sage Advice**
> "Difficulties increase the nearer we approach the goal."
> *Goethe*

> **Sage Advice**
> "Force never moves in a straight line, but always in a curve vast as the universe, and therefore eventually returns whence it issued forth, but upon a higher arc, for the universe has progressed since it started."
> *Kabbalah*

no matter what is going on in your life. If someone you loved just died be grateful and happy you had the chance to know them. No matter what just happened remember these are the good old days. You've no doubt heard the saying, "Some day we are going to look back at this and smile." That is very true so why wait? Smile about it today.

Don't make yourself miserable searching for happiness, it isn't something you can find because it is something you already have.

Letting Go Of Attachments

So often we are so attached to the way a thing is supposed to look that when it shows up we don't notice it. Recently I was watching the movie Jacobs Ladder again. In the movie, one of the characters talks about the difference between heaven and hell. When you're still attached to your life you think you're in hell you see demons ripping your life away from you. But when you let go of your attachments to your life you see angels guiding you home.

Attachments to form, to other people, to our feelings, and to the things in our life causes us to live our lives in hell. As long as we hold onto our attachments we can't get into heaven, our mind won't let us. The only place heaven and hell exists is right between your ears. It is so hard to see that when we still believe our thoughts are real. They aren't, thoughts create your experience of reality, but they are only as real as you make them. If you really believe you are miserable you will be. If you know you are happy you will be.

When I studied with don Miguel he talked about breaking free from this reality. I thought that would look dramatic and I would find myself walking around in an alternate universe. Breaking free of this reality is as simple as not believing your thoughts. What you really break free of is your mind. My mind might say something like, "You're ridiculous, who do you think you are to write this book?" Now say I believed that thought and started thinking about it, and I let it grow. I'd lie awake at night telling myself I had no right to write this book. I'd doubt myself and before too long I'd worry about every word I wrote. It wouldn't take too long before I couldn't write this book or any other for that matter.

Sage Advice
"The fates lead the willing, and drag the unwilling."
Seneca

Clarity Corner
Budda said many times that all human suffering is due to our **attachments.** We can form attachments to people, places, things, feelings, thoughts, beliefs, and a way of being. It is our attachment to our old way of being that causes most of our limitations. We are often so attached to the idea of being right, that we make ourselves miserable rather than say "I'm sorry. I was mistaken."

What do you tell yourself you can't do? Do you believe yourself? Is there anything you tell yourself you can't have? What do you tell yourself about life, happiness, joy, and all of your other emotions? Are some more real than the other? Is an emotion that appears spontaneously more real than one you generate by telling yourself something?

Changing the Channel

If you wake up feeling sad, then start talking positively to yourself, and you start feeling better which feeling is real? Are you doing something wrong? Are you suppressing your emotions? Are you attached to any of your old, limiting beliefs? Are you attached to your filter system?

Life is such an incredible gift. It will consistently mirror our attachments to anything in our lives. As soon as we are attached to something we will begin to be afraid of losing it. If we are attached to happiness, we will start worrying about no longer being happy, and suddenly we're no longer happy.

> **Sage Advice**
> "One life – a little gleam of time between two eternities."
> *Carlyle*

Relationships go through a series of phases, the first being the honeymoon stage. We could stay in that phase if we weren't afraid of losing the object of our affection, if we weren't attached to the relationship. We could be happy if we stopped being attached to our belief that our happiness comes to us through that person. We want to keep them and as soon as we want to keep the relationship we try to control the other person and ourselves. And low and behold we're no longer happy.

Don't Worry, Be Happy

Happiness can only exist in the moment. And no matter how hard you try, this moment is going to change into the next, and the next after that. If you're attached to any particular moment you're not going to be happy because each moment is fleeting. If you just let your thoughts flow and don't get attached to any particular one you can choose to be happy moment-by-moment. But if you start thinking about being happy, trying to create it, or avoid unhappiness you've grabbed hold of one of those thoughts and it's taken you for a ride. As soon as you notice you're not in the moment stand still again and watch your thoughts go by.

> **Spiritual Shortcuts**
> Make a list of all the things that make you happy. After each thing write down what you tell yourself about it that makes you happy. Separate happiness from the object. Puppies make me happy. I feel good inside when I watch them play, smell their breath, feel their tiny tongues on my face, and feel their energy. I feel good because I tell myself positive things, which in turn opens my heart when I experience each of those events. Some people hate puppies. They experience the same events but they tell themselves something else, which closes their heart. What do you tell yourself that makes you happy? Once you know make it a point to tell it to yourself more often.

Staying happily in the moment can be a frustrating process if you judge not being happily in the moment. It takes a great deal of discipline and dedication to stay in the moment. And that doesn't mean you can't be happy until you're in the moment. You can notice you're terrible unhappy and be happy about that.

Be happy that you're alive and the moment you're dead be happy you're dead. Take all of your attachments off the state of being happy and it will be a lot easier to be happy.

> **Sage Advice**
>
> "Serenity, regularity, absence of vanity, sincerity, simplicity, veracity, equanimity, flexibility, non-irritability, adaptability, humility, tenacity, integrity, nobility, magnanimity, charity, generosity, purity. Practice daily these eighteen 'ities' and you will soon attain immortality."
>
> *Sivananda*

All emotions are the same; they all depend on what we are telling ourselves. No events have emotions attached to them, every event is emotionally neutral until we attach an emotion to it by what we tell ourselves. If we don't like the way we are feeling, we just have to attach different emotions to the event.

But we get attached to the way we think about things and we often have a hard time just letting go of the belief. When we are in the midst of an emotional time it sure doesn't seem as simple as telling ourselves something different. It is simple it's just that sometimes it isn't very easy to do. At times it isn't easy to let go of the way we are feeling, we want to be right and not necessarily happy.

When Your Inside and Your Outside Matches

You can't get spiritual until you're spiritual about something. You may know you can choose to be happy but until you can be happy you have to feel whatever you're feeling. That sounds like a contradiction and it isn't. The moment you chose to be happy you will be but it may take months or years of unraveling old limiting beliefs before you can be free to make that choice. And you don't have to be miserable in the meantime.

Allowing yourself to feel sad, or angry takes the power out of the emotions. Trying to be something you're not only makes it more painful and harder to change.

If you're wearing a huge, ruffled dress on the inside it is hard to put a tight pair of pants over it. If you are hurt and wounded it is hard to put on a happy face. First you have to heal the old wounds then it becomes easier to make the choice to be happy.

> **Sage Advice**
>
> "Rhythm is the basis of life, to steady forward progress. The forces of creation, destruction, and preservation have a whirling, dynamic interaction."
>
> *Kabbalah*

My favorite poster was of a man surrounded by alligators. The caption read, "It's hard to remember your initial objective was to drain the swamp when you're up to your ass in alligators." You have to remember what your initial objective is. If your initial objective was to connect with your spiritual essence, healing your emotional wounds will allow you to make that connection. You'll also feel happier because healing your emotional wounds will make it easier for you to make the choice to be happy.

If your objective is to be happy you'll still have to heal your emotional wounds because you can't just cover them up. You've already tried that and since you're reading this book I assume it didn't work. And in the process your spiritual connection will deepen.

Either way your insides and your outsides will begin to match. When you put an ice cube into a hot cup of tea eventually both the ice cube and the tea have the same temperature. The same thing happens to us, the more our internal life matches our external life the more likely we are to be happy and at peace. I don't imagine the ice cube rants and raves about its fate or tries to be something it isn't. It just surrenders and melts. That ice cube can teach you a lot.

Inner Peace

What constitutes inner peace? I don't believe there is one set of definitions that is going to work for everyone. We each define inner peace differently. I love nothing better than to sit quietly. My mother had to be active or she was miserable. I love to be touched while some people find being touched very uncomfortable. We are all different.

Sage Advice
"Integrity has no need of rules."
Albert Camus

As we near the end of this book you will find that the only one who has the answers to the important questions is you. Until you find out what makes you feel peaceful it doesn't matter. Ultimately what you tell yourself is what makes you feel peaceful but doing certain things will make it easier for you to tell yourself you're at peace. I have a chair that hangs from the beams in front of my home, when you sit in it you feel like your hanging in the trees. It is very easy for me to feel peaceful when I am sitting there. Do I have to sit there to feel peaceful? No. Do I always feel peaceful sitting there? No, but I am more likely to.

One of the requirements of inner peace is a peaceful inner dialog. That could mean that you've quieted your mind or it could mean that your thoughts are more peaceful. There are many ways to achieve inner peace and the only one that really matters is the one you choose, the way that you find inner peace.

Life could be so simple if we'd let it be. Speak softly to yourself and others, be gentle, and loving at all times, don't judge yourself or others, take care of yourself, and live a balanced life. How simple that is yet it is so hard for us to do even for a single day because we're out of practice. Practice doing those things moment-by-moment and you'd be amazed at what a wonderful life you'd have in no time at all.

And the gift life brings you is the opportunity to choose again if you fall short. Your life will willingly illuminate any limiting beliefs that will stop you from being loving at all times. The problem is we judge ourselves and the results we're getting instead of using them as an opportunity to adjust our course. Imagine what would happen to a pilot if instead of adjusting the course of the airplane he sat in the cockpit, with his hand pressed to his forehead, judging himself for going off course? A plane is off course more than it's on course the autopilot simply adjusts the course so the plane arrives at its destination.

> **Spiritual Shortcuts**
>
> When I first tried to find inner peace I was clueless. A friend told me to keep trying things until I felt peaceful. Here is a partial list of suggestions; try them, add to the list, and feel free to find a list all your own. Go for a ride in the car, roll up the windows, and scream as loud as you can until you feel done. Call a friend. Sit in the cemetery, contemplate the alternatives. Meditate. Go for a long swim. Jog until you can't jog anymore. Spend the day in silence. Go to a church and pray. Find a sacred place and spend time there. Make a hot cup of tea and watch the sunrise. Climb to the top of a mountain. Go to the movies and sit alone in the darkness. Mail a card to yourself and be filled by love when you get it. Play your favorite music. Dance in the moonlight. Sing as loud as you want.

Set Yourself Free

The only one who can set you free is yourself. No one else's opinion of you matters unless you give them a vote. Freedom is really the ability and the courage to walk to the beat of your own drum. Happiness is whatever you define it to be. You could define happiness to be grief and for you that would be so. Years ago my definition of personal freedom included a good paying job. My aunt still wonders when I am going to get a real job. To her a job meant working for someone else, with health insurance, and a good retirement package. I do meaningful work but by her standards I don't have a job. I don't care though, I have meaningful work that pays the bills, and I love every minute of it.

> **Sage Advice**
>
> "The finest gift you can give to anyone is encouragement. Yet, almost no one gets the encouragement they need to grow to their full potential. If everyone received the encouragement they needed to grow, the genius in most everyone would blossom and the world would produce abundance beyond our wildest dreams."
> Sidney Madwed

What do you need in order to feel free? Before I moved to Hawaii I was seeing a counselor. I tend to do things and not think about the consequences. He suggested I have a nest egg before I moved to Hawaii so it would be less stressful. I agreed at first. We decided I would save at least several thousand dollars before I moved. One day during my meditation I was thinking about the money and I realized I didn't need money to feel safe. What was several thousand dollars in a bank account anyway, besides an external symbol? I remembered I could feel as safe as I wanted to regardless of the money. The money gave my mind something to hold onto, I could make money as real or as illusionary as I wanted.

A few weeks later I boarded a plane to Hawaii without the money. I arrived in paradise with eight hundred dollars and everything worked out fine. I wasn't able to get an apartment immediately and times were lean but by the time my dog got out of quarantine I had a great place for the two of us to live. SO if your answer to the question is you need money or a relationship to feel safe think again. You don't need anything external to be free. You only need to know what the external circumstances allow you to say to yourself. Then repeat those words to yourself regardless of your external circumstances.

Remember there really is no out there. Out there is a magnificent mirror. Hold up words of encouragement and love and that is what will be reflected back to you. Shout words of judgment and fear and those will be reflected back to you as well.

Smoke & Mirrors

One of the biggest traps our mind can set is to believe we need something external to be free. I used to believe I needed money, a place to live, and a means of transportation to be free. Before I knew I didn't need anything outside of myself, the very things I thought would free me enslaved me. Once I knew I didn't need them, I was free to have them but not be enslaved by them, and I no longer had to work hard to keep them.

You Already Have It

Whatever it is you already have it. When I first began my spiritual journey someone told me you couldn't desire something you didn't already have because you wouldn't know it existed. That made very little sense to me then. I knew things existed because I saw them in ads. I found it easier to understand when it came to human behaviors then I did for things. If I didn't have the capacity to be kind I wouldn't notice kindness so I couldn't desire to be kind.

If you read about serial killers many of them don't have the capacity to feel compassion so they can kill with very little regard for their victims. None of them desire compassion because they don't have it to begin with.

Spiritual Shortcuts

First, clearly decide what you want. Next, describe it in as minute detail as possible. Then write about how having that will make you feel. If there is a short cut take it. If having a particular thing will make you feel safe skip the object and allow yourself to feel safe. If it is something concrete like a certain type of car buy it. If you don't have the money for it keep processing until you are really clear about what you want, why you want it, and why you won't let yourself have it.

I wanted a Mustang Convertible for years. Part of the desire was because I was promised a Mustang if I graduated from high school. Once I separated the emotional wound from the actual desire to have a convertible it was much simpler for me to buy one. Until I did that I drove cars that simply got me from one place to another. When I finally bought the Mustang I had the opportunity to continue processing a lot of old feelings and I also got to enjoy riding with the top down.

Now, What Do You Really Want?

If I want to be at peace yet I tell myself unsettling things the truth is I want to be unsettled. Our reality never lies. Whatever is in your life is there because you want it there. Whatever isn't in your life isn't there because you don't want it there. That is the truth, and it is often hard to accept, especially when you really think you want something.

For years I said I wanted abundance yet I consistently spent more money than I made. I wanted to spend more money, which was clear because I spent more money. But I didn't really care about paying my bills on time because I didn't pay my bills on time. When I finally started to care more about paying my bills on time than I did for spending more money I paid my bills on time. When I got clear that I wanted to live more abundantly I did that as well.

Once I decided not to spend money unless I actually had it I went for a walk through the mall. I hadn't done that for years. I went window-shopping. I looked at all the wonderful things that were available and decided I wanted to be able to afford to buy them easily and effortlessly. It took a few months to change the way my mind thought but once I did my income increased and I could buy what I wanted without borrowing on my future income.

You have exactly what you want right now. If you're not happy with your life figure out what you've really been wanting. Here's a hint look at what you've been getting. Now change what you really want. It took me years to realize what my money issues were really about. Once I did it took a very short time to change the results.

Change is a lot like turning around a giant ocean liner. It takes miles for a big ship to turn around, the ride gets a bit rough as the boat goes back over its own wake but then the sailing is easier because it is riding in its old wake. So it is whenever we change something about ourselves. It gets bumpy for a while and then life gets so much easier.

In light of all you've read spend some time deciding what it is you really want. I used to think I wanted a Porsche and all the trappings that go with it. Now I know the things that really matter to me are the people in my life, how I feel about myself, and my spiritual connection. That doesn't mean I can't have the Porsche it's just that right now I'm enjoying my little Mustang convertible.

As I allow my happiness to manifest from the inside out the outside gets brighter too. Spirituality and poverty aren't synonymous. The more I connect to my true essence the fuller and more joyous my life becomes. I used to think the person with the most toys won. Now I know the person the least attached to their toys tends to be the happiest one and that doesn't mean you have to have less toys.

Sage Advice

"There was something differentiated and yet complete, which existed before heaven and earth. Soundless and formless, it depends nothing and does not change. It operates everywhere and is free from danger. It may be considered the mother of the universe."

Lao Tse

Sage Advice

"Life is a language in which certain truths are conveyed to us; if we could learn them in some other way, we should not live.."

Schopenhauer

The Least You Need to Know

- You can be happy as soon as you decide to be happy.
- Attachments to things cause your pain not the things themselves.
- It is an inside job.
- You already have what you want but you may want to want something else.

Part 7
A Vision For The Future

In the early seventies I got involved with social causes because it was a whole lot easier to focus on healing the world than looking at my own issues. Many of us do that, we try to fix other people, the environment, corruption in the government, or some other external things rather than face our own inner pain and turmoil.

But once we've begun our spiritual healing looking at the bigger picture and being of service to the planet is the next logical step. We don't live in a vacuum. And at some point you need to ask yourself what you want to see reflected in your world. Do you want a world where violence is an everyday occurrence and people starve on a regular basis? Do you want social equality? Do you want to be aligned with anger and hatred or love and forgiveness? None of us can save the world but we certainly can bend over and pick up the piece of litter in front of us. You can make a difference in your corner of the world. We can all make a big difference together.

What do you want the future to look like?

Chapter 27

Planetary Healing

> **In This Chapter**
>
> ➤ Your safety comes from vulnerability.
>
> ➤ Separation is an illusion.
>
> ➤ Healing each other to heal ourselves.
>
> ➤ Helping ourselves by helping the earth.

We live in a global community. What we need and what the world needs is really one in the same. People often focus on healing the world when what they really need to focus on is their emotional healing. If you focus on changing the world when you actually need to work on yourself you are avoiding the real issue. But part of healing ourselves is healing our world.

Imagine how nice it would be to live in a world where everyone made all their decisions based on love. People would care for the earth, the rivers, and the air would no longer be polluted. Balance would be restored in our lives and to the ecosystem we call planet earth.

Who Put the Lines on the Map?

I have a poster hanging in my office composed of children's letters to God. One of the little boys wrote to God and asked him who put the lines around the countries. I'd never really given that much thought. We all live on this rather small sphere called earth floating around in the blackness of space. Each country has different customs, food preferences, different languages or dialects, and laws. Millions and millions of people have died because of conflicts over artificial boundaries.

Sage Advice

"This we know: the earth does not belong to man, man belongs to the earth. All things are connected like blood unites us all. Man does not weave the web of life, he is merely a strand in it. Whatever he does to the web, he does to himself."

— Chief Seattle

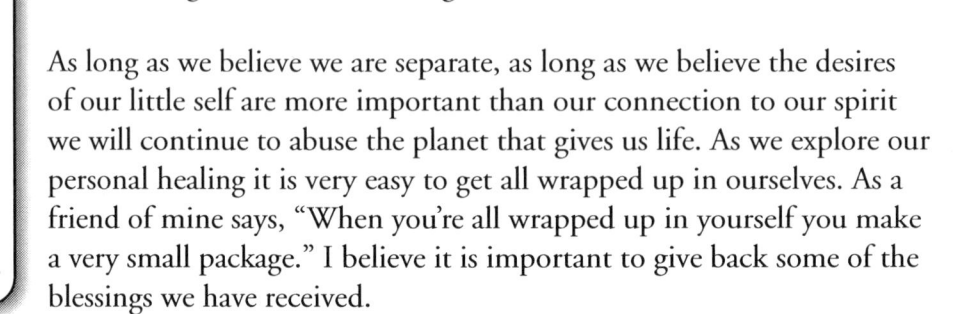

Clarity Corner

What would happen if we all realized we were part of a global community instead of residents of a particular country? If we all became citizens of the earth, wars, prejudice, boundary disputes, and racial hatred would become much less likely. We are all residents of the planet called earth; when are be going to become good stewards of that planet?

What does this need for boundaries mirror about ourselves as a species? The Native American Indians were very perplexed by the white people's belief or desire to own the land. How is it we can feel separate from the very thing that gives us life? The people of earth are all one just as we as individuals are one with our spirit and with each other. It is our belief in separation that causes most of our pain and discomfort. Think of the wars that have been waged, the lives lost and destroyed, the pain and the suffering because of our arrogance.

As long as we believe we are separate, as long as we believe the desires of our little self are more important than our connection to our spirit we will continue to abuse the planet that gives us life. As we explore our personal healing it is very easy to get all wrapped up in ourselves. As a friend of mine says, "When you're all wrapped up in yourself you make a very small package." I believe it is important to give back some of the blessings we have received.

Part of our healing is developing a sense of responsibility to our global community. It helps us as much as it helps others to reach out. As Mother Teresa said, "If we worry too much about ourselves we don't have time for other people." As we heal we begin to reach out to others. I suggest people give some of their time to their community. Participate in cleaning up the environment, work at a homeless shelter, plant a garden, or visit a sick friend.

We have become so callused as a society. We can walk by a homeless person and be annoyed by their presence or ignore them rather than be appalled that in such a rich society we allow people to be homeless. If we healed our society as well as ourselves there would be no homeless people. Our world would be a safe place for young children and animals, the most vulnerable members of our society.

As you learn to love yourself how do you think that will affect the way you view the world? If your life isn't filled with fear how do you think that will affect your thoughts and your decisions? When your heart is full of love you have room to care about others.

Creating a Loving, Supportive Community

As we proceed on our journey of personal exploration and healing it helps to be surrounded by loving and supportive people or at least people who understand what we are going through. Finding a group of like-minded people can make this journey much easier.

I was fortunate to find friends that were also on a spiritual quest. There are also twelve step programs where you can receive support as you connect with your spiritual self. You can get involved with environmental groups or other groups of people who are trying to make a difference in their lives and the lives of others.

Unity Churches often have a listing of classes or groups interested in exploring their spirituality and healing. Alternative healing practitioners often will be aware of groups in the area. There are often community bulletin boards in shops that sell crystals or new age bookstores. If you check around in your community you will find places to connect with others on their own path of spiritual healing. Read your alternative newspapers and just be open, classes and groups will appear in the most unlikely manner.

Try a group a few times before you make a decision whether it's for you or not. Use your powers of discernment and follow your heart. You are definitely not alone on your search for inner peace, love, and self-acceptance.

There is a tiny country named Bhutan that lies between China and India. It is based on spiritual principles and its leaders guide the country based on that spiritual connection. When people began climbing their mountains the local farmers complained about the intrusion. The mountains were sacred and these people were disturbing their peace. The country could have profited from the climbers but listened to their farmers and banned climbing. They talk about their Gross National Happiness rather than the products and profit. We could learn a lot from them.

> **Sage Advice**
>
> "Even a caterpillar, when coming to an end of a blade of grass, reaches out to another blade of grass and draws itself over to it, in the same way the Soul, leaving the body and unwisdom behind, reaches out to another body and draws itself over to it."
>
> *Upanishads*

> **Spiritual Shortcuts**
>
> Create a network of friends; create a network of people who care. Imagine how different your life would be if all your decisions were made based on love; what if you really loved yourself passionately and fully – now what if everyone else felt the same way about themselves. What do you think would happen to our global community? If people truly made all their decisions from love we could end all pain and suffering.

Your Legacy

What do you want your legacy to be? How would you define success for yourself? What do you want to be remembered by in your local community?

Unfortunately one of the legacies of our collective thinking is to let the government do it. We look around at society as a whole and we often feel powerless. The majority of people don't even vote in the United States. When asked why, most people express a belief that their vote wouldn't matter any way. Imagine if all governments were composed of elders, people that had shown a basic sense of wisdom and compassion, that would lead based on that rather than on getting votes to be re-elected.

What could you do in your local community that would make a difference? When I first moved to Vermont most communities were governed by Town meetings. In March the town would get together and decide collectively what needed to be done and how their taxes would be spent. Before welfare they had an Overseer of the Poor. They knew which families were in need and took care of them by buying them food. Often people in the community would help to take care of their other needs. People cared about their neighbors. Today we may live next door for years and not even say hello.

How could you reach out in your community? How could you make a difference? On the Internet every morning I log onto a site that sends money to the United Nations to feed the hungry. When you click on each sponsor sends the equivalent of a quarter of a cup of rice to help feed the hungry. It was an idea someone had that helps the world as a whole. They took the time to implement their idea and now it is making a difference. If each of us picked up a piece of litter our streets would be clean. It only takes each of us doing a small thing for the world to really change.

Every time you step on the earth you are leaving a little bit of energy behind. What are you leaving behind in your footsteps? Love? Fear? Apathy? Compassion? Next time you start to judge yourself or someone else ask yourself if that is what you want to leave behind and be loving instead.

Coming Together

In the seventies I was part of a group that started a co-op. We were a bunch of hippy, idealists who wanted to make a difference. By coming together in a group we did. The sum of the whole is always greater than the individual parts. Mob mentality is very powerful for both loving and hateful purposes. In Hawaii we have certain days designated for beach cleanups. Hundreds of people come out and clean the beaches. In cities all over the country people have come together and cleaned

---

Sage Advice

"The way of heaven does not compete and yet it skillfully achieves victory. It does not speak, and yet skillfully responds to things. It comes to you without your invitation. It is not anxious about things and yet plans well. Heaven's net is indeed vast. Though its meshes are wide, it misses nothing."

Lao Tse

Sage Advice

"Great ideas come into this world quietly as doves. Perhaps then, if we listen attentively, we shall hear among the uproar of empires and nations a faint fluttering of wings, the gentle stirrings of life, peace, and hope."

Albert Camus

up their neighborhoods. They have organized community gardening spaces. There are so many things that can be done and often it just takes one person to take the time to organize things.

Some communities have listings of places that need volunteers. There are so many places to come together and make a difference, not only in your life but also in the lives of others. I know when I stop focusing myself long enough to reach out and help someone I feel better.

Spend time loving yourself but also take time to love others and let others love you. One of my mentors told me to make sure I always kept my own cup full and to give others of the overflow. One of the things I found was the more I shared the more I had to give. Find out what nurtures you, do it, and the give to your fellow travelers.

Sage Advice
"How does the meadow flower its bloom unfold? Because the lovely little flower is free down to its roots, and in that freedom bold."
Wordsworth

The Earth Will Be Fine; We're in Danger

I am often perplexed when people talk about saving the planet. The earth will be fine, it is the human species that is in danger. We have to clean up the environment for ourselves not for the earth. The earth will cleanse itself eventually the real question is if our species will be around to see it. If we continue to poison the water we drink and the air we breathe, who will suffer? How long before human beings are on the endangered species list?

We can all do our part. We can recycle, we can be vigilant about our consumption, and we can support companies that are environmentally friendly. We can do simple things like conserve water, walk instead of drive, carpool, stop littering, stop smoking, make sure our car is running efficiently, plant a garden or a tree, the list can go on and on. The important thing is to be part of the solution instead of the problem.

Smoke & Mirrors
The planet earth will be fine if we continue to pollute the air and the water. Human beings as a species will not be; if we continue doing what we've been doing, we will become extinct before too long. The planet won't be able to support our ever-increasing population, and just as our practices have caused hundreds of species to become extinct, we will cause our own extinction.

From The Inside Out

Just as we must heal from the inside out so must society. Society is merely a collection of individuals. If the individuals change so will society and unless the individuals change society can't. Most people complain about politics and politicians but seldom do anything about it. How could you make a difference? Do you vote? Do you take time to get involved with your neighborhood boards? What about listening to a friend or writing a letter to the editor?

What changes would you like to see happen in your life? What changes would you like to see happen in your neighborhood? One day when I first moved to Hawaii I took my dog for a walk, I was feeling lonely.

A woman walked by, smiled broadly at me, and said hello. Her smile warmed my heart. Sometimes something as simple as a smile can make a difference in someone's life.

If each of us added a little bit of love to the world each day by loving ourselves and reaching out to someone else, what do you think would happen? When I was a little girl I wanted the world to be a better place because I had been born. Now I know that was because I felt so alone and powerless but as an adult I can make the conscious decision to leave love behind instead of hatred and fear.

We Are All One

The basic concept of spirituality is that we are all one; we are all part of the creative force of this universe and there is no such thing as separation except in our mind. When I look at you as the problem or as a threat I cut myself off not only from you but from myself as well. Fear is what makes us think we are separate.

Our inability to feel love is what keeps us addicted to fear. The emotions we call negative fear, anger, sadness are strong emotions. They capture our attention. Love is softer and gentler. Feeling love requires us to open our heart and be vulnerable. We can feel the so-called negative emotions while our walls are still up and our hearts are closed. We don't have to be vulnerable to feel those emotions and we don't feel safe enough to feel the love. The irony is we can only feel truly safe when we are connected to our true self, to our spirit, and our spirit is love. Once we lose that connection we move further and further away from ourselves and deeper and deeper into fear.

So take the risk to reach out in love. Take the risk to reach out and connect with those around you and to your own true nature. At the level of spirit we are all one. It is only when we are surrounded by fear that we feel alone, that we feel the need to protect ourselves, and reach out in fear and anger to the people around us. We push away love because we are afraid to open up and feel it; there really is nothing to fear except fear itself.

Safety really lies in absolute vulnerability. When we are vulnerable our hearts are open and we can connect to the love. When we are guarded we are only open to fear. We are much more likely to be hurt when our walls are up than when they are down. When we are totally vulnerable

---

Sage Advice
"What folks think is impossible is just stuff they haven't seen before."
Robin Williams character in "What Dreams May Come"

Sage Advice
"When you were born, you cried and the world rejoiced. Live your life so that when you die, the world cries and you rejoice."
Cherokee Saying

Sage Advice
"Pray to God, but keep rowing to shore."
Russian Proverb

we have nothing to defend, which means we have nothing to hide. We are free and we are safe. Love always keeps us safe. Love is an act of giving. When love is flowing outward with no expectation of reward nothing can get in to hurt you. It is like a giant faucet flowing outward with great pressure, nothing can get back in to contaminate the faucet. But when we are really bargaining, when we are giving love to receive love we love from a place of fear. We aren't really sharing love at all. Loving from a place of fear isn't being vulnerable and we are often hurt when we do that. Then we use our pain as an excuse not to love at all.

Love. Just love yourself and others at a profound level. You'll be amazed at the world love can build.

> **Sage Advice**
> "The important thing is not to stop questioning."
> *Einstein*

It Starts With You

This journey can only start with one person – you. There is no one else in your world except you and there is no one who can take this journey for you. We seem to be born alone and die alone because we live in a world based in fear. In a world based in love we are always surrounded and filled with our spiritual connection to everyone and everything. We are never alone in a world based on love. How can you create that world of love for yourself? It really is possible. Your life would be totally transformed if you loved yourself deeply and passionately. The entire world would change completely if you openly shared that love with those about you.

When I was a student one of the commitments I had to make was to share the knowledge with others. At the time that made very little sense to me but now that I know the transformative power of love it makes perfect sense. Love needs to be as freely given as it is received. The more you give away the more there is to give. When you live in a world filled with love there is no fear, lack, or limitation so why wouldn't you share what you have?

> **Sage Advice**
> "Do not go gentle into that good night,
> Old age should burn and rave at the close of day
> Rage, rage against the dying of the light.."
> *Dylan Thomas*

Learn how to love and then show others how to love as well. Be a shinning light and let the world rejoice in your presence. Love is real everything else is an illusion but it sure does seem real. I believe it was Emily Dickerson who said, "It is better to light a candle than curse the darkness." Love as passionately as you can love. Give as freely as you can give. Love and give not from a place of fear but from your fullness of spirit, from the place of the beautiful light that you really are.

The rest of this book is about that healing journey this chapter is about giving back what you received during your journey. What do you want to do with your life? How do you want to make a difference? How do you want your life to be different?

Imagine All the People

Our imaginations are very powerful. What we believe is what we'll see and what our experiences will be based on. John Lennon wrote a beautiful song called Imagine. If you've never heard it take the time to listen to it. If you've heard it before listen to it again and really allow yourself to feel the words and let them move you.

What kind of a world would you like to imagine? What would Utopia look like to you? What would your role be in that world? What would the world be like if everyone took the time to do their emotional healing? Join me in creating that world one person at a time.

Creating the World of Our Dreams

Take a few deep breaths and mentally give yourself permission to relax. Really focus your full attention on your breath and as you inhale breathe in relaxation and as you exhale release anything unlike relaxation. Allow yourself to fully experience your breath as it moves in and out of your body. As your breath fills your body with life sustaining air relax the muscles in your chest and let go. Let the feeling of relaxation flow into your stomach and let go of anything unlike relaxation in your chest or your stomach.

Relax your jaw and all the muscles in your face. Breathe in through your mouth and out through your nose, slowly, deeply, and rhythmically. Relax your shoulders and your neck, allow yourself to feel totally relaxed. Allow your consciousness to drift gently moving you into a place of total relaxation. You feel as if you're about to drift off to sleep.

Imagine yourself standing in the center of a beautiful clearing in an ancient forest. The air smells fresh and clean, it is heavy with the musky smell of wet earth after a gentle rain. You find yourself slowly walking around the clearing. It feels familiar and safe. You feel yourself surrounded by the energy of love. A shaft of light fills the clearing with a magical light.

Slowly people begin to fill the clearing. As each one enters the clearing they reach out and hug you. You feel full and connected and at peace. Before long the entire clearing is full of people holding each other's hand, sharing love, and feeling connected and at peace. You look around at the faces; they are all different ages, races, shapes, and sizes.

You look around and you notice their hearts are beaming with light. A beautiful pink light emanates from their heart, joining with the light of those around them. You mentally see them moving through their lives making all of their choices based on love. They are free of fear; you are free of fear. Love guides your way; love surrounds you and fills your very being.

You see a world in which everyone is free of fear; in which the band of fear is removed from their hearts and their minds. It is a world in which all people realize they are one; in which all people make their choices based on love and mutual respect. It is a world free of hatred, free of prejudice. The air is clear and the water clean. Everyone, including the heads of state and the leaders of industry make their decisions based on the good of the planet and all people great and small.

Take a few moments to envision that world and then know it could be even more magnificent than you could possible picture. Allow it to be grand, glorious, and free. Imagine your life in that world. Imagine yourself doing what you love as your livelihood. Imagine all your wants and needs being effortlessly met. Imagine that for everyone everywhere in the world.

Imagine all people living in peace and harmony. Imagine a world of love. Imagine a world that is safe, loving, supportive, and nurturing to all of its inhabitants.

Now let it be so. Let that world take form in your mind and begin to materialize in your life. Let yourself know what you need to do to make it so and decide to do it.

Take a few minutes to let your mind wander in its creation and when you are ready gently bring yourself back to your room.

Now write about your vision. What do you need to do to allow that world to manifest in your life? Does your mind think its possible? What beliefs do you need to let go of? What actions do you need to take in your life?

It is possible and it can begin with you.

Remember to be vigilant in meeting your own needs and healing your emotional wounds so you have a full cup. I believe we all came here for a reason to share ourselves in a profound manner. If your cup is full we will be able to do what you came here to do. You will be able to let your light shine freely and share it freely.

The Least You Need to Know

> - **Love is an act of giving; the more freely you give the more freely you receive.**
> - **You can make a difference.**
> - **You are never alone if you live in a world based on love.**
> - **Fear really is an illusion.**

Appendix A

Suggested Reading

There are thousands of wonderful books out there. This is a list of a few of my favorites. When I was in the midst of doing my healing every so often I would 'feel called' to go to the bookstore. I would wander around the stacks and the best way I can describe it is a certain book would call to me. Try some of the books on this list or wander around your local bookstore and let the book you need to read next find you. I hope you enjoy some of my favorites as well.

Many of the authors listed here have also written other wonderful books. I recommend them as well.

Channeled

Emmanuel's Book, Bantam Books, 1985
Emmanuel's Book II, Bantam Books, 1989
Emmanuel's Book III, Bantam Books, 1994
I Come As A Brother, Bartholomew, High Mesa Press, 1986
Reflections of An Elder Brother, Bartholomew, High Mesa Press, 1989

Emotional Healing

Adult Children, John & Linda Friel, Health Communications, 1988
Fire In The Soul, Joan Borysenko, PH.D., Warner Books, 1993
Legacy of The Heart, Wayne Muller, Fireside, 1992

Healing

Anatomy of the Spirit, Caroline Myss, PhD, Harmony Books, 1996
A Touch of Hope, Dean & Rochelle Kraft, Berkley, 1999
Back to Eden, Jethro Kloss, Back to Eden Books, 1985
Earthway, Mary Summer Rain, Pocket Books, 1990
Joy's Way, W. Brugh Joy, M.D., Jeremy P. Tarcher, 1979
Light Emerging: The Journey of Personal Healing, Barbara Ann Brennan, Bantam Books, 1993
You Can Heal Your Life, Louise L. Hay, Hay House, Inc., 1984

Inspirational

A Path With Heart, Jack Kornfield, Bantam Books, 1993
A Return to Love, Marianne Williamson, Harper Collins, 1992
Conversations With God Book I, G.P. Putnam's Son, 1995
Joshua, Joseph F. Girzone, Macmillan, 1987
Peace is Every Step, Thich Nhat Hanh, Bantam Books, 1991
The Alchemist, Paulo Coelho, Harper Collins, 1993
The Four Agreements, Don Miguel Ruiz, Amber-Allen, 1997
The Laws of Spirit, Dan Millman, H J Kramer, 1995
Touching Peace, Thich Nhat Hanh, Parallax Press, 1992
Way of The Peaceful Warrior, Dan Millman, H J Kramer, 1984

Novels

The Celestine Prophecy, James Redfield, Warner Books, 1993
Illusions, Richard Bach, DeLacorte Press/Eleanor Friede, 1977
The Oversoul Seven Trilogy, Jane Roberts, Amber-Allen, 1995

Prosperity

Creating Money, Sanaya Roman & Duane Packer, H J Kramer, 1988
The Dynamic Laws of Prosperity, Catherine Ponder, DeVorss, 1984

Relationships

Love and Awakening, John Welwood, Harper Collins, 1997

Shamanism

Dance of Power, Dr. Susan Gregg, Llewellyn, 1993
Finding the Sacred Self, Dr. Susan Gregg, Llewellyn, 1995

Mastering Your Hidden Self, Serge Kahili King, Theosophical, 1985
The Path of Power, Sun Bear, Wabun, & Barry Weinstock, Prentice Hall, 1987
The Teachings of Don Carlos, Victor Sanchez, Bear & Co., 1995
A Toltec Path, Ken Eagle Feather, Hampton Roads, 1995
Urban Shaman, Serge Kahili King, PH.D., Fireside, 1990
Woman At The Edge of Two Worlds, Lynn V. Andrews, Harper Collins, 1993

Appendix B

Organizations

This is a list of organizations you might find helpful. The Internet is a wonderful resource for information on all sorts of healing. Any of the search engines will provide you with a wealth of information. The sites come and go so rapidly a list I provided you with today would be out dated tomorrow so as the saying goes seek and yea shall find.

Acupuncture

American Academy of Medical Acupuncture
5820 Wilshire Boulevard, Suite 500
Los Angeles, CA 90036
(213) 937-5514

American Association of Acupuncture and Oriental Medicine
433 Front Street
Catasauqua, PA 18032
(610) 226-1433

American Foundation of Traditional Chinese Medicine
505 Beach Street
San Francisco, CA 94133
(415) 776-0502

The National Commission for Certification of Acupuncturists
1424 16th Street NW, Suite 501
Washington, DC 20036
(202) 232-1404

The Alexander Technique

North American Society of Teachers of the Alexander Technique
3010 Hennepin Avenue South, Suite 10
Minneapolis, MN 55408
(610) 824-5066 or (800) 473-0620

Art Therapy

American Art Therapy Association
1202 Allanson Road
Mundelein, IL 60060
(847) 949-6064

Ayurveda

California College of Ayurveda Center for Optimal Health
1117A East Main Street
Grass Valley, CA 95945
(916) 274-9100

Chopra Center for Well-Being
7630 Fay Avenue
LaJolla, CA 92037
(888) 424-6772

Educational Service of Maharishi Ayurveda International
PO Box 49667
Colorado Springs, CO 80949
(800) 843-8332

Chinese Herbalism

American Association of Acupuncture and Oriental Medicine
433 Front Street
Catasauqua, PA 18032
(610) 226-1433

Chiropractic

American Chiropractic Association
1701 Clarendon Boulevard
Arlington, VA 22209
(703) 276-8800

Federation of Straight Chiropractors and Organizations
642 Broad Street #9
Clifton, NJ 07013
(800) 521-9856

International Chiropractors Association
1110 North Glebe Road, Suite 1000
Arlington, VA 22201
(800) 423-4690

World Chiropractic Alliance
2950 North Dobson Road #1
Chandler, AZ 85224
(800) 347-1011

Craniosacral Therapy

The Upledger Institute
11211 Prosperity Farms Road, Suite D325
Palm Beach Gardens, FL 33410
(5610 622-4334

The Feldenkrais Method

The Feldenkrais Guild
PO Box 489
Albany, OR 97321-0143
(541) 926-0981 or (800) 775-2118

Healing

The Barbara Brennan School of Healing
PO Box 2005
East Hampton, NY 11937
(516) 329-0951

Ecumenical Society of Psychorientology
(Holistic Faith Healing)
1407 Calle del Norte
Laredo, TX 78041
(210) 7226391

Nurse Healers Professional Associates
1211 Locust Street
Philadelphia, PA 19107
(215) 545-8079

Hellerwork

Hellerwork International
406 Berry Street
Mount Shasta, CA 96067
(916) 926-2500 or (800) 392-3900

Homeopathy

The American Institute of Homeopathy
1585 Glencoe
Denver, CO 80220
(303) 898-5477

The National Center for Homeopathy
801 North Fairfax Street, Suite 306
Alexandra, VA 22314
(703) 548-7790

Iridology

Iridologists International
24360 Old Wagon Road
Escondido, CA 92027
(760) 749-2727

Kirlian Photography
c/o Linda Wiggin
PO Box 1114
Provincetown, MA 02657
(508) 487-9873

Magnetic Therapy

Bio-Electro-Magnetics Institute
2490 West Moana Lane
Reno, NV 89509-3936
(702) 827-9099

Meditation

Insight Meditation Society
1030 Pleasant Street
Barre, MA 01005
(508) 355-4378

Maharishi Ayur-Ved Products International, Inc.
PO Box 49667
Colorado Springs, CO 80949-9667
(800) 255-8332

Naturopathy

American Association of Naturopathic Physicians
601 Valley Suite 105
Seattle, WA 98109
(206) 298-0125

Network Chiropractic

Association for Network Chiropractic
444 North Main Street
Longmont, CO 80501
(303) 678-8101

Osteopathy

American Academy of Osteopathy
3500 DePauw Boulevard
Suite 1080
Indianapolis, IN 46268
(317) 879-1881

American Osteopathic Association
142 East Ontario Street
Chicago, IL 60611
(312) 280-5800

The Cranial Academy
8606 Allisonville Road
Indianapolis, IN 46350
(317) 594-0411

Polarity Therapy

American Polarity Therapy Association
2888 Bluff Street, Suite 149
Boulder, CO 80301
(303) 545-2080 or (800) 359-5620

Reflexology

American Academy of Reflexology
606 East Magnolia Boulevard, Suite B
Burbank, CA 91501
(818) 841-7741

International Institute of Reflexology
PO Box 12462
St. Petersburg, FL 33733
(813) 343-4811

Reiki

The Center for Reiki Training
29209 Northwestern Highway #592
Southfield, MI 48034
(800) 332-8112 or (810) 948-9534

Rolfing

The Rolf Institute of Structural Integration
205 Canyon Boulevard
Boulder, CO 80302
(800) 530-8875

Silva Method

Silva International Inc.
1407 Calle Del Norte
Laredo, TX 78041
(956) 722-6391

Sound Therapy

The Institute for Music, Health, and Education
PO Box 4179
Boulder, CO 80306
(303) 443-8484

Sound, Listening, and Learning Center
2701 East Camelback, Suite 205
Phoenix, AZ 85016
(602) 381-0086

Therapeutic Touch

Nurse Healers Professional Associates
1211 Locust Street
Philadelphia, PA 19107
(215) 545-8079

Touch For Health

Touch for Health Kinesiology Association
3223 Washington Boulevard, Suite 201
Marina del Rey, CA 90292
(800) 466-8342

Tragerwork

The Trager Institute
21 Locust Avenue
Mill Valley, CA 94941
(415) 388-2688

Yoga

American Yoga Association
513 South Orange Avenue
Sarasota, FL 34236
(941) 953-5859

Integral Yoga Institute
227 West 13th Street
New York, NY 10011
(212) 929-0586

International Association of Yoga Therapists
20 Sunnyside Avenue, Suite A243
Mill Valley, CA 94941-1928
(415) 332-2478

About the Author

Dr. Susan Gregg believes that life is meant to be happy and free of struggle – that life is an opportunity to remember our divine nature and to have fun.

The Hawaiians say there are many paths to the top of the mountain but the view from the top is the same for everyone. At the top of the mountain, no matter what path you take, you learn to love unconditionally and see the perfection in all of life. The Toltec tradition is one of the many paths that can help you reach the top so you can create a life that is a safe, joyous, loving and fun.

The Ancient Ones were men and women of knowledge in Teotihuacán, Mexico. Their spiritual teachings have been handed down for over two thousand years through generations of shamans, referred to as Naguals. For many years Susan studied with don Miguel Ruiz and his mother Sister Sarita. After she completed her apprenticeship don Miguel told her to go and teach in her own way. With deep gratitude to her mentor, don Miguel, she shares these powerful teachings with others.

Transformation is perhaps the best word to use when describing the life of Susan Gregg. Born and raised in New York City, Susan found her teenage world turned upside down when her parents moved to a small, rural town in northern Vermont.

Susan pinpoints a survived suicide attempt (doctors were amazed she lived after ingesting cyanide) as the turning point in her life. She realized at a profound level that she could no longer run from life's problems and that there are no outside solutions. Susan became willing to do whatever it took to create happiness and personal freedom for herself. From a very early age Susan always felt there was something beyond what she experienced with her five senses. That feeling sparked the exploration of human potential that led to Susan's life work.

After graduating from the University of Vermont with a B.A. in mathematics, Susan began to research human behavior and creativity in the mid-seventies. In the mid-eighties she moved to San Diego where she connected with don Miguel Ruiz and Sister Sarita. Sarita and Ruiz schooled Susan in the ancient Toltec Tradition. That training totally changed her inner landscape and her experience of life. She went from being a depressed, lonely, fearful, and unhappy person to a woman who lives life passionately and has a life filled with magic and miracles, joy and happiness.

After receiving her doctorate in clinical hypnotherapy in 1989, Susan moved to Hawaii and started a private practice. Her first book was *Dance of Power*. She also wrote *Finding the Sacred Self, The Complete*

Idiot's Guide to Spiritual Healing, The Toltec Way, Mastering the Toltec Way: a Daily Guide to Happiness, Freedom, and Joy,, The Complete Idiot's Guide to Short Meditations, and *The Complete Illustrated Encyclopedia of Magical Plants.* Her latest book is *Encyclopedia of Angels, Spirit Guides and Ascended Masters: A Guide to 200 Celestial Beings to Help, Heal, and Assist You in Everyday Life* .

Her love of healing and her desire to continue to deepen her connection with her divinity led to the exploration of Reiki. She is now a certified Reiki Teacher and Karuna® Master. She has also been studying ancient Hawaiian Spirituality with Mahealani Kuamo'o-Henry. She is a Kumu 'Elele (teacher and messenger) for her ancestors and an incredibly warm, loving and caring woman. The combination of traditions creates a powerful synthesis. Susan has dedicated her life to being of service and helping others experiencing all the wonders life has to offer.

When not writing or working with clients, Susan likes to spend time with the neglected and injured animals she has rescued over the years. Her love of animals also includes the dolphins she swims with and the turtles she sees while scuba diving. Susan recently moved to the Big Island of Hawaii after living on Oahu for many years.

If you'd like more information you can visit her website at http://susangregg.com

Printed in Great Britain
by Amazon